Emotional Cognition

Advances in Consciousness Research

Advances in Consciousness Research provides a forum for scholars from different scientific disciplines and fields of knowledge who study consciousness in its multifaceted aspects. Thus the Series will include (but not be limited to) the various areas of cognitive science, including cognitive psychology, linguistics, brain science and philosophy. The orientation of the Series is toward developing new interdisciplinary and integrative approaches for the investigation, description and theory of consciousness, as well as the practical consequences of this research for the individual and society.

Series B: Research in progress. Experimental, descriptive and clinical research in consciousness.

Editor

Maxim I. Stamenov
Bulgarian Academy of Sciences

Editorial Board

David Chalmers, *University of Arizona*
Gordon G. Globus, *University of California at Irvine*
Ray Jackendoff, *Brandeis University*
Christof Koch, *California Institute of Technology*
Stephen Kosslyn, *Harvard University*
Earl Mac Cormac, *Duke University*
George Mandler, *University of California at San Diego*
John R. Searle, *University of California at Berkeley*
Petra Stoerig, *Universität Düsseldorf*
† Francisco Varela, *C.R.E.A., École Polytechnique, Paris*

Volume 44

Emotional Cognition: From brain to behaviour
Edited by Simon Moore and Mike Oaksford

Emotional Cognition
From brain to behaviour

Edited by

Simon C. Moore
University of York

Mike Oaksford
University of Cardiff

John Benjamins Publishing Company
Amsterdam / Philadelphia

∞™ The paper used in this publication meets the minimum requirements of American National Standard for Information Sciences – Permanence of Paper for Printed Library Materials, ANSI Z39.48-1984.

Library of Congress Cataloging-in-Publication Data

Emotional cognition: From brain to behaviour / edited by Simon Moore, Mike Oaksford.
    p. cm. (Advances in Consciousness Research, ISSN 1381–589X ; v. 44)
    Includes bibliographical references and index.
    1. Emotions and cognition. I. Moore, Simon C. II. Oaksford, M. (Mike) III. Series.

BF311.E486   2002
152.4-dc21   2002066613
ISBN 90 272 5168 1 (Eur.) / 1 58811 244 6 (US) (Hb; alk. paper)
ISBN 90 272 5164 9 (Eur.) / 1 58811 224 1 (US) (Pb; alk. paper)

© 2002 – John Benjamins B.V.
No part of this book may be reproduced in any form, by print, photoprint, microfilm, or any other means, without written permission from the publisher.

John Benjamins Publishing Co. · P.O. Box 36224 · 1020 ME Amsterdam · The Netherlands
John Benjamins North America · P.O. Box 27519 · Philadelphia PA 19118-0519 · USA

Table of contents

CHAPTER 1
Emotional Cognition 1
   Simon C. Moore and Mike Oaksford

CHAPTER 2
The role of the human amygdala in emotional modulation of
long-term declarative memory 9
   Tony W. Buchanan and Ralph Adolphs

CHAPTER 3
Associative representations of emotionally significant outcomes 35
   Simon Killcross and Pam Blundell

CHAPTER 4
Neurons with attitude 75
   Eamon P. Fulcher

CHAPTER 5
Affect and processing dynamics 111
   Piotr Winkielman, Norbert Schwarz and Andrzej Nowak

CHAPTER 6
Consciousness, computation, and emotion 137
   Jesse J. Prinz

CHAPTER 7
Emotion and reasoning to consistency 157
   Keith Oatley and P. N. Johnson-Laird

Chapter 8
Expected feelings about risky options 183
Alan Schwartz

Chapter 9
Motivational underpinnings of utility in decision making 197
Jerome R. Busemeyer, James T. Townsend, and Julie C. Stout

Chapter 10
An informational value for mood 221
Simon C. Moore and Mike Oaksford

Chapter 11
The effects of positive affect and arousal on working memory and executive attention 245
F. Gregory Ashby, Vivian V. Valentin and And U. Turken

Chapter 12
Integration of emotion and cognitive control 289
Jeremy R. Gray and Todd S. Braver

Name index 317

Subject index 329

CHAPTER 1

Emotional Cognition
An introduction

Simon C. Moore and Mike Oaksford

There has been a marked shift in the perceived role of emotion in human behaviour. Plato sought to dispel the detrimental influence of emotion on human reason and the Stoics went as far as proposing training programmes to achieve this (Birley 1987). In contrast, recently Goleman (1996) has advocated developing our emotions as a means to intelligent behaviour. Although the contrast between reason (good) and emotion (bad) has significantly diminished since Plato's day, the importance of emotional processing in human cognition has yet to penetrate all areas of Cognitive Psychology. One reason for this situation is that the goal of cognitive theory is to develop formal computational models of cognitive processes. But such well-defined models are rare in the area of emotional effects on cognition. *Emotional Cognition* seeks to address this imbalance by presenting a collection of papers on computational models of emotion. To fully understand how we think *Emotional Cognition* makes a unique contribution to the emotion-cognition debate it is necessary to consider some of the background history.

Perhaps the most influential contribution to the emotion debate in modern times was Darwin's *The Expression of Emotions in Man and Animals* in 1872. Darwin suggested that there were fundamental emotions that found their expression in overt behaviour in animals *and* in humans. In so arguing, Darwin led to the view of the universality of emotion and that emotions were part of the natural order of things: biological systems expressed emotion as part of their natural context. For Darwin, there was no involvement of the 'higher' functions of reason, those functions that the earlier philosophers tried to protect from the influences of emotion, in expressing an emotion. Emotion was a remnant of our pre-sapient inheritance. For Darwin, it was enough to describe emotion in this irreducible form, without attending to its antecedents.

For example, 'hate' affected behaviour and, following Plato, cognition was not involved in driving one to act on that hatred. Emotion and cognition were still regarded as separate, unrelated, processes when William James published his seminal paper 'What is an Emotion?' (James 1884).

For James, we feel sad because we cry. The sensation of tears on the face constitutes the emotion of sadness. Our perception of visceral changes, the interaction between the body and the context it was in, determined how we felt. Our heart beating fast, perspiration, an increased rate of respiration, a flushed face, these were the building blocks of our emotions. James's thesis, together with C. G. Lange's similar ideas, led researchers to seek out the bodily changes associated with our emotions (e.g. Ekman, Levenson, & Friesen 1983; Lang, Greenwald, & Bradley 1993). However, a consequence of this research was that emotion was further separated from the mind. Emotion was reduced to a sort of visceral sensation, akin to hunger, and divorced from thought and reason. Although this research has contributed enormously to our understanding of emotion, theories of how emotions and cognition interacted were still lacking. One reason may be related to a legacy of the behaviourist paradigm that cognitive psychology replaced.

The Behaviourism of the early to mid-twentieth century sought to examine *observable* behaviour and in so doing removed the topic of emotion from inquiry completely. Whereas cognitivism implicated the thoughts and beliefs of an organism as determinants of its actions and experiences, behaviourists only dealt with the objective and the observable. Yet Behaviourism left research in cognition an important legacy: methodological behaviourism. It is still the objective and the observable that informs much cognitive theorising. For example, reaction times and participant choices are still the primary data that serve as the bedrock of cognitive theories and both can be precisely measured. Emotion, however, is still seen as subjective and somehow inaccessible to accurate measurement. In emotion research there has been a tendency to assume some measurable aspect of the environment is in direct correspondence with the intensity of an elicited emotion: fear is talked of as 'fear of a dog.' Thus the emotion 'fear' is equated with a measure of the dog's dangerousness and a measure of the action carried out to avoid that danger. Dangerousness and behaviour are measurable, but it seems there is no role for felt emotions, which still remains penetrable only to subjective measures.

An influential development in recent years has been research into the neuroanatomical substrates of emotion and cognition. This research has exploited more sophisticated imaging equipment that has allowed insight into the hardware of the mind and an increased interest in the relation between the mind and the brain. This hardware approach has circumvented some of the measurement problems associated with emotion. Even though we do not know precisely how happy or sad someone is, at least we could see differential activation in the brain. For example, Damasio (1994) argues that reason and emotion go hand in hand, without one we would not have the other and suggests this interaction occurs in the frontal lobes. Whereas LeDoux (1994) has documented the specific neuroanatomical circuits involved with the representation of fear and has implicated the amygdala. Both LeDoux and Damasio's work, amongst others, has brought emotion and cognition back together. However, they have done so only by utilising one approach: by looking at how the hardware of the brain relates to the interaction of emotion and cognition. This is only part of the story.

Contemporary cognitive psychology assumes a computational approach. Computational explanation, according to Marr (1982), involves three interacting levels of explanation. At the computational level, the functions that the cognitive system needs to compute are specified. Such theories are constrained to be both normatively justified and descriptively adequate. At the algorithmic level, the cognitive processes that compute these functions, and the representations over which they operate are specified. Finally at the implementational level, the actual hardware in which the algorithms are implemented is outlined. Relating cognition-emotion interactions only to brain function deals only with this last level of providing a computational explanation. Marr originally proposed that it was a logical priority to sort out the computational level first, as only with this level in place, would one know what algorithms to look for and what kinds of brain mechanisms would be needed. These days, these levels are usually thought of as non-autonomous and mutually constraining. So it is useful to know something of the computationally relevant aspects of the hardware of the brain as they might constrain the possible algorithms that can be implemented and may influence their complexity profiles, e.g., how long they take to compute a given function. *Emotional Cognition* seeks to provide a more rounded picture of computational approaches to emotion and cognition by looking also at the algorithmic and computational levels. We hope, therefore, that *Emotional Cognition* presents a broader and more complete picture of the relation between cognition and emotion from a cognitive psychological, and hence computational, perspective.

In keeping with Marr's framework, the chapters in *Emotional Cognition* cross the different levels he proposed with many contributors, although starting from one or other position, also speculating on how their work might be extended into the others. The book begins with Buchanan and Adolphs (*The

Role of the Human Amygdala in Emotional Modulation of Long-Term Declarative Memory) mechanistic account of the role of the amygdala in the emotional modulation of long-term declarative memory. It makes perfectly good sense to remember aspects of the environment that lead to a happy or sad experience: you might wish to avoid events that made you sad and seek out those that make you happy. Unsurprisingly, there is a large literature that shows that long-term memory is modulated by emotion (e.g. Christianson 1992). Buchanan and Adolphs address how emotion influences the way that material is stored in relation to the current emotional state. In so doing they review what is currently known about the physiology of emotion and memory, providing important insights into this complex relationship.

Killcross and Blundell (*Associative Representations of Emotionally Significant Outcomes*) consider the amygdala's role in acquiring associative representations of emotionally significant outcomes. The amygdala has long been regarded as a central component of emotion (LeDoux 1992) and they suggest that the amygdala plays a vital role in the formation of a representation that integrates sensory and motivational properties of goals or rewards. They further explicate the nature of these representations and how they are formed in an associative-cybernetic model of instrumental action.

Under the right circumstances, using backward masking, it is possible to show someone an emotive picture without them being consciously aware of what they have been shown. Even under these circumstances people appear to have some representation of the emotional content of that picture (Ladavas, Cimatti, Del Pesce, & Tuozzi 1993). This would suggest that evaluative processes may be located very early in information processing and may be a fundamental aspect of how we see the world. Fulcher's chapter (*Neurons with Attitude*) examines how stimuli are evaluated and incorporates a detailed neural network model of how these evaluations are learnt, one that defines the subject matter and makes testable predictions. The key to Fulcher's account is the observation that evaluative information is extracted quickly and without awareness.

This issue is examined further by Winkielman, Schwarz and Nowak (*Affect and Processing Dynamics*) who suggest that perceptual fluency, the amount of effort put into processing information, may be responsible for eliciting an emotion. Evaluation, which involves the emotions, is a way of coming to understand the world (Plato was wrong, we do not come to understand the world through reason alone). This is an important issue as it subtly moves research away from the view that emotion is some post hoc reaction to our deliberations towards the view that emotion is related to how we come to understand the world.

Are feelings emotions? This is an important question, examined by Prinz (*Somatic Appraisals and Emotional Consciousness*), and directly relates to the claim that emotion is separate from cognition. It does seem reasonable to assume that emotions are feelings that are in turn sensations. With a change in emotion we are aware of some physiological changes such as an increase in ones heart rate. However, much goes *unfelt*, such as changes in, say the activity of the brain. But what is essential is that none of these changes are paradigmatic of one, and only one, emotion (Boiton 1996; Ekman et al. 1983). So how do we know we are in one emotional state rather than another when so much that constitutes an emotion is outside of our awareness? Prinz presents, at a philosophical/computational level, his AIR theory of consciousness to address this issue.

Beliefs and goals are the mainstay of cognitivism but we live in an uncertain world, one where we are confronted with more and more information. Employing our beliefs to accurately navigate our world and attain our goals, is fraught with difficulty. This difficulty is compounded by the limitations imposed by our cognitive system (Gigerenzer & Goldstein 1996). Oatley and Johnson-Laird (*Emotion and Reasoning to Consistency*) suggest that emotions are elicited when things go wrong and errors are made. Importantly, Oatley and Johnson-Laird place goals and beliefs as central to emotion. This is a marked shift from how emotion was initially conceived by Plato and Darwin (see above). Emotion is now seen as a consequence of cognition, rather than a visceral sensation. Further, Oatley and Johnson-Laird suggest that emotion acts as a heuristic that biases the cognitive system to resolve the inconsistencies with which it is confronted.

According to classical economic theory, the decisions we make are those that maximise our subjective utilities. However, we also have preferences for our emotions and generally prefer to remain happy than experience sadness. This is the focus of Schwartz's (*Expected Feelings about Risky Options*) chapter and he makes the claim that people can gauge how they will feel given some decision and that these anticipated feelings influences their choice. What is more, he presents data suggesting people are swayed by how they anticipate they will feel as much as the objective returns given some option. Although intuitive, we often invest considerable time and money securing our happiness, this is at odds with traditional economic theory.

Although decision theory is also central to Busemeyer, Townsend and Stout's chapter (*Motivational Underpinnings of Utility in Decision Making*) they use an extension of decision field theory (Busemeyer & Townsend 1993) to examine the influence of emotion on decision-making. Decision field theory represents an important extension of decision theory, which assumes our perceived utilities are static and fixed. In contrast, decision field theory makes the intuitive claim that our perceived values vary under differing circumstances, levels of consumption and so forth. Using decision field theory, Busemeyer and Townsend examine decision-making in a variety of experimental contexts and hypothesise that emotional plays an important role in determining the decision-makers subjective utilities.

Moore and Oaksford (*An Informational Value for Mood: Negative Mood Biases Attention to Global Information in a Probabilistic Classification Task*) examine how emotion can be represented in relation to a classification task. In this empirical chapter they present data suggesting that negative mood biases visual attention towards information located at low visual spatial frequencies under conditions of maximal uncertainty. They further suggest that, and contrary to the view that mood has no information value compared to emotion, one effect of mood may be to act as an attentional weight in the dimensional representation of information, one that has its strongest effect under conditions of uncertainty.

Ashby, Valentin and Turken (*The Effects of Positive Affect and Arousal on Working Memory and Executive Attention*) examine the effects of positive affect and arousal on working memory and executive attention via a neural network model of the hardware involved in creative problem solving tasks (Dunkers Candle Task, Remote Associates Task and a words association task). To achieve this they consider a wide range of normally disparate literatures. For example, dopamine has long been associated with emotion (Schildkraut & Kety 1967) and positive mood has been associated with creativity (Isen 1987). To determine the relationship between mood, behaviour and the brain they propose a neural network model that captures the behavioural effects of dopamine (associated with more positive moods) and show how the model can account for the effects of mood on behaviour.

Goal states are an important feature of many of the chapters in this volume. Gray and Braver's chapter (*Integration of Emotion and Cognitive Control: A Neurocomputational Hypothesis of Dynamic Goal Regulation*) deals with rewards and punishments and their relationship to approach and withdrawal goals. Starting with a psychologically plausible account of why we should avoid punishment and approach rewards they posit an informal computational model whereby emotion prioritises one or other of the two goal states (approach and withdrawal). Drawing on research on the anatomical substrates of working memory (Smith & Jonides 1999) their computational model is then applied to research on the neuroanatomical substrates of emotion and cognition. They suggest that different emotions serve to prioritise different goal states and suggest how this relationship is realised anatomically.

As a whole, *Emotional Cognition* attempts to present the reader with an up to date overview of the current state of emotion and cognition research that is striving for computationally explicit accounts of the relationship between these two domains. Many different areas are covered across a range of cognitive research, from the neurosciences through mathematical models to philosophy. We think that the emergence of such an integrative, computational, approach in emotion and cognition research is an exciting development. And we hope that this collection will stimulate even more research in the same vein.

Acknowledgements

We would like to thank the contributors to this volume for their enthusiasm about the project and for their timely delivery of the manuscripts that has made our job so much easier. We also thank Maxim Stamenov at John Benjamin for soliciting this volume and for their support generally. Finally we thank our families, SCM: Jo, Katherine, Sue and Paul, MO: Karen, for their patience and forbearance while we have been involved in this project.

References

Birley, A. R. (1987). *Marcus Aurelius: A Biography*. London: Batsford.
Boiton, F. (1996). Autonomic response patterns during voluntary facial action. *Psychophysiology, 33*, 123–131.
Busemeyer, J. R., & Townsend, J. T. (1993). Decision field theory: A dynamic-cognitive approach to decision making in an uncertain world. *Psychological Review, 100*(3), 432–459.
Christianson, S. A. (1992). *The Handbook of Emotion and Memory: Research and Theory*. Hillsdale, NJ: Lawrence Erlbaum Associates.
Damasio, A. R. (1994). *Descartes Error: Emotion, Reason, and the Human Brain*. New York: Avon Books.
Ekman, P., Levenson, R. W., & Friesen, W. V. (1983). Autonomic nervous system activity distinguishes among emotions. *Science, 221*, 1208–1210.
Gigerenzer, G., & Goldstein, D. G. (1996). Reasoning the fast and frugal way: Models of bounded rationality. *Psychological Review, 103*(4), 650–669.

Goleman, D. (1996). *Emotional Intelligence: Why it can Matter More than IQ.* London: Bloomsbury.

Isen, A. M. (1987). Positive affect, cognitive processes, and social behavior. *Advances in Experimental Psychology, 20,* 203–253.

James, W. (1884). What is an emotion? *Mind, 9,* 188–205.

Ladavas, E., Cimatti, D., Del Pesce, M., & Tuozzi, G. (1993). Emotional evaluation with and without conscious stimulus identification: Evidence from a split-brain patient. *Cognition and Emotion, 7*(1), 95–114.

Lang, P. J., Greenwald, M. K., & Bradley, M. M. (1993). Looking at pictures: Affective, facial, visceral, and behavioral reactions. *Psychophysiology, 30,* 261–273.

LeDoux, J. E. (1994). In search of an emotional system in the brain: Leaping from fear to emotion and consciousness. M. S. Gazzaniga (Ed.), *The Cognitive Neurosciences* (pp. 1049–1061). Cambridge, MA: MIT Press.

LeDoux, J. E. (1992). Emotion and the Amygdala. J. P. Aggleton (ed.), *The Amygdala: Neurobiological Aspects of Emotion, Memory, and Mental Dysfunction.* New York: Wiley Liss, Inc.

Marr, D. (1982). *Vision: A Computaional Investigation into the Human Representation and Processing of Visual Information.* New York: Freeman.

Schildkraut, J. J., & Kety, S. (1967). Biogenic amines and emotion. *Science, 156,* 21–30.

Smith, E. E., & Jonides, J. (1999). Storage and executive processes in the frontal lobes. *Science, 283,* 1657–1661.

CHAPTER 2

The role of the human amygdala in emotional modulation of long-term declarative memory

Tony W. Buchanan and Ralph Adolphs
University of Iowa College of Medicine

It seems obvious that some events are better remembered than others are. The emotional salience of a situation often determines the subsequent memory for that situation. Ultimately the role of emotion is to support survival and well-being in an organism's interactions with the environment (Adolphs & Damasio 2000). There would seem to be survival value in creating stronger associations during emotional situations – it would be adaptive for an organism to remember the location of a water source or a predatory attack over less relevant information. The nervous system has evolved mechanisms that facilitate the formation of emotional memories in the service of survival. The neural basis of emotional memory has been studied extensively in animal models. Examination of the neural basis of human emotional memory is a relatively recent endeavor that has been fostered by interdisciplinary research in the field of cognitive neuroscience. A major thrust of this research has been a focus on the role of the amygdala in the formation of long-term declarative memory for emotionally arousing material. This chapter will focus on the role of the human amygdala in the formation of long-term emotional declarative memories. Following an introduction to the effect of emotion on human long-term declarative memory, we will review neurobiological studies that have used the lesion method, functional neuroimaging and pharmacological probes in the investigation of emotional memory.

Throughout the history of the study of emotions and memory there has been controversy concerning the nature of the association between these phenomena. The psychodynamic concept of repression states that memories associated with negative emotional states are not remembered as well as emotionally neutral memories. This repression was proposed as a mechanism to shield the conscious mind from emotional trauma. Contrary to this view, research illustrates that emotional memories are not repressed at all, but are more vivid and better recalled than memories which are not associated with emotion (Schwartz & Reisberg 1991). So-called flashbulb memories are an example of this enhancement of memory for emotional events (Brown & Kulick 1977). This phenomenon is characterized by a heightened sense of vividness and clarity regarding an individual's personal experiences upon hearing emotionally activating news. In spite of the enhanced clarity of the memory trace, these memories are not necessarily accurate (Schmolck, Buffalo, & Squire 2000).

Two lines of evidence are relevant to the discussion of flashbulb memories as a modulation of memory by emotion. The first came out of animal research and is known as the Easterbrook hypothesis (Easterbrook 1959). This hypothesis proposes that emotional arousal causes a narrowing of the range of attention (or range of cue utilization in Easterbrook's terminology) such that low arousal would lead to a greater amount of information taken in, including relevant and irrelevant information. Conversely, high arousal should lead to a narrowed focus of attention to relevant cues, resulting in improved memory performance for highly salient cues and less to peripheral cues due to the exclusion of distraction. This would suggest an attentional mechanism whereby more attention is focused on one aspect of a situation leading to improved memory for that aspect and diminished memory for those details in the periphery.

The second line of evidence is derived from human research on eyewitness testimony (Loftus 1979). The emotional nature and memory demands of eyewitness testimony make it an externally valid means of examining the effect of emotion on memory. A common phenomenon reported anecdotally is known as the 'weapon focus.' The prototype of this phenomenon involves an eyewitness to a crime focusing primarily on the weapon used by the perpetrator to the exclusion of other aspects of the incident. This fits with the Easterbrook hypothesis in that it involves an increased memory for one aspect of a situation and diminished memory for peripheral details.

What aspect of emotion is most important for the modulation of declarative memory? Evidence so far indicates that it is primarily emotional arousal, as opposed to valence (or pleasantness). Some psychological theories of emotion have argued that valence and arousal are two orthogonal factors that may capture the entire spectrum of basic emotions (Lang, Greenwald, Bradley, & Hamm 1993; Russell 1980; Russell & Bullock 1985; Russell, Lewicka, & Niit 1989). Several studies have shown that emotions, as depicted both in facial expressions and in verbal labels, can be represented in a two dimensional space with valence and arousal as orthogonal axes (Lang et al. 1993; Russell 1980; Russell & Bullock 1985; Russell et al. 1989). Using this framework, studies have shown that stimuli are remembered better the more emotionally arousing they are (Bradley, Greenwald, Petry, & Lang 1992; Hamann, Cahill, & Squire 1997). These findings have led to the hypothesis that it is emotional arousal, and not valence, that is the major factor contributing to how well material is encoded into declarative memory. This hypothesis has been directly tested by manipulating arousal, either pharmacologically (Cahill, Prins, Weber, & McGaugh 1994) or through the use of a specific context (Cahill & McGaugh 1995) in normal human subjects. In the remainder of the chapter the term 'emotional memory' will be used to describe the effect of emotional arousal during encoding on subsequent recollection of the arousing materials.

The aforementioned examples illustrate the complexity of the relationship between emotion and memory. The experience of emotion appears to modulate memory by alternately enhancing or impoverishing memory performance depending upon the details involved in the test of memory. It would seem that the experience of flashbulb memories are at odds with the position espoused in the Easterbrook hypothesis and the phenomenon of weapon focus (Heuer & Reisberg 1990). Flashbulb memories are thought to be vivid due to the inclusion of a great many peripheral details, which is just the opposite of the Easterbrook/weapon focus claim which states that memory for peripheral details is reduced while central information is enhanced. Heuer and Reisberg (1990) suggest that while emotion leads to vivid recollections, these recollections may not be accurate and could be the result of post-hoc reconstructions of the emotional event. This contention is consistent with Loftus' work on the fallibility of eyewitness testimony (Loftus 1979).

Heuer and Reisberg (1990) designed an experiment to assess the impact of emotional arousal on both central and peripheral memory. In the study, subjects watched a series of slides accompanied by a narrative. Each participant was randomly assigned to either the neutral or arousing version of slides. In the neutral version, the slides featured a story about a boy and his mother going to visit his father at a garage. The arousal version also features a story about a boy and his mother visiting the father at work, however in this version, the father is a surgeon at a local hospital and several of the slides feature graphic portrayals of surgery scenes. The slides were roughly matched for structure and layout. The participants were not told that their memory for the slides would be tested, instead they were told that the purpose of the experiment was to assess heart rate responses to the different slide presentations. A third group of participants, however, saw the neutral slides and was told to attempt to memorize the details of the slides. Participants were asked to return two weeks later at which time a surprise memory test was given. The memory test consisted of both recall and recognition questions regarding central and peripheral material contained within the two slide presentations. Results showed that those in the arousal group had increased memory for both central and peripheral aspects of the slide presentation compared to those who watched the neutral slides.

Additionally, the arousal group showed increased memory compared to the memorizing group in peripheral details. The authors discuss this finding as a contrast to the idea that the arousing material may have been more interesting and therefore, more time would have been spent thinking about the material. The memorizing group were those most likely to rehearse the information that they saw prior to memory assessment, and yet their performance on recall of peripheral details was worse than the arousal group. These data fit with the data on flashbulb memories, but do not support the claims of the Easterbrook hypothesis. This study illustrates that both central and peripheral details of an emotional situation are better remembered than details from a neutral situation.

Cahill and McGaugh (1995) point out a possible confound of these findings in regard to the effect of emotional arousal on memory. In the Heuer and Reisberg (1990) study, participants in the emotional arousal group were exposed to stimuli that were not presented to the other group. It is therefore possible that the differences in memory performance between groups may be due to different features of the stimuli other than their emotional content (differences due to story effects versus emotion effects). Cahill and McGaugh designed a study to address this possible confound (Cahill & McGaugh 1995). All participants were exposed to the same slides (similar to the slides from the arousal condition in the Heuer and Reisberg study), different only in narration, to create two different stories, one neutral and one arousing. The only difference between the two conditions consisted of the narration during the middle phase of each slide presentation. In the neutral condition, the narration describes the son watching his father conduct mock surgery during a disaster drill at the hospital. In the arousal condition, the boy is badly injured on the way to the hospital and a surgeon attempts to save the boy's life. Graphic pictures of surgery in the neutral condition were described as being an actor made up to appear badly injured, whereas the arousal condition narration described the slides as actual surgery on the boy. As in the earlier study, participants returned two weeks later expecting to see a new set of slides, but were presented with an unexpected memory test consisting of recall and recognition questions. Results of this study showed that both groups had identical performance for the neutral portions of the slide narration. The arousal group, however, had markedly increased performance for the arousal portion of the narration both in free recall and recognition tests compared to the neutral group. Additionally, participants who reported greater emotional reaction to the emotional slides also showed better performance. The authors interpret these findings as showing a specific effect of emotional arousal on subsequent memory performance.

Findings from these studies illustrate that emotionally arousing stimuli – including both central and peripheral details – are better remembered than neutral stimuli. A question that arises from these results is: What are the neurobiological underpinnings of emotional memory?

Neurobiology of emotional memory

By virtue of its position in the brain, the amygdala has been the focus of much interest as a possible site of learning and memory for many years (Squire 1987). It was originally thought to play an integral role in the formation of declarative memories. More careful study has revealed the role of the amygdala to be separate from the traditional 'medial temporal lobe memory system', which includes the hippocampus and adjacent cortex (Murray 1992; Zola-Morgan, Squire, Alvarez-Royo, & Clower 1991; Zola-Morgan, Squire, & Amaral 1986). There is now evidence, however, that the amygdala plays a modulatory rather than an essential role in declarative memory formation. This evidence is derived from a model of the amygdala's role in memory formation derived from animal research (McGaugh 2000). In this model, the amygdala is part of a neurobiological system – including stress hormones – that regulates the formation of memory for emotionally salient events via its influence on other brain structures – including the hippocampus and caudate/putamen (Packard & Teather 1998). Within this model, the amygdala is not the site of memory storage, but is involved only in the formation of memories. Also according to this model, the amygdala is not involved in the retrieval of memories – emotional or otherwise – but only in modulating initial encoding and consolidation of memories. While the specifics of this model are controversial (Cahill, Weinberger, Roozendaal, & McGaugh 1999; Fanselow & LeDoux 1999), both animal and human research supports the idea of a selective role of the amygdala in the formation of emotionally significant long-term memories. Additionally, there is evidence that the amygdala is involved in storage of non-declarative emotional memory, for example auditory fear conditioning (Maren 2000).

While our review will focus on emotional memory in humans, we briefly mention studies in animals. A large literature from such studies has demonstrated that the amygdala critically influences both the acquisition and the expression of emotional memories. Much of the evidence to support this claim comes from studies of motivated learning, using both appetitive as well as aversive stimuli. In these experiments, clear evidence has been obtained that the behavioral expression of emotionally motivated learning depends on the integrity of the amygdala during a narrow and highly specific window of time (McGaugh 2000). Notably, the amygdala appears to play a critical role immediately after acquisition of the behavior, and for some time thereafter. These findings have been interpreted as evidence for the amygdala's role specifically in the consolidation processes of motivated learning that are influenced by emotional arousal, a finding also consistent with studies in humans (see below; McGaugh 2000). Direct manipulations of neural activity in the amygdala with reversible pharmacological lesions have shown that the amygdala exerts its modulatory effect on secondary structures, such as the hippocampus, that are directly involved in memory consolidation (McGaugh & Izquierdo 2000; Packard & Teather 1998; Roozendaal 2000).

Lesion studies of emotional memory

As with most brain-behavior relationships, our primary source of information on the role of the amygdala in human behavior has come from patients with specific lesions. This pattern holds true for the relationship between the amygdala and emotional declarative memories as well. While selective bilateral lesions of the amygdala are rare, the few cases that have been reported are illustrative. In addition to bilateral temporal lobectomies, two disorders have been described that result in the bilateral destruction of the amygdala: 1) Urbach-Wiethe disease and 2) Herpes simplex encephalitis. Urbach-Wiethe disease (also known as lipoid proteinosis) is a rare hereditary disorder characterized by the deposition of hyaline material in the skin and mouth areas, and is associated with bilateral mineralization of medial temporal lobe structures in about half of the cases. Herpes simplex encephalitis is an inflammation of neural structures following viral infection. While this disease may result in widespread pathology throughout the nervous system, its earliest pathology almost invariably includes the amygdalae. Additionally, unilateral temporal lobectomy is commonly employed in the surgical treatment of intractable epilepsy. Here we report on studies of long-term declarative memory of emotional events from subjects with both bilateral and unilateral amygdala damage.

One of the cases of bilateral amygdala damage that has been best characterized was originally reported by Tranel and Hyman (Tranel & Hyman 1990). The patient (SM046) had been diagnosed with Urbach-Wiethe disease. Computerized tomography (CT) and magnetic resonance imaging (MRI) confirmed the mineralization of both amygdalae, as well as minimal damage to anterior entorhinal cortices, but no other structural abnormality. Neuropsychological evaluation of this patient revealed normal general intellect, language and verbal memory function. These results are in stark contrast to the profound declarative memory impairment following hippocampal damage (Squire 1987). Follow-up research with patient SM046 and others with amygdala damage has highlighted the modulatory role in declarative memory formation played by the amygdala. While no explicit tests of emotion or emotional memory were originally documented, later work with this patient (described below) has addressed her emotional memory function.

The results of a conditioning study conducted by Bechara and colleagues (Bechara et al. 1995) illustrate the separable roles of the amygdala and hippocampus in the memory formation. The ability of patient SM046 to show conditioned autonomic responses to conditioned stimuli (CS) paired with an aversive sound (unconditioned stimulus; US) was tested in comparison to a patient with bilateral hippocampal damage as well as a patient with bilateral damage to both amygdalae and hippocampi. Results illustrated that while SM046 was impaired in the production of conditioned autonomic responses to the CS, she was able to form declarative memories for which stimulus was paired with the aversive sound. The patient with hippocampal damage displayed the opposite pattern, showing no declarative knowledge of the CS-US contingency, but exhibiting normal conditioned autonomic responses to the CS presentation. The patient with damage to both amygdala and hippocampus failed to form either associative or declarative memories during the task. In this study, declarative memory for the CS-US contingency was not dependent on the amygdala. While both the amygdala and hippocampus are necessary for the 'normal' performance of these tasks, bilateral damage to either structure results in a dissociable pattern of deficits.

Markowitsch and colleagues have examined emotional memory formation in two patients with Urbach-Wiethe disease (Markowitsch et al. 1994). Both patients showed bilateral mineralization of the amygdala. Neuropsychological evaluation revealed that while neither patient had a general impairment of declarative memory, they were slightly impaired on several specific tests of memory (e.g., Auditory Verbal Learning). Memory for emotional material was similarly depressed, with one patient (C.P.) showing more impairment than the other (B.P.). Specifically, in a word stem completion task of previously presented emotional or neutral words, C.P. remembered the neutral words better than the emotional words, while B.P. showed roughly equivalent performance for neutral and emotional stimuli, as compared to control subjects who tend to remember the emotional stimuli better. Similarly, in a recognition test of previously presented emotional pictures, C.P. recognized neutral pictures better than emotional pictures in contrast to normal controls who showed enhanced recognition performance of the emotional materials. This study was one of the first to examine the relationship between emotional memories and the amygdala using the lesion method. Subsequent work has refined the experimental stimuli and conditions in order to better address this relationship.

Two studies have provided a follow-up experiment, all using the same task in rare patients with selective bilateral amygdala damage (Adolphs et al. 1997; Cahill et al. 1995). Subjects completed a task that shows a reliable effect of emotional content on memory performance in normal human participants, the 'Reisberg Task' mentioned earlier (Cahill & McGaugh 1995; Heuer & Reisberg 1990). In the task, participants are presented with 12 slides with an accompanying narration. The slides depict a mother and son going to visit the boy's father at a local hospital. While on route to the hospital, they are involved in a traffic accident and the boy is rushed to the hospital where a surgeon attempts to save the boy's life. The story of the slides and narration may be divided into three phases: phase 1 contains non-arousing material (e.g., the boy and mother on their way to the hospital), phase 2 contains emotionally arousing material (scenes of surgery), and phase 3 again contains neutral materials (mother leaving the hospital). Participants were told only to play close attention to the slides, but no mention of a memory test was made. All studies found a similar impairment in subjects with bilateral amygdala damage. For example, in the study by Adolphs et al. (1997), immediately after viewing the slides, subjects were asked to rate their emotional reactions to the story; all subjects rated the story equally on this measure. Twenty-four hours after exposure to the slides, memory for the stimuli was tested using a multiple-choice questionnaire. While normal participants remembered slides from phase 2 significantly better than the other two phases, neither amygdala damaged patient showed this pattern. Specifically, the one slide remembered best by the control participants (a slide showing the surgically reattached legs of a car-crash victim) was the slide on which the two patients deviated most from the controls' scores (see Figure 1). The pattern of impaired facilitation of memory for emotionally arousing material in the face of otherwise normal overall memory performance in subjects with bilateral amygdala damage contrasts sharply with the performances given by amnesic subjects. Subjects with hippocampal or diencephalic amnesia are impaired in their overall memory performance, but show a normal (albeit smaller absolute magnitude) enhancement when the subject matter is emotionally arousing (Hamann et al. 1997).

Using the same task, Adolphs and colleagues examined the pattern of emotional memory performance following unilateral amygdala damage (Adolphs, Tranel, & Denburg 2000). Eight subjects with unilateral amygdala damage consequent to temporal lobectomy (6 left; 2 right), 9 brain damaged controls with no damage to the anterior temporal lobe, and 7 normal controls participated in the study. In this experiment, each slide in the story was rated on scales of emotional valence, arousal, unusualness, and complexity. There were no group differences in slide ratings. As in the previous study, both normal con-

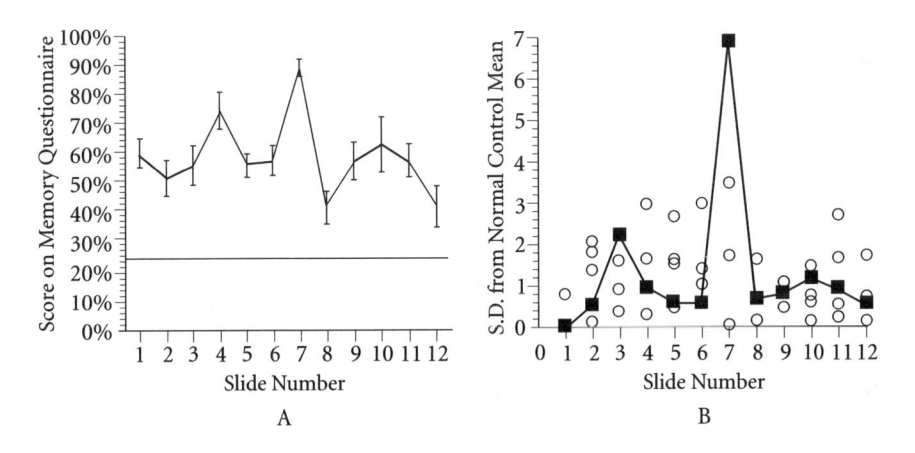

Figure 1. Bilateral damage to the human amygdala impairs declarative memory for emotionally arousing material. Subjects were shown a series of 12 slides that varied in emotional arousal. Slide 7 was the most arousing slide, showing surgically reattached legs of a car-crash victim. A, Data from seven normal control subjects, showing memory score on a questionnaire about each slide. Chance is at 25% (solid line). B, Data from six brain-damaged control subjects with no damage to amygdala (circles) and from subject SM (solid line), plotted as differences from the control data, SM differed most from controls on the most emotional slide, an impairment not shown by any of the brain-damaged control subjects. (Reprinted from Adolphs, Cahill, Schul, & Babinsky. Impaired declarative memory for emotional material following bilateral amygdala damage in humans. Learn Mem 1997; 4: 291–300. Copyright ©1997 Cold Spring Harbor Laboratory Press.)

trols and brain damaged controls showed enhanced memory for phase 2 of the slide/narrative story, specifically for the most highly arousing slide. This pattern was also found for the 2 subjects with right amygdala damage. Those subjects with left amygdala damage, however, failed to show enhanced memory for this slide, showing the same pattern as previously reported for subjects with bilateral amygdala damage. These findings suggest a role for the left amygdala in the consolidation of declarative memory for emotionally arousing stimuli.

Further studies have addressed the role of unilateral amygdala damage in the formation of memory for emotional words. Phelps and colleagues examined emotional memory formation in 26 subjects following unilateral temporal lobectomy (Phelps, LaBar, & Spencer 1997). In experiment 1, subjects were presented with a list of 27 words (9 positive, 9 negative, and 9 neutral) while skin conductance responses (SCRs) were recorded. A surprise recall test was administered 1 minute after the presentation of the word list. Results illustrated that the left temporal lobectomy group had the worst recall of the word list, but this effect was not statistically significant. Each group recalled the negative and positive words better than the neutral words, but there was no difference among the groups in terms of the pattern of slide recall. The authors noted that the words used in the negative ('victim') and positive ('comedy') categories were perhaps not salient enough to produce the emotional arousal necessary to show any group differences in emotional memory performance. In fact, the SCR data illustrated that the neutral word category elicited a greater response than did either emotion word category. In light of these findings, these investigators report a subsequent study designed specifically to address the role of the arousal dimension in memory consolidation (LaBar & Phelps 1998). In this follow-up study, 22 temporal lobectomy patients (10 left, 12 right) were presented with a list of 40 words (20 arousing, 20 neutral). The arousing words chosen in this study consisted of 'profanities, sexually explicit words, and words depicting social taboos.' These words were successful in producing increased SCRs and were rated as significantly more arousing than neutral words in controls and in both temporal lobectomy groups. Free recall for the words was assessed both immediately and at 1 hour post-encoding. The results were assessed in terms of 'forgetting rates' between the immediate and delayed free recall tests. Only the control group showed a differential forgetting rate for the arousing versus neutral words, showing increased recall for the arousing words at the delayed recall test. Both the right and the left temporal lobectomy group showed decreased memory for the arousing words at delayed recall. Consistent with the two previously reported studies, the left temporal lobectomy group showed the poorest levels of recall; their performance was significantly worse than both controls and the right temporal lobectomy group. This effect was not, however, specific to emotionally arousing material, as the left temporal lobectomy group showed reduced overall performance, but not a specific impairment on memory for emotional stimuli. While these results are consistent with previous research showing a left-hemisphere dominance for verbal memory, they do not address a specific role of the right or left amygdala in memory for verbal versus visual emotional stimuli.

A recent study in this lab has attempted to address this issue (Buchanan, Denburg, Tranel & Adolphs 2001). Participants consisted of 20 subjects with unilateral amygdala damage following temporal lobectomy for treatment of epilepsy (11 left, 9 right) and 25 brain damaged controls with unilateral lesions outside the temporal lobe. Additionally, 35 normal control subjects were recruited for participation. Participants were tested on two days, on the first session 15 pictures differing in emotional salience (5 pleasant, 5 unpleasant, 5 neutral) were presented along with a one-sentence verbal narrative description (e.g., accompanying a picture of two parents with their new twin babies was the narrative: 'After the babies were born, both parents were very happy, although a bit exhausted.'). During picture presentation, SCRs were recorded. Subjects were told to watch attentively while the emotional responses to the stimuli were recorded, no mention of a follow-up memory test was made. Twenty-four hours after the first session, subjects' memory for the slides was assessed with free recall, multiple choice and 4-alternative forced choice recognition tests. Within both free recall and multiple choice tests, memory for both narrative and picture information was assessed. The recognition test assessed only recognition of visual detail. Results illustrated that the group with left amygdala damage was specifically impaired on memory for emotional narratives relative to memory for neutral narratives. Interestingly, this group was not impaired on memory for emotional picture information. The right amygdala group, on the other hand, were impaired on visual recognition memory; however this impairment was not specific to emotional pictures. These findings support a role of the left amygdala in the processing of verbal emotional stimuli and a role of the right amygdala in processing visual emotional stimuli, corroborating previous work describing the separable language versus visuospatial processing roles for the left and right hemispheres, respectively. These data replicate previous work illustrating a deficit in verbal emotional memory in individuals with left amygdala damage (LaBar & Phelps 1998; Phelps et al. 1997) while illustrating a lateralized pattern of the amygdala's influence on emotional memory. Future work should further examine the lateralization of amygdala involvement in the processing of emotional memory (Cahill et al. 2001).

Neuroimaging studies of emotional memory

Functional neuroimaging has provided another tool with which to examine the role of the human amygdala in the formation of emotional memories. Several recent studies have been able to test specific hypotheses derived from both animal research and studies in humans with amygdala lesions using positron emission tomography (PET) and functional magnetic resonance imaging (fMRI).

The first study to examine the role of the human amygdala in the formation of emotional memories using functional neuroimaging was conducted by Cahill and colleagues (Cahill et al. 1996). Healthy participants viewed emotionally arousing and neutral videos during PET scanning. Three weeks later, participants were asked to recall all the information that they could remember from each video. As expected, participants recalled significantly more information from the emotionally arousing video than from the neutral video. Correlation analyses revealed a significant positive correlation between the glucose metabolic rate of the right amygdala and the number of emotional film clips recalled ($r = 0.93$). Further analyses showed no such association with recall of neutral film clips. These findings suggest that the amygdala is activated during the encoding of emotionally arousing events and is involved in the translation of these events into long-term memory. A follow-up study corroborated the finding that amygdala activity is not involved in the formation of declarative memory for nonemotional material (Alkire, Haier, Fallon, & Cahill 1998). This study did, however, document an association between hippocampal activity and the formation of memory for a nonemotional word list. These two studies further illustrate the dissociation of memory functions between the hippocampus and amygdala, and highlight a specific role of the amygdala in the formation of emotional memories.

Two recent studies have extended these findings to show an association between bilateral amygdala activity during encoding and memory for both emotionally pleasant and unpleasant stimuli using both PET (Hamann, Ely, Grafton, & Kilts 1999) and fMRI (Canli, Zhao, Desmond, Glover, & Gabrieli 1999). The study by Hamann and colleagues additionally tested the emotional specificity of the amygdala's influence on memory by including a stimulus category of interesting and memorable pictures. These interesting pictures included a chrome rhinoceros and a scene from a surrealist painting. Presumably, if the amygdala is involved in general memory enhancement, then amygdala activity should be associated with memory for memorable yet nonemotional stimuli. Results from this study illustrate that while these interesting pictures were better remembered than neutral and pleasant pictures at 4 weeks after encoding, this enhancement was unrelated to amygdala activity that was specifically related only to memory for aversive and pleasant stimuli (a finding also consistent with studies in monkeys, which have failed to find any effect of amygdala lesions on the von Restorff effect – enhanced memory for especially unusual or distinctive stimuli in a set; (Parker, Wilding, & Akerman 1998). These results highlight the specific role of the amygdala in the enhancement of memories for emotionally significant material.

A recent event-related fMRI study has shown that only those stimuli rated as the most emotionally intense are associated with increased amygdala activity and increased memory performance (Canli, Zhao, Brewer, Gabrieli, & Cahill 2000). In this study, 10 female volunteers were exposed to a selection of neutral and emotionally negative pictures while the fMRI response was recorded for each picture. Immediately after viewing each picture, subjects rated their emotional response on a scale from 0 indicating 'not emotionally intense at all' to 3 indicating 'extremely emotionally intense.' Analysis of the fMRI response illustrated that bilateral amygdala activity was correlated with increased ratings of emotional intensity, such that the greater the emotional intensity, the greater the amygdala response. Three weeks later, subjects returned for a surprise memory test in which they were asked to report whether they were certain that they remembered a slide, whether the slide seemed familiar or whether they did not remember the slide. Performance data illustrated that those slides rated as 'extremely emotionally intense' were remembered significantly better than those rated as less intense. Additionally, the degree of left amygdala activation during picture encoding was correlated with subsequent memory for the pictures (see Figure 2). Those pictures that tended to produce the greatest response in the left amygdala were also those that were remembered most often.

Results from lesion studies and neuroimaging investigations would suggest that the amygdala enhances the encoding of emotional stimuli and that this enhancement translates into improved memory performance for these materials. In addition to encoding, long-term memory involves other processes including consolidation and retrieval. The designs of the aforementioned studies have not allowed for the assessment of the role of the amygdala in these other processes of memory for emotional events. Two neuroimaging studies have addressed the role of the amygdala in the recognition of previously presented emotional stimuli (Dolan, Lane, Chua, & Fletcher 2000; Taylor et al. 1998). Taylor and colleagues report a study in which PET scans were taken during the encoding of emotionally unpleasant and neutral pictures and subsequent recognition of these stimuli. Initial encoding of the unpleasant pictures resulted in increased left amygdala activity, but the recognition of these

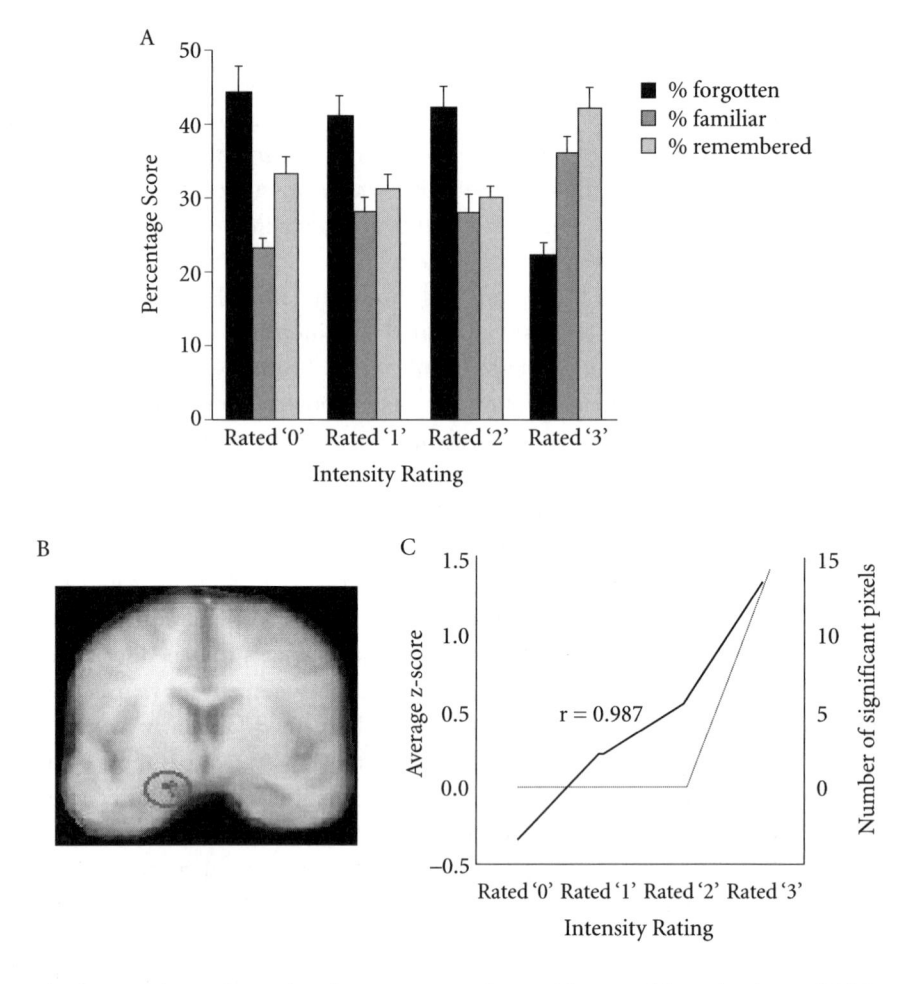

Figure 2. Enhanced emotional memory correlates with amygdala activation to highly emotionally intense stimuli. *A*, Behavioral data on memory performance as a function of subjects' ratings of emotional intensity. *B*, Cluster of significant correlation between amygdala activation and subjects' memory for scenes rated as emotionally highly intense (rated 3). Left side of the image is left side of the brain. *C*, Correlation between left amygdala activation and memory for emotional items increases with greater emotional intensity. Black solid line shows higher z-score averages across the amygdala with higher emotional intensity ratings. Z-scores represent the strength of correlation between amygdala activation and subsequent memory for emotional stimuli. The gray line shows that there were no pixels within the amygdala that reached statistically significant z-score level ($z > 1.96$) for scenes that were rated 0 to 2, but there were 14 significant pixels for scenes that were rated 3. (Reprinted with permission from Canli, Zhao, Brewer, Gabrieli, & Cahill, Event-related activation in the human amygdala associates with later memory for individual emotional experience. J. Neurosci 2000, 20 (RC99), 1–5. Copyright ©2000 Society for Neuroscience.)

same pictures did not affect amygdala activity. Areas associated with recognition included prefrontal and anterior cingulate cortices. These findings fit with the aforementioned model of the role of the amygdala in memory formation derived from animal research (McGaugh 2000) which suggests that the amygdala is involved in the acquisition and consolidation, rather than the retrieval of emotional memory. However, a recent study provided some evidence against this model by examining amygdala activity during the recognition of emotional pictures while controlling for the emotional reaction to the pictures (Dolan et al. 2000). Dolan and colleagues presented emotionally pleasant, unpleasant and neutral pictures to subjects prior to a PET scan during which two different tasks were performed: memory and judgment. In the memory condition, recognition for these pictures was tested using a target detection task. The judgment condition consisted of looking at the same pictures as in the memory condition, but instead of indicating recognition the subjects were instructed only to decide whether the pictures depicted indoor or outdoor scenes. Results illustrated increased left amygdala activity during the recognition of emotional pictures compared to the judgment condition. These findings provide some preliminary evidence that in addition to the previously described role of the amygdala in the encoding of emotional memory, it may also play a role in the retrieval of emotional events.

Findings from several of these studies have illustrated different patterns of lateralized amygdala activity in males (Cahill et al. 1996; Hamann et al. 1999) who showed predominantly right lateralized activation versus females (Canli et al. 1999; Canli et al. 2000) who showed left lateralized activation. These gender differences have recently been addressed in a study utilizing both men and women (Cahill et al. 2001) and using identical experimental conditions as previously used with men only (Cahill et al. 1996). Results from this study illustrated the same gender-specific lateralized pattern of activation previously documented across separate studies with right amygdala activity predicting enhanced emotional memory performance in men while in women, left amygdala activity predicted enhanced emotional memory. The authors suggest that these gender differences may reflect different cognitive strategies between men and women in the processing of these stimuli. These intriguing findings clearly warrant the inclusion of gender and laterality as factors in future work on the relationship between the amygdala and emotional memory.

Pharmacology of emotional memory

The effect of drugs on emotional memory has been studied extensively in animals (McGaugh 2000; McGaugh & Izquierdo 2000) and human research on the topic has been accumulating recently (Buchanan & Lovallo 2001; Cahill et al. 1994; O'Carroll, Drysdale, Cahill, Shajahan, & Ebmeier 1999b; van Stegeren, Everaerd, Cahill, McGaugh, & Gooren 1998). Results from animal research have suggested a role of the stress hormones – both epinephrine and glucocorticoids – in the enhancement of memory by emotion. A great deal of work has characterized the influence of these chemicals on memory through pharmacological and neuroanatomical manipulations. This work has led to the postulation of a neurobiological system – involving both the stress hormones and the amygdala – which is active during arousing learning situations to enhance memory for these events (McGaugh 2000). Briefly, both epinephrine and glucocorticoids can enhance memory for aversive events, this enhancement can be blocked either by lesions of the amygdala or specific pharmacological antagonism of either the adrenergic or glucocorticoid system (Roozendaal 2000). It is proposed that the final common pathway of these hormones' influence on emotional memory is through β-adrenergic activation within the basolateral nucleus of the amygdala which regulates memory consolidation via the hippocampus and striatum (McGaugh 2000).

Human research has tested this model, extending the findings on both epinephrine and cortisol (the human glucocorticoid) to declarative memory for emotional materials. The first study to address this issue in humans examined the effects of β-adrenergic blockade on memory for emotionally arousing slides (the same task described previously; Cahill et al. 1994). Results showed that those individuals receiving the β-blocker did not show enhanced memory for the emotionally arousing slides as the placebo group did. There was no effect of the drug, however, on memory for emotionally neutral slides. These findings illustrate that β-adrenergic activity plays a role in the enhancement of memory for emotional stimuli. Follow-up studies using the same task have illustrated that this effect is dependent on central, but not peripheral adrenergic blockade (van Stegeren et al. 1998; O'Carroll, Drysdale, Cahill, Shajahan, & Ebmeier 1999a) and that enhancement of adrenergic function can enhance the emotional-modulation of memory (O'Carroll et al. 1999b). Specifically, O'Carroll and colleagues (1999b) gave participants either yohimbine, a central noradrenergic agonist, or metoprolol, a central noradrenergic antagonist or placebo prior to viewing the slide series. Results showed a modest, but significant increase in emotional memory in those who received yohimbine and reduced emotional memory performance in those receiving metoprolol. These studies point to a role of central adrenergic activity in the enhancement of memory by emotional events.

A recent study has addressed the role of glucocorticoids in the formation of emotional memory in humans (Buchanan & Lovallo 2001). In this study, separate groups of participants received either 20 mg of cortisol or placebo and viewed both emotionally arousing and neutral pictures. One week later, participants' memories for the pictures was examined using free recall, cued recall and recognition tests. The cortisol group recalled more of the arousing slides compared to the placebo group while the groups did not differ in recall of neutral slides (see Figure 3). Although research has suggested that chronically elevated corticosteroids may impair memory for emotionally neutral materials (Lupien & McEwen 1997), these results suggest that acute elevations in the hormone enhances long-term memory for emotionally arousing stimuli. These findings extend a great deal of animal research which suggests that acute elevation of glucocorticoids can enhance memory performance for emotionally arousing situations (Roozendaal 2000).

Taken together, human studies involving the pharmacological manipulation of epinephrine and glucocorticoids have supported the hypothesis that these compounds are involved in the enhancement of memory by emotion. While these human studies do not directly assess the effects of these compounds on amygdala function, their correspondence with animal research would suggest that the amygdala is a putative site of action in this phenomenon. Future research will no doubt address this relationship.

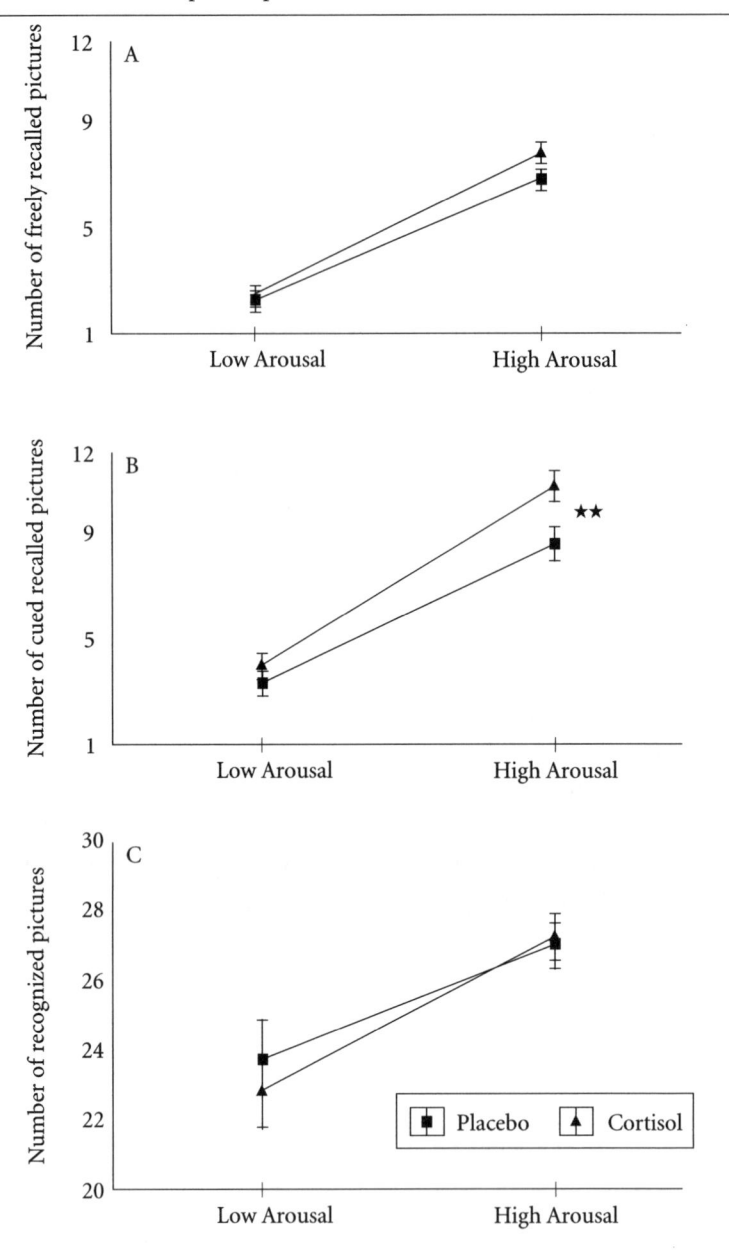

Figure 3. Effects of cortisol and emotional arousal on picture recall and recognition. Subjects who received cortisol (20 mg) recalled more highly arousing material than did the placebo group. A, Correct free recall as a function of a median split of arousal ratings. B, Correct cued recall, ** = significant group difference at p < 0.02. C, Correct recognition. (Reprinted with permission from Buchanan & Lovallo, Enhanced memory for emotional material following stress-level cortisol treatment in humans. Psychoneuroendocrinology 2001, 26, 307–317. Copyright ©2001 Elsevier Science Ltd.)

Summary and integration

The studies reviewed in this chapter illustrate the complex nature of the role of the amygdala in the modulation of memory by emotion. Findings from lesion studies and neuroimaging work suggest that amygdala activity is necessary for the enhanced memory of emotionally arousing stimuli. Further, pharmacological studies illustrate that both catecholamines and glucocorticoids play a role in emotional memory. What mechanistic role might the amygdala play in facilitating the memory of emotional material? What other brain regions are involved in this process? How do the stress hormones interact? We shall address these questions in this section of the chapter by attempting to place the aforementioned studies within the context of mechanistic animal research and suggest future research that may further elucidate the role of the amygdala in emotional memory.

In addition to the immediate effect of emotion on survival-related behaviors, enhanced long-term memory of this emotional situation would serve to aid the organism in potential future encounters. Numerous brain structures – including the amygdala, hypothalamus, hippocampus, cingulate, insular, and orbitofrontal cortices, among others – are involved in both the appreciation of and response to emotional stimuli. The various structures involved in this process imbue the emotion-eliciting stimulus with affective properties that, in addition to producing the appropriate response, lead to an enhanced representation of that stimulus as a memory trace. Thus, in response to emotion, the activity of the same brain structures are at the service of both response output and memory formation. That enhanced activity of response systems – autonomic, endocrine and skeletal motor activity – accompanies increased mnemonic representation illustrates the coordinated activity of these brain structures in the service of survival.

The amygdala receives both rudimentary (LeDoux 2000) as well as highly processed sensory information (Amaral, Price, Pitkänen, & Carmichael 1992) that allows for quick and specific activation of response systems that influence behavior and subsequent memory formation. The specific role of the amygdala in this process appears to be that of instigator, the catalyst that initially imbues incoming stimuli with emotional significance triggering other neural regions to react accordingly. This view of the amygdala's role in emotional memory formation fits with its role in classical fear conditioning. In this paradigm the amygdala is involved in the initial formation of the contingency between the biologically meaningful stimulus (US) and predictive stimulus (CS), but once this contingency is established the amygdala is no longer actively involved in the memory process (Buchel, Morris, Dolan, & Friston 1998; LaBar, Gatenby, Gore, LeDoux, & Phelps 1998; Wilensky, Schafe, & LeDoux 1999). The role of the amygdala in explicit emotional memory formation seems also to be modulatory and time limited: influencing the formation and storage of memory in other brain regions – the hippocampus, caudate and putamen, for example (McGaugh 2000) – while not being involved in the subsequent retrieval of these memory traces.

The role of the amygdala as an instigator of the formation of emotional memories is supported by the aforementioned functional imaging and lesion studies in humans. The lesion studies described suggest that the amygdala is necessary for the enhancement of memory for emotionally arousing stimuli (most specifically the left amygdala due, perhaps, to the verbal nature of the testing procedures). The inactivation of one or both amygdalae (either due to disease or surgery) results in reduced memory for emotionally arousing materials. The nature of these studies do not allow for the assessment of consolidation or retrieval effects, but clearly implicate the amygdala in the encoding of emotional material into memory. Similarly, the functional neuroimaging studies have most consistently pointed to encoding as the memory stage at which the amygdala exerts its effects (although Dolan et al. 1998 also report amygdala activity associated with retrieval). Recent research suggests that both storage and retrieval may be susceptible to modulation by emotion under certain circumstances in which reconsolidation is occurring (Nader, Schafe, & Le Doux 2000; Sara 2000). Regardless of the caveats such as gender and laterality effects (Cahill et al. 2001), and the potential effects of reconsolidation (Sara 2000), the most consistent finding from the discussed studies is an association between amygdala activity during encoding and the enhancement of subsequent memory. The activation of the amygdala would seem to be a potent predictor of memory performance.

In light of the established role of the medial temporal lobe memory system – that includes the hippocampus and adjacent cortex (Cohen & Eichenbaum 1993) – how does the amygdala fit in? The detection and experience of emotion increases the processing of the emotional stimuli by focusing attention and enacting response systems (Frijda 1987; Lang, Bradley, & Cuthbert 1990). The amygdala plays an integral role in this enhanced processing through influence over numerous brain structures including the hippocampus, hypothalamus, brain stem arousal centers, as well as bidirectional connections with neocortex (Amaral et al. 1992). It appears that one pathway of the amygdala's influence is to augment the activity of the medial temporal lobe memory system by imbuing explicit memories with affective tone. Animal research supports this view by showing that stimulation of the basolateral amygdala enhances long-term potentiation (LTP) – a process widely considered to be a cellular underpinning of memory formation – in both the dentate gyrus (Ikegaya, Saito, & Abe 1995) and insular cortex (Escobar, Chao, & Bermudez-Rattoni 1998). Interestingly, and in relation to the aforementioned role of catecholamines, β-adrenergic blockade within the basolateral amygdala reduces dentate gyrus LTP (Ikegaya, Nakanishi, Saito, & Abe 1997). Human neuroimaging results from Hamann and colleagues (1999) extend this notion by showing that both amygdala and hippocampal activity during the encoding of emotional material was correlated with subsequent emotional memory performance. These findings place the amygdala in a modulatory position of the traditional medial temporal lobe memory system, its activity influencing memory formation only under conditions of emotional arousal.

Another pathway through which the amygdala may influence memory performance is via hormonal output. The previously described pharmacological studies have illustrated the effect of manipulations of both catecholamines and glucocorticoids on emotional memory performance. Direct connections between the amygdala and the hypothalamus mediate the release of both epinephrine and cortisol during emotionally arousing situations (Davis 1997). Following their release, these hormones exert actions throughout the central nervous system and specifically at the level of the amygdala (Honkaniemi et al. 1992; Shepard, Barron, & Myers 2000). A great deal of animal research has focused on the bidirectional nature of the relationship between the amygdala and stress hormones (McGaugh & Izquierdo 2000; Roozendaal 2000). Enhancement of either adrenergic or glucocorticoid activity improves while blockade of these hormones reduces memory performance. The final common pathway of these hormones' effects on memory performance appears to be at the level of the amygdala – specifically via noradrenergic neurotransmission in the lateral/basolateral nuclei (Quirarte, Roozendaal, & McGaugh 1997). As previously mentioned, manipulations of this activity within these nuclei influences hippocampal and cortical function (Escobar et al. 1998; Ikegaya et al. 1997), providing a potential mechanism whereby the actions of these hormones at the level of the amygdala could influence the formation of emotional memories. While human research has yet to show a relationship among stress hormones, amygdala activity and emotional memory, animal research suggests such a relationship and future work will no doubt focus on elucidating this relationship.

In line with the relationship between systemic hormones influencing subsequent amygdala activation, one mechanism through which the amygdala could influence memory is via perception of the physiological response in the body. Vagal stimulation in both animals (Clark, Krahl, Smith, & Jensen 1995) and humans (Clark, Naritoku, Smith, Browning, & Jensen 1999) results in increased memory performance. Specifically, Clark and colleagues (1999) stimulated the vagus nerve in human patients immediately following verbal learning. This stimulation resulted in enhanced recognition memory for target words previously seen in the encoding phase. While in this experiment the study materials were not emotionally arousing, the authors propose that vagal stimulation resulted in enhanced arousal via influence on the amygdala and thus enhanced memory. In fact, the sensory role of the vagus nerve is proposed to be the mechanism whereby peripherally-released epinephrine – which does not readily pass the blood-brain-barrier – influences amygdala function in the formation of emotional memories (McGaugh 2000). These results illustrate that the influence of the amygdala on memory could occur at multiple stages: (a) through rapid initial responses influencing neural information processing, (b) indirectly via perception of the body's physiological response, or (c) by the experienced feeling of an emotion, even in the absence of an emotional stimulus (for instance, by asking subjects to volitionally induce a particular mood while they are encoding material). Most present studies have not permitted a separation of the emotion depicted in the stimulus, from the emotional reactions and feelings of the subject – the assumption has generally been that emotional stimuli will result in emotional states in the subject. A goal for the future will be to disentangle these issues.

The role of the amygdala in the formation of memories has long been a topic of research and debate in neuropsychology. Research presented in this chapter describes a modulatory role of the human amygdala – in combination with stress hormones – in the formation of emotional memories. This work has grown directly out of basic animal research that has outlined mechanistic models whereby the amygdala may influence memory (LeDoux 2000; McGaugh 2000). Both animal and human research are contributing to a more refined view of the role of the amygdala in long-term declarative memory that will inform our basic understanding of the processes of emotion and memory.

Acknowledgements

We thank Antonio and Hanna Damasio, Daniel Tranel, Natalie Denburg, and William Lovallo for their participation in some of the studies reviewed. Supported in part by an NRSA grant from the National Institute on Aging to T.W.B. and an NIH FIRST Award to R.A.

References

Adolphs, R., Cahill, L., Schul, R., & Babinsky, R. (1997). Impaired declarative memory for emotional material following bilateral amygdala damage in humans. *Learning & Memory, 4*, 291–300.

Adolphs, R., & Damasio, A. R. (2000). Neurobiology of emotion at a systems level. In J. C. Borod (Ed.), *The Neuropsychology of Emotion*. Oxford: Oxford University Press.

Adolphs, R., Tranel, D., & Denburg, N. (2000). Impaired emotional declarative memory following unilateral amygdala damage. *Learning and Memory, 7*(3), 180–186.

Alkire, M. T., Haier, R. J., Fallon, J. H., & Cahill, L. (1998). Hippocampal, but not amygdala, activity at encoding correlates with long-term, free recall of nonemotional information. *Proceedings of the National Academy of Science USA, 95*(24), 14506–14510.

Amaral, D. G., Price, J. L., Pitkänen, A., & Carmichael, S. T. (1992). Anatomical organization of the primate amygdaloid complex. In J. P. Aggleton (Ed.), *The Amygdala: Neurobiological Aspects of Emotion, Memory, and Mental Dysfunction* (pp. 1–66). New York: Wiley-Liss.

Bechara, A., Tranel, D., Damasio, H., Adolphs, R., Rockland, C., & Damasio, A. R. (1995). Double dissociation of conditioning and declarative knowledge relative to the amygdala and hippocampus in humans. *Science, 269*, 1115–1118.

Bradley, M. M., Greenwald, M. K., Petry, M. C., & Lang, P. J. (1992). Remembering pictures: pleasure and arousal in memory. *Journal of Experimental Psychology: Learning Memory and Cognition, 18*(2), 379–390.

Brown, R., & Kulick, J. (1977). Flashbulb memories. *Cognition, 5*, 73–99.

Buchanan, T. W., Denburg, N. L., Tranel, D., & Adolphs, R. (2001). Verbal and nonverbal emotional memory following unilateral amygdala damage. *Learning & Memory, 8*, 326–335.

Buchanan, T. W., & Lovallo, W. R. (2001). Enhanced memory for emotional material following stress-level cortisol treatment in humans. *Psychoneuroendocrinology, 26*(3), 307–317.

Buchel, C., Morris, J., Dolan, R. J., & Friston, K. J. (1998). Brain systems mediating aversive conditioning: an event-related fMRI study. *Neuron, 20*(5), 947–957.

Cahill, L., Babinsky, R., Markowitsch, H. J., & McGaugh, J. L. (1995). The amygdala and emotional memory [letter]. *Nature, 377*, 295–296.

Cahill, L., Haier, R. J., Fallon, J., Alkire, M. T., Tang, C., Keator, D., Wu, J., & McGaugh, J. L. (1996). Amygdala activity at encoding correlated with long-term, free recall of emotional information. *Proceedings of the National Academy of Science USA, 93*(15), 8016–8021.

Cahill, L., Haier, R. J., White, N. S., Fallon, J., Kilpatrick, L., Lawrence, C., Potkin, S. G., & Alkire, M. T. (2001). Sex-related difference in amygdala activity during emotionally influenced memory storage. *Neurobiology of Learning and Memory, 75*(1), 1–9.

Cahill, L., & McGaugh, J. L. (1995). A novel demonstration of enhanced memory associated with emotional arousal. *Consciousness and Cognition, 4*(4), 410–421.

Cahill, L., Prins, B., Weber, M., & McGaugh, J. L. (1994). Beta-adrenergic activation and memory for emotional events. *Nature, 371*(6499), 702–704.

Cahill, L., Weinberger, N. M., Roozendaal, B., & McGaugh, J. L. (1999). Is the amygdala a locus of "conditioned fear"? Some questions and caveats. *Neuron, 23*(2), 227–228.

Canli, T., Zhao, Z., Brewer, J., Gabrieli, J. D., & Cahill, L. (2000). Event-related activation in the human amygdala associates with later memory for individual emotional experience. *Journal of Neuroscience, 20*(19), RC99.

Canli, T., Zhao, Z., Desmond, J., Glover, G., & Gabrieli, J. D. (1999). fMRI identifies a network of structures correlated with retention of positive and negative emotional memory. *Psychobiology, 27*(4), 441–452.

Clark, K. B., Krahl, S. E., Smith, D. C., & Jensen, R. A. (1995). Post-training unilateral vagal stimulation enhances retention performance in the rat. *Neurobiology of Learning and Memory, 63*(3), 213–216.

Clark, K. B., Naritoku, D. K., Smith, D. C., Browning, R. A., & Jensen, R. A. (1999). Enhanced recognition memory following vagus nerve stimulation in human subjects. *Nature Neuroscience, 2*(1), 94–98.

Cohen, N. J., & Eichenbaum, H. (1993). *Memory, Amnesia, and the Hippocampal System.* Cambridge: MIT Press.

Davis, M. (1997). Neurobiology of fear responses: the role of the amygdala. *Journal of Neuropsychiatry and Clinical Neuroscience, 9*(3), 382–402.

Dolan, R. J., Lane, R., Chua, P., & Fletcher, P. (2000). Dissociable temporal lobe activations during emotional episodic memory retrieval. *Neuroimage, 11*(3), 203–209.

Easterbrook, J. A. (1959). The effect of emotion on cue utilization and the organization of behavior. *Psychological Review, 3*, 183–201.

Escobar, M. L., Chao, V., & Bermudez-Rattoni, F. (1998). In vivo long-term potentiation in the insular cortex: NMDA receptor dependence. *Brain Research, 779*(1–2), 314–319.

Fanselow, M. S., & LeDoux, J. E. (1999). Why we think plasticity underlying Pavlovian fear conditioning occurs in the basolateral amygdala. *Neuron, 23*(2), 229–232.

Frijda, N. H. (1987). Emotion, cognitive structure, and action tendency. *Cognition and Emotion, 1*, 115–143.

Hamann, S. B., Cahill, L., & Squire, L. R. (1997). Emotional perception and memory in amnesia. *Neuropsychology, 11*(1), 104–113.

Hamann, S. B., Ely, T. D., Grafton, S. T., & Kilts, C. D. (1999). Amygdala activity related to enhanced memory for pleasant and aversive stimuli. *Nature Neuroscience, 2*(3), 289–293.

Heuer, F., & Reisberg, D. (1990). Vivid memories of emotional events: the accuracy of remembered minutiae. *Memory and Cognition, 18*(5), 496–506.

Honkaniemi, J., Pelto-Huikko, M., Rechardt, L., Isola, J., Lammi, A., Fuxe, K., Gustafsson, J. A., Wikstrom, A. C., & Hokfelt, T. (1992). Colocalization of peptide and glucocorticoid receptor immunoreactivities in rat central amygdaloid nucleus. *Neuroendocrinology, 55*(4), 451–459.

Ikegaya, Y., Nakanishi, K., Saito, H., & Abe, K. (1997). Amygdala beta-noradrenergic influence on hippocampal long-term potentiation in vivo. *Neuroreport, 8*(14), 3143–3146.

Ikegaya, Y., Saito, H., & Abe, K. (1995). Requirement of basolateral amygdala neuron activity for the induction of long-term potentiation in the dentate gyrus in vivo. *Brain Research, 671*(2), 351–354.

LaBar, K. S., Gatenby, J. C., Gore, J. C., LeDoux, J. E., & Phelps, E. A. (1998). Human amygdala activation during conditioned fear acquisition and extinction: a mixed-trial fMRI study. *Neuron, 20*(5), 937–945.

LaBar, K. S., & Phelps, E. A. (1998). Arousal-mediated memory consolidation: Role of the medial temporal lobe in humans. *Psychological Science, 9*(6), 490–493.

Lang, P. J., Bradley, M. M., & Cuthbert, B. N. (1990). Emotion, attention, and the startle reflex. *Psychological Review, 97*(3), 377–395.

Lang, P. J., Greenwald, M. K., Bradley, M. M., & Hamm, A. O. (1993). Looking at pictures: affective, facial, visceral, and behavioral reactions. *Psychophysiology, 30*(3), 261–273.

LeDoux, J. E. (2000). Emotion circuits in the brain [In Process Citation]. *Annual Review of Neuroscience, 23*, 155–184.

Loftus, E. (1979). *Eyewitness Testimony*. Cambridge, MA: Harvard University Press.

Lupien, S. J., & McEwen, B. S. (1997). The acute effects of corticosteroids on cognition: integration of animal and human model studies. *Brain Research Review, 24*(1), 1–27.

Maren, S. (2000). Auditory fear conditioning increases CS-elicited spike firing in lateral amygdala neurons even after extensive overtraining. *European Journal of Neuroscience, 12*(11), 4047–4054.

Markowitsch, H. J., Calabrese, P., Wurker, M., Durwen, H. F., Kessler, J., Babinsky, R., Brechtelsbauer, D., Heuser, L., & Gehlen, W. (1994). The amygdala's contribution to memory – a study on two patients with Urbach-Wiethe disease. *Neuroreport, 5*, 1349–1352.

McGaugh, J. L. (2000). Memory-a century of consolidation. *Science, 287*(5451), 248–251.

McGaugh, J. L., & Izquierdo, I. (2000). The contribution of pharmacology to research on the mechanisms of memory formation. *Trends in Pharmacological Science, 21*(6), 208–210.

Murray, E. A. (1992). Medial temporal lobe structures contributing to recognition memory: The amygdaloid complex versus the rhinal cortex. In J. P. Aggleton (Ed.), *The Amygdala: Neurobiological Aspects of Emotion, Memory, and Mental Dysfunction* (pp. 453–470). New York: Wiley-Liss.

Nader, K., Schafe, G. E., & Le Doux, J. E. (2000). Fear memories require protein synthesis in the amygdala for reconsolidation after retrieval. *Nature, 406*(6797), 722–726.

O'Carroll, R. E., Drysdale, E., Cahill, L., Shajahan, P., & Ebmeier, K. P. (1999a). Memory for emotional material: a comparison of central versus peripheral beta blockade. *J Psychopharmacology, 13*(1), 32–39.

O'Carroll, R. E., Drysdale, E., Cahill, L., Shajahan, P., & Ebmeier, K. P. (1999b). Stimulation of the noradrenergic system enhances and blockade reduces memory for emotional material in man. *Psychological Medicine, 29*(5), 1083–1088.

Packard, M. G., & Teather, L. A. (1998). Amygdala modulation of multiple memory systems: hippocampus and caudate-putamen. *Neurobiology of Learning and Memory, 69*(2), 163–203.

Parker, A., Wilding, E., & Akerman, C. (1998). The Von Restorff effect in visual object recognition memory in humans and monkeys. The role of frontal/perirhinal interaction. *Journal of Cognitive Neuroscience, 10*(6), 691–703.

Phelps, E. A., LaBar, K. S., & Spencer, D. D. (1997). Memory for emotional words following unilateral temporal lobectomy. *Brain and Cognition, 35*(1), 85–109.

Quirarte, G. L., Roozendaal, B., & McGaugh, J. L. (1997). Glucocorticoid enhancement of memory storage involves noradrenergic activation in the basolateral amygdala. *Proceedings of the National Academy of Science USA, 94*(25), 14048–14053.

Roozendaal, B. (2000). 1999 Curt P. Richter award. Glucocorticoids and the regulation of memory consolidation. *Psychoneuroendocrinology, 25*(3), 213–238.

Russell, J. A. (1980). A circumplex model of affect. *Journal of Personality and Social Psychology, 39,* 1161–1178.

Russell, J. A., & Bullock, M. (1985). Multidimensional scaling of emotional facial expressions: similarity from preschoolers to adults. *Journal of Personality and Social Psychology, 48,* 1290–1298.

Russell, J. A., Lewicka, M., & Niit, T. (1989). A cross-cultural study of a circumplex model of affect. *Journal of Personality and Social Psychology, 57,* 848–856.

Sara, S. J. (2000). Retrieval and reconsolidation: toward a neurobiology of remembering. *Learning and Memory, 7*(2), 73–84.

Schmolck, H., Buffalo, E. A., & Squire, L. R. (2000). Memory distortions develop over time: Recollections of the O.J. Simpson trial verdict after 15 and 32 months. *Psychological Science, 11*(1), 39–45.

Schwartz, B., & Reisberg, D. (1991). *Learning and Memory.* New York: W. W. Norton.

Shepard, J. D., Barron, K. W., & Myers, D. A. (2000). Corticosterone delivery to the amygdala increases corticotropin-releasing factor mRNA in the central amygdaloid nucleus and anxiety-like behavior. *Brain Research, 861*(2), 288–295.

Squire, L. (1987). *Memory and Brain.* New York: Oxford University Press.

Taylor, S. F., Liberzon, I., Fig, L. M., Decker, L. R., Minoshima, S., & Koeppe, R. A. (1998). The effect of emotional content on visual recognition memory: a PET activation study. *Neuroimage, 8*(2), 188–197.

Tranel, D., & Hyman, B. T. (1990). Neuropsychological correlates of bilateral amygdala damage. *Archives of Neurology, 47,* 349–355.

van Stegeren, A. H., Everaerd, W., Cahill, L., McGaugh, J. L., & Gooren, L. J. (1998). Memory for emotional events: differential effects of centrally versus peripherally acting beta-blocking agents. *Psychopharmacology (Berlin), 138*(3–4), 305–310.

Wilensky, A. E., Schafe, G. E., & LeDoux, J. E. (1999). Functional inactivation of the amygdala before but not after auditory fear conditioning prevents memory formation. *Journal of Neuroscience, 19*(24), RC48.

Zola-Morgan, S., Squire, L. R., Alvarez-Royo, P., & Clower, R. P. (1991). Independence of memory functions and emotional behavior: separate contributions of the hippocampal formation and the amygdala. *Hippocampus, 1*(2), 207–220.

Zola-Morgan, S., Squire, L. R., & Amaral, D. G. (1986). Human amnesia and the medial temporal region: enduring memory impairment following a bilateral lesion limited to field CA1 of the hippocampus. *Journal of Neuroscience, 6*(10), 2950–2967.

CHAPTER 3

Associative representations of emotionally significant outcomes

Simon Killcross and Pam Blundell
School of Psychology, Cardiff University / Department of Psychology, University of York

The aim of this chapter is to investigate the way in which contemporary learning theory has conceptualised the role of the reinforcer in emotional learning and memory, and how this role may be characterised in the context of models of emotional behaviour. We will briefly outline some fundamental distinctions that have made between different forms of learning in animals, and highlight the different role of the reinforcer in each of these types of learning. Then we will examine the way in which neuroscience has chosen to look at emotional learning, before going on to examine one particular brain structure, the basolateral amygdala (by which we mean the lateral nucleus of the amygdala, together with the basal and basal accessory nuclei – see Amarel et al. 1992), in different forms of emotional learning in rats. Experimental work will be examined that suggests that current models of neural bases of emotional learning fail to account for the multiple roles of the reinforcer in emotional learning and do not match the level of theory dictated by purely behavioural examinations of reinforcer function. Finally, we will present a model of reinforcer function that draws on concepts from animal learning theory and accounts for much of the current literature detailing the role of the basolateral amygdala in emotional memory. This model suggests a selective role for the basolateral amygdala in the association or representation of the sensory and hedonic properties of reinforcers, but not their motivational properties.

Types of emotional learning in animals

Although there are undoubtedly a very wide range of behaviours in animals that may be described as emotional, we are going to take the view that learning about emotionally significant stimuli takes two forms: that dictated by Pavlovian contingencies, and that described as instrumental. Our reasons for adopting some form of two-process view is unimportant to the current argument and is well-rehearsed elsewhere (Rescorla and Solomon 1967; Dickinson 1980; Mackintosh 1983; Dickinson 1994). A Pavlovian conditioning procedure typically describes a situation in which an animal is exposed to a correlation of external events. An initially neutral stimulus (the conditional stimulus or CS) predicts, to some greater or lesser degree, the occurrence of an emotionally significant event (the unconditional stimulus, or US). Classically, and in many of the examples we discuss below, this will involve the pairing of an auditory signal, such as a pure tone, with a food reward. As a consequence of this correlation between CS and US, the CS comes to elicit conditional responses (CRs) during presentations of the CS. The precise form of these CRs may, contrary to many descriptions in classic textbooks, be related, partially related, or totally unrelated, to the response elicited by the US. Hence, delivery of food after a tone may elicit conditioned orienting behaviours to the tone (head-jerking), locomotor activity, approach to the food source, and ingestive responses appropriate to the consumption of a palatable foodstuff (see Holland 1990; Boakes 1979; Konorski 1967; Holland and Straub 1979).

In contrast, instrumental learning refers to learning that occurs as a consequence of the experimental arrangement of a causal relationship between performance of some action by an animal and occurrence of an emotionally significant event. In the traditional learning theory environment this might be the delivery of a food pellet reinforcer consequent upon an animal pressing a lever in a Skinner box. Although the distinction between Pavlovian and instrumental conditioning is one that appears obvious at an operational level, it is not nearly so easy to produce a formal distinction between the two; many of the contingencies arranged in a Pavlovian learning situation are also present in instrumental learning tasks, and debate about distinctions between the two has received considerable attention for the past seventy-five years (see Mackintosh 1983; Solomon and Rescorla 1967; Rescorla 1980). It is not our intention to examine this work in this chapter, but it is an issue that should be highlighted here as it may have implications for broader consideration.

Having accepted the distinction, at least in principal, between Pavlovian and instrumental learning, we may now address the issue of the role of the reinforcer in each of these forms of emotional learning.

The reinforcer in Pavlovian conditioning

To a certain level of analysis, the role of the US in Pavlovian conditioning appears relatively straightforward. In associationist terms, correlated presentation of a CS and US leads to the formation of associations between mental representations of the CS and US, such that presentation of the CS comes to elicit associatively-generated activation of the US representation, and so to performance of CRs. However, a moment's consideration suggests that this cannot be the whole story. Presentation of the US itself is likely to lead to a wide variety of behaviours, each related in some way to the varied properties of the US. Actual presentation and consumption of food will lead an animal to experience the physical properties of that food – its appearance, smell, taste, consistency – as well as the fact that this is a substance that may influence the animal's state of hunger or thirst. It should come as no surprise then that the CS should be able to form an association with each of these varied aspects of the US representation. We have already suggested above that a CS comes to elicit a wide range of CRs over the course of Pavlovian conditioning, and to some extent these CRs reflect the formation of these varied US associations. This distinction in generation of CRs and properties of URs has not gone unnoticed in theories of learning. Konorski (1967) put forward the idea of dissociable preparatory and consummatory aspects of Pavlovian CRs, and suggested that these reflect dissociable influences of the US. Protopathic properties reflect the primary affective properties of the US – that is, the ability of the US to produce immediate and direct change in affective or motivational states. Second, he identified idiopathic properties of the US – those properties that are unique to the precise nature of the US. Here we refer to the sensory properties of the US, its taste, smell etc. This distinction has been reflected in a variety of theories seeking to account for the involvement of emotional or motivational factors in associative learning (Dickinson and Dearing 1978; Wagner and Brandon 1989). In Konorski's terms, associative activation of the protopathic properties of the reinforcer leads to the generation of CRs that are preparatory in nature. Preparatory responses are therefore generalised responses that reflect the affective nature of the reinforcer – for example appetitive or aversive. Such responses might include the general increase in locomotor activity in the presence of stimuli associated with reward (e.g. Holland and Rescorla 1975), or the heightened responsivity to startle stimuli that accompanies stimuli associated with mild electric shock (Davis 2000). In contrast, associative activation of the idiopathic properties of the US leads to the generation of consummatory CRs that are directed towards, and shaped by, specific sensory properties of the US. Particular examples of this include the unique patterns of pecking response in pigeons receiving either solid grain or liquid water reinforcement (Moore 1973), or in the patterns of salivation evoked by stimuli predictive of food or acid (Pavlov 1927). Some more recent models of associative learning maintain this distinction (e.g. Brandon and Wagner 1989).

The reinforcer in instrumental learning

In the case of instrumental learning, recent evidence has begun to highlight the importance of consideration of reinforcement and motivational processes (see Balleine 2000; Balleine, & Dickinson 1994). Traditional theory might suggest that the reinforcer in instrumental learning is just that – solely an event that reinforces, or strengthens, an association between stimuli in the environment and responses made in that environment that increase the likelihood of reinforcer presentation. This is, of course, an S-R view of instrumental performance (Thorndike 1911; Skinner 1932). The reinforcer has no status other than as an event in the world that, for reasons of apparent biological destiny, comes to have the ability to increase or decrease the likelihood of responses that lead to its presentation. Here there is virtually no role reserved for the affective properties of the reinforcer in the formation of S-R associations – there is little sense in which an event's reinforcing properties are a consequence of its ability to evoke emotional responses or anything to do with its specific properties. Any specificity in an S-R system comes about through a general drive theory of motivation – particular responses only come to be selected over others to the extent that internal drives may act as stimuli to bias production towards particular responses, a bias that is capitalised upon by the overall energising effect of the drive itself.

In opposition to this view are theories that suggest that animals do encode, in some manner, the specific outcome of their actions. This is to say that actions are performed, at least in some sense, precisely because of their consequences (Dickinson 1989; Tolman 1949). Considerable evidence has now accumulated that renders this stance superior in many ways to S-R theories. Outcome devaluation studies show clearly that animals do encode the consequences of their actions. For example, Colwill and Rescorla (1985; see also Adams and Dickinson 1981) trained a group of rats to make two responses (pulling a chain and pressing a lever), one response leading to one outcome (food pellets) and the second response to a second outcome (sucrose solution). After acquisition of these responses a mild aversion was conditioned to one of the outcomes by pairing free consumption of the outcome with gastric nausea induced by injection of lithium chloride (LiCl). A test session in which the animals were allowed to make the two responses in the absence of reinforcement (i.e. an extinction test) revealed that animals made more responses on the manipulandum that led to the non-poisoned outcome than on the manipulandum that previously produced the outcome that was poisoned. This pattern of results is most simply explained by suggesting that animals form associations between their actions and outcomes (A-O associations). Devaluation of the outcome renders it no longer attractive and so the response that led to an expectation of the devalued outcome will be performed at a lower rate on test than responses leading to activation of a representation of the non-devalued outcome. The benefit of this within-subject design is that the training and dissociation of two responses allows any possible Pavlovian influences to be equated across responses and outcomes, thereby avoiding a possible alternative explanation of the finding: Pavlovian-instrumental transfer experiments readily demonstrate the possibility that cues uniquely paired with a particular outcome could serve to increase or decrease performance of a response also associated with that outcome (e.g., Colwill and Rescorla 1988). Indeed we make use of this fact later in this chapter to help us to reveal exactly what animals know about the consequences of their actions.

Within this A-O framework there has been much work examining the way in which outcomes achieve and maintain their desirability as goals of instrumental actions. It is not the intention of this chapter to examine this work, but it certainly appears that the value of reinforcers does not seem to be innate, but must be learnt during experience with the reinforcer and experience of its effects in different motivational circumstances (see Dickinson and Balleine 1994; Balleine 1992). What we shall seek to outline here is the manner in which these various aspects of the reinforcer may be represented neurally, and to what extent there is a generality across the different forms of reinforced learning. This is a matter that warrants serious consideration in the realm of emotional or motivational processing. Many of the behaviours we observe, both in humans and non-human animals, are undoubtedly the combination of many different aspects of emotionally-significant events – their arousing properties, their valence and so forth. Many of the behaviours examined in animal models of emotion (e.g., fear conditioning) examine responses that may have a rather uncertain status with respect to exactly what aspects of emotion are being examined (see Nader and LeDoux 1997; Killcross et al. 1997b; LeDoux 2000). It may be relatively easy to generate an animal that no longer freezes – it is an entirely different matter to demonstrate that it is no longer frightened. In the same manner, it may be straightforward to demonstrate that an animal will no longer respond for a particular reward, but determining why this might be is another task altogether. Here we describe a series of experiments designed to examine the functions of the basolateral nucleus of the amygdala in appetitive learning in rats. This relatively simple approach proves to provide substantial insight into the nature of representations of emotionally-significant events and the ways in which behaviour comes to be controlled by them.

The role of the amygdala in emotion

For many years, the amygdala, a small structure lying under the temporal lobe of the brain, has been implicated in emotional processing. The evidence for this involvement comes from a wide variety of sources, including cognitive psychology, neuropsychology and behavioural neuroscience. First we shall detail a number of studies that provide the background for regarding the amygdala as central to some aspects of emotional processing. Then we will report some recent studies we have conducted that combine contemporary animal learning theory with behavioural neuroscience, and complement studies in normal humans and patient populations to provide a highly detailed level of understanding of amygdala function that generates testable hypotheses.

The amygdala

The amygdala is a small, sub-cortical structure lying deep within the temporal region of the brain. However, this relatively small structure has a vastly complicated neuroanatomy. It receives an enormous range of neural inputs from a wide variety of areas of the brain, both cortical areas and sub-cortical structures. It is a heterogeneous structure, comprising many different nuclei, and it is largely because of historical precedent that these different structures are considered to be part of the same structure. The different nuclei within the amygdala are often divided into groups of similar nuclei based on location, the cells of which they consist, their embryonic origin and the neurotransmitter systems they contain. Many different classification systems have been proposed for the various amygdala nuclei. Johnston (1923) introduced the fundamental description of amygdala structure most widely used today (Swanson & Petrovich 1998), suggesting that the nuclei of the amygdala should be divided into two groups, a primitive group associated with the olfactory system (central, medial and cortical nuclei, and nucleus of the olfactory tract), and a phylogenetically more recent group (lateral and basal nuclei). Swanson and Petrovich (1998) argue that current data suggests the amygdala should be considered as a heterogeneous region, one part of which is a specialised ventromedial expanse of the striatum (central and medial nuclei, and rostral regions), a second part of which is caudal olfactory cortex (the nucleus of the lateral olfactory tract, cortical nucleus and postpiriform and piriform amygdalar areas), and a third part of which is a ventromedial extension of the claustrum (lateral, basal and posterior nuclei). Alheid (1988) includes a new structure in the amygdala – the extended amygdala, which occupies the ventricular floor in the form of the bed nucleus of the stria terminalis.

Much of the information received by the amygdala is of a highly processed nature – information that has undergone a great degree of manipulation, combination and recombination in other regions of the brain. For a detailed review of amygdala connectivity, the reader is referred to Pitkänen (2000). The major projections to the amygdala come from the thalamus and cortex (Turner & Herkenham 1991). From the thalamus, the amygdala receives rich auditory and viscerosensory information (Turner & Herkenham 1991). There are heavy projections to the basal nucleus of the amygdala from thalamic areas with presumed viscerosensory function. The central, lateral and basal accessory nuclei of the amygdala receive auditory information by projections from the medial geniculate. The amygdala also receives inputs from all main subdivisions of the cerebral cortex, including visual, auditory and somatosensory areas. Generally, it is innervated by higher-order association cortical areas towards the end of cortical processing streams, rather than directly by primary sensory areas. For example, there is no amygdala innervation from the primary auditory cortex, but there is from rat temporal cortex area 3, which itself is innervated by primary auditory cortex. Most cortical projections terminate in the deep nuclei of the amygdala, particularly the lateral and basomedial nuclei. However, there are also projections to other nuclei, for example visceral and gustatory information are transmitted from dysgranular cortex to the lateral section of the central nucleus, as well as to the basolateral complex. Similarly, prefrontal and hippocampal areas of cortex convey polymodal sensory information to the amygdala. The basal nucleus of the amygdala is the main target of projections from the prefrontal cortex. While many areas of prefrontal cortex also project to lateral and/or basomedial nucleus, only the infralimbic cortex projects to any great degree to the superficial nuclei and central nucleus. The amygdala receives olfactory inputs directly from the olfactory bulb and also from the olfactory allocortex. In the rat the principle targets of olfactory projections are the cortical amygdaloid nucleus and the periamygdaloid cortex.

Overall, the amygdala receives multimodal sensory information from cortex and thalamus. Other areas also project to the amygdala including the hippocampal formation, areas of pons, midbrain, striatum, basal forebrain and hypothalamus. With these connections, the amygdala receives highly processed information from the visual system, the auditory cortex, the olfactory and gustatory neocortex and the somatosensory cortex. In short it is informed about each of our five senses – sight, hearing, smell, taste and touch. By its projections from prefrontal cortex and hippocampus it also gains more highly processed polymodal information about the relationship between different objects and events in the world. Finally, the range of sub-cortical input structures are important in presenting information relating to a variety of internal bodily states such as hunger and thirst.

In addition to this vast array of inputs, the amygdala also projects to a wide variety of areas, including reciprocal connections to many of the cortical areas just mentioned, as well as to sub-cortical areas involved in motor output, and hypothalamic and brainstem regions involved in the coordination of autonomic, endocrine and behavioural responses. The lateral nucleus of the amygdala projects to many areas of cortex, including the ventral and dorsal perirhinal cortices, infralimbic and prelimbic cortices. There are direct inputs to the hippocampal formation and to the entorhinal cortex, a light projection to the hypothalamus and a substantial input to the nucleus accumbens, particularly to the lateral part of the shell region. The basolateral nucleus projects to the perirhinal cortex, the prefrontal cortex, the frontal cortex, (including the medial and lateral orbital cortices), the hippocampal formation and the olfactory tubercle. The basolateral nucleus also sends substantial topographically organized inputs to the mediodorsal thalamic nucleus, and is the major source of amygdaloid inputs to both the core and shell of the nucleus accumbens, and the caudate-putamen. Finally, the substantia innominata, claustrum, and bed nucleus of the stria terminalis also receive a heavy input from the basolateral nucleus. In contrast, the central nucleus of the amygdala has projections to several nuclei in the midline thalamus, the hypothalamus, the substantia innominata, the lateral septum and the bed nucleus of the stria terminalis, as well as to the midbrain, pons and medulla, including all sections of the substantia nigra, and many other brainstem areas.

In summary, all amygdala nuclei have numerous efferent and afferent projections. Areas such as the lateral nucleus and the basolateral nucleus have substantial connections with cortical areas, including primary sensory and association areas representing a wide variety of uni- and polymodal sensory information, from all of the sensory modalities. In contrast, areas such as the medial and central nucleus have substantial projections to midbrain and brainstem structures, and receive most of their input from other amygdalar nuclei and from some areas conveying information from gustatory centres. Projections from these two areas allows information flow to brainstem areas concerned with reflexive endocrine, autonomic and motor responding, as well as to higher-order motor centres via the striatum and cortex. The amygdala is well-placed to integrate sensory information and pass this information on to systems concerned with directed actions and reflexive responses.

The amygdala and emotion

There is a substantial body of work examining the role of the amygdala in emotion that makes use of patients with selective damage to this region. This may occur due to surgery, for example to destroy the epileptic focus in the case of intractable epilepsy, or in some very rare cases due to congenital defects that lead to the progressive calcification of limbic structures sometimes restricted to the amygdala – Urbech-Wiethe disorder. More recent studies have made excellent use of emerging imaging technology, employing positron emission tomography (PET) and functional magnetic resonance imaging (fMRI) of healthy participants to examine brain systems underpinning learning and emotion.

One striking finding that has been replicated a number of times is that relating amygdala damage in patients to deficits in the recognition of facial expressions of emotion (e.g., Calder et al. 1996). Using both pictures of actors simulating emotions, and computer-generated morphed images of different prototypical emotional expressions, research has demonstrated that patients with damage to the amygdala, although normal in the vast majority of respects, have difficulty recognising facial expressions of emotion. Moreover, this deficit appears to be selective to expressions of fear, anger and disgust but not happiness, sadness and surprise, a finding replicated several times.

Similarly, although patients with amygdala damage show surprisingly few deficits across a wide range of neuropsychological tests, and can function well in everyday life, recent studies have started to pick out specific problems with social and emotional judgement (Adolphs, Tranel, & Damasio 1998; Adolphs & Tranel 2000). Here, researchers examined three individuals with highly selective damage to the amygdala, testing their ability to make judgements about the approachability of individuals based on photographs. In comparison to control judgements they were far more likely to rate individual characters as approachable. This finding provides solid empirical evidence to back up anecdotal observations made by patients' families, a number of clinicians, and others working with these groups that their ability to make personal judgements was abnormal.

Finally, recent work has been carried out examining the role of the amygdala in responding to emotionally-significant events with PET and fMRI studies of Pavlovian conditioning in humans (e.g., Morris, Ohman, & Dolan 1998; Dolan 2000). In one such study, individuals received pairings of pictures of angry faces with an intense and aversive burst of white noise. Following these pairings, participants were presented with just the pictures of angry faces, whilst undergoing PET analysis of their neural activity. Very brief presentations of the angry face were immediately followed by presentation of a neutral face. This procedure served to 'mask' awareness of the angry face so that participants were not even conscious they had seen it. Nevertheless, two important findings emerged. First, participants showed a change in skin conductance response during the subliminal presentations of the angry face, demonstrating that it was capable of generating an emotional response, by virtue of previous Pavlovian conditioning even when subjects were unaware of it. Second, and just as striking, they found a selective activation of the right amygdala following such presentations, again demonstrating the central role of the amygdala in responding in emotionally significant situations.

In summary, there is much evidence to associate the amygdala with emotion, and with learning about emotionally significant events. It is involved in a wide variety of emotional responses, including responding to linguistic threat, facial and vocal expressions of emotion, memory for emotional events, and even simple responding to pleasant and aversive stimuli, including music. The evidence of its primary involvement in emotion is overwhelming, although in each instance it should be noted that the deficits observed following selective damage to the amygdala are rather subtle, and perhaps not as dramatic as one might imagine following destruction of a structure that appears so critically connected to such a wide variety of other brain regions.

In fact, these findings reflect earlier work in animals that similarly revealed the involvement of the amygdala in emotion. Perhaps most well-known are classic studies by Kluver and Bucy (1939) which demonstrated that damage to the temporal lobe in monkeys led to a wide variety of symptoms which they characterised as disruptions in normal emotional responding. These included tameness, visual agnosia, increased exploratory behaviour, compulsive oral behaviour, and hypersexuality collectively known as Kluver-Bucy syndrome. Similar findings have since been reported in humans with gross damage to the temporal lobe. However it is now widely recognised that several of the components of this syndrome are not due to damage to the amygdala, but rather to overlying cortical areas, or due to damage to nerve fibre projections through the damaged region. More recent and more careful studies have revealed that deficits following discrete damage to the amygdala are both subtle and mild (e.g., Malkova et al. 1996).

Finally, work in laboratory rats, as with work examining humans and non-human primates, has indicated that deficits following discrete amygdala damage (in many cases limited to specific sub-nuclei of the amygdala such as the central and basolateral nuclei) are rather variable. There appears to be a clear deficit in learning about some aversive events, such as a simple Pavlovian conditioning situation where a signal such as a tone is paired with an aversive event such as mild footshock and a behavioural measure such as freezing or fear-potentiated startle is examined (LeDoux 1996; Davis 1992). In fact, selective sub-nuclei appear to influence different aspects of behavioural control by footshock, with the basolateral amygdala controlling instrumental choice in which selective responding increases or decreases the likelihood of footshock, and the central nucleus mediating behavioural suppression cessation of responding during presentation of a signal for footshock (see Killcross et al. 1997a). These results have recently been replicated using an alternative procedure (Amorapanth et al. 2000). Possible reasons for this pattern of results are discussed more fully later in this chapter.

In contrast to these findings, there appears to be little change in the ability of animals with lesions of the basolateral amygdala to learn about pleasant events – see Figure 1 – in this case animals were trained in a simple Pavlovian conditioning procedure, learning that a signal such as a tone predicts the delivery of food pellets. There is clearly no deficit in this task. So is it the case that the amygdala is important only for learning about aversive events? Overall we can see that damage to the amygdala produces some deficits in learning about the emotional significance of events in the world, although these effects are quite subtle, and rather varied. Whilst the amygdala is important in emotions and emotional learning, we have yet to produce a clear and accurate characterisation of its function in relation to the representation of emotionally-significant events–reinforcers. What is it about the representation of reinforcers that is affected by lesions of the amygdala? Earlier in the chapter we attempted to outline the various aspects of reinforcers that have been highlighted by recent research

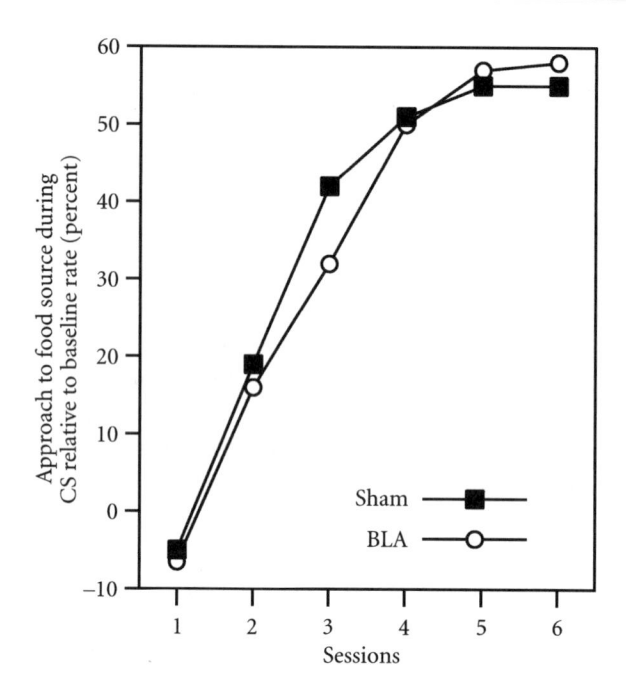

Figure 1. Acquisition of conditioned approach to a food magazine by animals with lesions of the basolateral amygdala (BLA) and sham-lesioned controls (SHAM), measured as percent increase over baseline rates.

in processes of animal learning. The experiments that follow attempt to reveal the role of the basolateral amygdala in these varied aspects.

Development of representations for event outcomes and goals

One feature of animals with damage to the amygdala that has been noted by a number of researchers is that, although these animals appear to learn well that a particular signal or response predicts the imminent arrival of rewarding food, they do not seem to retain as much knowledge about this food as normal animals. To take a specific example from recent work (see also Hatfield et al. 1996), when normal animals have learnt the relationship between a response or stimulus and a reward, changes in the value of that reward (for example, reducing its value by prefeeding the animal on that reward – a phenomenon known as sensory-specific satiety) will produce predictable changes in the animals' responses to the predictor of that reward (in this example a reduction in the level of lever pressing for that reward). As in the example given above, this is most clearly demonstrated when animals have a choice of responses to make, one response leading to one type of reward (say, a pellet of food) and second response leading to another type of reward (delivery of sucrose solution). Prefeeding an animal with food pellets preserves responses that led to sucrose solution but practically eliminates responses that led to food pellets. It is generally accepted that satiation is effective as it reduces the value of internal representations of the goal or predicted outcome and thus reduces the vigour of responding (see Balleine 2000; Dickinson 1994). Animals with damage to the basolateral amygdala fail to show sensitivity to these changes in the value of reward. In a recent experiment (Willoughby and Killcross 1998; Blundell 2001) two groups of rats, one with excitotoxic (quinolinic acid) lesions of the basolateral amygdala and the other with control sham-lesions, were trained in an autoshaping procedure. The experimental chambers contained two levers, one either side of a central recess in which two different rewards (food pellets and sucrose solution) could be presented. On any trial, a 10-sec presentation of one of the levers was followed by delivery of one of the rewards. Hence presentation of a specific lever came to predict presentation of a specific reward – note that this is a Pavlovian procedure, even though levers served as the cue for reward. Over the course of 16 sessions all animals came to approach and respond on the levers as a consequence of their pairings with reward (see Davey & Cleland 1981). As with previous findings, there was no difference in the rate of conditioned responding in control and lesioned animals (Figure 1). At the end of this training, animals were given a series of choice extinction trials in which both levers were presented simultaneously for 10 sec. Prior to each of two such test sessions animals were sated on one or other of the reinforcers, receiving free consumption of one of the rewards for an hour immediately before test. Figure 2 shows the results of these test sessions, collapsed across satiety conditions. Clearly, control sham-lesioned animals came to bias their conditioned responding as a consequence of the specific satiety treatment – they were more likely to respond towards the lever that had cued presentation of the reward on which they were not sated, over the lever that cued the sated reward. However, animals with lesions of the basolateral amygdala showed no such sensitivity to the satiety treatment on test. They responded at an equal level towards both levers. This was not because the satiety treatment was ineffective in these animals – a free consumption test immediately after extinction testing showed that lesioned animals rejected the sated food to the same degree as sham-lesioned control animals. We have also found a very similar effect in a purely instrumental choice procedure in which rats were trained to press one lever in order to get

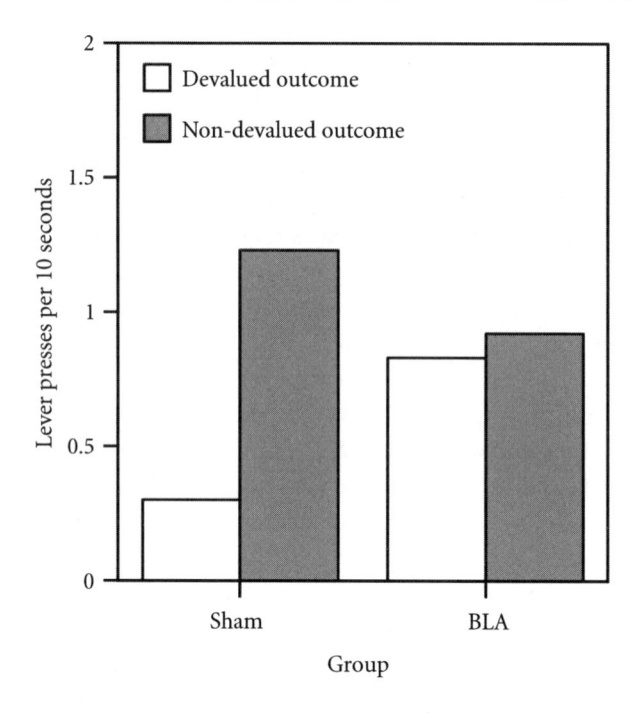

Figure 2. Choice extinction test performance in lesioned and control animals. Animals were trained with differential autoshaping pairings of left or right lever presentation and food or sucrose before devaluation of one or other of the outcomes prior to the choice test. Open bars indicate responding on the lever that was paired with the devalued outcome, filled bars indicate responding on the lever paired with the non-devalued outcome.

food pellets and to pull a chain to get sucrose solution (Balleine, Killcross, & Dickinson, submitted). For control animals, as in the autoshaping procedure, devaluation of one of the outcomes by specific satiety reduced performance on the manipulandum that produced that devalued outcome. However animals with excitotoxic lesions of the basolateral amygdala once again failed to show this discriminative performance, despite showing sensitivity to the devaluation procedure in a subsequent consumption test. Hence, in both Pavlovian and instrumental procedures, lesions of the basolateral amygdala produce deficits in devaluation of reinforcers in extinction tests.

However, to take the particular example of lever pressing for food, failure of response-reward learning to control behaviour could occur for a variety of reasons. First, animals may fail to discriminate between representations of the two actions. Second, animals may fail to discriminate between representations of the two rewards. Let us address each of these in turn.

Can these animals discriminate between the two actions? Clearly an explicit test of this is required, and is provided most simply by training the animals to perform a simple chain of instrumental responses. If an animal can distinguish between two responses then it ought to be able to learn to perform one action followed by a second, *in a particular order*, to get food reward. For example, pressing a lever followed by pulling a chain leads to food (A1–A2), but any other order of responding (leverpress-leverpress, chainpull-chainpull, chainpull-leverpress; A1–A1, A2–A2, A2–A1) does not. Normal animals readily learn this and in the above example are far more likely to perform a chainpull after a leverpress than any other combination of responses. That is, examining the probability of A2 as a function of the time since A1 was performed reveals that the probability of A2 peaks within a couple of seconds of performance of A1, whereas the probability of A1 remains consistently low after performance of A2, as does the probability of performing a second A1 response, or the probability of an A2 response after any other A2 response. In a previous study (Balleine, Killcross and Dickinson, submitted) we initially trained animals, again with either excitotoxic lesions of the basolateral amygdala or sham control lesions, on a random-interval 2-sec schedule of reinforcement for chain-pulls and lever-presses in separate sessions. After this all animals were trained on the chain schedule A1-A2 such that food pellets were delivered according to schedule, contingent upon the performance of A2 provided that A1 had been performed at least once after the reinforcer became available. Three sessions were run with increasing random-interval schedules of 2, 15 and 30 sec. The results from this study are shown in Figure 3 and confirmed that animals with lesions of the basolateral amygdala, despite failing to show sensitivity to selective reward devaluation in an instrumental choice procedure, could tell the difference between their instrumental actions – that is, they showed a greater probability of performing A2 immediately after performance of A1, whereas the probability of all other response combinations remained consistently low. As animals with amygdala damage can learn these sequences, we have ruled out the possibility, at least in the instrumental domain, that they fail to indicate their ability re-value food reward because they cannot discriminate between responses.

So can these animals distinguish between different rewards? We have applied a similar logic in determining this. If animals can learn about the different nature of rewards, they ought to be able to make use of that information to help them to get around the world. One way in which knowing about the difference

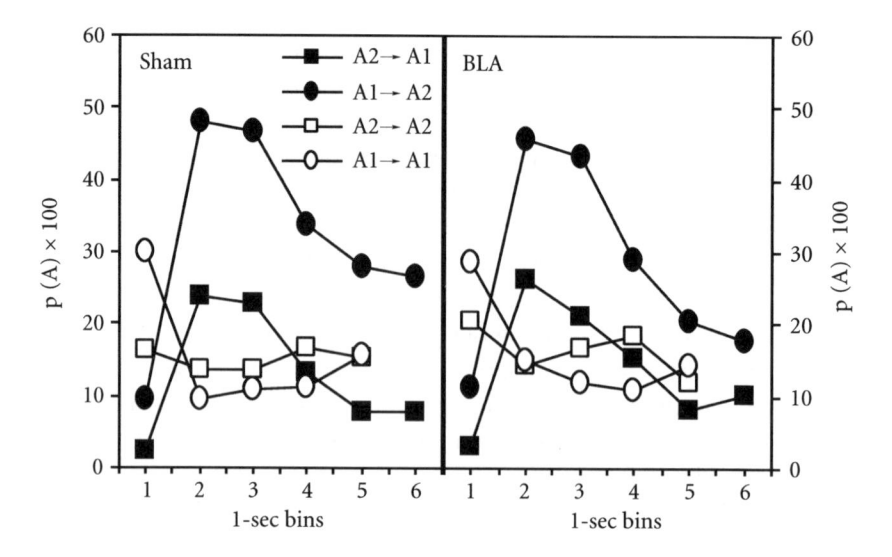

Figure 3. Conditional probability of performance of specific response chains across six, 1-sec bins following performance of the initial component of the response chain in sham- (left panel) and BLA-lesioned (right panel) animals. Only performance of action A2 following action A1 was reinforced.

between rewards helps animals is in discriminating between events that lead to those rewards. An animal will more readily learn to tell one frequency of tone from another if the two tones lead to different rewards (say food pellets and sucrose solution) than if they lead to the same reward. Trapold (1970) first reported this differential outcomes procedure. He compared the performance of two groups of animals in learning a discrete-trial instrumental conditional discrimination. On each trial the rats were presented with two levers, along with either a tone or click stimulus. In the control group, correct responses in the presence of either stimulus were always rewarded by delivery of the same type of reward (a food pellet for some animals, sucrose solution for the others). In the experimental group correct responses in the presence of one stimulus were consistently reinforced by one reward; correct responses in the presence of the other stimulus were consistently reinforced by the other reward. The animals in the experimental group learned the discrimination faster than those in the control group. There are a variety of possible explanations for the differential outcomes effect, but on the whole they all assume that the more rapid acquisition of the conditional discrimination in the experimental group is due to associations forming between the discriminative stimuli and the different reinforcers.

We made use of this finding by training rats on a task in which they had to learn to press one lever (say, the left-hand lever) in the presence of one type of auditory signal, but another lever (the right-hand lever) in the presence of a second auditory signal. In both cases, correct presses were followed by reward, incorrect presses (i.e. those on the opposite lever) by nothing. Rats readily solved this discrimination, but solved it even more easily if correct presses on one lever produced sucrose and correct presses on the other produced food pellets. These results are shown for sham-lesioned control animals in the left-hand panel of Figure 4. Rats in both reward-inconsistent and reward-consistent groups came to respond more on the correct lever than on the incorrect lever as training proceeded. However, acquisition of the discrimination was retarded in the Inconsistent group who had responded at a higher rate on the incorrect lever and a lower rate on the correct lever than the reward-consistent group; that is, the sham-lesioned rats showed the differential outcomes effect. The right-hand panel of Figure 4 shows acquisition of the conditional discrimination in the BLA-lesioned groups. Again, across training sessions, rats in both reward-inconsistent and reward-consistent groups came to respond more on the correct lever than on the incorrect lever. Hence BLA lesions do not prevent acquisition of the conditional discrimination. There was, however, no difference between the performance of the reward-inconsistent and the reward-consistent groups; that is, BLA lesions eliminated the differential outcomes effect. Although rats with excitotoxic lesions of the basolateral amygdala could learn the overall discrimination readily enough, they failed to show any benefit from having two different rewards. Finally, it is important to note that an extinction test confirmed that the animals were discriminating between responses on the basis of the two signals, and all animals' failure to show any discrimination in a test in which the outcomes alone were presented (in the absence of signals) further supported this interpretation. It might also be added that this experiment also confirmed that the BLA-lesioned rats show no deficit in basic instrumental or Pavlovian conditioning.

But what is it about the two rewards they cannot distinguish? Again there are a number of competing alternatives. First, the animals may not represent the reward as an outcome at all. This might seem to suggest that the animal cannot learn anything at all (and therefore would predict a failure of basic conditioning which is not observed – as we have already observed in Figure 1 and in the acquisition of autoshaped lever approach). However, there are likely to be several different forms of learning that can occur following the pairing of a stimulus and a reward. As reviewed earlier, the rat might learn some form of S-R habit. Here, the function of a reward is conceived solely as strengthening

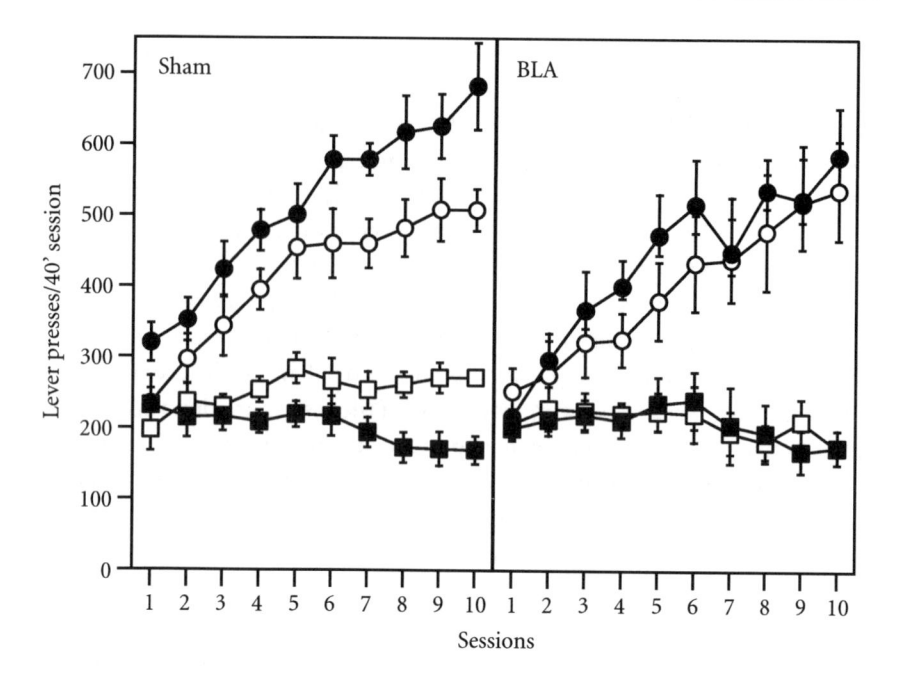

Figure 4. Acquisition of a conditional lever-press discrimination in sham- (left panel) and BLA-lesioned (right panel) animals. Circles indicate performance on the correct lever, squares performance on the incorrect lever. Closed symbols indicate discrimination in which each of the two rewarded responses (left or right) was consistently followed by a particular outcome (food pellets or sucrose) – the differential outcomes condition. Open symbols indicate discrimination in which the two rewarded responses were randomly followed by either food pellets or sucrose solution.

the likelihood that a stimulus will elicit a response. Responding is therefore not mediated by a representation of the reward, but by a direct connection between stimulus and response. This is in contrast to the outcome-based interpretation of responding given above where performance is held to be mediated by activity in a representation of reward as a consequence of some predictive event. The S–R interpretation predicts that animals will not change their behaviour in response to changes in the value of the reward, and further, they will not be sensitive to the exact nature of the reward – but merely to its capacity to reinforce the S–R habit. This is, of course, the pattern of data discussed so far – rats with amygdala damage could be behaving solely on the basis of S–R habits. A second possible account of the failure of these rats to be sensitive to the nature of reward might suggest that they are failing to generate a proper associative representation of the rewards. That is, their performance is mediated by a representation of the reward, but this representation is impoverished in some way. More specifically, they may not be able to represent the sensory properties of the reward along with its motivational properties. In order to understand how this might produce the pattern of deficits described so far, we have to investigate further the likely different functions of different associative representations of reinforcers.

We have already considered the fact that the protopathic, or motivational, properties of a reinforcer seem likely to be able to support certain forms of conditioned behaviours – those which are often labelled preparatory. Of course, there is a great risk of circularity here – those behaviours which are termed preparatory are those which depend on protopathic properties, and protopathic properties are those which support preparatory conditioned behaviours. The same is also true of the relationship between consummatory responses and the idiopathic, or sensory, properties of reinforcers. The search for explicit and objective definitions of behavioural classes or categories is reflected in the wide array of different, yet overlapping attempts to capture the essence of alternative learning or response systems (Mowrer 1947; Konorski 1967; Vandercar & Schneiderman 1967; Wagner & Brandon, 1989; Thompson et al. 1984; Lennartz & Weinberger, 1992; Boakes 1979, 1977). There are also several situations in which it is observed that different behaviours are controlled by dissociable properties of the reinforcer (Balleine, Garner, Gonzalez, & Dickinson 1995; Adams 1982), and still further emerging evidence that these reinforcement learning systems are likely to be dissociable at a neural and pharmacological level (Killcross et al. 1997a; Balleine & Dickinson 1994; Balleine, Ball & Dickinson 1994; Berridge 1996; Wyvell & Berridge 2000; Berridge & Robinson 1998; Thompson et al. 1984; Powell, Hernandez, & Buchanan 1985).

Berridge (1996) drew a distinction between brain substrates of wanting and liking. By this he was attempting to deconfound aspects of reinforcers that folk psychology has long placed together. It seems natural to assume that if one likes something, then one will want it – and similarly if one wants a particular outcome, then that outcome must, surely, be liked. Drawing on a background of drug-addiction literature, and in line with the venerable history of differential reinforcer-response associations outlined above, Berridge suggested that this was not necessarily the case. In the drug-addiction world it is common to talk of needs without desires, and further studies have gone on to demonstrate that wants and likes are dissociable at neural, as well as psychological levels (Berridge & Robinson 1998). To follow this line of argument, rats with lesions of the basolateral amygdala may fail in tests which require them to respond on the basis of the nature of rewards because although they want the reward, they are no longer able to represent whether or not the reward is liked, or has hedonic value. The failure to show an effect of specific satiety occurs because representations of the sensory hedonic properties of the reward are no longer available. In the absence of such representations, changes in the palatability and hedonics of the outcome as a consequence of satiety treatments will no longer influence the motivational properties of the outcome (see Balleine 2000). Similarly, failing to represent properties of outcomes based on their individual characteristics – their ideopathic properties – means that rats cannot make use of this information to help them solve discriminations.

Both of these theories, the S–R interpretation and the failure to represent sensory properties of rewards along with their motivational properties, predict the pattern of results we have discussed to date. So can they be dissociated? Indeed they can, and here we appeal to a third procedure from learning theory – a transfer of control design (Kruse et al. 1983). Experiments of this type combine all the various aspects of Pavlovian and instrumental conditioning we have already discussed. Pavlovian CSs can strongly influence instrumental behavior (Rescorla & Solomon 1967; Kruse et al. 1983). For example, presentation of a CS that has been paired with reward will, in some circumstances, potentiate instrumental responding that has been reinforced by that reward. This potentiation of responding is reinforcer specific – if an animal has a choice of two responses and consequent differing outcomes, when a CS is presented it will increase responding more on a lever that resulted in the delivery of the reward that has followed the CS than on a lever that previously led to a different reward. For example, a CS that has been paired with food pellets will cause a greater increase in responding on a manipulandum that has been reinforced by the same food pellets than on one that has been reinforced by a different appetitive reinforcer (Kruse et al. 1983).

We used this phenomenon to study the associations that are formed during Pavlovian and instrumental conditioning in rats following basolateral amygdala lesions. There are two aspects to the potentiation of responding caused by presentation of a Pavlovian CS – a general enhancement in instrumental responding by virtue of the CS's association with arousing, motivational aspects of the US, and the reinforcer-specific potentiation by virtue of the CS's association with the specific sensory aspects of the reward. If rats with lesions of the basolateral amygdala were simply S–R animals, incapable of forming associations between a cue and any aspect of the reinforcer, then we would not expect them to show any potentiation of responding due to superimposing a CS on instrumental responding. In fact, we might expect a reduction in responding, as the response normally elicited by presentation of a CS (food-magazine approach) is likely to interfere with lever pressing. However, if animals with basolateral amygdala lesions form associations between CSs and the motivational, but not sensory, aspects of a reward, then we would expect instrumental responding to increase during presentation of CSs, but not to increase specifically on the response that had previously earned the same reward as that predicted by the CS. In the particular design we used, animals received pairings of two auditory stimuli, a tone and a train of clicks, with, for example, food pellets and sucrose solution, respectively. In independent sessions animals were also trained to perform left or right lever presses for food pellets or sucrose solution, respectively. Test sessions then examined the effect of superimposing presentations of the tone or click stimuli on animals' pressing on both levers in a choice extinction test.

We predicted that sham-lesioned rats would show an increase in responding on both levers during the tone and the click-train, (by virtue of their conditioned arousing effects) but that the increase would be greater on the lever that had previously resulted in delivery of the same reward as was predicted by the stimulus. The question of interest was whether BLA-lesioned rats would show a general increase in responding during presentation of the CSs, and if they did, would that increase be reinforcer specific?

What we found was that whereas sham-lesioned animals responded as expected, showing both selective and general elevation of responding, animals with selective damage to the basolateral amygdala showed a general elevation in responding during a signal for food, but this increased responding was not selective to the reward being earned. These results are shown in Figure 5. The measure used to assess transfer is an elevation ratio based on responding during the presence of a Pavlovian cue, compared to responding in its absence. Although animals with lesions of the basolateral amygdala showed a general transfer effect (their elevation ratios were greater than 1), this transfer was not selective to the response that had previously predicted the same outcome as the Pavlovian cue present.

We may now distinguish between the two possible theories of function following lesions of the basolateral amygdala. As lesioned animals showed a general, but not selective, Pavlovian-instrumental transfer, we are left to conclude that these animals are not merely S–R animals, but are in fact animals who can no longer represent certain selective aspects of reinforcers – those ideopathic features that are responsible for patterns of consummatory responses directed at the reinforcer, as well as for the generation of palatability effects and hedonic judgements.

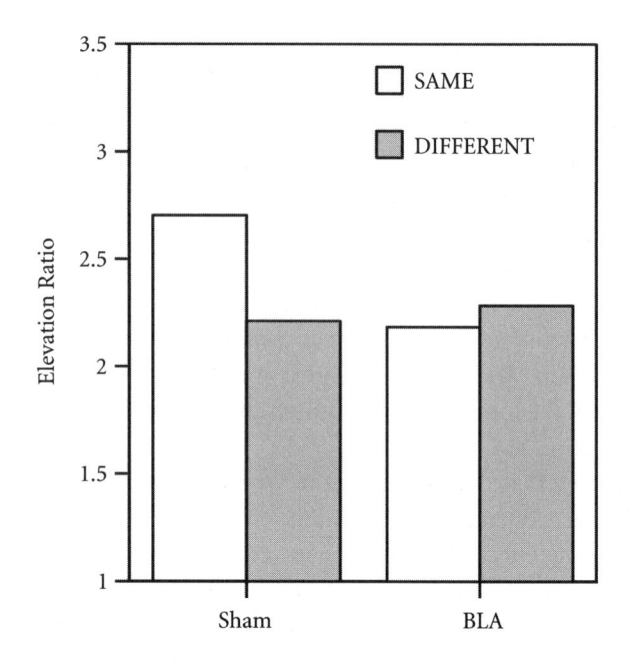

Figure 5. Elevation of lever press responding during presentation of Pavlovian conditional stimuli, relative to baseline rates of pressing, in sham- and BLA-lesioned animals. Open bars indicate performance of the response that produced the same outcome as that predicted by the stimulus present. Closed bars indicate performance of the response that produced the alternative outcome to that predicted by the stimulus present.

To present a simplified case, in normal animals, when a CS is paired with a US, several different associations may form (Konorski 1967; Dickinson & Dearing 1978). CS presentation evokes an internal CS representation (initially sensory in nature, see Wagner and Brandon 1989). US presentation activates both sensory (US_S) and motivational (US_M) representations, which elicit their own characteristic responses (consummatory and preparatory, respectively). The CS representation may form associations with both US_S and US_M, and/or with the responses these produce. Whereas US_S is conceived as being specific to the particular outcome, US_M reflects a more general motivational impact. Although BLA lesions do not interfere with simple Pavlovian conditioning, amygdala-lesioned rats are not sensitive to post-conditioning changes in the reward value (Hatfield et al. 1996). Since reward devaluation by LiCl injection is likely to act via US_S (Holland 1990; Berridge 1991, 1996; Balleine 2000; Garcia 1989; see also Balleine & Dickinson 1998a), reducing palatability and hedonic evaluation of the reward, we suggest that CS–US$_S$ associations are not formed in BLA-lesioned animals. Rather, conditioned responding depends on the formation of associations between CS and response, or between CS and US$_M$. We should be explicit about what we mean by US$_S$ in contrast to US$_M$. By US$_S$ we refer to those aspects of the reinforcer that are specific to the individual outcome. Substantial evidence (see Balleine 2000) suggests that reinforcers are represented by a number of sensory features to which incentive value is ascribed. This value is manifest by changes in hedonic evaluation, palatability, and subsequent desirability, of the reinforcer (Balleine 2000; Berridge 1996). Animals with BLA lesions are incapable of forming, or utilizing, associative US$_S$ representations, and cannot respond in accordance with associatively activated changes in hedonic evaluation or palatability. Note that BLA lesions do not disrupt direct perception of changes in palatability; their ability to show rejection of devalued foods in consumption tests is maintained (Dunn & Everitt 1988; Hatfield et al. 1996; Willoughby & Killcross 1998). This contrasts with US$_M$, by which we mean the arousing aspects of motivation that lead to alterations in preparatory activity and to changes in the strength, but not direction, of Pavlovian modulation of instrumental performance (Dickinson & Dearing 1979).

The differential outcomes effect occurs because the discriminative stimulus forms an association with the specific properties of the food that accompanies it (Trapold 1970; Trapold & Overmier 1972; Rescorla 1994). According to the analysis presented above, rats with lesions of the basolateral amygdala do not show this effect because the discriminative stimulus cannot form associations with a representation that includes the sensory properties of the reward. Accordingly, animals with lesions of the basolateral amygdala do not show any advantage of differential reinforcement in discrimination learning. A similar logic explains the results of our transfer experiment. During Pavlovian conditioning, associations form between CS and reward, but in animals with lesions of the basolateral amygdala, this does not include US$_S$. When the CS is presented during an extinction test in which animals are making instrumental responses, the CS creates the expectation of reward (US$_M$), but does not activate a representation of the specific sensory aspects of that reward (US$_S$). Hence, there is a general increase in responding, but no selective effect based on specific response-reward relationships.

This analysis can also account for the results of previous research examining the role of the amygdala in learning. Consider second-order conditioning. In a design used by Hatfield et al. (1996), one CS (CS$_1$) was paired with reward in the first phase, and in the second phase a second CS (CS$_2$) was followed by CS$_1$. There are (at least) three proposed mechanisms that have been put forward to account for the acquisition of responding in second-order conditioning. First, animals may form an association between CS_2 and CS_1, which, by virtue of an associative chain and the existing CS_1–reward association, will produce responding during CS_2 (S-S learning – Rescorla 1982; Rescorla 1980; Rescorla 1979; Rashotte et al. 1977). Second, animals may form an S–R association between CS_2 and any response evoked by CS_1, increasing responding during CS_2 (S–R learning – Holland & Rescorla 1975; Rizley & Rescorla 1972). Finally, animals may learn a direct association between CS_2 and the representation of reward evoked by presentation of CS_1 (Ross 1986).

There is substantial evidence in favor of S-S and S-R interpretations, but rather less favoring CS_2-reward associations (indeed, theories of learning (e.g., Wagner 1976) suggest that associations between CSs and evoked representations are difficult to form – but see Holland 1981). Whether S-R or S-S associations form depends largely on the parameters of the experiment – the similarity between CS_1 and CS_2 (Rescorla 1982) and the capacity of CS_1 to evoke a response during CS_2–CS_1 pairings (Rescorla 1973). Hence, the failure of animals with lesions of the basolateral amygdala to show second-order conditioning can be accounted for in two ways: First, if animals with lesions of the basolateral amygdala cannot learn about the sensory properties of motivationally significant events, then during phase 2 they will have difficulty in forming the association between CS_2 and CS_1, (note that CS_1 will have acquired motivational significance due to first-order associations with US_M.) Second-order conditioned responding based on an associative chain would not be possible. Second, if animals with lesions of the basolateral amygdala were unable to show S-R learning, they would thus be unable to form associations between CS_2 and the response evoked by CS_1. The first of these explanations fits with our interpretation in terms of the failure of lesioned animals to represent the sensory properties of motivationally significant events. However, an account based on failure of S-R learning in lesioned animals has problems accounting for the deficits following reinforcer devaluation (Figure 2, see also Hatfield et al. 1996) and the reinforcer-specificity effects (Figures 4 and 5) outlined above. If appetitive conditioning proceeds normally, but is insensitive to reward devaluation, animals must either be learning by S-R mechanisms or with an impoverished representation of the US. If the former explanation is invoked to account for normal appetitive conditioning, then a disruption of S-R learning cannot then be used to explain deficits in second-order conditioning. For these reasons we favor the parsimonious explanation that animals with lesions of the basolateral amygdala have a deficit in representing the sensory properties of motivationally significant events.

We can apply a similar explanation to the finding that basolateral amygdala lesions disrupt the ability of Pavlovian CSs to act as reinforcers for instrumental conditioning – studies of second-order conditioning and conditioned reinforcement. As CSs are purely sensory stimuli with acquired motivational significance, rats with lesions of the basolateral amygdala will have difficulty learning lever press-CS associations, and acquisition of lever pressing rewarded by CSs will be disrupted. However, even if this associative chain mechanism is not functioning, acquisition could occur if animals still show S-R learning – formation of a stimulus-leverpress association reinforced by the acquired motivational properties of the CS. There is evidence that monkeys with lesions of the basolateral amygdala can show conditioned reinforcement (Malkova et al. 1996), that BLA-lesioned rats show only partial (Alderson et al. 2000; Burns et al. 1993; Cador et al. 1989; Everitt et al. 1989) or transient (Burns et al. 1999) deficits in conditioned reinforcement. One possibility that might explain the variable findings, especially in situations in which the original primary reinforcer is a drug of abuse such as cocaine, amphetamine or heroine, is the extent to which the reinforcer possesses both motivational and sensory properties and the extent to which these overshadow one another. Hence one might expect to see a lesser impact of lesions of the basolateral amygdala when the motivational properties of a reward far outweigh the impact of its sensory properties. We might also suggest that this provides an alternative framework to account for the selective effects of lesions of the basolateral amygdala on fear conditioning in the parallel aversive situation of conditioned punishment. We (Killcross et al. 1997a) have previously demonstrated that lesions of the basolateral amygdala, but not of the central nucleus of the amygdala, disrupt conditioned punishment, but not conditioned suppression. The opposite pattern of results was revealed following lesions of the central, but not basolateral, portion of the amygdala. We suggested that this double dissociation might depend upon the voluntary versus reflexive nature of the behavioural indices of fear used in punishment and suppression, respectively. A modification of this theory might suggest that the profound effects of lesions of the basolateral amygdala on punishment are due to the requirement of this operant procedure to maintain a representation of a signal for footshock as the outcome of an instrumental activity, a representation that depends more on the sensory aspects of the cue and the reinforcer than acquired motivational properties. In contrast, conditioned suppression, regarded by many as a classic preparatory fear response, depends more upon the motivational properties of the footshock than upon the ability of a cue for footshock to act as an outcome or dis-incentive for instrumental responding.

In summary, for rats with lesions of the basolateral amygdala, the ability of a CS to evoke representations of the motivationally arousing aspects of a US does not appear to be impaired. Rather, rats with basolateral amygdala lesions appear to be incapable of forming associations between events in the world and the sensory-specific aspects of motivationally significant stimuli. As suggested above, these sensory aspects of the reinforcer appear to play an important role in the hedonic evaluation of rewards and their palatability (Berridge 1996; Balleine 2000). Using this distinction it would seem that the basolateral amygdala is involved in aspects of 'liking' rather than 'wanting' (Berridge 1996; Simbayi, Boakes, & Burton 1986). As this would seem to provide support for the notion that the nature of reinforcer representations, and the role they play in learning, may differ in different conditioning paradigms, this provides a basis for attempting to put together an informal model that attempts to capture these selective aspects of reinforcement.

An informal model

Dickinson and Balleine (1993) put forward a putative associative architecture that was capable of generating actions (goal-directed behaviours) and responses (behaviours that appear, at least in part, insensitive to changes in goal-value) under appropriate conditions (see also Dickinson 1994). This model they termed the associative-cybernetic model (after Sutton & Barto 1981). Associative, as it holds that in the presence of certain stimuli activity will be evoked in representations of responses associated with those stimuli, which will in turn evoke activity in goal representations, and cybernetic, because it assumes that this evoked goal activity will feed back to boost the activity in response representations until such point as the responses are performed. The model contained two distinct routes to behaviour. All responses are dependent upon activity in evoked response representations in an S-R store, which in turn activates representations of the responses in the motor system. If activity in the motor system achieves some threshold, the response occurs. Goal-directed responses also activate response representations in an associative memory, which then activate representations of the goal associated with the response. In turn, activation of this goal representation feeds through a reinforcement or incentive system to provide feedback to the motor system and to the S-R store. This feedback both indiscriminately alters the threshold for activation of representations in the motor system, and also facilitates associations in S-R memory, ultimately leading to the development of goal-independent habits. Goal-directed behaviour occurs when sufficient associative strengths allow firing of motor units due to the *combined* influence of direct excitation of motor representations by matching S-R response elements and threshold alteration of these motor representations due to activity in the incentive system. Responses that are not goal-directed are conceived of as lacking a response representation in associative memory to match that in the S-R store. Hence evoked activity in the reinforcement system comes about not due to activation of a response-outcome association in associative memory, but rather due to a stimulus-outcome association.

As Dickinson and Balleine (1993) point out, this model is not without its problems – it assumes that both goal-directed actions and responses are mediated by a common representation of outcome in the associative memory – in the first case as part of an action-outcome association, in the latter as part of a stimulus-outcome association. That this is not the case may be inferred from work reviewed above – we might argue that the nature of an outcome in goal-directed responding requires that its representation provides information about the sensory, hedonics-generating properties of the reinforcer, rather than merely its motivational properties. In contrast, although undoubtedly sometimes encoded, this sensory information may be neither necessary nor sufficient to support Pavlovian learning. This would certainly seem to be in agreement with the now substantial literature detailing the sensitivity of instrumental actions to the process of incentive learning (Balleine & Dickinson 1991; Dickinson & Balleine 1995). In an elegant series of experiments Balleine, Dickinson and colleagues have demonstrated that in order for a change in the value of an instrumental outcome to have an impact on instrumental performance, animals must have experience of the outcome in its newly-valued form. For example, Balleine (1992) demonstrated that rats trained to respond for food pellets when sated, showed identical performance in an extinction test regardless of whether they were tested hungry or tested sated. That is, increases in primary motivation for food had no direct impact on responding that previously delivered food pellets. However, an impact of the shift in motivational state was observed if animals were given the opportunity to experience the food pellets when hungry. Simple non-contingent exposure to food pellets when hungry brought about the expected shift in performance – greater responding when tested hungry than when tested sated. One interpretation of this is that the exposure when hungry established in these animals a desire for the pellets – manifest by an increase in incentive value that is reflected in instrumental performance. Further experiments have established that this effect is dependent upon experience of the affective state produced by the outcome during incentive learning – reflecting taste properties, palatability and hedonic responses – rather than the relevance of the outcome to the primary motivational state (Balleine 2000; Balleine, Ball, & Dickinson 1994).

Similarly, dissociations appear in the requirements for incentive learning in Pavlovian and instrumental learning procedures. Whereas instrumental learning appears to require incentive learning for changes in the value of outcomes to influence performance, Pavlovian responding appears to be directly and instantaneously influenced by changes in reward value. Hence in the incentive learning experiments described above, magazine approach (which is likely to depend upon Pavlovian excitation) is directly influenced by changes in reward value even though lever press performance is not. However, it has been suggested that this is not due to Pavlovian or instrumental distinctions, but rather due to the proximity of the response to the reinforcer. This is supported by experiments examining the role of incentive learning in heterogeneous instrumental chains (Balleine, Garner, Gonzalez, & Dickinson 1995). Here, hungry rats were trained to perform a two-component instrumental chain in order to get food pellets (for example, chainpull-leverpress-pellets). This they readily learnt. However, subsequent manipulations of satiety prior to test again revealed an influence of incentive learning on instrumental performance, but this effect was largely restricted to the more distal component of the instrumental chain (in this example, chainpulling). In contrast, the proximal response was directly influenced by the change in motivational state. Although this echoes a similar lack of sensitivity of Pavlovian second-order conditioning to reinforcer devaluation (Holland & Rescorla 1975), whereby reinforcer devaluation prevented performance of Pavlovian conditioned responding to first-order CSs but had no impact on conditioned responding to second-order CSs, a parallel interpretation is unlikely to be true as the multiple devaluation trials used by Holland and Rescorla provided, by chance, an opportunity for incentive learning that was almost identical to the one used by Balleine et al. (1995) – but see Balleine (2000) for a possible unifying interpretation.

We have suggested that there is evidence that the basolateral amygdala mediates associatively activated representations of the sensory properties of outcomes, and that these sensory properties are those involved in representation of incentive value (see Balleine 2000). These incentive properties are required for the formation of action-outcome associations, but not for performance of conditioned responding based on stimulus-outcome associations (although they may be encoded in certain procedures). The influence of different properties of outcomes on responding also depends on the proximity of CSs and responses to the outcome, although the manner of this dependency may vary between Pavlovian and instrumental procedures. How might these various facts be incorporated into a model of performance?

An initial attempt at this is shown, in a very informal manner, in Figure 6. The basic elements of this structure owe a great deal to previous models of motivation-reinforcer interactions in learning (Konorski 1967; Dickinson & Dearing 1978; Dickinson & Balleine 1993). In the following description readers will recognize elements that correspond, more or less, to previous conceptualisations of reinforcement systems, preparatory and consummatory response systems, associative memory, motor memory and so forth. The fundamental assumption is that responding due to pairings of an event in the world (E1) and a motivationally significant outcome can arise in two ways. The first is due to the ability of the event to evoke a representation of the outcome (US_S) that then leads to either consummatory Pavlovian conditioned responding or instrumental responding based on an action-outcome association. In this sense development of these responses is much akin to that proposed in the associative-cybernetic model above (Dickinson & Balleine 1993). Here, associatively based activation of specific outcome representations (US_S) causes activation of motivational associates or attributes (US_M – similar to activation of a reinforcement system) which then influence the likelihood of responding (by a system of long-

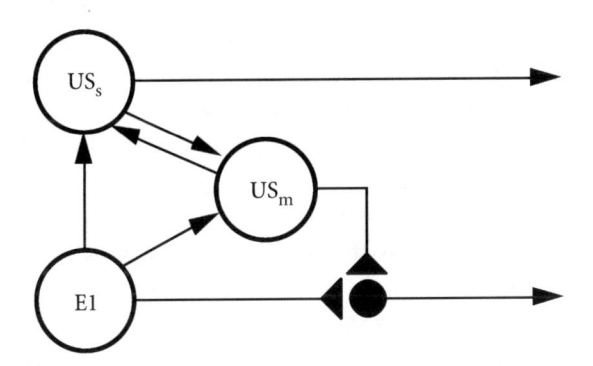

Figure 6. An informal model of response production (after Dickinson and Balleine 1993). An event in the world (E1) is capable of evoking activity in representations of different aspects of the outcome (US_S and US_M). Activity in US_S leads to outcome-specific responding (response R1). Activity in US_M (by either direct activation from E1 or indirect activation via US_S activity) leads to modulation of motor output systems activated by E1 (both long-term influences that reduce firing threshold and short-term conjoint activation that summates with sub-threshold activation from E1). Symbols indicate acquired excitatory connections (→), motor output units (•), and modifiable connections (◄).

term modulation and conjoint activation due to representational activity of the initiating event, as would be effected by interaction of an S-R store and motor system). Second, the initiating event can itself directly produce activation of the reinforcement system, altering the likelihood of responding *independently* of the activity of the specific outcome representation. A central feature of the model is the suggestion that the relative importance of these different forms of activation depends on the precise nature of the learning situation. The basic idea would be that the role of the *directly* evoked activation of US_M (i.e., by the initiating event) is rather stronger for Pavlovian learning contingencies than for instrumental conditioning. After all, the initiating event in a Pavlovian learning situation is actual presentation of CS, whereas the initiating event in instrumental learning (following the associative-cybernetic model) is likely to be an action pattern representation evoked by some salient stimulus in an S-R store. The consequence of this assumption is that performance of instrumental actions is largely mediated by the sensory or incentive representation of the reinforcer (US_S), which in turn may activate reinforcement systems, whereas Pavlovian responding is mediated by direct activation of *both* the incentive representation *and* the reinforcement system (US_M).

This differential involvement has a number of implications for the development of different forms of responding and their differential sensitivity to shifts in reinforcement value. If we consider the case that might arise in Pavlovian learning (the left-hand panel of Figure 7) then we see that the ability of a Pavlovian cue S1 to enter into direct association with reinforcement systems allows performance of conditioned responses that depend upon the nature of S1, rather than the nature of the US. This is in accordance with a wide variety of findings highlighting the distinction between sign-directed and goal-directed behaviours (and a variety of similar distinctions e.g., Boakes 1977, 1979; Davey, Oakland, & Cleland 1981; Holland 1980). A further consequence of the fact that S1 will be able directly to evoke US_M is that higher-order stimuli (e.g., S2) will be able to produce responding due to both S2-S1-US_S associations and direct reinforcement of S2-mediated responding by the associatively based reinforcing properties of S1 (here termed $S1_M$) – effectively an S-R process. The designation of $S1_M$ is not intended to indicate that the properties of this representation are necessarily different from those of US_M, but rather that this representation is evoked due to activity in S1 rather than US_S. A natural consequence of this structure is that changes in the value of the US, which might operate by the interaction of US_S and US_M (hence the bi-directional connection – see Balleine 2000), will have little impact on behaviours evoked by higher-order stimuli (Holland & Rescorla 1975). It might be stressed however, that the nature of this model is not to be overly prescriptive with respect to the scope of influence of associations. Hence it is likely that activity in US_M will have some ability to influence behaviours due to S2, and, presumably to a lesser extent, S3 and so forth. Neither is it intended that S1, S2 etc., refer necessarily to explicit, experimentally defined stimuli. It is possible for example that S1 might be incidental cues (e.g., the sight of a food magazine) predictive of food delivery, whereas S2 might be the explicit CS used in a particular experimental procedure. The idea is that a continuum of stimuli control a continuum of behavioural responses, each point in these continua influencing, and influenced by, the graded impact of associative relationships. An attempt is made to indicate this in the arrows indicating a final common pathway of behavioural responses leading from preparatory to consummatory. A further possible consequence of this structure is that the nature of the devaluation is likely to differentially affect different forms of responding. Devaluation procedures that might be conceived as influencing the hedonic aspects of the US (perhaps LiCl-induced nausea) are more likely to influence more consummatory forms of responding, whereas alternative forms of devaluation (e.g. rotation) may influence behaviours more distal (preparatory) to the US (see Holland and Straub 1979).

The basic outline for instrumental performance (the right-hand panel of Figure 7) is very similar to that for Pavlovian learning, with the important distinction that the ability of action representations to produce activity in reinforcement systems is achieved primarily through only the specific representation of the reinforcer. This is again not intended to be overly prescriptive. Action representations may come to be able to influence US_M directly, but the tendency for this to occur is considerably less than is the case in Pavlovian learning. In fact, as for the associative-cybernetic model, it is this direct form of modulation that, over time, leads to the development of S-R habits. It is not that either one or another of the associations is formed, but rather that they contribute differentially to the control of behaviour. Indeed, it may be the case that this interaction is competitive and the absence of one mechanism boosts the salience or importance of the other in controlling responding. The bias towards processing via US_S in instrumental learning has a number of effects. First, the majority of activation of motor outputs occurs via activation of the specific representation of the reinforcer, the incentive representation. Second, as associations between actions and US_M are weak there is correspondingly less opportunity for the formation of direct higher-order associations between more distal actions in an instrumental chain and the reinforcement system. Hence, although activity in the reinforcement system can modulate the likelihood of

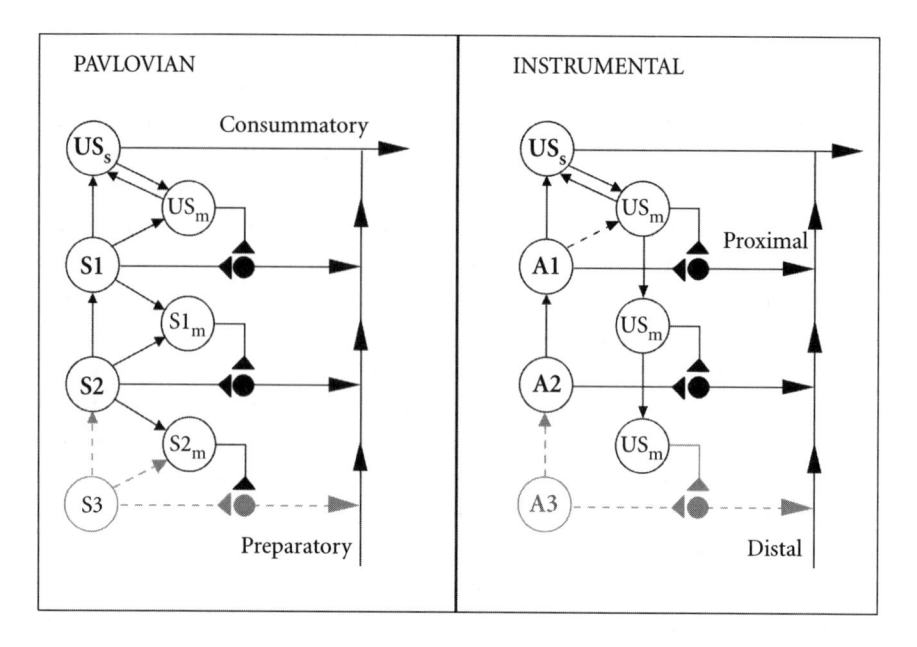

Figure 7. Impact of differential activation of US_S and US_M in Pavlovian and instrumental learning. S1, S2, S3 and A1, A2, A3 refer to sequences of stimuli and actions, respectively. Dotted lines and a fading and greying of connections and symbols indicates a weakening of the influence of the primary reinforcer over initial components of the event sequence. The arrowed line to right indicates a behavioural output cascade controlled by initial, through to terminal, aspects of the event sequence. Other symbols as for Figure 6.

multiple events in an instrumental chain, this is nevertheless achieved primarily by activation of the incentive representation of the outcome. Furthermore, as activation of US_M by actions occurs by this associative chain, the influence of directly evoked activity in US_M over more distal actions is assumed to decline the more distal the action becomes to US_S. Consequently, more distal components of a chain should be slower to become habit-based, and should maintain a stricter requirement for modification of the value of the incentive representation by experience to produce changes in behaviour. As outlined above, this latter point is certainly supported by previous experiments (Balleine, Garner, Gonzalez & Dickinson 1995). Similarly, it is the more proximal responses that, with extended training and the gradual development of modulation of actions by direct activation of the reinforcement system by evoked action representations, become both habit-like, and less dependent on incentive learning –

again suggestions supported by previous findings (Dickinson, Balleine, Watt, Gonzalez, & Boakes 1995).

In summary, we are not suggesting that Pavlovian and instrumental systems make use of either the same, or radically different, representations of outcomes. Rather, we are suggesting that the two forms of learning differ in the extent to which they rely upon different aspects of the incentive and reinforcing properties of outcomes. The application of this theory to the neuroscientific studies outlined above should be fairly self-evident. We would suggest that lesions of the basolateral amygdala disrupt processes concerned with the ability of animals to represent the US_S aspects of outcomes, be they concerned with Pavlovian or instrumental learning. This evaluative function is likely to be dependent upon connections between the basolateral amygdala and the insular cortex (Balleine & Dickinson 1998) and perhaps also the core subregion of the nucleus accumbens (Corbit et al. 2001). In contrast, other data would suggest that alternative neural systems are involved in the formation of associations that subserve the activation of reinforcement systems – those more akin to wanting than liking. Previous work suggests that the central nucleus of the amygdala is involved in 'wanting' rather than 'liking' (Berridge 1996; Galaverna et al. 1993; Robledo et al. 1996), perhaps mediated by interactions with the shell region of the nucleus accumbens (Corbit et al. 2001). These neural relationships remain at this stage speculative, but an increasing number of studies are addressing these issues. It already seems clear that there are dissociable aspects of reinforcement that come to control behaviour in different ways, and that many behaviours are the consequence of multiple levels of interaction with these dissociable aspects of reinforcement. Further research should allow us to examine the relationship between these alternative representations of outcomes, the ways they combine to influence learning about emotionally significant events and the way they might relate to different aspects of our emotional life – for example how might different aspects of reinforcement relate to the arousal and valence dimensions often used to characterize emotion?

Acknowledgements

SK would like to thank Andrew Delamater for discussions relating to this work, and Tony Dickinson and Bernard Balleine for continuing conversations on this topic over several years.

References

Adams, Chris, D. (1982). Variations in the sensitivity of instrumental responding to reinforcer devaluation. *Quarterly Journal of Experimental Psychology, 34B*, 77–98.

Adams, Chris, D. & Anthony Dickinson (1981). Instrumental responding following reinforcer devaluation. *Quarterly Journal of Experimental Psychology, 33B*, 109–122.

Adolphs, Ralph & Daniel Tranel (2000). Emotion, recognition and the human amygdala. In J. P. Aggleton (Ed.), *The amygdala: A functional analysis.* New York: Oxford University Press.

Adolphs, Ralph, Daniel Tranel, & Anthony R. Damasio (1998). The human amygdala in social judgement. *Nature, 393*, 470–474.

Alderson, Helen L., Trevor W. Robbins, & Barry J. Everitt (2000). The effects of excitotoxic lesions of the basolateral amygdala on the acquisition of heroin-seeking behavior in rats. *Psychopharmacology, 153*, 111–119.

Alheid, G. F. & Heimer, L. (1988). New perspectives in basal forebrain organization of special relevance for neuropsychiatric disorders: The striatopallidal, amygdaloid, and corticopetal components of substantia innominata. *Neuroscience, 27*, 1–39.

Amaral, David G., Joseph L. Price, Asla Pitkänen, & Carmichael S. Thomas. (1992). Anatomical organisation of the primate amygdaloid complex. In J. P. Aggleton (Ed.), *The amygdala: Neurobiological aspects of emotion, memory, and mental dysfunction* (1–66). New York: Wiley.

Amorapanth, P., Joseph E. LeDoux, & Karim Nader (2000). Different lateral amygdala outputs mediate reactions and actions eleicited by a fear-arousing stimulus. *Nature Neuroscience, 3*, 74–79.

Balleine, Bernard W. (2000). Incentive processes in instrumental conditioning. In R. R. Mowrer & S. B. Klein (Eds.), *Handbook of contemporary learning theories* (307–366). Mahwah, NJ: Lawrence Erlbaum Associates.

Balleine, Bernard W. (1992). The role of incentive learning in instrumental performance following shifts in primary motivation. *Journal of Experimental Psychology: Animal Behavior Processes, 18*, 236–250.

Balleine, Bernard W., James Ball, & Anthony Dickinson (1994). Benzodiazepine-induced outcome revaluation and the motivational control of instrumental action. *Behavioral Neuroscience, 108*, 573–589.

Balleine, Bernard W. & Anthony Dickinson (1998a). The role of incentive learning in instrumental outcome revaluation by specific satiety. *Animal Learning and Behavior, 26*, 46–59.

Balleine, Bernard W. & Anthony Dickinson (1998b). Goal-directed instrumental action: contingency and incentive learning and their cortical substrates. *Neuropsychopharmacology, 37*, 407–419.

Balleine, Bernard W. & Anthony Dickinson (1994). The role of cholecystokinin in the motivational control of instrumental action. *Behavioral Neuroscience, 108*, 590–605.

Balleine, Bernard W. & Anthony Dickinson (1991). Instrumental performance following reinforcer devaluation depends upon incentive learning. *Quarterly Journal of Experimental Psychology, 43B*, 279–296.

Balleine, Bernard W., Clare Garner, Feli Gonzalez, & Anthony Dickinson (1995). Motivational control of heterogeneous motivational chains. *Journal of Experimental Psychology: Animal Behavior Processes, 21,* 203–217.

Balleine, Bernard W., Simon Killcross, & Anthony Dickinson (2001). Effects of lesions of the basolateral amygdala on instrumental learning. *Journal of Neuroscience,* manuscript submitted.

Berridge, Kent C. (1996). Food reward: Brain substrates of wanting and liking. *Neuroscience and Biobehavioral Reviews, 20,* 1–25.

Berridge, Kent C. (1991). Modulation of taste affect by hunger, caloric satiety, and sensory-specific satiety in the rat. *Appetite, 16,* 103–120.

Berridge, Kent C. & Terry E. Robinson (1998). What is the role of dopamine in reward: Hedonic impact, reward learning, or incentive salience? *Brain Research Reviews, 28,* 309–369.

Blundell, Pamela J. (2001). *The effects of lesions of the basolateral amygdala on appetitive conditioning in the rat.* Unpublished PhD thesis, University of York.

Boakes, Robert A. (1979). Interaction between type I and type II processes involving positive reinforcement. In A. Dickinson & R. A. Boakes (Eds.), *Mechanisms of Learning and Motivation: A memorial volume to Jerzy Konorski* (233–268). Hillsdale, NJ: Erlbaum.

Boakes, Robert A. (1977). Performance on learning to associate a stimulus with positive reinforcement. In H. Davies & H. M. B. Hurwitz (Eds.), *Operant-Pavlovian interactions.* Hillsdale NJ: Erlbaum.

Burns, Lindsey H., Barry J. Everitt, & Trevor W. Robbins (1999). Effects of excitotoxic lesions of the basolateral amygdala on conditional discrimination learning with primary and conditioned reinforcement. *Behavioural Brain Research, 100,* 123–133.

Burns, Lindsey H., Barry J. Everitt, & Trevor W. Robbins (1993). Differential effects of excitotoxic lesions of the basolateral amygdala, ventral subiculum and medial prefrontal cortex on responding with conditioned reinforcement and locomotor activity potentiated by intra-accumbens infusions of d-amphetamine. *Behavioural Brain Research, 55,* 167–183.

Cador, Martine, Trevor W. Robbins, & Barry J. Everitt (1989). Involvement of the amygdala in stimulus-reward associations: interaction with the ventral striatum. *Neuroscience, 30,* 77–86.

Calder, Andrew, J., Andrew W. Young, Rowland, D., Perrett, David, Hodges, J. R., & Etcoff, N. L. (1996). Facial emotion recognition after bilateral amygdala damage: Differentially severe impairment of fear. *Cognitive Neuropsychology, 13,* 699–745.

Colwill, Ruth, M. & Robert A. Rescorla (1988). Associations between the discriminative stimulus and the reinforcer in instrumental learning. *Journal of Experimental Psychology: Animal Behavior Processes, 14,* 155–164.

Colwill, Ruth, M. & Robert A. Rescorla (1985). Postconditioning devaluation of a reinforcer affects instrumental responding. *Journal of Experimental Psychology: Animal Behavior Processes, 11,* 120–132.

Corbit Laura H., Janice L. Muir, & Bernard W. Balleine (2001). The role of the nucleus accumbens in instrumental conditioning: Evidence of a functional dissociation between accumbens core and shell. *Journal of Neuroscience, 21,* 3251–3260.

Davey, Graham, C.L. & Gary G. Cleland (1981). Topography of signal-centered behavior in the rat: Effects of deprivation state and reinforcer type. *Journal of the Experimental Analysis of Behavior, 38*, 291–304.

Davey, Graham, C. L., Gary G. Cleland, & David A. Oakley (1981). Applying Konorski's model of classical conditioning to signal-centred behavior in the rat: Some functional similarities between hunger CRs and sign-tracking. *Animal Learning and Behavior, 10*, 257–262.

Davis, Michael (2000). The role of the amygdala in unconditioned and conditioned fear and anxiety. In J. P. Aggleton (Ed.), *The amygdala: A functional analysis* (213–288). New York: Oxford UP.

Davis, Michael (1992). The role of the amygdala in conditioned fear. In J. P. Aggleton (Ed.), *The Amygdala: Neurobiological aspects of emotion memory and mental dysfunction* (255–306). New York: Wiley-Liss Inc.

Dickinson, Anthony (1994). Instrumental conditioning. In N. J. Mackintosh (Ed.), *Animal learning and cognition* (45–80). San Diego: Academic Press.

Dickinson, Anthony (1989). Expectancy theory in animal condtioning. In S. B. Klein & R. R. Mowrer (Eds.), *Contemporary learning theories: Pavlovian conditioning and the status of traditional learning theory* (279–310). Hillsdale, NJ: Lawrence Erlbaum Associates.

Dickinson, Anthony (1980). *Contemporary animal learning theory* [Problems in the Behavioural Sciences]. Cambridge: CUP.

Dickinson, Anthony & Bernard W. Balleine (1995). Motivational control of instrumental action. *Current directions in Psychological Science, 4*, 162–167.

Dickinson, Anthony & Bernard Balleine (1994). Motivational control of goal-directed action. *Animal Learning and Behavior, 22*, 1–18.

Dickinson, Anthony, & Bernard W. Balleine (1993). Actions and responses: The dual psychology of behaviour. In N. Eilan, R. McCarthy, & W. Brewer (Eds.), *Spatial representation: Problems in philosophy and psychology* (277–293). Oxford: Blackwell.

Dickinson, Anthony, Bernard W. Balleine, Andrew Watt, Feli Gonzalez and Robert A. Boakes (1995). Motivational control after extended instrumental training. *Animal Learning and Behavior, 23*, 197–206.

Dickinson, Anthony & Michael F. Dearing (1978). Appetitive-aversive interactions and inhibitory processes. In A. Dickinson & R. A. Boakes (Eds.), *Mechanisms of Learning and Motivation: A memorial volume to Jerzy Konorski* (203–231). Hillsdale, NJ: Erlbaum.

Dunn, L. T. & Barry J. Everitt (1988). Double dissociations of the effects of amygdala and insular cortex lesions on conditioned taste-aversion, passive-avoidance, and neophobia in the rat using the excitotoxin ibotenic acid. *Behavioral Neuroscience, 102*, 3–23.

Everitt Barry J., Martine Cador, & Trevor W. Robbins (1989). Interactions between the amygdala and ventral striatum in stimulus reward association: studies using a second-order schedule of sexual reinforcement. *Neuroscience, 30*, 63–75.

Galaverna, O. G., Seeley, R. J., Kent C. Berridge, Grill, H. J., Epstein A. N., & Schulkin J. (1993). Lesions of the central nucleus of the amygdala. 1. Effects on taste reactivity, taste-aversion learning and sodium appetite. *Behavioral Brain Research, 59*, 11–17.

Garcia, J. (1989). Food for Tolman: Cognition and cathexis in concert. In T. Archer & L-G. Nilsson (Eds.), *Aversion, avoidance and anxiety* (45–85). Hillsdale, NJ: Lawrence Erlbaum Associates.

Hatfield, Tammy, Han, J. S., Conley, M., Michela Gallagher, & Peter C. Holland (1996). Neurotoxic lesions of basolateral, but not central, amygdala interfere with Pavlovian second-order conditioning and reinforcer devaluation effects. *Journal of Neuroscience, 16*, 5256–5265.

Holland, Peter C. & James J. Straub (1979). Differential effects of two ways of devaluing the unconditioned stimulus after Pavlovian appetitive conditioning. *Journal of Experimental Psychology: Animal Behavior Processes, 5*, 65–78.

Holland, Peter C. (1990). Event representation in Pavlovian conditioning – image and action. *Cognition, 37*, 105–131.

Holland, Peter C. (1981). Acquisition of representation-mediated conditioned food aversions. *Learning and Motivation 12*, 1–18.

Holland, Peter C. (1980). Influence of visual conditioned stimulus characteristics on the form of Pavlovian appetitive conditioned responses in rats. *Journal of Experimental Psychology: Animal Behavior Processes, 6*, 81–97.

Holland, Peter C. & Robert A. Rescorla (1975). Second-order conditioning with food unconditioned stimulus. *Journal of Comparative and Physiological Psychology, 88*, 459–467.

Johnston, J. B. (1923). Further contributions to the study of the evolution of the forebrain. *Journal of Comparative Neurology, 35*, 337–481.

Killcross, Simon, Barry J. Everitt, & Trevor W. Robbins (1997a). Different types of fear-related behaviour mediated by separate nuclei within amygdala. *Nature, 388*, 377–380.

Killcross, Simon, Barry J. Everitt, & Trevor W. Robbins (1997b). Is it time to invoke multiple fear systems in the amygdala? A reply to Nader and LeDoux. *Trends in Cognitive Sciences, 1*, 244–247.

Kluver, H. & Bucy, P. C. (1939). Preliminary analysis of the functions of the temporal lobes in monkeys. *Archives of Neurological Psychiatry, 42*, 979–997.

Konorski, Jerzy (1967). *Integrative activity of the brain: An interdisciplinary approach.* Chicago, IL: University of Chicago Press.

Kruse, John M., Overmier J. Bruce, Wilbert A. Konz, & Eric Rokke (1983). Pavlovian conditioned stimulus effects upon instrumental choice behavior are reinforcer specific. *Learning and Motivation, 14*, 165–181.

LeDoux, Joseph (2000). The amygdala and emotion: A view through fear. In J. P. Aggleton (Ed.), *The amygdala: A functional analysis* (289–310). New York: Oxford UP.

LeDoux, Joseph (1996). *The emotional brain: The mysterious underpinnings of emotional life.* New York: Touchstone.

Lennartz Robert C. & Norman M. Weinberger (1992). Analysis of response systems in Pavlovian conditioning reveals rapidly versus slowly acquired conditioned responses: Support for two factors, implications for behavior and neurobiology. *Psychobiology, 29*, 93–119.

Mackintosh, Nicholas J. (1983). *Conditioning and associative learning.* New York: Oxford University Press.

Malkova, L., David Gaffan, Elizabeth A. Murray (1997). Excitotoxic lesions of the amygdala fail to produce impairment in visual learning for auditory secondary reinforcement but interfere with reinforcer devaluation effects in rhesus monkeys. *Journal of Neuroscience, 17*, 6011–6020.

Moore, B. R. (1973). The role of directed Pavlovian reactions in simple instrumental learning in the pigeon. In R. A. Hinde & J. Stevenson-Hinde (Eds.), *Constraints on Learning* (159–186). London: Academic Press.

Morris, J. S., Ohman, A., & Raymond J. Dolan (1998). Conscious and unconscious emotional learning in the human amygdala. *Nature, 393*, 467–470.

Mowrer, O. H. (1947). On the dual nature of learning – A reinterpretation of 'conditioning' and 'problem-solving'. *Harvard Educational Review, 17*, 102–148.

Nader, Karim & Joseph LeDoux (1997). Is it time to invoke multiple fear systems in the amygdala? *Trends in Cognitive Sciences, 1*, 241–243.

Pavlov, I. P. (1927). *Conditioned Reflexes*. New York: Oxford University Press.

Pitkänen, A. (2000). Connectivity of the rat amygdaloid complex. In J. P. Aggleton (Ed.), *The amygdala: A functional analysis* (31–115). New York: Oxford UP.

Powell, David A., Hernandez, L., & Buchanan, S. L. (1985). Intraseptal scopolamine has differential effects on Pavlovian eyeblink and heart rate conditioning. *Behavioral Neuroscience, 99*, 75–87.

Rashotte, M. E., Griffin, R. W., & Sisk, C. L. (1977). Second-order conditioning of the pigeon's key peck. *Animal Learning and Behavior, 5*, 25–38.

Rescorla, Robert A. (1994). Transfer of instrumental control mediated by a devalued outcome. *Animal Learning and Behavior, 22*, 27–33.

Rescorla, Robert A. (1982). Simultaneous second-order conditioning produces S-S learning in conditioned suppression. *Journal of Experimental Psychology: Animal Behavior Processes, 8*, 23–32.

Rescorla, Robert A. (1980). *Pavlovian second-order conditioning: Studies in associative learning*. Hillsdale, NJ: Erlbaum.

Rescorla, Robert A. (1979). Aspects of the reinforcer learned in second-order Pavlovian conditioning. *Journal of Experimental Psychology: Animal Behavior Processes, 5*, 79–95.

Rescorla, Robert A. (1973). Second-order conditioning: Implications for theories of learning. In F. J. McGuigan & D. B. Lumsden (Eds.) *Contemporary approaches to conditioning and learning*, New York: Wiley.

Rescorla, Robert A., & Solomon, R. L. (1967). Two-process learning theory: Relationships between Pavlovian conditioning and instrumental learning. *Psychological Review, 74*, 151–182.

Rizley, R. C. & Robert A. Rescorla (1972). Associations in second-order conditioning and sensory preconditioning. *Journal of Comparative and Physiological Psychology, 81*, 1–11.

Robledo, Patricia, Trevor W. Robbins, & Barry J. Everitt (1996). Effects of excitotoxic lesions of the central amygdaloid nucleus on the potentiation of reward-related stimuli by intra-accumbens amphetamine. *Behavioral Neuroscience, 110*, 981–990.

Ross, Robert T. (1986). Pavlovian second-order conditioned analgesia. *Journal of Experimental Psychology: Animal Behavior Processes, 12*, 32–39.

Simbayi, L. C., Robert A. Boakes, & Burton, M. J. (1986). Effects of basolateral amygdala lesions on taste aversions produced by lactose and lithium chloride in the rat. *Behavioral Neuroscience, 100*, 455–465.

Skinner, B. F. (1932). On the rate of formation of a conditioned reflex. *Journal of General Psychology, 7*, 274–285.

Sutton Richard S. & Andrew G. Barto (1981). Toward a modern theory of adaptive networks: Expectation and prediction. *Psychological Review, 88*, 135–170.

Swanson, L. W. & Petrovich, G. (1998). What is the amygdala? *Trends in Neurosciences, 21*, 323–331.

Thorndike, E. L. (1911). *Animal intelligence: Experimental studies.* New York: Macmillan.

Thompson, Richard F., Clerk, G. A., Donegan, N. H., Lavond, D. G., Lincoln, J. S., Madden, J., Mamounas, L. A., Mauk, M. D., McCormick, D. A., & Thompson, J. K. (1984). Neuronal substrates of learning and memory: A 'multiple-trace' view. In G. Lynch, J. L. McGaugh, & N. M. Weinberger (Eds.), *Neurobiology of learning and memory* (137–164). New York: The Guilford Press.

Tolman, E. C. (1949). The nature and functioning of wants. *Psychological Review, 56*, 357–369.

Trapold, Milton, A. & Overmier, J. B. (1972). The second learning process in instrumental learning. In A. H. Black & W. F. Prokasy (Eds.), *Classical conditioning II: Current research and theory* (427–452). New York: Appleton-Century-Crofts.

Trapold, Milton, A. (1970). Are expectancies based upon different positive reinforcing events discriminably different? *Learning and Motivation, 1*, 129–140.

Turner, B. H. & Herkenham, M. (1991). Thalamoamygdaloid projections in the rat: A test of the amygdala's role in sensory processing. *Journal of Comparative Neurology, 313*, 295–325.

Vandercar, D. H. & Schneiderman, N. (1967). Interstimulus interval functions in different response systems during classical discrimination conditioning of rabbits. *Psychonomic Science, 9*, 9–10.

Wagner, Alan, R. (1976). Priming in STM: an information-processing mechanism for self-generated or retrieval-generated depression in performance. In T. J. Tighe, R. N. Leaton (Eds.), *Habituation: perspectives from child development, animal behavior and neurophysiology* (95–128). Hillsdale, NJ: Erlbaum.

Wagner Alan, R. & Susan E. Brandon (1989). Evolution of a structured connectionist model of Pavlovian conditioning (AESOP). In S. B. Klein & R. R. Mowrer (Eds.), *Contemporary learning theories: Pavlovian conditioning and the status of traditional learning theory* (149–189). Hillsdale, NJ: Lawrence Erlbaum Associates.

Willoughby, Pamela J. & Simon Killcross (1998). The role of the basolateral amygdala in appetitive conditioning. *Journal of Psychopharmacology, 12*, A5.

Wyvell, Cindy L. & Kent C. Berridge (2000). Intra-accumbens amphetamine increases the conditioned incentive salience of sucrose reward: Enhancement of reward 'wanting' without enhanced 'liking' or response reinforcement. *Journal of Neuroscience, 20*, 8122–8130.

Chapter 4

Neurons with attitude
A connectionist account of human evaluative learning

Eamon P. Fulcher
University College Worcester

Several theories of emotional information processing postulate an evaluative mechanism that operates early in sensory processing and is automatic, in the sense that it occurs rapidly, without deliberate intention, and without awareness. In addition, such evaluations are said to guide attention, learning, and behaviour in a variety of ways. The aim of this chapter is to tackle the difficult questions of how a stimulus comes to acquire an evaluation, the extent of awareness of the process, and the degree of stability of acquired evaluations. These questions are the central concerns of evaluative learning research and although several theoretical accounts of this form of learning have been outlined, none is expressed in sufficient detail. As such, they are difficult to test, and data are too often open to different interpretations. An attempt is made here to provide a detailed theory of evaluative learning and one expressed as a computational model. Such an enterprise forces an explicit statement of assumptions, requires specification of extreme detail, and can yield predictions that may otherwise have been overlooked.

The model is based on an analysis of a number of observations in evaluative learning and collectively these place certain psychological constraints on the plausibility of its processes and mechanisms. Various ways in which an evaluative response may be expressed are experimented with and how such variations impinge on theoretical issues are examined. An illustration of the generality of the model is its application to what appears to be an unrelated area of research, namely, attentional bias for threat-related information in anxiety. The model also makes predictions concerning the influence of evaluative learning in anxiety, one of which has since been confirmed empirically. In doing so, the model brings together two areas of research that were previously unconnected and, if nothing else, raises the importance of evaluative learning in anxiety research.

An overview of evaluative learning: theory and data

Evaluative learning focuses on the evaluation of a stimulus as good or bad, liked or disliked, pleasant or unpleasant. There are sound reasons for not considering more complex evaluations since positive and negative valence appears to be the most ubiquitous type of evaluations that people make (Osgood, Suci, & Tannenbaum 1957; Lazarus 1966). In an evaluative learning experiment, a neutral stimulus (one previously rated as neither liked nor disliked, but neutral, henceforth the NS, plural NSi) is paired up with an evaluative stimulus (one rated as either strongly liked or disliked, henceforth the ES, plural ESi). Participants are then asked to rate the NSi on a like/dislike scale. Either during paired presentation or after the ratings phase awareness of the relationship between each NS and its paired ES is also assessed. The two main tests are whether the ratings of the NSi are influenced by the valence of the ESi and whether the participant is aware of any of the NS-ES pairings (a test of contingency awareness). The issue of awareness is critical: if evaluative learning involves an automatic stimulus evaluation then one should expect evaluative changes in the absence of contingency awareness.

In one of the earliest studies, Levey and Martin (1975) used picture postcards as the stimuli and assessed awareness through a recognition test where participants had to select the ES that had been previously paired with each NS. They found that NSi paired with positive ESi were more liked than NSi paired with negative ESi. Analysis of recognition scores suggested to Levey and Martin that evaluative learning had occurred without awareness. Many subsequent studies claim to provide further evidence for the view that awareness, in the form of explicit memory for the pairs, is not required in evaluative learning.

Contingency awareness has been assessed through a number of different ways: In some studies participants have been interviewed about the various aspects of the experiment or have been given tests of recognition for the relevant pairs, and in others the long-term effects of evaluative learning and contingency awareness have been assessed. In the former type, the amount of contingency awareness measured does not appear to affect the magnitude of evaluative learning (Baeyens, Eelen, & Van den Bergh 1990; Hammerl & Grabitz 1996). In the latter type, when participants are re-tested several weeks after the initial learning sessions evidence for stable evaluative memory with weakened contingency memory has been obtained. In Fulcher and Cocks (1997), evaluative ratings of NSi were unchanged and remained biased by their corresponding ESi at re-test, but memory for the pairings had dropped from 30% to 6%. This result has since been successfully replicated (Fulcher, Mathews, Mackintosh, & Law 2001) and similar findings have been reported elsewhere (Baeyens, Crombez, Van den Bergh, & Eelen 1988). Taken together these studies suggest that evaluative learning does not depend on contingency awareness.

In many studies it is assumed that contingency awareness is reduced by exposure to a large number of stimuli and with only a handful of learning trials of each stimulus pair. However, reliance on recognition tests to assess awareness is problematic since awareness may exist in some non-verbal form (Shanks & St. John 1994); furthermore, since the recognition test is usually carried out *after* the rating phase, more contingency memory may be present during the rating phase than is revealed in the recognition phase (Fulcher & Cocks 1997). An alternative method that circumvents some of these problems is to present the ES subliminally, which is an attempt to eliminate contingency awareness at the outset. In De Houwer, Baeyens, and Eelen (1994) neutral words were paired with subliminal masked presentations (under 30 ms) of either emotionally positive or negative words. For the participants who were unable to detect the valence of the subliminally presented words through a forced recognition task, evaluative changes in ratings of the initially neutral words were observed. This result has been replicated in *some* of the experiments reported in a later study (De Houwer, Hendrickx, & Baeyens 1997), and a meta-analysis indicated that evaluative learning had occurred with subliminal presentation across the 5 experiments. Although using a different preparation, Öhman and Soares (1998) found evidence of subliminal autonomic conditioning in the absence of conscious recognition, as measured by the inability to detect the features of the masked neutral stimuli. Although the replication failures are disappointing, these studies give at least some credence to the suggestion that subliminal presentation of the ES can result in evaluative learning without contingency awareness.

Several other studies that have used more optimal presentation times have addressed the awareness issue by requesting recall of only the valence of the ES for each NS. Using tactile stimuli and a distracter task to reduce awareness, Hammerl and Grabitz (2000) found that pairing neutral haptic stimuli with either neutral haptic stimuli or stimuli pleasant to touch, evaluative learning occurred in participants who could not recall the valence of the ES. This again would appear to lend support for the evaluative-learning-without-awareness hypothesis.

Although implicit evaluative learning would be theoretically interesting in itself, there are significant implications of the learning of evaluative or emotional information without being able to consciously report on its source. For example, if feelings towards stimuli can be acquired non-consciously, then it may be difficult to unlearn such feelings, as has been reported in Baeyens et al. (1988). Further, the implication is that people make judgements based on information acquired non-consciously. Indeed, in many evaluative learning studies when participants are asked to justify their preferences, they frequently report basing their feelings on structural features of the stimuli or on previous associations with personal experiences. Yet their preferences have clearly been biased by the experimental manipulation (at least for the most methodologically sound demonstrations). Another consequence of evaluative learning may be that attention to the neutral stimulus is subsequently increased. In the Fulcher et al. (2001) study, which is discussed later, we found that under certain conditions the neutral stimulus interfered with an ongoing task after it had been paired with an unpleasant stimulus. This is interesting because it occurred for participants who had no explicit knowledge of information about the stimulus contingencies (based on a recognition test), and we conjecture that they were perhaps trying to rationalise their preferences, providing plausible reasons for them.

From this brief review of the relationship between contingency awareness and evaluative learning, we can tentatively conclude that the weight of the evidence seems to favour the contention that evaluative learning can occur without contingency awareness. Our caution concerns the desire for more convincing evidence and the need to address a number of methodological issues raised by Shanks and St. John (1994), Field and Davey (1997), and more recently in Shanks and Lovibond (2002).

What is learned in evaluative learning?

A second area of debate concerns the question of *what* is learned. The referential hypothesis (Davey 1994; Shanks & Dickinson 1990; Shanks & St. John 1994; see also Holland 1990, for a similar discussion in animal learning) is that the evaluation of the NS is the result of a learned association that is re-activated on presentation of the NS. Thus, the NS is said to be a cue for the memory of the ES and the resultant evaluation is a response to that reactivated memory. Hence for this view, a structural link between the NS and ES is responsible for any observed shift in evaluation of the NS.

An alternative hypothesis (Levey & Martin 1975; Baeyens et al. 1990; Krosnick 1992; Betz, Jussim, & Lynn 1994; Martin & Levey 1994; De Houwer et al. 1997) is that the change in valence becomes intrinsic to the stimulus: its new evaluation is activated on subsequent occasions without any involvement of or reference to the internal representation of the previously paired ES. For the intrinsic hypothesis, then, the evaluative perception of the NS has been altered – it is said to have witnessed a 'hedonic shift' and hence is 'immediate in the sense that it does not require cognitive mediation, decision processes, or chains of inference' (Levey & Martin 1987, p. 122).

The evidence of evaluative learning in the absence of contingency awareness could be taken as support for the intrinsic hypothesis. However, the lack of awareness does not refute the referential hypothesis since the ES may exert its influence on the NS non-consciously. Likewise, the presence of explicit awareness does not refute the intrinsic hypothesis since there may be some third variable that correlates with the magnitude of intrinsic changes and the strength of contingency awareness, such as the intensity of the ES.

There are only a handful of studies that have attempted to pull apart the intrinsic and referential hypotheses. One way in which the possible influences of any structural NS-ES link may be revealed is to test whether the valence of the NS tracks subsequent changes to the valence of the ES, changes that occur in the absence of the NS. The rationale, borrowing an idea from animal learning, is that if the NS evaluation is based on a structural NS-ES link then changes to the ES evaluation should affect the subsequent evaluation of the NS. In a study by Baeyens, Eelen, Van den Bergh, and Crombez (1992b), after a number of acquisition trials, participants were re-presented with the ESi, which were human faces, and given personality descriptors of each face, some of which altered the participants' evaluation of the ESi. These re-evaluations affected the acquired NSi evaluations and can be interpreted as demonstrating that an NS-ES link in memory does contribute to the evaluation of the NS. In one of our own studies, we first presented neutral photographs with words that cued personal events from the participants' recent history. We then altered the participant's feelings towards these events through the 'counterfactual' procedure, in which the participant imagines how an event may have had a better or worse outcome. Ratings of the images created through counterfactual thinking indicated that feelings towards the events had shifted. We then assessed the influence of the initial event images on ratings of the neutral items and the influence of the counterfactual procedure. While a main effect of the initial valence of the event image was found, so too was a main effect of the shifted valence of the event images after counterfactual thinking. Thus, revaluation of the ESi did influence the ratings of the NSi even though the NSi and the shifted ESi were never directly paired.

In sum, these findings tend to support the referential hypothesis; however we present evidence in later sections that is difficult for this hypothesis, such as some failures to obtain effects of revaluation. An alternative theory is advanced over the next section, which argues that there are aspects of both hypotheses that can account for the range of data. The composite theory that is presented is that an evaluative response is the combination of both the intrinsic evaluation acquired by the NS during acquisition and the evaluation of the NS whose representation has become at least partially re-instated. It is argued that this composite hypothesis best captures the essential features of the data. The network model of evaluative learning presented here is designed to simulate expressions of the intrinsic, referential and composite theories with the aim of comparing the model's performance in each of the three forms. From there, we then go on to evaluate the network as a model of emotional information processing by considering one important aspect of emotion, namely attention to affective stimuli, especially cognitive biases in anxiety.

The network

History

Apart from characteristics such as categorization and generalization, much of the impetus for developing connectionist models was due to interest in the properties of self-organisation and potential solutions to difficult control problems. The latter features drove the development of the present model, since, for many connectionist models, learning was controlled, rather unrealistically, by distinct learning and recall phases (learning was managed by the programmer, who inserted code that instructed the system when and when not to update its connection weights). In attempting to answer the question of how a system could manage its own learning, it became apparent that such a system might require an internal model of its environment and one that is continually updated with experience. An important aspect of the internal model appears to be the detection of both stimuli that are significant for the system, and stimuli that, while intrinsically innocuous, bring about or cause the occurrence of significant stimuli. In Fulcher (1992), it was shown that an evaluative mechanism, which continuously evaluates incoming stimuli for significance or potential significance, could fashion a system capable of controlling its own learning.

While the model was shown to provide a solution to difficult control problems, such as balancing a pole and finding goal locations in complex environments, it was also shown to capture important aspects of animal learning (e.g., spatial memory and classical conditioning phenomena). The idea of an evaluative mechanism and its importance for emotion in human information processing is the basis of the model presented below.

Overview

As indicated above, a basic assumption of the model is that early in the information processing sequence, incoming stimuli are evaluated for their affective significance prior to more elaborate forms of processing. At this early stage, stimuli are processed in parallel, and while they begin to activate richer representations, they are already being evaluated for emotional significance in a separate module termed the *evaluative map*. When a match is found with preexisting evaluative representations (through a parallel search), the evaluative map provides output that (1) boosts the activity of the corresponding perceptual representations, thus increasing the amount of attentional processing of the stimulus, and (2) increases the rate of learning between the stimulus representation and any other stimulus representation in working memory. Initially matching representations would be biologically prepared, such as loud noises or sudden movements, but then the contents of the evaluative map will be updated constantly as the system adapts to new information. In this way, matches will occur for events that were neutral originally but which have gained significance by association with strongly evaluated items or have acquired affect via higher-level processes.

The amplification and inhibition of perceptual representations by an evaluative map also models both top-down and bottom-up aspects of attention. Representations of affective stimuli are amplified by immediate feedback from the evaluative map; hence, strongly affective stimuli are able to capture attention rapidly. Conversely, an evaluative map primed by internal influences will in turn prime the perceptual representations of certain (target) stimuli that are presented to the network. In this way, external input of a target will receive immediate amplification from an already primed evaluative map. The rationale for this scheme is the observation that some affective states, e.g., anxiety, modulate attention in significant ways. For example, there is now considerable evidence that threatening stimuli are able to capture selective attention in high (e.g., clinical) but not low state anxiety and that, furthermore, after therapy this attentional bias often disappears.

In accordance with the referential hypothesis, a temporal relationship between the neutral stimulus and the evaluative stimulus representation is modelled, such that future activation of the representation of the neutral stimulus will activate the representation of the evaluative stimulus. When re-activated, the ES representation excites a match in the evaluative map. The temporal weight between the NS and the ES is assumed to correlate with the degree of contingency awareness or the ability to recall the ES on presentation of the NS. When this weight is small, contingency awareness is low, and perhaps below the level of activation required for explicit recall, but ES activation via this weight is still sufficient to excite the evaluative map.

In contrast, the intrinsic hypothesis is based on changes within the evaluative map itself. Thus, by mere temporal contact, the neutral stimulus acquires some of the properties of the evaluative stimulus. In this scheme, all perceptual representations are immediately evaluated via modifiable evaluative weights. When representations of affectively neutral stimuli are active in close temporal proximity to strongly evaluated stimuli the weights of the affectively neutral stimuli are updated. On future presentations of the NS, a direct match is activated in the evaluative map.

A modular network

A visual stimulus, when presented to the network activates a set of perceptual units that correspond to the presence of particular stimulus features of the input. These inputs propagate through a layer of weights, exciting a layer of stimulus units that represent early categorization of the stimulus features (see Figure 1). Through previously acquired connection weights between these perceptual units and the layer of stimulus units, one stimulus unit, unit S_i, will receive the greatest amount of excitation. The net external input into unit S_i is then the sum of the product of each input unit I_p and the categorization weights c_{pi}:

$$\text{net external input to unit } S_i = \sum c_{pi} I_p.$$

Through this process, more than one unit may become active, each one representing a plausible categorization of the input. Typically, one unit will be more active than the rest, representing the best match in the absence of further information. At this stage there is no mutual inhibition between stimulus units and several representations may be active at the same time. This is consistent with the view that there is an unlimited capacity for processing information, but that the reason for selectivity in attention, and hence inhibition of some sensory representations, is that the system has goals and intentions that are given temporal priority at any one time (Allport 1987). In the model these top-down influences, such as task goals, current concerns, and longer-term dispositions, exert their influence on stimulus units via feedback from the evaluative map and other task-relevant salience maps, such as those involved in visual search. Before these take effect, active signals in the stimulus units are propagated to the evaluative map, which then feeds back to corresponding stimulus units via evaluative weights. These weights represent learned primary positive and negative evaluations of stimuli, and they amplify corresponding stimulus units and inhibit all other stimulus units, modelling increases and decreases in attention to particular stimuli. Thus, the net external input to unit S_i is gated by the evaluative significance of stimulus I, denoted e_i:

$$\text{gated input to } S_i = e_i \sum c_{pi} I_p.$$

The net result of this evaluative gating is to influence categorization according to stimulus significance. Thus, if S_1 and S_2 units are both good matches of the visual input then the activation of the unit with the greater evaluative weight will be higher. This models some elementary aspects of emotional information processing, such as automatic attention capture of liked and disliked attitude objects (e.g., Fazio, Sanbonmatsu, Powell, & Kardes 1986).

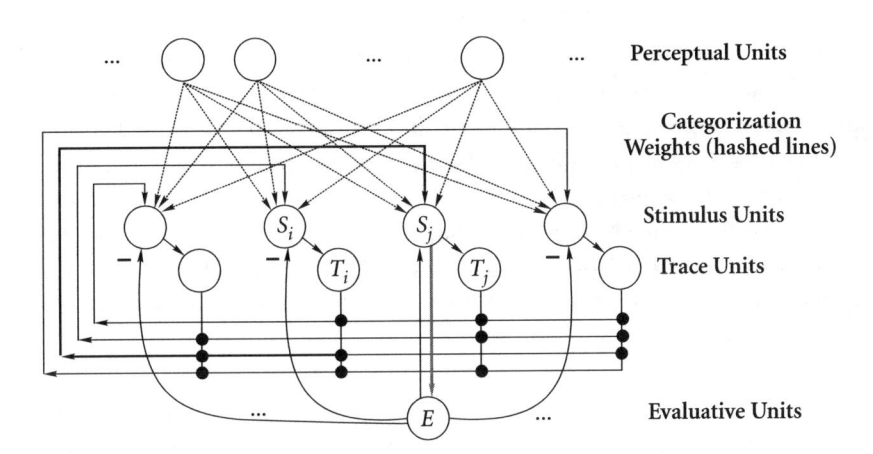

Figure 1. Diagram of the network. Dots indicate a large number of other units that are not shown. All connections that are shown are excitatory, unless indicated. The heavy line indicates the direction of the signal gated by the temporal weight w_{ij}. The grey line indicates the direction of the signal gated by the evaluative weight e_j.

The activation of stimulus unit S_i, a_i, is then the result of the propagation of the input via categorization weights boosted by evaluative excitation, internal feedback, and an evaluative inhibition function gated by a constant, H:

$$a'_i = \alpha a_i + (1-\alpha)\left[e_i \sum c_{pi} I_p - H \sum_{i \neq k} e_k \right] \quad (1)$$

where α is a constant such that $0 \ll \alpha < 1$. Equation 1, then, represents the position that, and without consideration of ongoing tasks or concerns, attention is directed towards the stimulus with the greatest affective significance. Since, much of behaviour is goal- or task-directed, there is additional top-down priming that attempts to increase the strength of task-relevant representations. For example, in visual search the evaluative strength of specific units that correspond to target features are amplified. The search for a target X proceeds by priming unit X and inhibiting other stimulus units. The likelihood that the activation of unit S_x will be the maximally active unit on the subsequent external presentation of X is increased by its priming and by the inhibition of other stimulus units. Similar models of attention have been proposed elsewhere (see Allport 1987), but unlike the model presented here, they have focused on other aspects of attention rather than on attention guided by emotional significance.

Learning

In order to model the acquisition of NS-ES associations in memory, we include a set of weights between units that represent learned associations. Thus, if stimuli I and J are presented serially, then this relationship is modelled through updates to a temporal weight w_{ij} between their two units. A central feature of models of temporal processing is the representation of memory traces of stimuli whose offset coincides, or thereabouts, with the onset of other stimuli with which a temporal association is to be learned. Thus, the activity, b_i, of trace unit T_i mimics the activity of unit S_i but with a slow decay rate. The activation is determined by:

$$b'_i = \alpha b_i + (1-\alpha) a_i \quad (2)$$

where α is a constant such that $0 \ll \alpha < 1$. Trace units are then able to excite stimulus units, through a temporal weight that reflects the extent of their temporal association. Temporal weights connect trace units to stimulus units, so that on presentation of stimulus I, the network goes through the activation sequence $S_i > T_i > w_{ij} > S_j$. The level of activity of S_j is then also a function of the connection weight w_{ij}. Therefore, Equation 1 is re-written as:

$$a'_i = \alpha a_i + (1-\alpha)\left[e_i \sum c_{pi}I_p - H\sum_{i\neq k} e_k + \sum_{i\neq j} w_{ji}\right]. \quad (1b)$$

The temporal weight is updated according to a delta learning rule that specifies w_{ij} moves in the direction of the activation level of unit S_j, i.e., a_j, which models the assumption that the weight is dependent upon the amount of attention captured by stimulus J. It further models the assumption that the rate of the increase to this weight is modulated by the evaluative significance of stimulus J, namely, e_j. The latter models the assumption that the rate of learning of an association between two stimuli is dependent upon the significance of the second item in the sequence (thus, it is more important to learn that X leads to Y when Y is extremely aversive, than when Y is innocuous). w_{ij} is updated by the rule:

$$w'_{ij} = (1 - ke_j)w_{ij} + ke_j a_j \quad (3)$$

where k is a constant such that $0 < k \ll 1$. The evaluative weight e_i is a relatively simple learning rule, which is a function of the temporal overlap between the activities of unit S_i and unit S_j, and the evaluative weight e_j. The idea is that when one stimulus is presented alongside an evaluative stimulus, the evaluative weight of the latter can modify the evaluative weight of the former. An additional assumption is that separate units exist for positive and negative evaluations, such that unit S_i has the capacity to excite positive and negative evaluative units via a separate connection with each. While there are sound anatomical reasons for this, there are several psychological observations that make this arrangement more plausible than one that posits a one-dimensional evaluation that is able to cross zero (see Bouton 1994). Thus, for positive evaluative weights, when both stimulus units are active:

$$e'_i(pos) = \alpha e_i(pos) + (1-\alpha)e_j(pos) \quad (4a)$$

and for negative evaluative weights:

$$e'_i(neg) = \alpha e_i(neg) + (1-\alpha)e_j(neg) \quad (4b)$$

The value e_x in Equation 1 and Equation 3 is the sum of $e_x(pos)$ and $e_x(neg)$, thus the amount of attention paid to a stimulus representation and temporal learning weights are dependent upon the overall evaluative strength of a stimulus, including cases where the stimulus has both positive and negative evaluative weights. Although there clearly are asymmetries in positive and negative evaluations of stimuli and events (e.g., Kahneman & Tversky 1984), in most of the following simulations we discuss an evaluation without specifying its direction. Valence is considered in other simulations when the data being modelled requires it, such as in the simulations of information processing in anxiety.

The evaluative response

When making an evaluative response (*ER*) to stimulus *I*, which has been previously paired with stimulus *J*, we assume that active representations in the evaluative map are computed directly and indirectly. According to the intrinsic theory, an evaluative response to stimulus *I* (ER_i) may be a function of the stimulus-intrinsic evaluation: a direct measure of the evaluative weight, e_i. However, for the referential hypothesis, ER_i is a function of a referential-based evaluation: an indirect measure of the evaluative weight e_j. In the case of the latter hypothesis, the indirect evaluation is computed as a function of the temporal weight w_{ij}. However, it is possible to define a general case in which the ER_i is a composite of both stimulus-intrinsic and referential-based evaluations, with an additional parameter, ρ, that can be adjusted according to either hypothesis:

$$ER_i = \rho e_i + (1 - \rho) w_{ij} e_j \tag{5}$$

For the referential hypothesis, $\rho = 0$ and the first term is redundant, while for the intrinsic hypothesis $\rho = 1$, which makes the second term redundant. However, for the composite theory, the parameter ρ may take on a value between 0 and 1; thus both terms may contribute to the *ER*. The advantage of adopting this approach is that it may enable researchers to identify the conditions under which one or other of the two terms dominates. In terms of whether evaluative learning can occur without contingency awareness, the composite hypothesis is compatible with the notion that as contingency awareness increases, so too does the evaluative response (i.e., the product $w_{ij}e_j$). Furthermore, both learning equations (updates to w_{ij} and e_i) are based on the notion that as e_j increases, so too does contingency awareness as represented by w_{ij} and the intrinsic evaluation acquired by stimulus *I*, e_i. However, once an intrinsic evaluation is acquired, the composite hypothesis predicts that it can remain even if contingency awareness should return towards 0 (i.e., $w_{ij} \rightarrow 0$).

In the next section, we compare simulations of behavioural data with the model in each of its three forms (with $\rho = 0, \rho = 0.5$, and $\rho = 1$). We consider some of the essential data that needs to be modelled, such as the rate of acquisition, the temporal ordering of stimuli, the presentation rate of the evaluative stimulus, and some pertinent findings from our own laboratory. The discussion then moves on to how the model has inspired research in the area of cognitive bias in anxiety and how simulations of the model can account for inconsistent findings in this field.

Acquisition of an evaluative response

Studies that have assessed the rate of learning with increased number of trials have shown that the evaluative response generally increases up to about 10 trials, as does contingency awareness as measured by correct recognition of NS-ES pairs (Baeyens, Eelen, Van den Bergh, & Crombez 1992b; Stuart, Shimp, & Engle 1987; Boss & Bonke 1998). We simulated acquisition by first by pre-setting some of the categorization weights so that one stimulus unit would become active on presentation of the first stimulus (the NS) and a second would become active on presentation of the second stimulus (the ES). Evaluative weights of the stimuli were set at 0.1 and 0.8, respectively. The NS onset was set at iteration 0 and offset at 100, and the ES onset was set at iteration 100 with offset at 200. During NS presentation, the activity of the S_{NS} unit rapidly approaches maximum amplitude as does its corresponding trace unit T_{NS}, but delayed in time. At NS offset, the S_{NS} unit begins to decay but the T_{NS} unit remains active. At this time, the S_{ES} unit becomes active with ES onset and the weight w_{NS-ES} and e_{NS} increase until unit T_{NS} is no longer active. Parameters were set according to α (Equation 1 & Equation 2) = 0.95, H (Equation 1b) = 0.1, k (Equation 3) = 1 x 10^{-4}, α (Equation 4) = 0.9997. The evaluative response was computed according to each hypothesis. The results of 20 simulated acquisition trials are shown in Figure 2. As can be seen, the evaluative response computed for each hypothesis (intrinsic, referential, and composite) displays the similar rates of increase. These rates of increase are comparable with that found in the literature, with one or two exceptions. In some of these studies there is a sharp fall in the strength of the evaluative response in the condition exposed to the most learning trials. This curious dip suggests that at least some relationship may exist between contingency awareness, or w_{ij}, and the magnitude of ER. We defer a discussion of possible explanations for this effect to a later section where the relationship between learning and awareness is examined further.

88   Eamon P. Fulcher

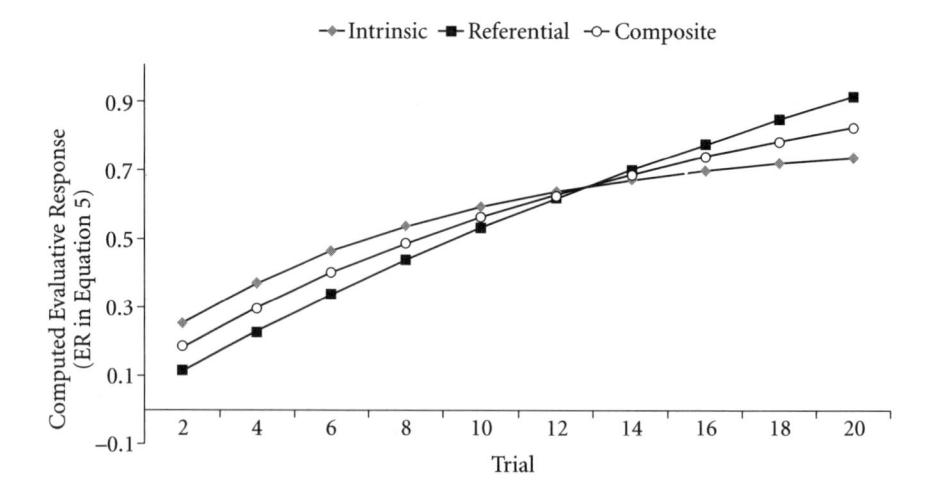

Figure 2. Simulation results of evaluative learning with forward pairing and 'supraliminal' ES presentation.

Backward pairing

The architecture of the model is designed to maximise learning when the presentation of the neutral stimulus precedes that of the evaluative stimulus (forward pairing), rather than the other way around (backward pairing). This is a constraint that comes from studies comparing the two types of stimulus arrangements: backward pairing is significantly weaker than forward pairing (e.g., Hammerl & Grabitz 1993; Boss & Bonke 1998; Stuart et al. 1987).

We simulated backward pairing by reversing the presentation of each stimulus, with the ES onset occurring before NS onset, all other parameters were set to the same values as in the previous simulation. The results of these simulations are shown in Figure 3. Note that since the ES precedes the NS in the presentation order there is only a small temporal overlap between the T_{NS} unit and the S_{ES} unit, hence the temporal weight acquired between them is small. However, the temporal overlap between the S_{NS} and the S_{ES} units is about the same as in forward pairing, hence the evaluative weights for both are the same. Because of the differences in the size of the temporal weights, the referential and composite hypotheses, but not the intrinsic hypothesis, model the data that forward pairing produces stronger evaluative learning than does backward pairing.

Although there are too few studies that have compared forward and backward pairing in evaluative learning, some recent evidence from the animal learning literature provide empirical support for the hypothesis that some

→ Intrinsic ■ Referential -○- Composite

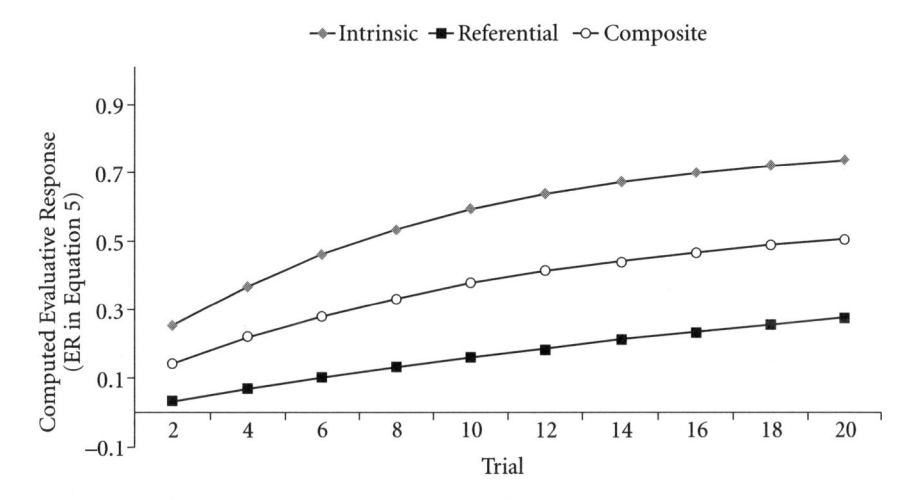

Figure 3. Simulation results of evaluative learning with backward pairing and 'supraliminal' ES presentation.

learning does occur in backward pairing. Cole and Miller (1999) compared the effects on behaviour of backward learning with increasing number of trials. They found that backward pairing did not support signal learning in that the neutral stimulus was not an elicitor of an anticipation of the evaluative stimulus. Clearly, this is because the neutral stimulus did not predict the onset of the evaluative stimulus. However, the neutral stimulus did acquire evaluative significance since it supported second-order conditioning: it could act as a secondary reinforcer. These findings can be explained in the model as representing acquisition of an evaluative weight but not a temporal weight. In classical conditioning the effects of backward conditioning may not be immediately obvious since acquired evaluations need not affect an involuntary reflex, but nonetheless, the neutral stimulus may become endowed with evaluative significance. Levey and Martin (1987) and others have argued that more than one type of learning can occur in classical conditioning: signal learning (learning that the CS predicts the onset of the UCS) and evaluative learning (that the CS acquires properties of the UCS, such as being able to support secondary conditioning). In this case, evaluative learning is present after backward pairing even though it may not influence the anticipatory CR.

Subliminal evaluative learning

We repeated forward and backward simulations this time with a brief presentation rate of the ES, mimicking evaluative learning with a subliminally presented evaluative stimulus. In order to simulate this, the ES is set to 1 for only 10 iterations; this represents 10% of the number of iterations used in simulations of supraliminal learning. These simulations indicate stronger subliminal evaluative learning with backward pairing than with forward pairing (see Figures 4 and 5). The reason for this reversion is due to the temporal dynamics of evaluative inhibition and the activity of trace units. In forward learning and with brief presentation of the ES, at ES onset the NS stimulus unit has acquired significant stimulation to reach maximum amplitude. This activity declines rapidly at NS offset but this rate is accelerated through a large evaluative inhibition from the ES. With brief ES presentation prior to NS onset, the ES stimulus has acquired significant stimulation to reach its maximum amplitude but at ES offset/NS onset, the evaluative inhibition on the NS is stronger than it is on the ES. Thus, in backward pairing, the ES stimulus unit decays more slowly than it does in forward learning while the build up in the activity of the NS is more gradual. Thus, when the ES precedes the NS there is a longer temporal overlap between both stimulus units, and the amount of overlap will be much larger than it is when the ES is presented after the NS. The result is that a larger evaluative weight is acquired during backward pairing than during forward pairing. Notice that this has more implications for the intrinsic and composite hypotheses than for the referential hypothesis, since the evaluative weight is predicted to make a contribution to the evaluative response.

The literature tends to agree with the results of these simulations. Studies in the *affective priming* literature report a much stronger and more reliable effect than the subliminal evaluative learning studies described in De Houwer et al. (1997). For example, in Murphy and Zajonc (1993) and Winkielman, Zajonc, and Schwarz (1997), evaluative stimuli were presented prior to the neutral stimuli, in the manner of backward pairing. Their results indicate more reliable shifts in evaluations brought about by the affective, or evaluative, prime. However, a comparison between these studies may be unwarranted since the affective priming method involves immediate ratings of the neutral stimuli, while the De Houwer et al. (1997) study involved rating the neutral stimuli in a separate phase after acquisition trials. Because of this difference, this author ran a series of experiments to compare forward and backward subliminal evaluative learning with immediate versus delayed rating (Fulcher, submitted). Digitised photographs of smiling and angry faces were presented subliminally

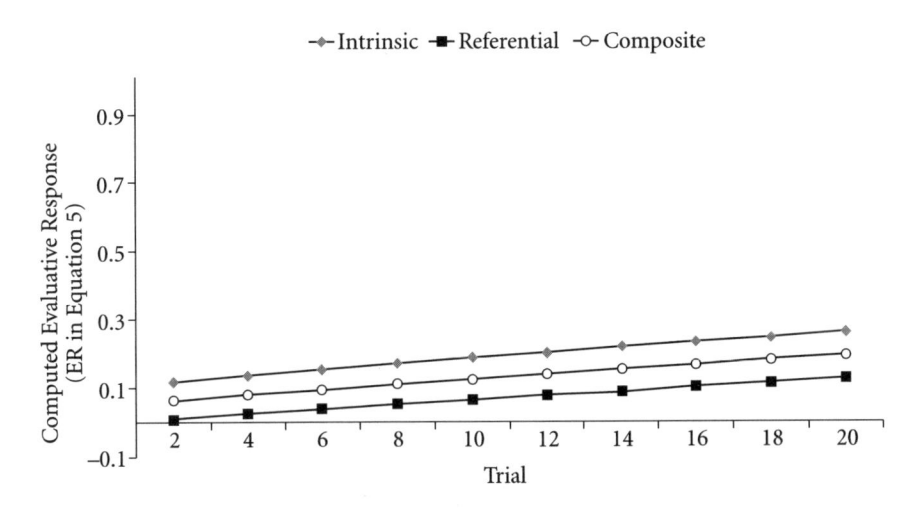

Figure 4. Simulation results of evaluative learning with forward pairing and 'subliminal' ES presentation.

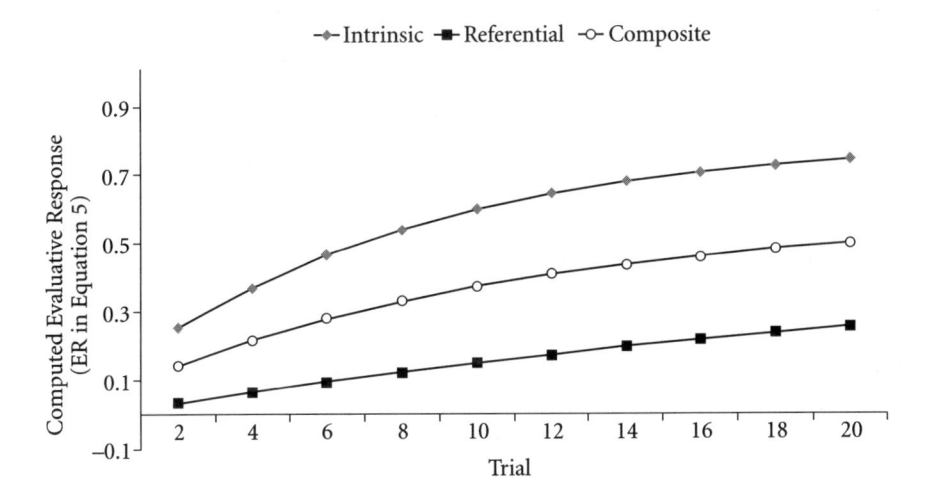

Figure 5. Simulation results of evaluative learning with backward pairing and 'subliminal' ES presentation.

and paired with digitised images of hand drawn Japanese ideographs. In the first experiment, we compared immediate rating (rating each ideograph immediately after its pairing with one of the faces) with delayed rating (rating the set of ideographs together after acquisition trials are completed). Interestingly, we found that the time of rating made no difference to learning, suggesting that evaluative learning appears to occur in affective priming (a position recognised by Winkielman et al. 1997). However, in a comparison of forward and backward pairing, the latter produced reliable evaluative learning but forward pairing consistently produced a contrast effect; that is, ratings of ideographs paired with smiling faces were *less* liked than ideographs paired with angry faces. Thus, the prediction of the simulations is upheld.

Conscious control of the evaluative response

The contrast effect in forward pairing reported in our study was contrary to expectations, though entirely consistent with the seemingly weaker effect of forward subliminal evaluative learning. This surprising result was followed up in a subsequent study in which the emergence of contrast effects reappeared when attempts were made to encourage contingency awareness through detailed instructions to the participant (Fulcher & Hammerl 2001). We designed an evaluative learning experiment around the basic logic of Jacoby's exclusion–inclusion task (Jacoby 1991; Merickle, Joordens, & Stolz 1995), in which a dissociation between familiarity and recognition is demonstrated. In one study, we increased awareness by informing the participants of the nature of evaluative learning and by encouraging them to learn the NS-ES pairs (Experiment 1). Compared with participants whose awareness was reduced by use of a distracter task (and not informing them of the nature of evaluative learning), the increase in awareness was mirrored by a decrease in evaluative learning. While unaware participants showed the expected assimilation effect, aware participants showed a contrast effect. Thus, the influence of the evaluative stimulus seems to be inhibited by increased awareness. There are sound reasons for thinking that this inhibition is an attempt to discount this influence. When awareness is partial, discounting may be based on an overestimate of the influence of the evaluative stimulus, resulting in a contrast effect. Evidence from Winkielman et al. (1997) further indicates that when awareness of the ES is low, as in its subliminal presentation, attempts to discount are ineffectual.

In our latest study, we again used the logic of the exclusion-inclusion task but this time we modified the Merickle et al. (1995) design. In that study, the presentation time of the critical stimuli was varied and instructions were given to either to exclude or include the stimulus in selecting a response. We varied the presentation time of the ES from 12.5 ms through to 125 ms with two instruction conditions. In the first, participants were not informed about the likely influence of the ES when later asked to rate the NS (normal condition), but in the second (contrast condition), they were. In addition, the contrast group were told to rate NSi in the *opposite direction*, i.e., when rating the NS items, they were told to first try to recall the valence of the ES prime and then to rate the ES in the opposite direction. For example, if they thought that the NS was paired with a positive prime, then they were to rate it as *unpleasant*. The logic is that at if participants were unaware of the primes at, say, 12.5 ms, then attempts by the contrast condition to rate in the opposite direction would be overridden by unconscious influences of the ES during learning, and hence, they should show evaluative learning. Conversely, if participants are aware of the primes at, say, 125 ms, then attempts to contrast are more likely to be effective since conscious processes will override unconscious processes. Participants were given immediate forced-choice recognition tests throughout, to assess whether they had detected the primes. Our predictions were supported: For the normal condition, evaluative learning was present at the shortest presentation rate but was absent at the longer presentation rates. However, for the contrast condition, the data show strong evaluative learning at 12.5 ms and contrast effects at both 50 and 125 ms. Figure 6 displays the mean evaluation index (computed by subtracting mean ratings of NSi paired with negative ES primes from those paired with positive ES primes) for both conditions as the duration of the ES is increased (data for 12.5 ms and 25 ms presentations includes only those participants whose detection rates were at chance levels, suggesting that they did not see the prime, and data for 50 ms and 125 ms presentation rates includes only those participants whose detection rates were *better* than chance, indicating that they did see the prime). These results provide more compelling support for the notion that evaluations can be acquired unconsciously and can resist conscious control. However, when the evaluative stimuli are consciously perceived, awareness can serve to reduce their impact. Further, when given motivation to do so and when at least some awareness is present, the influence of the evaluative stimulus can be consciously controlled.

These results are problematic for the claim that evaluative learning is *dependent* upon awareness; moreover, they indicate that contingency awareness can exert an inhibitory effect on the magnitude of the evaluative response. This conclusion is further supported by studies that compared subliminal presentation of the ES with clearly visible, or unmasked, presentations (Murphy & Zajonc 1992; Fulcher & Hammerl 2001, exp. 3). In these studies, subliminal presentation resulted in significantly stronger evaluative learning than did unmasked presentations. Clearly, then, *ER* does not monotonically increase with increased awareness.

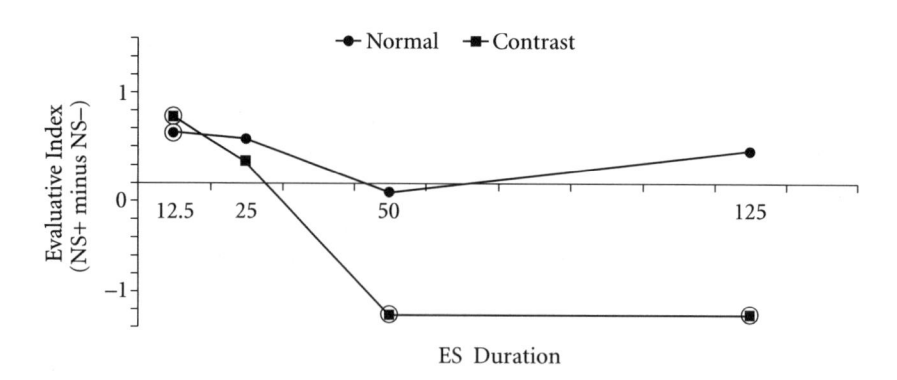

Figure 6. Experimental results of evaluative learning with varied exposure durations of the ES, and normal instructions compared with contrast instructions. (Circled data points indicate evaluative indeces that are statistically significant).

It is suggested here that these pattern of results can be explained by an additional function, which makes corrections to the evaluative response as the strength of w_{NS-ES} increases. A similar explanation for the effects of increased awareness of an evaluative stimulus is described in Murphy and Zajonc (1993). In their account, the influence of the prime is based on both its conscious and unconscious evaluations. Where both evaluations can be congruent, the evaluations are cumulative, and where they are incongruent, the one is 'diluted' by the other. However, extrapolating their model to a broader range of evaluative learning data is difficult as their model is based on competing evaluations of a stimulus: the rapid, non-conscious evaluations may be of the gross positive or negative impressions of the stimulus, and the slower, conscious evaluations may include more detailed affective analyses of the stimulus. These may be incongruent when the stimulus is displayed for longer durations. However, the model makes no reference to conscious or unconscious influences of the evaluative stimulus on the neutral stimulus with which it is paired, but only on how the evaluation of a stimulus may alter with variations of exposure time. Nonetheless, their development of a model of competing conscious and unconscious influences is a useful starting point for speculating that with increased awareness of the NS-ES relationship, there can be competing evaluations of the NS.

Suppose that when evaluating the NS, there is a motivation to deny the influence of the ES. This is most likely to occur where there is explicit knowledge of the relationship and where there is a clear absence of a causal relationship between the two stimuli: if the NS is not a *cause* of an unpleasant event, then there may be little to gain in disliking it. So, when two stimuli are presented merely contiguously, there might be an attempt to inhibit or discount the second term in Equation 5. Although most studies that attempt to measure awareness use a binary classification of awareness (and correspondingly label participants as aware or unaware), awareness is most likely to exist on a continuum (hence, a recognition failure might not mean that awareness was completely absent, Shanks & Lovibond, in preparation). Since awareness might often be partial, then attempts to discount will be based on incomplete information. We can conceptualise this assertion within the model by saying that as $0 < w_{NS-ES} < 1$ (contingency awareness is partial), attempts to discount can only be based on an estimate of e_{ES}, with accuracy dependent on w_{NS-ES}. When w_{NS-ES} is very low, the relative contribution of the referential-associative evaluation (that based on re-activation of the ES) may be *underestimated*. The result is that the second term in Equation 5 can contribute to the *ER* without much inhibition. However, as w_{NS-ES} increases, so too does the knowledge of the ES. As a result, the discounted value gradually equals the value of the temporal weight, and the second term of Equation 5 is cancelled out. It is possible to conceive of a function where, when w_{NS-ES} is moderately high, the relative contribution of the referential-associative evaluation is even an *overestimate*, which can result in a discounted value that is greater than the temporal weight. This type of function could generate a contrast effect.

The estimated influence of the ES is assumed to be (i) sigmoidal, reflecting under- and over-estimations, and (ii) a function of the associative weight w_{NS-ES}, reflecting the accuracy of the estimation:

$$z(x) = \frac{1}{1 + e^{-A(Bx-1)}}$$

where $x = w_{NS-ES}$, A and B are constants, and e is the exponential operator. We can now write Equation 5 as:

$$ER_i = \rho e_i + (1 - \rho)\left[w_{ij} - z(x)\right] e_j \qquad (6)$$

and for accuracy, where $x = w_{ij}$. Thus, Equation 5 is a non-compensatory formulation of the evaluative response, and Equation 6 includes a non-linear compensatory function representing the effort to discount the influence of the evaluative stimulus. When A is set to 5.0 and B is set to 2, an idealised graph is produced that yields contrast effects with high contingency awareness, and when B is reduced to 1.4, the inhibition term cancels out the influence of the ES produced by the temporal weight (see Figure 7). The values of these parameters may vary depending upon individual differences in reactions to evaluative learning, such as those suggested by the theory of *psychological reactance*

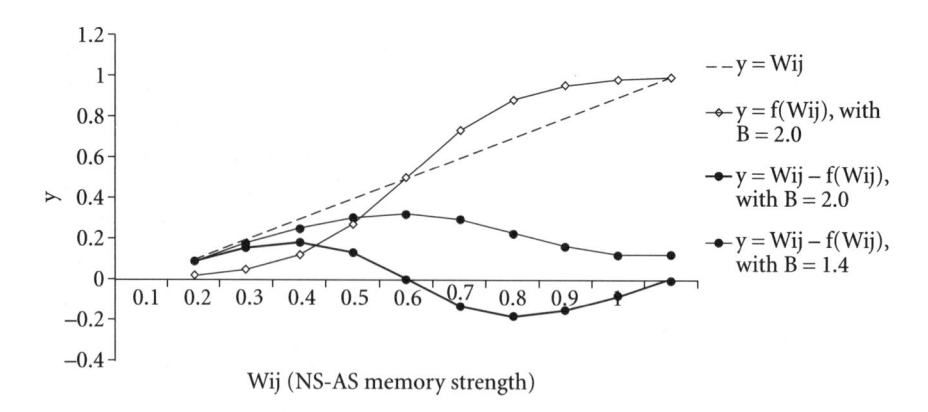

[Figure 7 plot showing curves for y = Wij, y = f(Wij) with B = 2.0, y = Wij − f(Wij) with B = 2.0, and y = Wij − f(Wij) with B = 1.4, plotted against Wij (NS-AS memory strength) on the x-axis from 0.1 to 0.9 and y on the vertical axis from −0.4 to 1.2.]

Figure 7. Idealised compensation functions, f(Wij).

(Brehm 1966). Some support for this possibility was obtained in (Fulcher & Hammerl 2001, exp. 3) where we found that whereas low reactance individuals showed strong evaluative learning, high reactance individuals showed a contrast effect.

The function developed above, then, accounts for our most recent data and in doing so produces a straightforward account for the anomalies reported earlier. By experimenting with the constants A and B in the inhibition function, we repeated the earlier simulations in an attempt to reproduce a fall in evaluative learning when contingency awareness is high. When A is set to 5.0 and B is set to 1.4, a dip in the simulated evaluative response (forward 'supraliminal') is produced that corresponds to the observed data (see Figure 8). However, this dip occurs for both the composite hypothesis and the referential hypothesis, and the function does not therefore, discriminate between them.

Simulations of subliminal learning with forward and backward pairing were carried out next, and the evaluative response was computed according to Equation 6 (augmented evaluative response). These agreed with the earlier simulations, producing stronger learning with backward rather than forward pairing. The inhibitory function described advances the earlier formulation of the model and provides an explanation for the contradictory findings in the literature on the relationship between contingency awareness and evaluative learning. A further test of the model might be to determine whether it can successfully simulate other evaluative learning phenomena. In the next section, we examine long-term retention of an evaluative response and a change to the NS evaluation brought about through a change to the ES evaluation.

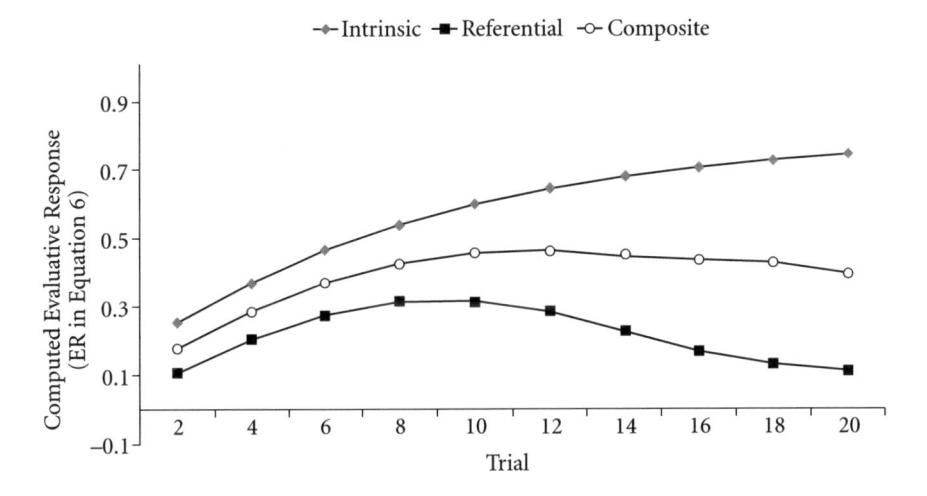

Figure 8. Simulation results of evaluative learning (using Equation 6) with forward pairing and 'supraliminal' ES presentation.

Long-term retention and revaluation of the ES

Since evaluative weights and temporal weights are stored separately, then according to the dissociation principle, their learning or forgetting rates may be dissimilar. As reported in the introduction, one way in which this might be observed is after a long retention interval, and in Fulcher and Cocks (1997) we found that while memory for precise NSi-ESi pairings dropped by some 60%, evaluations of the stimuli remained relatively stable, with even a slight increase in the effect size. Similar findings were replicated in Fulcher et al. (2001).

Since ratings during re-test were still biased by the ESi, then it poses problems for the referential hypothesis, which predicts that the means should return towards baseline. In the next simulation we model the Fulcher et al. data and repeat the simulations described above for forward pairing with 'supraliminal' presentation. The evaluative responses were computed using Equation 5 and Equation 6 for a comparison. Although learning was simulated over 20 trials, we consider the values corresponding most closely to the Fulcher and Cocks (1997) and Fulcher et al. (2001) data, namely when w_{NS-ES} reached 0.34 (time t). For the re-test data the weight was then reduced to about 5% (time $t + 1$). These studies reveal that the evaluative response is remarkably stable and we look to see for which hypothesis does the computed ER at $t + 1$ remain closest to its time t value.

For the intrinsic hypothesis, no changes occur through time (since it is unaffected by changes to the temporal weight), it therefore represents one explanation for stability of evaluative learning over time. For the referential hypothesis, the *ER* falls from 0.34 to 0.056 (an 83% drop); for the augmented referential hypothesis, the *ER* falls from 0.272 to 0.047 (an 82.7% drop); for the composite hypothesis, the drop is from 0.4 to 0.259 (35%); and for the augmented composite hypothesis, the drop is from 0.367 to 0.254 (30.8%). A similar pattern of comparisons occurred throughout the 20-trial simulations, with the augmented composite hypothesis consistently showing the lowest fall in the *ER* (see Figure 9). So, while all but the intrinsic hypothesis tend to show a decrease in the evaluative response over time, the augmented composite hypothesis comes closest to the data, and this is because as the weight decreases, so too does the effect of the compensatory function, and the dominant term at re-test, is e_{NS}, that is, the intrinsic evaluation of the NS.

Revaluation studies were mentioned in the introduction as representing stringent tests of the referential hypothesis. This is whether the valence of the NS would track a subsequent change to the valence of the ES, changes that would occur in the absence of the NS. The evidence reviewed indeed indicated that evaluative ratings can be dependent upon NS-ES associations (albeit at some pre-attentive level). However, one of our own studies sheds further light on the issue and offers some difficult data for the referential hypothesis.

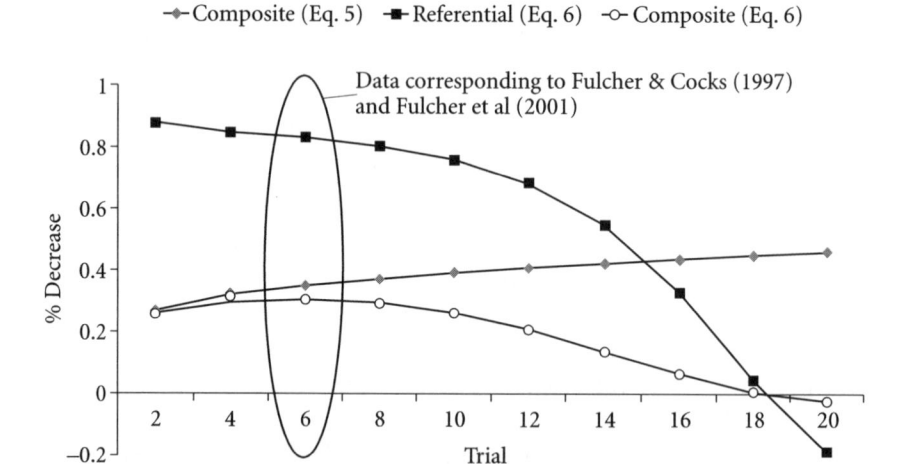

Figure 9. Simulation results of evaluative rating taken immediately after learning and after a retention interval. (Graph shows % decrease in the computed ER from time t to time t+1).

We supposed that the strongest test of the referential hypothesis would be revaluation of the ES after it had been paired with the NS through subliminal presentation. Thus, smiling and angry faces were presented subliminally while viewing neutral Japanese ideographs. As expected, this method produced evaluative learning in that the ratings of the ideographs were biased by the subliminal primes. In a later phase, the faces were given various personality descriptors that presented the individual in a pleasant or an unpleasant light. Thus, some smiling faces were paired with pleasant descriptors and others with unpleasant descriptors. This also applied to the angry faces. Analysis of the ideograph ratings showed that they were influenced by the revaluation procedure. Thus, even with subliminal presentation of the ES, a structural NS-ES link may be formed. However, there was one exception: While NS ratings were influenced by revaluation in forward learning, they were not in backward learning. This result is compatible with the composite hypothesis since in the earlier simulations it was demonstrated that backward subliminal learning might yield an intrinsic shift with little or no associative memory being formed. Hence if the ES is altered in backward pairing, the evaluation of the NS can remain unaffected. Given the importance of this result for the composite hypothesis, a replication study is required to be more convincing.

Although both the composite and referential hypotheses fair well against the available evidence, the simulations so far indicate that the composite hypothesis is slightly ahead since it consistently accounts for a broader range of data, and especially with the addition of the compensatory function. At the very least, this implies that proponents of the referential hypothesis cannot so easily rule out intrinsic shifts in the evaluation of a stimulus following evaluative learning.

One testable prediction emerging from the above discussions is that evaluative learning can emerge after a retention interval even when it is not observed immediately after acquisition trials. If full contingency awareness during acquisition was induced, for example through repeated trials until learning reaches some criterion, then we would expect to observe little or no evaluative learning due to the operation of the compensatory function. However, after a retention interval, contingency memory will decline significantly and the compensation function will relax its inhibition of the contribution of the evaluative stimulus. In this case, evaluative learning should emerge at re-test when it was not observed in the earlier session. This kind of prediction arises from the detailed specification of the composite theory, and it is doubtful whether the intrinsic and referential theories cited in the literature could have arrived at a prediction such as this.

Selective attention and emotional states

An assumption of the model is that while stimulus units can accommodate more than one representation at any one time, the stimulus unit with the strongest evaluative weight will receive most of the attentional resources, all else being equal. Moreover, an exceptionally strong evaluative weight will inhibit the representations of other stimuli. Studies such as Fazio et al. (1986) and Roskos-Ewoldson and Fazio (1992) have demonstrated that strongly liked and disliked attitude objects tend to distract attention away from a target object considerably more than do neutral objects. The implication is that even when a stimulus is in the focus of attention and the task demands attention to it, objects in the periphery of the field of vision that are of greater evaluative significance can momentarily distract attention away from the task.

There is other evidence that particular kinds of stimuli can attract attention dependent upon the emotional state of the individual. For example, there is now a substantial body of evidence that attention can be biased towards threatening information in states of anxiety (see Mathews, & MacLeod 1994 for a review). For example, when an emotionally threatening word and a neutral word are presented simultaneously, anxious or depressed patients are faster to detect a probe stimulus that replaces the threatening word than are normal controls (MacLeod, Mathews, & Tata 1986; Mathews, Ridgeway, & Williamson 1996). These observations imply that the patients were more likely to have been attending to the location of the negative emotional word. If the threatening word is a to-be-ignored distracter, then any attention it attracts is likely to slow responses to other stimuli. For example, in the emotional Stroop task, when participants are required to name the colour of a word while ignoring its content, threatening words cause slowing in anxious but not non-anxious individuals (Williams, Mathews, & MacLeod 1996). It is reasoned that attentional resources are selectively captured by the emotional word content in individuals prone to anxiety, and this leads to interference when the task requires attending to another stimulus.

Attentional bias is quite specific in terms of the type of material exposed to and is influenced by the emotional preoccupation of the individual. For example, those whose worries relate to physical illness preferentially attend to stimuli related to disease and socially anxious individuals preferentially attend to social threats (Mathews, & MacLeod 1994). It seems, then, that attention is primed by the current emotional state to seek out particular stimuli in the environment. This notion of negative priming in anxious states may be similar to the priming of evaluative maps in a task-dependent manner, and this assumes that vigilance for particular types of threat is either a long- or short-term goal of the system. Primed negative evaluative maps have the effect of amplifying those stimulus units that have the strongest evaluative match and inhibiting the weaker ones. In this way, attention is directed towards the threat and away from innocuous stimuli, and task-dependent stimuli will compete for attention with the threat.

To model the effects of a distracter item on a simple decision task, we introduce evaluative priming according to task-relevance that amplifies the activity of task related units. For example, one task that we have developed is the simple detection of the direction of an arrow on a visual display. We assume that such a task primes representations relating to the concepts *arrow* and *direction*. With practice, the participant learns that the arrow always has the same appearance and is pointing either to the left or to the right and the attentional process is refined such that fewer representations need to be primed. This is not unlike the assumptions behind the model of attention described by Matthews and Harley (1996) and involves increasing the activity of a stimulus unit that represents the task stimulus. The arrows are presented simultaneously with pictures in the background of either pleasant, unpleasant, or innocuous images. It is expected that on occasion, the picture will operate as a distracter item that reduces the amount of attention paid to the location of the arrow. We know that in anxiety, the perceived negativity of a stimulus is increased (e.g., Lang, Bradley, & Cuthbert 1990; Fulcher et al. 2001), and we assume that the effect of anxiety is therefore to inflate the values of negative evaluative weights. Since representations of task-related stimuli and those of negative stimuli are both primed, the location of the arrow and the negative information in unpleasant pictures will compete for attentional priorities. The representations of the negative stimuli may momentarily become more active than those of the task-relevant stimuli, and in doing so, detection of the direction of the arrow is slowed. This is reflected in longer reaction times to press a button indicating the detection of the direction of the arrow. Anxious individuals are slower to react to targets superimposed on unpleasant pictures than they are to pleasant ones.

In order to model this phenomenon, there is no need to make significant changes to the architecture, other than to introduce the priming function. Negative evaluative weights are inflated by the term: $e_i(\text{primed}) = e_i(1 + X)$, where X is a function of the level of anxiety, and we assume a similar term for the priming of the evaluative weight of the target stimulus. In the following simulation, the task evaluation in the simulation is set to 0.9, which is its inflated or primed value. We assume that reaction time is a linear function of the level of activity of the target stimulus unit, and in the simulations target detection is given by the number of iterations it takes for the task unit to reach a certain threshold. The evaluative weight of the negative distracter item is varied from 0.1 to 1.0 over the set of simulations and with values of X ranging from 0.0 to 2.0. The results are shown in Figure 10.

The most marked effect of the distracter is with high anxiety, which in this case has the effect of dramatically inhibiting attention away from the task stimulus. While strongly negative items may draw attention away from the target regardless of anxiety level, the effect is most exaggerated with high anxiety, and this accords with the data (Mogg, Mathews, Bird, & Macgregor-Morris 1990). Interestingly, since positive evaluations, we assume, are unaffected by anxiety, distracter items with positively evaluated stimuli have little effect on the amount of attention given to the task unit, even with high anxiety. However, these simulations deviate from the observed results in a subtle but important way. The data provided by MacLeod et al. (1986) indicates an attentional *avoidance* in low anxiety for mildly threatening stimuli. Thus, for low anxiety, as the severity of the threat increases, so too does an avoidance strategy. This occurs only until the threat is so severe that it then promotes vigilance. We interpret this as a result of increased controlled effort aimed at reducing the impact of the emotional stimulus. Individuals may monitor their performance continuously so that when a noticeable interference occurs, controlled effort can increase up to a point. Anxious individuals may differ from low anxious individuals in that their efforts to control attention away from a negative stimulus are more vigorous; hence, with low or moderately negative distracters, highly anxious individuals are better able to inhibit them. However, there may be upper limits in the extent to which such efforts successfully inhibit the distracter, and for

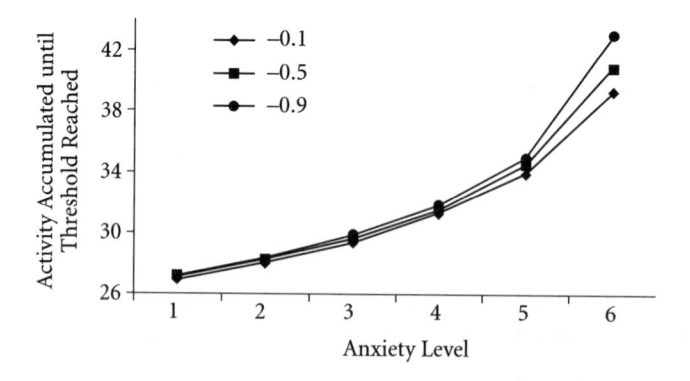

Figure 10. Simulated reaction time to respond to a task with a negative distracter item of varying intensity and with increasing anxiety level.

more intensely negative stimuli, the effort required will exceed this limit and lead to disruptions in task performance.

One modification that can capture this aspect of the data is to model demand awareness as initially low but variable within a trial. In addition, a mechanism is included that detects whether or not the task unit is 'winning', and if it is, then no increase in demand strength is required, but if it is not then demand strength is incremented. Thus, task demand can be adjusted on a moment-by-moment basis, but may not exceed an upper limit.

The results of the new simulations are shown in Figure 11. For low anxiety, a U-curve is formed with an initial slowed reaction time for low intensity distracters. However, with increases in the strength of the distracter, reaction time to the task is speeded (reflecting avoidance), but then begins to slow as the strength increases further (reflecting vigilance). For high anxiety, with increases in the strength of the distracter, reaction time increases exponentially and, as in the previous simulations, differences between high and low anxiety are most exaggerated with strong distracters.

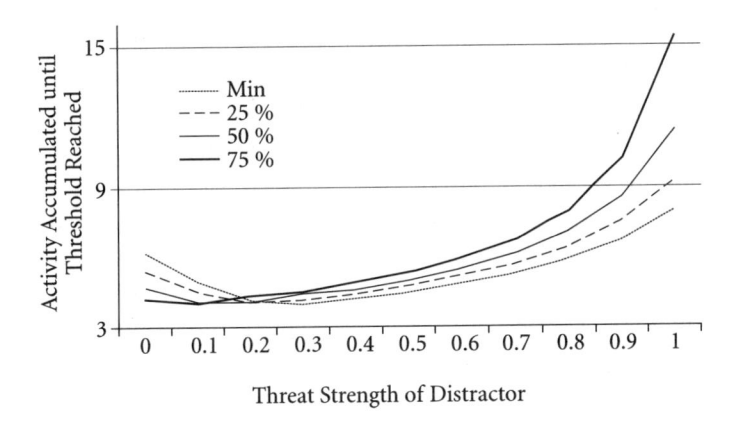

Figure 11. RT Analogue with varied distractor strength for different anxiety levels.

Evaluative learning and the allocation of attention in anxiety

The model makes an important prediction that bridges research in both evaluative learning and attentional bias in anxiety. If the amount of attention given to a stimulus is a direct function of its evaluation, then a stimulus that has acquired a negative evaluation through evaluative learning should itself come to attract attention. This effect should be most apparent in high anxiety. We put this to the test in Fulcher et al. (2001) using the method of Fulcher and Cocks (1997) in learning trials. Neutral stimuli were paired with word labels that corresponded to pleasant and unpleasant events in the participant's personal history. This method ensures that the ESi are highly pertinent to ongoing concerns, which appears to be one prerequisite for observing attentional bias. After acquisition trials, the previously neutral stimuli were then subjected to the attentional task described above in which the task is to detect the direction of an arrow on a visual display, and to respond by pressing a key as quickly as possible. Instead of presenting the ESi in the background, the NSi were displayed. The results over two experiments indicate that highly anxious individuals were slower to respond to targets superimposed over NSi that had been previously paired with unpleasant ESi than they were for targets on NSi that had been paired with pleasant NSi. This suggests that for highly anxious participants, a neutral stimulus previously paired with a negative stimulus can capture attention as though the neutral stimulus was itself affective. The data also indicated a trend for the opposite effect in low anxious individuals, who were marginally slowed by NSi paired with pleasant stimuli.

The importance of this result is that firstly, it demonstrates how the range of stimuli capable of provoking anxiety can be increased through evaluative learning. Attention in anxiety may then develop from being biased towards a narrow range of stimuli to a much broader range through evaluative learning. Secondly, it provides support for the predictions of the model, and the contention that evaluative processes in learning and those that guide attention arise from a common mechanism. Further support for this contention is the finding that a neutral picture paired with a shock can enhance the startle-probe response in a similar way, as can overtly unpleasant pictures (Hamm, Greenwald, Bradley, & Lang 1993; Lipp, Fitchett, & Siddle 1996). Thus, the magnitude of the startle-probe is another measure of the evaluative strength of the NS-ES composition.

Interpretational bias

One result of evaluative priming is that there will be the tendency to highlight the most threatening aspects of a stimulus array. This corresponds to what Mineka (1992) termed "adaptive conservatism": that it is less costly to erroneously perceive a stimulus as threatening than it is to fail to detect a real threat. Indeed, another cognitive bias in anxiety is the negative interpretation of ambiguous information. For example, when presented with information (e.g., a homograph such as "stroke") that could have a threatening meaning (e.g., "disease") or a benign one (e.g., "caress"), anxious individuals are more likely to interpret the information with the threatening meaning (Mathews, Richards, & Eysenck 1989; Richards, & French 1992). It might be the case that this interpretational bias occurs simply because of the more frequent exposure to the negative interpretation than to the benign one. However, the inflation of negative evaluations in anxiety is sufficient to explain this bias since it promotes increases in the potential activity levels of negative representations. Moreover, we rule out a learning component since we have failed in over 14 experiments (8 of them unpublished) to find a bias in evaluative learning that favours negative associations in anxious participants (e.g., Fulcher et al. 2001). This and the data obtained on the acquired attentional bias to previously neutral stimuli, together suggest that with equal learning experiences, anxious individuals process negative information differently than do non-anxious individuals.

Conclusions

It has been contended that theories of evaluative learning can be better understood through the design and simulation of a connectionist network that maps the evaluation of an incoming stimulus. The result, we argue, is that a new composite hypothesis best accounts for the learning phenomena. In terms of evaluative processing in anxiety, we argue that it compares favourably with the model of Matthews and Harley (1996), which was designed specifically to capture attentional bias but does not address the acquisition of emotional information. While the initial purpose of the model presented here was to better understand the acquisition of emotional information, it was found to be able to offer an account of how attention can be selectively biased towards negative emotional information with little modification to the basic model. Thus the model may also be useful for generating ideas and predictions concerning the acquisition and processing of emotional information.

Although the model was inspired by psychological rather than neuropsychological findings, we suspect that the amygdala implements aspects of negative evaluative maps. For example, in humans, amygdala damage can impair acquisition of aversive associations but leave contingency memory in tact (Bechara, Tranel, Damasio, Adolphs, Rockland, & Damasio 1995), and patients with damage to the amygdala show disturbances in the acquisition of preferences (Johnsrude, Owen, White, Zhao, & Bohbot 2000). These findings are analogous to disorders of evaluative maps. Furthermore, it is now well documented that the amygdala is specialized for the detection of negative stimuli and plays a critical role in the acquisition of fears (LeDoux 1993; Davidson, & Irwin 1999). The hypothesis that negative evaluative maps are primed in anxiety is entirely consistent with recent theories of the amygdala, such as Rosen & Schulkin (1998) who suggest that while the amygdala is activated by fearful stimuli, when interacting with anxious states it becomes *hyperexcitable* and is not dampened by normal inhibitory processes. It is significant, then, that a psychological model inspired by questions of self-organisation in connectionist systems, and one based on evaluative processing of relatively moderate stimuli, should converge on a similar mechanism as neurophysiological models of pathological fear.

Finally, computational models can be arrived at either through a top-down approach, in which theory drives the modelling process, or through a bottom-up process, in which the observed data provides the necessary constraints, or through a combination of the two approaches. The initial formulation of the model was inspired by the question of how a system can organise its own learning. It was then adapted according to the general theoretical positions of the intrinsic and referential hypotheses of evaluative learning. Its final re-shaping was then determined by several empirical observations, and we arrived at an alternative hypothesis of evaluative learning, which is specified in detail. To develop more confidence in the model, it will be necessary to obtain more data; however, the data from these studies should inspire further developments of the model. The modelling process has already provided an impetus for several new studies, as have been reported here, and it is hoped will continue to spur on future research.

Acknowledgments

Preparation of this manuscript was supported by a Wellcome Trust award (Grant No. 051027). Andrew Mathews, Bundy Mackintosh, and Marianne Hammerl are gratefully acknowledged for their valuable suggestions on an earlier version of this manuscript.

References

Allport, D. A. (1987). Selection for action: Some behavioural and neurophysiological considerations of attention and action: In H. Heur & F. Sanders (Eds.), *Perspectives on perception and action*. Hillsdale, N. J.: Lawrence Erlbaum Associates.

Baeyens, F., Crombez, G., Van den Bergh, O., & Eelen, P. (1988). Once in contact always in contact: Evaluative conditioning is resistant to extinction. *Advances in Behaviour Research and Therapy, 10,* 179–199.

Baeyens, F., Eelen, P., & Van den Bergh, O. (1990). Contingency awareness in evaluative conditioning: A case for unaware affective-evaluative learning. *Cognition and Emotion, 4,* 3–18.

Baeyens, F., Eelen, P., Crombez, G., & Van den Bergh, O. (1992a). Human evaluative conditioning: Acquisition trials, presentation schedule, evaluative style and contingency awareness. *Behaviour Research and Therapy, 30,* 133–142.

Baeyens, F., Eelen, P., Van den Bergh, O., & Crombez, G. (1992b). The content of learning in human evaluative conditioning: Acquired valence is sensitive to US-reevaluation. *Learning and Motivation, 23,* 300–224.

Bechara, A., Tranel, D., Damasio, H., Adolphs, R., Rockland, C., & Damasio, A. R. (1995). Double dissociation of conditioning and declarative knowledge relative to the amygdala and hippocampus in humans. *Science, 269,* 1115–1118.

Boss, M., & Bonke, B. (1998). When seemingly irrelevant details matter: Hidden covariation detection reexamined. *Consciousness and Cognition, 7,* 596–602.

Bouton, M. E. (1994). Context, ambiguity, and classical conditioning. *Current Directions in Psychological Science, 3,* 49–52.

Brehm, J. W. (1966). *A theory of psychological reactance.* New York: Academic Press.

Cole, R. P., & Miller, R. R. (1999). Conditioned excitation and conditioned inhibition acquired through backward conditioning. *Learning and Motivation, 30,* 129–156.

Davey, G. C. L. (1994). Is evaluative conditioning a qualitatively distinct form of classical conditioning? *Behaviour Research and Therapy, 32,* 291–299.

Davidson, R. J., & Irwin, W. (1999). The functional neuroanatomy of emotion and affective style. *Trends in Cognitive Sciences, 3,* 11–21.

De Houwer, J., Baeyens, F., & Eelen, P. (1994). Verbal evaluative conditioning with undetected US presentation. *Behaviour Research and Therapy, 32,* 629–633.

De Houwer, J., Hendrickx, H., & Baeyens, F. (1997). Evaluative learning with "subliminally" presented stimuli. *Consciousness and Cognition, 6,* 87–107.

Fazio, R. H., Sanbonmatsu, D. M., Powell, M. C., & Kardes, F. R. (1986). On the automatic activation of attitudes. *Journal of Personality and Social Psychology, 50,* 229–238.

Field, A. P., & Davey, G. C. L. (1997). Conceptual conditioning: Evidence for an artifactual account of evaluative learning. *Learning and Motivation, 28,* 446–464.

Fulcher, E. P. (1992). The construction of evaluative maps in classical and operant conditioning. *Unpublished Ph.D. thesis.* University of London.

Fulcher, E. P. (Submitted). Spontaneous displacement of valence through subliminal evaluative learning.

Fulcher, E. P., & Cocks, R. P. (1997). Dissociative storage systems in human evaluative conditioning. *Behaviour Research and Therapy, 35,* 1–10.

Fulcher, E. P., & Hammerl, M. (2001). When all is revealed: A dissociation between evaluative learning and contingency awareness. *Consciousness and Cognition, 10,* 524–549.

Fulcher, E. P., Mathews, A., Mackintosh, B., & Law, S. (2001). Evaluative learning and the allocation of attention in anxiety. *Cognitive Therapy and Research, 25,* 261–280.

Hamm, A. O., Greenwald, M. K., Bradley, M. M., & Lang, P. J. (1993). Emotional learning, hedonic change, and the startle probe. *Journal of Abnormal Psychology, 102*, 453–465.

Hammerl, M., & Grabitz, H.-J. (In press). Affective-evaluative learning in humans: A form of associative learning or only an artifact? *Learning and Motivation*.

Hammerl, M., & Grabitz, H.-J. (1996). Human evaluative conditioning without experiencing a valued event. *Learning and Motivation, 27*, 278–293.

Hammerl, M., & Grabitz, H.-J. (1993). Human evaluative conditioning: Order of stimulus presentation. *Integrative Physiological and Behavioral Science, 28*, 191–194.

Holland, P. C. (1990). Event representation in Pavlovian conditioning: Image and action. *Cognition, 37*, 105–131.

Jacoby, L. L. (1991). A process dissociation framework: Separating automatic from intentional uses of memory. *Journal of Memory and Language, 30*, 513–541

Johnsrude, I. S., Owen, A. M., White, N. M., Zhao, W. V., & Bohbot, V. (2000). Impaired preference conditioning after anterior temporal lobe reseaction in humans. *Journal of Neuroscience, 20*, 2649–2656.

Kahneman, D., & Tversky, A. (1984). Choices, values, and frames. *American Psychologist, 39*, 341–350.

Krosnick, J. A., Betz, A. L., Jussim, L. J., & Lynn, A. R. (1992). Subliminal conditioning of attitudes. *Personality and Social Psychology Bulletin, 18*, 152–162.

Lang, P. J., Bradley, M. M., & Cuthbert, B. N. (1990). Emotion, attention, and the startle reflex. *Psychological Review, 97*, 377–395.

Lovibond, P. F., & Shanks, D. R. (2002). The role of awareness in Pavlovian conditioning: Empirical evidence and theoretical interpretations. *Journal of Experimental Psychology: Animal Behaviour Processes, 28*, 3–26.

Lazarus, R. S. (1966). Psychological stress and the coping process. New York: McGraw-Hill.

LeDoux, J. E. (1996). *The Emotional Brain*. Simon and Schuster.

Levey, A. B., & Martin, I. (1975). Classical conditioning of human "evaluative" responses. *Behaviour Research and Therapy, 13*, 221–226.

Levey, A. B., & Martin, I. (1987). Evaluative conditioning: A case for hedonic transfer. In H. J. Eysenck & I. Martin (Eds.). Theoretical Foundations of Behaviour Therapy (pp. 113–131). New York: Plenum Press.

Lipp, O. V., Fitchett, H., & Siddle, D. A. T. (1996). Blink startle as a measure of evaluative conditioning. *International Journal of Psychology, 31*, 375.

MacLeod, C., Mathews, A., & Tata, P. (1986). Attentional bias in emotional disorders. *Journal of Abnormal Psychology, 95*, 15–20.

Martin, I., & Levey, A. B. (1994). The evaluative response: Primitive but necessary. *Behaviour Research and Therapy, 32*, 301–305.

Mathews, A., & MacLeod, C. (1994). Cognitive approaches to emotion and emotional disorders. *Annual Review of Psychology, 45*, 25–50.

Mathews, A., Richards, A., & Eysenck, M. (1989). Interpretation of homophones related to threat in anxiety states. *Journal of Abnormal Psychology, 98*, 31–34.

Mathews, A., Ridgeway, V., & Williamson, D. A. (1996). Evidence for attention to threatening stimuli in depression. *Behaviour Research & Therapy, 34*, 695–705.

Matthews, G., & Harley, T. A. (1996). Connectionist models of emotional distress and attentional bias. *Cognition and Emotion, 10*, 561–600.

Merickle, P. M., Joordens, S., & Stolz, J. A. (1995). Measuring the relative magnitude of unconscious influences. *Consciousness and Cognition, 4*, 422–439.

Mineka, S. (1992). Evolutionary memories, emotional processing, and the emotional disorders. In D. Medin (Ed.), *The psychology of learning and memory* (pp. 161–206). New York: Academic Press.

Mogg, K., Mathews, A., Bird, C., & Macgregor-Morris, R. (1990). Effects of stress and anxiety on the processing of threat stimuli. *Journal of Personality and Social Psychology, 59*, 1230–1237.

Murphy, S. T., & Zajonc, R. B. (1993) Affect, cognition, and awareness: Affective priming with optimal and suboptimal stimulus exposures. *Journal of Personality and Social Psychology, 64*, 723–739.

Öhman, A., & Soares, J. F. (1998) Emotional conditioning to masked stimuli: Expectancies for aversive outcomes following nonrecognised fear-relevant stimuli. *Journal of Experimental Psychology: General, 127*, 69–82

Osgood, C. E., Suci, G. J., & Tannenbaum, P. H. (1957). *The measurement of meaning.* Urbana: University of Illinois Press.

Richards, A., & French, C. C. (1992). An anxiety-related bias in semantic activation when processing threat/neutral homographs. *Quarterly Journal of Experimental Psychology: Human Experimental Psychology, 45*, 503–525.

Rosen, J. B., & Schulkin, J. (1998). From normal fear to pathological anxiety. *Psychological Review, 105*, 325–350.

Roskos-Ewoldson, D. R., & Fazio, R. H. (1992). On the orienting value of attitudes: Attitude accessibility as a determinant of an object's attraction of visual attention. *Journal of Personality and Social Psychology, 63*, 198–211.

Shanks, D. R., & Dickinson, A. (1990). Contingency awareness in evaluative conditioning: A comment on Baeyens, Eelen, and van den Bergh. *Cognition and Emotion, 4*, 19–30.

Shanks, D. R., & St. John, M. F. (1994). Characteristics of dissociable human learning systems. *Behavioral and Brain Sciences, 7*, 367–447.

Stuart, E. W., Shimp, T. A., & Engle, R. W. (1987). Classical conditioning of consumer attitudes: Four experiments in an advertising context. *Journal of Consumer Research, 14*, 334–349.

Williams, J. M. G., Mathews, A., & MacLeod, C. (1996). The emotional Stroop task and psychopathology. *Psychological Bulletin, 120*, 3–24.

Winkielman, P., Zajonc, R. B., & Schwarz, N. (1997). Subliminal affective priming resists attributional interventions. *Cognition and Emotion, 11*, 433–465.

CHAPTER 5

Affect and processing dynamics
Perceptual fluency enhances evaluations

Piotr Winkielman, Norbert Schwarz and Andrzej Nowak
University of Denver / University of Michigan / University of Warsaw

Research in psychology and neuroscience increasingly paints us as the "evaluating human," whose interactions with the world are facilitated by a variety of evaluative mechanisms. Traditionally, psychologists studying evaluations viewed them as resulting from the slow and careful consideration and integration of relevant stimulus attributes (e.g., Anderson 1981; Fishbein & Ajzen 1975). In contrast, recent psychological research suggests that evaluative judgments are often formed without such considerations, for example, by consulting one's apparent affective response to the stimulus (e.g., Schwarz 1990). Moreover, it is now widely accepted that people evaluate objects in their environment automatically and without conscious intention, extracting evaluative information from stimuli quickly and efficiently (e.g., Bargh 1996; Winkielman, Zajonc, & Schwarz 1997; Zajonc 2000). These observations are echoed by research in psychophysiology and neuroscience. For example, researchers have mapped out neuronal circuits allowing for rapid evaluative response (e.g., LeDoux 1996) and have highlighted the importance of quick affective feedback in decision making (e.g., Damasio 1994).

This chapter expands the portrayal of the evaluating human by reviewing our research on the relation between affect and the dynamics of information processing. We organize the presentation as follows. We first discuss differences between evaluative responses based on stimulus attributes and evaluative responses based on processing dynamics. Next, we review empirical findings that illustrate that ease of processing (high fluency) is consistently associated with more positive evaluations. Subsequently, we discuss why this might be the case and offer some speculations about possible computational mechanisms and neural instantiations. Finally, we address some boundary conditions governing the impact of processing dynamics on affect and evaluative judgment.

Feature-based and fluency-based sources of evaluative responses

Evaluative reactions can be based on multiple mechanisms that draw on different inputs. One source of relevant information are stimulus features. The analysis of such features, of course, can differ in complexity. On one end of the spectrum, there are simple affective responses to environmentally relevant stimuli, such as facial expressions or snakes, which require extraction of only few basic features (LeDoux 1996; Oehman, Flykt, & Lundqvist 2000; Zajonc 2000). On the other end, there are sophisticated emotions, such as hope or regret, which require intricate appraisals of the stimulus and its context (Frijda 1988; Ortony, Clore, & Collins 1988). Between these extremes are evaluative responses occurring during processes such as impression formation that involve integration of information from multiple features (e.g., Anderson 1981; Fishbein & Ajzen 1975).

Recently, researchers began collecting evidence suggesting another source of information underlying evaluative reactions, namely information provided by the dynamics of information processing itself. As we review below, this research shows that ease of processing, typically referred to as *high fluency*, tends to elicit a positive evaluative response that can be captured through self-reports as well psychophysiological measures. Before we review this evidence in more detail, it is useful to discuss a few conceptual differences between feature-based and fluency-based evaluative responses. An example may help here. Suppose you walk down a busy street and recognize one passing face as a neighbor who is smiling at you. One source of your pleasant affect might be the stimulus' descriptive features (i.e., your neighbor's smile). The other source of evaluative response, however, might be the fluency accompanying the processing of the stimulus (i.e., the ease of recognizing your neighbor's face). As we elaborate below, easy processing can trigger pleasant affect because it indicates that the stimulus is familiar or typical, and thus relatively likely to be positive. Further, easy processing can trigger pleasant affect because it indicates that your attempt at recognition is likely to be successful.

Although fluency-based affective reactions emerge in the course of processing stimulus features, they are *not* a function of these features in the same way that other affective reactions are. Most important, fluency-based evaluative reactions can be elicited by variables that are unrelated to the features of the stimulus itself, but influence the ease with which the stimulus can be processed. Accordingly, variables that are known to influence the speed of stimulus recognition – like visual priming, stimulus repetition, and exposure duration – have been found to consistently influence evaluative responses. Of course, certain intrinsic features of a stimulus, like figure-ground contrast, symmetry, or semantic predictability may themselves facilitate fluent processing. However, in such cases, the affective reaction may not derive from analysis of the implications of stimulus features, but from the influence of such features on the processing dynamics. Finally, it is also worth noting that the assumption that fluency-based affective reactions do not derive from stimulus features is fully compatible with the assumption that affective reactions are *perceived* by people as a response to features of the stimulus. As research in social psychology points out (see Higgins 1998), people "by default" assume that feelings they experience while thinking about a target bear on that target – or why else would they be experienced at this point in time? However, we may expect that the influence of fluency-based affective reactions on evaluative judgment is eliminated when people become aware that their feelings may be due to a source other than the stimulus, as has been observed in other investigations of affective influences, like moods and emotions (e.g., Schwarz & Clore 1983; see Schwarz & Clore 1996, for a review).

Perceptual fluency enhances liking

Historically, the interest in the fluency-evaluation link was stimulated by research into the mere-exposure effect, i.e., the observation that repeated exposure enhances liking for an initially neutral stimulus (for reviews see Bornstein 1989; Zajonc 2000). Several authors proposed that the mere-exposure effect might reflect changes in perceptual fluency (e.g., Bornstein & D'Agostino 1994; Jacoby, Kelley, & Dywan 1989; Seamon, Brody, & Kauff 1983). This proposal is consistent with the observation that repeated exposure speeds up stimulus recognition and enhances judgments of stimulus clarity and presentation duration, which are indicative of processing facilitation (e.g., Haber & Hershenson 1965; Jacoby & Dallas 1981; Witherspoon & Allan 1985; Whittlesea, Jacoby, & Girard 1990). If so, we may expect that any variable that facilitates processing results in increased liking, even under conditions of a single exposure. Our initial studies were designed to test this possibility.

In one of these studies (Reber, Winkielman, & Schwarz 1998, Study 1), participants were exposed to pictures of everyday objects (e.g., a desk, bird, or plane). The fluency with which these target pictures could be processed was manipulated through a subliminal priming procedure that exposed participants to visual contours. Some target pictures were preceded by matched contours (e.g., contour of a desk followed by a picture of the desk), whereas others were preceded by mismatched contours (e.g., contour of a desk followed by a picture of a bird). We expected that matched contours would facilitate target processing, consistent with the finding that subliminal visual primes enhance recognition of related targets (e.g., Bar & Biederman 1998). Some participants were asked to indicate how much they liked the target pictures; other participants were asked to press a button as soon as they could recognize the object in the picture, thus providing an independent measure of processing ease. The data were consistent with our predictions: Pictures preceded by matched contours were recognized faster, indicating higher fluency, and were liked more than pictures preceded by mismatched contours. Importantly, participants were unaware of the priming manipulation, thus eliminating the possibility of strategic responding to pictures preceded by various primes.

Additional studies replicated and extended these findings. First, we wanted to show that perceptual fluency enhances liking even when it is manipulated by means other than priming. This is important since priming procedures require previous exposure to at least some form of the target stimulus, thus raising interpretational issues surrounding the effect of repetition on liking (Zajonc 1998). Second, we wanted to show that liking can be increased by manipulations that do not rely on inhibitory influences. This is important since priming with matched versus mismatched stimuli can either increase or decrease fluency. Reflecting these considerations, we conducted several studies using other manipulations of perceptual fluency. In one study (Reber et al. 1998, Study 2), we manipulated fluency through different degrees of figure-ground contrast, a variable that has been shown to influence identification speed (Checkosky & Whitlock 1973). Again, participants liked the same stimulus more when it was presented with higher contrast, and hence could be processed more fluently. In another study (Reber et al. 1998, Study 3), we manipulated fluency through subtle increases in presentation duration, taking advantage of the observation that longer presentation durations facilitate the extraction of information (Mackworth 1963). As expected, participants evaluated the same stimulus more positively when it was presented for a longer duration, but were unaware that duration was manipulated. In combination, the above studies, based on visual priming, figure-ground contrast and presentation duration, consistently show that high perceptual fluency leads to more positive evaluations of the perceived stimuli.

Perceptual fluency selectively elicits positive evaluation

Different process assumptions are compatible with the observation that high processing fluency elicits more positive evaluations. On the one hand, we proposed that fluency is itself hedonically marked and experienced as positive (e.g., Reber et al. 1998; Winkielman et al., in press). On the other hand, several researchers suggested that fluency is affectively neutral and proposed accounts of the evaluative effects of fluency that draw on the logic of Schachter and Singer's (1962) two-factor theory of emotion.

One variant is the *non-specific activation model* by Mandler, Nakamura, and Van Zandt's (1987). According to this model, manipulations that increase processing fluency merely ensure a greater activation of the stimulus representation, and this "activation may then be related to any judgment about the stimuli that is stimulus relevant" (Mandler et al. 1987, p. 647). Similarly, the *fluency–attribution model* (e.g., Bornstein & D'Agostino 1994; Jacoby, Kelley, & Dywan 1989; Seamon, Brody, & Kauff 1983) assumes that fluency is affectively neutral and that participants try to arrive at "the most parsimonious and reasonable explanation" of "the experience of perceptual fluency, given situational constraints and the available contextual cues" (Bornstein & D'Agostino 1994, p. 106). In the process, participants will attribute the experience "to liking or, for that matter, to any variety of stimulus properties that the subject is asked to rate" (Bornstein & D'Agostino 1994, p. 107). Finally, the *familiarity–attribution model* proposes that high fluency elicits a vague feeling of familiarity (Bonanno & Stillings 1986; Klinger & Greenwald 1994; Smith 1998), which is also assumed to be affectively neutral and able to influence a variety of judgments, depending on contextual factors. Specifically, "in the context of performing liking judgments, misattributions to liking and disliking are likely because the goal of the subject is to form a preference" (Klinger & Greenwald 1994, p. 77). Such misattributions are considered likely because "subjects are highly susceptible to subtle suggestions as to the particular stimulus qualities that might be taken as the source of their subjective experience" (Smith 1998, p. 416).

Empirically, these two-step models are well supported by studies that assessed non-evaluative judgments. For example, Mandler et al. (1987) observed pronounced focus-of-judgment effects: when asked to assess the brightness of a stimulus, participants rated high fluency stimuli as brighter than low fluency stimuli; yet when asked to rate their darkness, they rated the same stimuli as darker. Similarly, Jacoby and his colleagues (for a review see Kelley & Jacoby 1998) observed that fluency influences a broad range of different judgments, from recognition to truth and fame. Importantly, however, these models did not fare well in the evaluative domain, paralleling the general fate of Schachter and Singer's (1962) two-factor theory of emotion (see Reisenzein 1983). For example, in Mandler et al.'s (1987) studies, as well as a follow-up by Seamon, McKenna and Binder (1998), higher perceptual fluency increased judgments of liking, but not judgments of disliking. This pattern contradicts two-step accounts, but is consistent with the assumption that fluency itself is positively marked. Our own studies reiterate this observation.

In one study (Reber et al. 1998, Study 2), we asked some participants to judge the "prettiness" of the targets, but asked other participants to judge the "ugliness" of the targets. In another study (Reber et al. 1998, Study 3), we asked some participants to make "liking" judgments, but asked others to make "disliking" judgments. In both studies, increased perceptual fluency resulted in higher judgments of "prettiness" and "liking" and lower judgments of "ugliness" and "disliking," as reflected in significant interactions of fluency and judgment focus. In combination, these findings indicate that increased fluency does not facilitate more extreme evaluations in general, but selectively enhances positive evaluations.

Note, however, that these studies are subject to the objection that judgments of disliking or ugliness may be less "natural" than judgments of liking and prettiness. In fact, Mandler et al. (1987) suggested that in their studies repeated exposure did not lead to high disliking because "disliking is a complex judgment, often based on the absence of a liking response. Linguistically, liking is the unmarked and disliking the marked end of the imputed continuum" (p. 647). Hence, participants may prefer to initially evaluate prettiness or likeability of stimuli and only later reverse their response to report it along an ugliness or disliking scale, which would thwart the attempt to induce a focus on ugliness or dislikeability. Although possible in principle, this explanation cannot account for results of Study 1 by Winkielman and Cacioppo (2001). In this study, participants were presented with pictures that varied in processing fluency, manipulated through a visual priming manipulation. Some participants were told to selectively monitor and report only the presence of positive affective reactions, whereas other participants were told to selectively monitor and report only the presence of negative affective reactions. We framed the question this way because it is very hard to argue that it is more "natural" for participants to monitor or report positive responses than negative responses, especially since participants have been able to provide such valence-specific reports in other research (see Cacioppo & Berntson 1994; Cacioppo & Gardner 1997 for reviews). As expected, the results showed a selective effect of the fluency manipulation on affective responses. Specifically, participants who focused on positive affective responses reported more positive evaluations of the stimuli under high rather than low fluency conditions. In contrast to the predictions of two-step models, however, participants who focused on negative affective responses did *not* report more negative evaluations under high rather than low fluency conditions.

In sum, studies that tested the predictions of two-step models in the evaluative domain, using initially neutral stimuli, failed to support the hypothesis that increased fluency may result in more positive as well as more negative evaluations, depending on the focus of the judgment task. Instead, the available findings are consistent with the assumption that fluency is positively marked and selectively enhances positive evaluations of the processed stimuli. The next set of studies takes this conclusion even farther.

Perceptual fluency triggers genuine positive affective responses

Another theoretically important question concerns the nature of the evaluative responses elicited by high fluency. If high fluency is itself hedonically marked, processing facilitation should lead to a genuine increase in positive affect. This increase, in turn, should appear on psychophysiological measures that tap into the positive affect system (Winkielman, Berntson, & Cacioppo, 2000). A demonstration of this is important for several reasons. The presence of genuine affective responses would strengthen our assumption that fluency makes a "hot" contact with the affective system, and is not purely based on "cold" inferences, as argued by proponents of the two-step models. Further, a demonstration of selective positivity of affective responses to fluency would strengthen our assumption that the fluency signal is hedonically marked. Finally, psychophysiological evidence is not subject to the complexities of self-reports, discussed above in the context of Mandler et al.'s (1987) findings.

To provide such evidence, Winkielman and Cacioppo (2001) measured affective responses to fluent stimuli with facial electromyography (fEMG). This technique relies on the observation that positive affective responses manifest themselves in incipient smiles, as reflected by higher activity over the zygomaticus major region (cheek muscle). On the other hand, negative affective responses manifest themselves in incipient frowns, as reflected by higher activity over the corrugator supercilii region (brow muscle). Importantly, fEMG can capture affective responses to subtle, everyday stimuli that do not produce overtly visible facial expressions (Cacioppo, Bush, & Tassinary 1992; Dimberg, Thunberg, & Elmehed 2000).

In the Winkielman and Cacioppo (2001) studies, participants saw pictures of everyday objects varying in fluency, manipulated through visual priming (Study 1) and presentation duration (Study 2), while their fEMG activity was recorded. Several seconds after the presentation of each picture, participants also reported their affective responses (as described above). The results of both studies were very consistent. High fluency was associated with stronger activity over the zygomaticus region (indicative of positive affect), but was not associated with stronger activity of the corrugator region (indicative of negative affect). This effect was obtained across both fluency manipulations and occurred in the first 3 seconds after the presentation of the stimulus, several seconds before participants made their overt judgments.

In sum, Winkielman and Cacioppo's (2001) findings suggest that manipulations of processing fluency have genuine affective consequences, consistent with our assumption that fluency is hedonically marked and closely connected to the affect system. Further, these findings suggest that the affect generated by processing facilitation is positive, thus providing another argument against the assumption of the two-step models that fluency is equally likely to elicit positive as well as negative responses.

Perceptual fluency and the mere-exposure effect

As noted earlier, research into the fluency-evaluation link was initially stimulated by research into the mere-exposure effect (Zajonc 1968). The studies reviewed above are consistent with the idea the repetition may be just one manipulation that leads to an enhancement of fluency. However, our studies also make clear that the role of fluency in the mere-exposure effect is not captured by the two-step models discussed earlier. Instead, it seems that the positive hedonic marking of the fluency signal is the crucial ingredient. This suggestion is consistent with the accumulating evidence that mere exposure elicits positive affect. For example in a recent study by Monahan, Murphy, and Zajonc (2000), participants were subliminally exposed to 25 pictures of Chinese ideographs, and were later asked to report their tonic mood. For some participants, each of the 25 ideographs was different, while for other participants, 5 different ideographs were repeated 5 times each. The results showed that participants who were subliminally exposed to repeated ideographs reported being in a better mood than participants exposed to 25 different ideographs. Moreover, Harmon-Jones and Allen (2001) observed that repeatedly presented stimuli elicited stronger EMG activity over the zygomaticus region, indicative of positive affect, without changing the activity over the corrugator region. In combination, the Monahan et al. (2000) and Harmon-Jones and Allen (2001) studies demonstrate that stimulus repetition can elicit a positive affective response, as has been observed for other manipulations of processing fluency.

The fluency-affect connection

A satisfying theoretical account of the above findings needs to answer two fundamental questions. First, how is the organism able to respond to changes in its own processing dynamics? Second, why is fluency associated with positive affect? A satisfying account must also offer a plausible model of the underlying processes, which should be consistent with the available neurophysiological data. Unfortunately, no available model fully satisfies all of these criteria. However, we suggest that current knowledge offers at least an outline of possible answers.

Cognitive monitoring and affect

Empirical and neurophysiological data suggest the existence of metacognitive mechanisms that provide internal feedback about ongoing processing operations (Metcalfe & Shimamura 1994; Mazzoni & Nelson 1998). These mechanisms may monitor not only the content of the representations being processed, but also the dynamical parameters of cognition. For example, research on the "feeling of familiarity" suggests that people are sensitive to the absolute and relative speed of various mental operations involved in stimulus recognition and categorization (Kelley & Jacoby 1998; Whittlesea & Williams 2001). Similarly, research on the "feeling-of-knowing" phenomenon suggests that people access the strength of their memory traces (Koriat 2000). Further, research on novelty monitoring show that people trace a nonspecific signal of a match between the incoming information and stored representations (Metcalfe 1993). Throughout, the available findings indicate that such non-specific signals about the quality of internal processing can be accessed independently of an explicit representation of the underlying representational content (e.g., Curran 2000). This allows for subjective states that are characterized primarily by a metacognitive experience, such as a feeling of fluency, knowing, or familiarity (see Koriat 2000).

We assume that metacognitive feedback signals are likely to carry both cognitive and affective information, consistent with approaches that view affect as involved in cognitive regulation (e.g., Carver & Scheier 1990; Oatley & Johnson-Laird 1987; Reisenzein 1998; Simon 1967). There are several reasons why metacognitive signals that indicate a high fluency of processing may be connected with positive affective responses. First, high fluency may indicate that an external stimulus is familiar and may therefore trigger a positive response due to a presumably biological predisposition for caution in encounters with novel, and thus potentially harmful, stimuli (Zajonc 1998). The available data support a close correspondence between the familiarity signal and positive affect. For example, fluency manipulations, which produce positive affect, also tend to produce memory illusions, which presumably reflect misattributions of familiarity (Whittlesea 1993; Winkielman et al., in press). Conversely, illusions of familiarity can be produced through unobtrusive inductions of positive affect (Garcia-Marques & Mackie 2000; Phaf, Rotteveel, & Spijksma 1998). Second, the fluency signal may be connected to affect by indicating the state of the ongoing processing operations. Thus, high fluency may indicate progress toward successful recognition and trigger positive affect due to the reinforcing value of maintaining the current, successful cognitive strategy and the ability to free resources for other tasks (Carver & Scheier 1990; Ramachandran & Hirstein 1999; Vallacher & Nowak 1999).[1] Third, fluency may indicate that the current processing is consistent with expectations. We surmise that many of these relations have their mirror images in connections between metacognitive signals of low fluency and negative affect. Thus, signals of cognitive error or violations of expectations have been shown to trigger negative affective responses (Derryberry & Tucker 1994; Fernandez-Duque et al. 2000). Finally, the above ideas converge with observations that mental states characterized by low coherence, such as cognitive dissonance, tend to be experienced as hedonically negative, as reflected in self-reports as well as physiological indices (Devine, Tauer, Barron, & Elliot 1999; Harmon-Jones 2000; Losch & Cacioppo 1990).

The assumed connection between the metacognitive monitoring system and the affect system is further supported by neuroimaging and electrophysiological data. Recent studies point to the brain midfrontal regions, and particularly the anterior cingulate, as one of the primary structures involved in metacognitive regulation (Fernandez-Duque et al. 2000). Interestingly, as part of the limbic system, the anterior cingulate is involved in emotion processes and emotional control (Lane et al. 1998). There are also very close links between circuits responsible for memory and emotion. For example, the hippocampus and amygdala jointly contribute to memory and form a basis of the limbic system (Squire 1992). Although it is still unclear whether the midfrontal region and the limbic structures form an integrated cognitive-emotional system or independent cognitive and emotional subsystems, the accumulating evidence renders a close relationship between metacognition and affect highly plausible.

Possible computational mechanisms

Until recently, the role of dynamical parameters has received surprisingly little research attention (Nowak & Vallacher 1998; Port & Van Gelder 1995). One notable exception is the neural network approach, or connectionism, in which cognition is viewed in terms of the passage of activation among simple, neuron-like units organized in large, densely interconnected networks (Rumelhart & McClelland 1986). The individual units function as simple processors that can influence each other through connections, which vary in strength and sign (facilitatory or inhibitory). This massively interconnected and parallel architecture gives the neural network approach a certain neurophysiological realism and makes it suitable for a wide variety of applications. For more biological applications one can conceptualize the network units as actual neurons, whereas for more psychological applications one can treat the units as blocks of neurons or functional sub-systems (O'Reilly & Munakata 2000). Several different neural network architectures have been proposed that utilize dynamical parameters. Below we focus on a proposal by Lewenstein and Nowak (1989), which illustrates the role of dynamical parameters in learning and recognition using a simple attractor neural network (Hopfield 1982). Importantly, similar mechanisms can be implemented in more complex networks that successfully deal with typical problems plaguing simple attractor networks, such as the plasticity-stability dilemma, and conform to more realistic biological assumptions about the network architecture (Murre, Phaf, & Wolters 1992; Norman, O'Reilly, & Huber 2000; Smith 2000). Further, although the models discussed here have been primarily designed to understand memory processes, similar mechanisms can shed light on the role of dynamical parameters in a variety of mental activities, including cognition-emotion interactions (Beeman, Ortony, & Monti 1995).

In a typical Hopfield network, representations are encoded as attractors of the network, i.e. states into which the network dynamics converge. The processing of information with the network can be seen as a gradual, evolving process, during which each neuron adjusts to the signal coming from other neurons. For example, when presented with a to-be-recognized pattern, the network goes through a series of adjustments and after some time approaches a stable state, an attractor, corresponding to the "recognition" of a particular pattern. Lewenstein and Nowak (1989) proposed that a typical Hopfield model can be extended with a simple control mechanism, which allows the network to monitor the dynamics of its own processing. Such a control mechanism can draw on a variety of dynamical parameters, such as volatility, signal strength, coherence, settling time, and so on. These formally related parameters can then be used by the network to roughly estimate the characteristics of the stimuli being processed as well as monitor the quality of its own processing (Lewenstein & Nowak 1989).

The available simulations focused on how monitoring the dynamical parameters of cognition can allow the network to estimate proximity to its closest attractor during the recognition process. This, in turn, allows the network to estimate the likelihood that the presented pattern is "known." Specifically, two dynamical parameters were identified. The first parameter is the network's "volatility," or the proportion of neurons changing their state at a given point. When the incoming, "to-be-recognized" pattern matches or closely approximates a known pattern, corresponding to one of the attractors (memories), the network is characterized by a relatively small proportion of neurons changing their state. When the incoming pattern is novel and thus does not approximate one of the attractors, the network is characterized by a large number of neurons changing their state. The second means of implementing a control mechanism involves checking the coherence of the signals received by the neurons. In the vicinity of an attractor (old pattern), the signals arriving from other neurons at a given neuron are consistent in dictating its state. However, when the network is far from an attractor (new pattern), the signals arriving from other neurons at a given neuron dictate conflicting states. A closely related criterion is the signal-to-noise ratio, or differentiation. In the vicinity of the attractor (old pattern), signals from other neurons typically add up, resulting in a relatively large summary signal dictating the state of a given neuron. However, far from an attractor (new pattern), signals from other neurons cancel each other, resulting in a relatively weak summary signal dictating the state of a given neuron. As a consequence, the processing of "old" patterns is characterized by a higher signal-to-noise ratio than the processing of "new" patterns.[2]

Both implementations of the control mechanism (via volatility or coherence/differentiation) allow the network to estimate whether a pattern is "new" or "old" (i.e., proximity to its closest attractor) within the first few processing steps. Specifically, the actual completion of the recognition process in the above model usually takes about 3–6 steps of a Monte Carlo simulation. Yet, it is possible to determine the novelty of incoming stimuli by monitoring how frequently a mere 10% of the neurons change their state at the first Monte Carlo step, which amounts to only 0.1 Monte Carlo step (Lewenstein & Nowak 1989).[3] Thus, these computations allow for an estimation of novelty that far precedes completion of the recognition process.

The assumptions of the above model are consistent with neuropsychological evidence. For example, early work on the orienting response shows that novel stimuli elicit a non-specific, undifferentiated activity, which gradually decreases with repetition (Skarda & Freeman 1987; Sokolov 1963). More recent studies using single cell recording and neuroimaging suggest that stimulus repetition tends to decrease non-specific activation and leads to more selective firing (Desimone, Miller, Chelazzi, & Lueschow 1995; Rolls, Baylis, Hasselmo, & Nalwa 1989). One interpretation of these data is that stimulus familiarization leads to a gradual differentiation of the neurons that represent the incoming stimulus from neurons that do not represent the stimulus (Norman et al. 2000). Such differentiation processes may occur on the perceptual as well as conceptual level (e.g., McClelland & Chappell 1998).

A simulation

The usefulness of the above model for thinking about the relation between processing dynamics and affect is suggested by its success in simulating actual human data. For example, Drogosz and Nowak (1998) used a dynamic attractor neural network to simulate the behavior of participants in a subliminal mere-exposure study by Seamon, Marsh, and Brody (1984). In their study, Seamon and colleagues exposed participants to 50 repetitions of polygons, presented at exposure times ranging from 2 to 48 milliseconds. As in other mere exposure experiments, participants showed an increased preference for repeated polygons, even when these polygons were only shown for a mere 2 or 8 milliseconds. Moreover, their preference increased with increasing exposure times, but reached asymptote at 24 milliseconds. In contrast, recognition was at chance at low durations (2 and 8 milliseconds), and then gradually increased up to 90% recognition at 48 milliseconds.

Drogosz and Nowak (1998) showed that these asymmetric effects of exposure time on preference and recognition can be closely simulated by assuming that the affective response represents a non-specific signal about the early dynamics of the network, as indexed by the number of changes of neuron states at the 0.1 MC step, whereas the recognition response represents a stabilization of the network on a specific pattern, at about the 6 MC step. A psychological interpretation that can be attached to these simulation data is that at very short presentation durations, the participants only have access to the non-specific fluency signal, which elicits positive affect and influences their preference judgments. With progressively longer presentation duration, the fluency signal (affective response) increases only marginally, whereas the recognition response continues to grow until it reaches nearly perfect performance.

The above simulations explored the role of dynamical parameters in the context of stimulus repetition, and are best suited to understanding the mere-exposure effect (Drogosz & Nowak 1998). Many prior exposures to a pattern establish a relatively strong memory for this pattern, whereas few prior exposures establish a relatively weak memory for the pattern. Test patterns with relatively stronger memories (i.e., stronger attractors) are processed with higher processing fluency (less volatility, more coherent signals) than test patterns with weaker or no memories. These differential fluency signals are picked up early on, as indicated by the simulation, and precede the extraction of stimulus information. Because the fluency signal is hedonically marked, it allows for evaluative responses prior to stimulus recognition, as initially reported by Kunst-Wilson and Zajonc (1980).[4]

Computational models of this type can also help us conceptualize the results of studies that used all novel patterns and manipulated the fluency of processing through procedures like priming, figure-ground contrast, and presentation duration. To account for these effects, the model requires only minimal modifications. Specifically, the above simulations were carried out in attractor networks composed of neurons with binary states, where a state of the neuron corresponds either to the presence or the absence of a feature encoded by this neuron (Hopfield 1982). However, the same "fluency" criteria (volatility, coherence, differentiation) apply to networks with continuous neurons, where the state of a neuron encodes the degree to which a feature is present or activated (Hopfield 1984; O'Reilly & Munakata 2000). In such networks, priming may correspond either to the pre-activation of neurons that encode the pattern (activation-based priming) or to the slight changes in weights between the neurons (weight-based priming). The effects of the prime and the actual target sum up in determining the state of neurons. This results in more extreme values of activation (i.e., better differentiation) of the neurons for primed versus non-primed patterns. The influence of presentation duration may be conceptualized as reflecting a similar process, in which patterns presented for a long time are represented by more extreme values of activation than patterns presented for a short time. Finally, manipulations such as figure-ground contrast or clarity of the perceived pattern should have similar effects on the "fluency" signal. Because salient features of the stimulus are encoded by more extreme states of neurons, perceiving a pattern characterized by a high contrast or high clarity results in more differentiated states of the neurons, and thus stronger signals in the network.

In sum, according to the above computational model, liking for novel and even completely unfamiliar (e.g., abstract) patterns may be influenced by manipulations such as priming, presentation duration, figure–ground contrast, and clarity because all these manipulations reduce the network's volatility and increase its signal-to-noise ratio. Presumably, such changes result in a signal of fluency, which in turn triggers a positive affective response via the mechanisms discussed above.[5] It is worth emphasizing that the above manipulations have a similar effect on processing dynamics as previous repetition. This again highlights the parallel between the work on the mere-exposure effect and our empirical findings presented above.

Extensions and boundary conditions

The principles discussed in the current chapter may be extended in several ways. One interesting question is whether the above notions can explain other important findings on preferences. For example, numerous studies show that people prefer stimuli that are average or prototypical, including faces, birds, cars, watches, and colors (e.g., Halberstadt & Rhodes 2000; Langlois & Roggman 1990; Martindale & Moore 1988; Rhodes & Tremewan 1996). Other studies show preferences for symmetrical facial and non-facial stimuli (e.g., Berlyne 1974; Palmer 1991; Rhodes, Proffitt, Grady, & Sumich 1998). These observations are often explained by assuming a biological, built-in mechanism (Etcoff 1999; Pinker 1998). This is a plausible hypothesis – after all, it has been shown in several species that symmetry and averageness are indicative of mate value (e.g., Thornhill & Gangstead 1993). However, average (prototypical) and symmetrical stimuli also are associated with more fluent processing, as shown in several empirical studies (Checkosky & Whitlock 1973; Posner & Keele 1968; Palmer 1991) as well as computer simulations (Enquist & Arak 1994; Johnstone 1994; Rumelhart & McClelland 1986).[6] Thus, preference for averageness and symmetry may be just another example of the affective marking of processing fluency. Of course, the reverse possibility is also logically possible. That is, the reason why one can elicit preferences by facilitating processing with means other than symmetry or prototypicality (or familiarity) may potentially be that these manipulations feed into mechanisms designed to track biologically relevant dimensions. Future studies may examine if preferences for symmetry and prototypicality can be fully accounted for by differences in perceptual fluency.

Another topic to be addressed in future studies is the role of conceptual fluency. Note that the studies discussed in the current chapter manipulated perceptual fluency, that is, the ease of low-level operations concerned primarily with processing of stimulus form. Accordingly, they used manipulations like visual priming, duration, figure-ground contrast, repetition, etc. However, the logic of our argument extends as well to conceptual fluency, that is, high-level operations concerned primarily with processing of stimulus meaning, and its relation to other semantic knowledge structures (McGlone & Tofighbakhsh 2000; Roediger 1990; Schacter 1992; Whittlesea 1993). We recently began to explore the effects of conceptual fluency on liking and memory judgments using manipulations like semantic priming and associative learning and obtained findings that are fully compatible with the logic offered in the present chapter (see Winkielman et al., in press).

Boundary conditions

As discussed above, the fluency signal is available at very early stages of information processing, allowing for a quick affective response. Therefore, fluency effects on preferences are likely to be strongest under conditions that limit the extraction of additional information, which may compete with the fluency signal in the computation of a preference judgment. Such conditions include time pressure, limited cognitive capacity and a lack of motivation to process the stimulus in sufficient detail. In fact, preliminary data from our labs suggest that fluency effects on evaluations increase under cognitive load conditions (Winkielman et al., in press) and decrease as more stimulus information is extracted (Reber & Schwarz 2001). Similarly, the fluency signal may be the most informative input when little other information can be extracted from the stimulus. Consistent with these assumptions, exposure frequency, exposure duration and figure-ground contrast have been found to have the strongest influence on preference judgments when the stimuli are novel, neutral and presented for relatively short durations (e.g., Bornstein 1994; Reber & Schwarz 2001).

When fluency derives from incidental variables, like exposure duration, exposure frequency or priming manipulations, awareness of these variables is likely to undermine the perceived informational value of fluency and its accompanying affective response. This is consistent with studies showing that mere-exposure effects decrease with increasing awareness of the manipulation (Bornstein & D'Agostino 1992). Further, recent data from our lab show that fluency effects on preferences disappear when the source of fluency is made salient or when participants are informed that their affective reactions may come from an irrelevant, external source (Winkielman et al., in press). These findings parallel similar observations with regard to other sources of experiential information (for a review see Schwarz & Clore 1996).

It is also likely that the impact of experienced fluency is moderated by the person's processing expectations, which provide context-dependent, implicit norms for processing ease associated with each item. Whittlesea and Williams (2001) observed, for example, that participants who initially expected a stimulus to be processed with low fluency were more likely to attribute high processing fluency to prior exposure than participants who initially expected the stimulus to be processed with high fluency. Hence, the former were more likely than the latter to conclude that they had seen the stimulus before. The extent to which processing expectations may moderate the influence of fluency on preference judgment has so far received no attention.

Under some specific conditions, it is also possible that high fluency may lead to more *negative* evaluations. Although this has not yet been observed, it is conceivable under two conditions. First, in an environment where, say, familiarity or prototypicality are associated with danger, fluency may become an automatic cue to negativity. Second, and less speculative, such reversal of the default positive influence may occur when people are lead to consciously believe that the experience of processing fluency is an indicator of negative value. In this case, their initially automatic positive reaction to high fluency may be overridden by deliberate, theory-driven inference processes that result in a negative judgment. That individuals' "naive" theories about the meaning of subjective experiences can determine which inferences they draw from cognitive feelings, such as recall difficulty or familiarity, is well documented (see Skurnik, Schwarz, & Winkielman 2000; Winkielman & Schwarz 2001), but has not yet been tested for the influence of fluency on evaluative judgments. Further, this possibility assumes that the fluency signal is strong and distinct enough to be consciously available and accessible to strategic inferences. Future studies may address this issue.

Finally, to avoid overgeneralization, it is worth emphasizing that some evaluative judgments, like complex aesthetic judgments or judgments of morality, are likely to involve extensive consideration of stimulus meaning, and may be based on sophisticated inferences from multiple sources of information.

In summary, this discussion of boundary conditions indicates that fluency-based affective reactions are likely to have most impact under the conditions that are also known to give rise to pronounced mood effects in evaluative judgment: When little other information is available; when the person's processing capacity or motivation are low, thus limiting more deliberate information search and integration; and when the informational value of the affect has not been called into question (for discussions see Schwarz 1990; Schwarz & Clore 1996). However, these parallels should not distract from the unique character of fluency-based affect. Most important, fluency-based affect is not based on an analysis of stimulus meaning, in contrast to specific emotions, which involve complex, meaning-based appraisals. Instead, fluency-based affect results from the dynamics of information processing itself. As such, the work described in the chapter adds another important piece to the mechanisms that make us the "evaluating human."

Author's note

We thank John Cacioppo, Tedra Fazendeiro, Yuko Munakata, Randy O'Reilly, Rolf Reber, and the University of Denver Cognitive Research Group for helpful discussions of these issues. Preparation of this chapter was partially supported by a fellowship from the Center for Advanced Study in the Behavioral Sciences to Norbert Schwarz and by the Internationalisation Grant from the University of Denver to Piotr Winkielman.

Notes

1. The possibility that positive affect is triggered by signals of "recognition progress" does not require an assumption that a person has to actually achieve the goal of recognition to experience positive affect. Instead, a signal indicating that the ongoing processing moves towards recognition should be sufficient. This suggestion distinguishes our view from proposals that link positive affective responses to achievement of cognitive sub-goals (Carver & Scheier 1990). Our interpretation fits the available data better than the "affect-as-achievement" interpretation. After all, in our studies, participants have no problem achieving the goal stimulus recognition, yet they experience different affective reactions depending on the fluency of the recognition.

2. In neural networks, the strength of a signal arriving at a neuron is a product of the state of the neuron that is sending the signal and the weight of the connection. For novel patterns, the connections among neurons are uncorrelated with the states of the neurons. Thus, the distribution of the summary signals received by neurons during recognition of a novel pattern resembles a normal distribution with a mean of zero and a standard deviation propor-

tional to 1/N, where N corresponds to the number of synapses transmitting the signal to a neuron.

3. Checking the coherence of incoming signals makes it possible to estimate not only the global novelty of the whole pattern, but also the novelty of fragments in the perceived pattern, such as elements of an object or objects in a scene (Zochowski, Lewenstein, & Nowak 1994).

4. The above simulations were conducted using very similar patterns, as is typical in the mere-exposure studies. Accordingly, the absolute processing fluency of a given pattern was a reliable indicator of its "oldness." For the fluency signal to be informative in a more realistic situation, in which stimuli differ widely in overall signal strength, the network needs to scale the absolute value of the fluency signal for the particular pattern against the expected value (Whittlesea & Williams 2001).

5. Our discussion of possible computational mechanisms is neutral on whether positive affect is triggered because high fluency indicates that a stimulus is likely to have been encountered before, because the stimulus is likely to be recognized, or because the processing is consistent with expectations. Our discussion also leaves open whether positive affect is directly triggered by the signal of fluency, without mediation of conscious awareness, or requires subjective mediation (i.e., a feeling that a stimulus is easy to process).

6. The effects of stimulus similarity (prototypicality) and symmetry are consistent with the above computational model (Lewenstein & Nowak 1989). Similarity between two patterns may be operationalized as the correlation between states of neurons representing the first and the second pattern. Accordingly, a novel pattern similar to one of the known patterns will trigger a stronger fluency signal than a dissimilar pattern. The same logic also suggests that novel patterns that follow the typical relations among neurons representing known patterns will trigger stronger fluency signals than novel patterns that violate typical relations among neurons. One example of such a case are symmetrical patterns. Objects in the real world typically are characterized by vertical symmetry (Palmer 1991). As a result, the connections between pairs of neurons representing the left and the right side of an object are typically positive. Accordingly, novel, but symmetrical patterns should produce a strong "fluency" signal because signals between the neurons that encode symmetrical features are coherent and thus add up.

References

Anderson, N. H. (1981). *Foundations of information integration theory.* New York: Academic Press.
Bar, M., & Biederman, I. (1998). Subliminal visual priming. *Psychological Science, 9,* 464–469.
Bargh, J. A. (1996). Automaticity in social psychology. In E. T. Higgins, & A. W. Kruglanski (Ed.), *Social Psychology: Handbook of Basic Principles* (pp. 169–183). New York: Guilford Press.

Beeman, M., Ortony, A., & Monti, L. A. (1995). Emotion-cognition interactions. In M. A. Arbib (Ed.), *The handbook of brain theory and neural networks* (pp. 360–363). Cambridge, MA: MIT Press.

Berlyne, D. E. (1974). *Studies in the new experimental aesthetics: Steps toward an objective psychology of aesthetic appreciation.* Washington, 1974: Hemisphere Co.

Bonanno, G. A., & Stillings, N. A. (1986). Preference, familiarity, and recognition after repeated brief exposures to random geometric shapes. *American Journal of Psychology, 99*, 403–415.

Bornstein, R. F. (1989). Exposure and affect: Overview and meta-analysis of research, 1968–1987. *Psychological Bulletin, 106*, 265–289.

Bornstein, R. F., & D'Agostino, P. R. (1994). The attribution and discounting of perceptual fluency: Preliminary tests of a perceptual fluency/attributional model of the mere exposure effect. *Social Cognition, 12*, 103–128.

Bornstein, R. F., & D'Agostino, P. R. (1992). Stimulus recognition and the mere exposure effect. *Journal of Personality and Social Psychology, 63*, 545–552.

Cacioppo, J. T., Bush, L. K., & Tassinary, L. G. (1992). Microexpressive facial actions as a function of affective stimuli: Replication and extension. *Personality and Social Psychology Bulletin, 18*, 515–526.

Carver, C. S., & Scheier, M. F. (1990). Origins and functions of positive and negative affect: A control-process view. *Psychological Review, 97*, 19–35.

Checkosky, S. F., & Whitlock, D. (1973). The effects of pattern goodness on recognition time in a memory search task. *Journal of Experimental Psychology, 100*, 341–348.

Curran, T. (2000). Brain potentials of recollection and familiarity. *Memory and Cognition, 28*, 923–938.

Damasio, A. R. (1994). *Descartes' error: Emotion, reason and the human brain.* New York: Grosset/Putnam.

Derryberry, D., & Tucker, D. M. (1994). Motivating the focus of attention. In P. M. N. & S. Kitayama (Eds.), (pp. 167–196). San Diego: Academic Press.

Desimone, R., Miller, E. K., Chelazzi, L., & Lueschow, A. (1995). Multiple memory systems in the visual cortex. In M. S. Gazzaniga (Ed.), *The cognitive neurosciences* (pp. 475–490). Cambridge, MA: MIT Press.

Devine, P., Tauer, J. M., Barron, K. E., & Elliot, A. J. (1999). Moving beyond attitude change in the study of dissonance-related processes. In E. Harmon-Jones & J. Mills (Eds.), *Cognitive Dissonance: Progress on a pivotal theory in social psychology* (pp. 297–323). Washington, DC: APA.

Dimberg, U., Thunberg, M., & Elmehed, K. (2000). Unconscious facial reactions to emotional facial expressions. *Psychological Science, 11*, 86–89.

Drogosz, M., & Nowak, A. (1998). Simulation theory of the mere exposure effect: The EXAC neural network model. *Unpublished manuscript.*

Enquist, M., & Arak, A. (1994). Symmetry, beauty and evolution. *Nature, 372*, 169–172.

Etcoff, N. (1999). *Survival of the prettiest: The science of beauty.* New York: Doubleday.

Fernandez-Duque, D., Baird, J. A., & Posner, M. I. (2000). Executive attention and metacognitive regulation. *Consciousness and Cognition, 9*, 288–307.

Fishbein, M., & Ajzen, I. (1975). *Belief, attitude, intention, and behavior: An introduction to theory and research.* Reading, MA: Addison-Wesley.

Frijda, N. H. (1988). The laws of emotions. *American Psychologist, 43*, 349–358.
Garcia-Marques, T., & Mackie, D. M. (2000). The positive feeling of familiarity: Mood as an information processing regulation mechanism. In H. Bless & J. Forgas (Eds.), *The message within: The role of subjective experience in social cognition and behavior* (pp. 240–261). Philadelphia: Psychology Press.
Haber, R. N., & Hershenson M. (1965). The effects of repeated brief exposures on growth of a percept. *Journal of Experimental Psychology, 69*, 40–46.
Halberstadt J., & Rhodes G. (2000). The attractiveness of nonface averages: Implications for an evolutionary explanation of the attractiveness of average faces. *Psychological Science, 4*, 285–289.
Harmon-Jones, E. (2000). A cognitive dissonance theory perspective on the role of emotion in the maintenance and change of beliefs and attitudes. In N. H. Frijda, A. R. S. Manstead, & S. Bem (Eds.), *Emotion and Beliefs* (pp. 185–211). Cambridge, UK: Cambridge University Press.
Harmon-Jones, E., & Allen, J. J. B. (2001). The role of affect in the mere exposure effect: Evidence from psychophysiological and individual differences approaches. *Personality and Social Psychology Bulletin, 27*, 889–898.
Higgins, E. T. (1998). The aboutness principle: A pervasive influence on human inference. *Social Cognition, 16*, 173–198.
Hopfield, J. J. (1982). Neural networks and physical systems with emergent collective computational abilities. *Proceedings of the National Academy of Sciences, 79*, 2554–2558.
Hopfield, J. J. (1984). Neurons with graded response have collective computational properties like those of two-state neurons. *Proceedings of the National Academy of Sciences, 81*, 3088–3092.
Jacoby, L. L. (1983). Perceptual enhancement: Persistent effects of an experience. *Journal of Experimental Psychology Learning, Memory, and Cognition, 9*, 21–38.
Jacoby, L. L., & Dallas M. (1981). On the relationship between autobiographical memory and perceptual learning. *Journal of Experimental Psychology: General, 110*, 306–340.
Jacoby, L. L., Kelley C. M., & Dywan J. (1989). Memory attributions. In H. L. Roediger & F. I. M. Craik (Eds.), *Varieties of memory and consciousness: Essays in honour of Endel Tulving* (pp. 391–422). Hillsdale, NJ: Erlbaum.
Johnstone, R. A. (1994). Female preference for symmetrical males as a by-product of selection for mate recognition. *Nature, 372*, 172–175.
Kelley, C. M., & Jacoby, L. L. (1998). Subjective reports and process dissociation: Fluency, knowing, and feeling. *Acta Psychologica, 98*, 127–140.
Klinger, M. R., & Greenwald A. G. (1994). Preferences need no inferences?: The cognitive basis of unconscious mere exposure effects. In P. M. Niedenthal & S. Kitayama (Eds.), *The heart's eye* (pp. 67–85). San Diego: Academic Press.
Koriat, A. (2000). The feeling of knowing: Some metatheoretical implications for consciousness and control. *Consciousness and Cognition, 9*, 149–171.
Kunst-Wilson, W. R., & Zajonc, R. B. (1980). Affective discrimination of stimuli that cannot be recognized. *Science, 207*, 557–558.

Lane, R. D., Reiman, E. M., Axelrod, B., Yun, L., Holmes, A., & Schwartz, G. E. (1998). Neural correlates of levels of emotional awareness: Evidence of an interaction between emotion and attention in the anterior cingulate cortex. *Journal of Cognitive Neuroscience, 10,* 525–535.

Langlois, J. H., & Roggman, L. A. (1990). Attractive faces are only average. *Psychological Science, 1,* 115–121.

LeDoux, J. E. (1996). *The Emotional Brain.* New York: Touchstone.

Lewenstein, M., & Nowak, A. (1989). Recognition with self-control in neural networks. *Physical Review, 40,* 4652–4664.

Losch, M. E., & Cacioppo, J. T. (1990). Cognitive dissonance may enhance sympathetic tonus, but attitudes are changed to reduce negative affect rather than arousal. *Journal of Experimental Social Psychology, 26,* 289–304.

Mackworth, J. F. (1963). The duration of the visual image. *Canadian Journal of Psychology, 17,* 62–81.

Mandler, G., Nakamura, Y., & Van Zandt, B. J. (1987). Nonspecific effects of exposure on stimuli that cannot be recognized. *Journal of Experimental Psychology: Learning, Memory, and Cognition, 13,* 646–648.

Martindale, C., & Moore, K. (1988). Priming, prototypicality, and preference. *Journal of Experimental Psychology: Human Perception and Performance, 14,* 661–670.

Mazzoni, G., & Nelson, T. O. (Eds.). (1998). *Metacognition and cognitive neuropsychology: Monitoring and control processes.* Mahwah, NJ.: Lawrence Erlbaum.

McClelland, J. L., & Chappell, M. (1998). Familiarity breeds differentiation: A Bayesian approach to the effects of experience in recognition memory. *Psychological Review, 105,* 724–760.

McGlone, M. S., & Tofighbakhsh, J. (2000). Birds of a feather flock conjointly (?): Rhyme as reason in aphorisms. *Psychological Science, 11,* 424–428.

Metcalfe, J. (1993). Novelty monitoring, metacognition, and control in a composite holographic associative recall model: Implications for Korsakoff Amnesia. *Psychological Review, 100,* 3–22.

Metcalfe, J., & Shimamura, A. P. (Eds.). (1994). *Metacognition: Knowing about knowing.* Cambridge, MA: MIT Press.

Monahan, J. L., Murphy S. T., & Zajonc R. B. (2000). Subliminal mere exposure: Specific, general, and diffuse effects. *Psychological Science, 6,* 462–466.

Murre, J. M. J., Phaf, R. H., & Wolters, G. (1992). CALM: Categorizing and learning module. *Neutral Networks,* 55–82.

Norman, K. A., O'Reilly, R. C., & Huber, D. E. (2000). Modeling hippocampal and neocortical contributions to recognition memory. *Poster presented at the Cognitive Neuroscience Society Meeting, San Francisco, CA.*

Nowak, A., & Vallacher R. R. (1998). *Dynamical social psychology.* New York: Guilford Press.

O'Reilly, R. C., & Munakata, Y. (2000). *Computational explorations in cognitive neuroscience: Understanding the mind by simulating the brain.* Cambridge, MA: MIT Press.

Oatley, K., & Johnson-Laird, P. (1987). Towards a cognitive theory of emotions. *Cognition and Emotion, 1,* 29–50.

Oehman, A., Flykt, A., & Lundqvist, D. (2000). Unconscious Emotion: Evolutionary perspectives, psychophysiological data and neuropsychological mechanisms. In R. Lane & L. Nadel (Eds.), *Cognitive Neuroscience of Emotion* (pp. 296–327). New York: Oxford University Press.

Ortony, A., Clore, G. L., & Collins, A. (1988). *The cognitive structure of emotions.* New York: Cambridge University Press.

Palmer, S. E. (1991). Goodness, gestalt, groups, and Garner: Local symmetry subgroups as a theory of figural goodness. In J. R. Pomerantz & G. R. Lockhead (Eds.), *Perception of Structure.* Washington, DC: APA.

Phaf, R. H., Rotteveel, M., & Spijksma, F. P. (under review). False recognition and affective priming.

Pinker, S. (1997). *How the mind works.* New York: Norton.

Poldrack, R. A., & Logan, G. D. (1998). What is the mechanism for fluency in successive recognition? *Acta Psychologica, 98,* 167–181.

Port, R. T., & van Gelder, T. (1995). *Mind as motion: Exploration in the dynamics of cognition.* Cambridge, MA: MIT Press.

Posner, M. I., & Keele S. W. (1968). On the genesis of abstract ideas. *Journal of Experimental Psychology, 77,* 353–363.

Ramachandran, V. S., & Hirstein, W. (1999). The science of art: A neurological theory of aesthetic experience. *Journal of Consciousness Studies, 6,* 15–51.

Reber, R., & Schwarz, N. (2001). The hot fringes of consciousness: Perceptual fluency and affect. *Consciousness & Emotion, 2,* 223–231.

Reber, R., Winkielman, P., & Schwarz, N. (1998). Effects of perceptual fluency on affective judgments. *Psychological Science, 9,* 45–48.

Reisenzein, R. (1983). The Schachter theory of emotion: Two decades later. *Psychological Bulletin, 94,* 239–264.

Reisenzein, R. (1998). A theory of emotions as metarepresentational states of mind. In A. H. Fischer (Ed.), *SRE'98. Proceedings of the 10th Conference of the International Society for Research on Emotions* (pp. 186–191). Faculty of Psychology: Amsterdam.

Rhodes, G., Proffitt, F., Grady, J. M., & Sumich, A. (1998). Facial symmetry and the perception of beauty. *Psychonomic Bulletin & Review, 5,* 659–669.

Rhodes, G., & Tremewan, T. (1996). Averageness, exaggeration, and facial attractiveness. *Psychological Science, 7,* 105–110.

Roediger, H. L. (1990). Implicit memory: Retention without remembering. *American Psychologist, 45,* 1043–1056.

Rolls, E. T., Baylis, G. C., Hasselmo, M. E., & Nalwa, V. (1989). The effect of learning on the face selective responses of neurons in the cortex in the superior temporal sulcus of the monkey. *Experimental Brain Research, 76,* 153–164.

Rumelhart, D. E., & McClelland, J. L. (Eds.). (1986). *Parallel Distributed Processes: Exploration in Microstructure of Cognition.* Cambridge, MA: MIT Press.

Schachter, S. E., & Singer J. (1962). Cognitive, social and physiological determinants of emotional state. *Psychological Review, 69,* 379–399.

Schacter, D. L. (1992). Understanding implicit memory: A cognitive neuroscience approach. *American Psychologist, 47,* 559–569.

Schwarz, N. (1990). Feeling as information: Informational and motivational functions of affective states. In E. T. Higgins & R. M. Sorrentino (Eds.), *Handbook of motivation and cognition* (pp. 527–561). New York: Guilford Press.

Schwarz, N. (1998). Accessible content and accessibility experiences: The interplay of declarative and experiential information in judgment. *Personality and Social Psychology Review, 2*, 87–99.

Schwarz, N., & Clore, G. L. (1983). Mood, misattribution, and judgments of well-being: Informative and directive functions of affective states. *Journal of Personality and Social Psychology, 45*, 513–523.

Schwarz, N., & Clore, G. L. (1996). Feelings and phenomenal experiences. In E. T. Higgins & A. W. Kruglanski (Eds.), *Social Psychology: Handbook of Basic Principles*. New York: The Guilford Press.

Seamon, J. G., Brody, N., & Kauff, D. M. (1983). Affective discrimination of stimuli that are not recognized: Effects of shadowing, masking, and cerebral laterality. *Journal of Experimental Psychology: Learning, Memory, and Cognition, 9*, 544–555.

Seamon, J. G., Marsh, R. L., & Brody, N. (1984). Critical importance of exposure duration for affective discrimination of stimuli that are not recognized. *Journal of Experimental Psychology Learning, Memory, and Cognition, 10*, 465–469.

Seamon, J. G., McKenna, P. A., & Binder, N. (1998). The mere exposure effect is differentially sensitive to different judgment tasks. *Consciousness and Cognition, 7*, 85–102.

Simon, H. A. (1967). Motivational and emotional controls of cognition. *Psychological Review, 74*, 29–39.

Skarda, C. A., & Freeman, W. J. (1987). How brains make chaos in order to make sense of the world. *Behavioral and Brain Sciences, 10*, 161–195.

Skurnik, I., Schwarz, N., & Winkielman, P. (2000). Drawing inferences from feelings: The role of naive beliefs. In H. Bless & J. P. Forgas (Eds.), *The message within: The role of subjective experience in social cognition and behavior* (pp. 162–175). Philadelphia: Psychology Press.

Smith, E. R. (1998). Mental representation and memory. In D. T. Gilbert, S. T. Fiske, & G. Lindzey (Eds.), *The Handbook of Social Psychology* (pp. 269–322). Boston, MA: The McGraw-Hill Companies, Inc.

Smith, E. R. (2000). Subjective experience of familiarity: Functional basis in connectionist memory. In H. Bless & J. P. Forgas (Eds.), *The message within: The role of subjective experience in social cognition and behavior* (pp. 109–124). Philadelphia: Psychology Press.

Snodgrass, J. G., & Vanderwart M. (1980). A standardized set of 260 pictures: Norms for name agreement, image agreement, familiarity, and visual complexity. *Journal of Experimental Psychology: Human Learning and Memory, 6*, 174–215.

Sokolov, E. N. (1963). *Perception and the orienting reflex*. NY: MacMillan.

Squire, L. R. (1992). Memory and the hippocampus: A synthesis from findings with rats, monkeys, and humans. *Psychological Review, 99*, 195–231.

Thornhill, R., & Gangestad, S. W. (1993). Human facial beauty: Averageness, symmetry, and parasite resistance. *Human Nature, 4*, 237–269.

Vallacher, R. R., & Nowak, A. (1999). The dynamics of self-regulation. In R. S. Jr. Wyer (Ed.), *Perspectives on behavioral self-regulation* (pp. 241–259). Mahwah: Lawrence Erlbaum Associates.

Whittlesea, B. W. A. (1993). Illusions of familiarity. *Journal of Experimental Psychology: Learning, Memory, and Cognition, 19,* 1235–1253.

Whittlesea, B. W. A., Jacoby L. L., & Girard K. (1990). Illusions of immediate memory: Evidence of an attributional basis for feelings of familiarity and perceptual quality. *Journal of Memory and Language, 29,* 716–732.

Whittlesea, B. W. A., & Williams, L. D. (2001). The Discrepancy-Attribution Hypothesis: I. The Heuristic Basis of Feelings of Familiarity. *Journal of Experimental Psychology: Learning, Memory, and Cognition, 27,* 3–13.

Winkielman P., Berntson, G. G., & Cacioppo, J. T. (2001). The psychophysiological perspective on the social mind. In A. Tesser & N. Schwarz (Eds.), *Blackwell Handbook of Social Psychology: Intraindividual Processes* (pp. 89-108). Oxford: Blackwell.

Winkielman, P., & Cacioppo, J. T. (2001). Mind at ease puts a smile on the face: Psychophysiological evidence that processing facilitation increases positive affect. *Journal of Personality and Social Psychology, 81,* 989–1000.

Winkielman, P., & Schwarz, N. (2001). How pleasant was your childhood? Beliefs about memory shape inferences from experienced difficulty of recall. *Psychological Science, 2,* 176–179.

Winkielman, P., Schwarz, N., Fazendeiro, T., & Reber, R. (in press). The hedonic marking of processing fluency: Implications for evaluative judgment. In J. Musch & K. C. Klauer (Eds.), *The Psychology of Evaluation: Affective Processes in Cognition and Emotion.* Mahwah, NJ: Lawrence Erlbaum.

Winkielman, P., Zajonc, R. B., & Schwarz, N. (1997). Subliminal affective priming resists attributional interventions. *Cognition and Emotion, 11,* 433–465.

Witherspoon, D., & Allan, L. G. (1985). The effects of a prior presentation on temporal judgments in a perceptual identification task. *Memory and Cognition, 13,* 103–111.

Zajonc, R. B. (1968). Attitudinal effects of mere exposure. *Journal of Personality and Social Psychology: Monograph Supplement, 9,* 1–27.

Zajonc, R. B. (1998). Emotions. In D. T. Gilbert, S. T. Fiske, & G. Lindzey (Eds.), *The Handbook of Social Psychology* (pp. 591–632). Boston, MA: McGraw-Hill.

Zajonc, R. B. (2000). Feeling and thinking: Closing the debate over the independence of affect. In J. P. Forgas (Ed.), *Feeling and thinking: The role of affect in social cognition* (pp. 31–58). Cambridge: Cambridge University Press.

Zochowski, M., Lewenstein, M., & Nowak, A. (1994). Local noise in neural networks with self-control. *International Journal of Neural Systems, 5,* 287–298.

CHAPTER 6

Consciousness, computation, and emotion

Jesse J. Prinz
Washington University

Emotions are characteristically conscious. That is to say they feel like something. It feels like something to be elated, irate, or disgusted. Some researchers think that emotions *must* be felt. They claim there is no such thing as an unconscious emotion. As we will see, this view is controversial. What is uncontroversial is the claim emotions are *often* conscious. To that extent, all emotion researchers need an explanation of emotional consciousness. How is it that emotions come to be felt?

To provide a theory of emotional consciousness, one must provide a theory of emotions, and one must provide a theory of consciousness. These are two of the greatest challenges facing cognitive science. At this stage in inquiry, any theory of emotional consciousness must be programmatic. A theory of emotional consciousness must rest on theories of emotion and consciousness that are, of necessity, speculative and incomplete. Speculations can be fruitful guides for future research. Therefore, I intend to speculate. Section 1 sketches a theory of emotion, Section 2 sketches a theory of consciousness, and Section 3 integrates these into a theory of emotional consciousness.

The theories of emotion and consciousness that I offer qualify as computational. As I use the term, a computational theory is one that explains a mental activity by appeal to inner representations, processes on those representations, and information flow between systems that carry out specific functions. I offer no formal computational models here, but my informal suggestions are computational in the broader sense. If my suggestions are right, emotions and emotional consciousness must be understood as computational processes.

Outline of a theory of emotions

Two traditions

A basic division exists between two kinds of theories of emotion: cognitive and non-cognitive. I will consider these in turn.

According to cognitive theories, emotions involve cognitive states essentially. There can be no emotion without a thought. Most of the psychologists who defend cognitive theories regard emotions as combinations of cognitive and non-cognitive states. For example, Schachter and Singer's (1962) two-factor theory defines emotions as states of arousal combined with cognitive "labels", which specify the significance of those states of arousal. Arousal is a physiological state caused by activity in the sympathetic part of the autonomic nervous system. A labeled state of arousal is an autonomic response that a person identifies to herself as falling into a particular emotion category.

In Schachter and Singer's famous study, participants were injected with adrenaline, which causes arousal, and subjected to environmental conditions that were consistent with elation, on the one hand, and anger, on the other. Despite being in similar physiological states, participants in the elation condition behaved in ways that are associated with positive affect, and participants in the anger condition behaved in ways that are associated with negative affect. Schachter and Singer conclude that the same physiological state can underlie distinct emotions. This conclusion has been challenged (see Reisenzein 1982). As we will see below, there is now evidence that distinct emotions correspond to distinct physiological states.

In recent decades, Schachter and Singer's two-factor cognitive theory has been overshadowed by cognitive appraisal theories. According to this approach, emotions are states (e.g., feelings, states of arousal, or action dispositions) that occur in response to appraisals (e.g., Arnold 1960; Roseman 1984; Scherer 1984; Lazarus 1990). An appraisal is a representation of one's relationship to the environment with respect to well-being (Lazarus 1990). For example, anger can be defined as the state that follows a judgment that one has been the victim of a demeaning offense. Fear can be defined as the state that follows a judgment that one is in danger. Lazarus (1990) calls such things as demeaning offenses and dangers "core relational themes". An emotion is a state that follows a cognition (e.g., a judgment) representing one of these themes.

Defenders of non-cognitive theories argue that emotions do not necessarily involve cognitive states (Zajonc 1984). Emotions can exist apart from thoughts. According to some non-cognitive theories, emotions are simply feelings. This view is sometimes attributed to James (1884). James has also been credited with an influential theory of where emotion feelings come from. We feel our emotions as a result of changes in bodily states, including visceral and musculoskeletal states. The feeling of anger is, in part, a feeling of our heart racing and our fists clenching. In other writings, James seems to assign a more central role to judgments in his theory of emotions, but history has largely read him as defending a non-cognitive view (see James 1894; Ellsworth 1994).

Damasio (1994) defends a variant of the theory associated with James. Like James, he says that emotions involve bodily changes, but Damasio does not claim that all emotions are felt. Brain states that unconsciously register bodily changes can qualify as emotions. Damasio distinguishes primary and secondary emotions. Both involve changes in bodily states but the latter are induced by thoughts. Primary emotions, which Damasio regards as biologically primitive, are triggered by responses in parts of the brain that are not associated with cognition. Damasio's claim that some emotions lack cognitive concomitants qualifies him as holding a non-cognitive theory.

Another non-cognitive approach identifies emotions with modes of processing. Oatley and Johnson-Laird (1987) say that basic emotions are constituted by characteristic patterns of memory, attention, categorization and so forth. As such, basic emotions may influence cognition, but they are not themselves identified with or individuated by any particular cognitive states. Oatley and Johnson-Laird claim that non-basic emotions are basic emotions that have been "elaborated" by cognitive states. Thus, they have a non-cognitive theory of basic emotions and a cognitive theory of non-basic emotions.

Ostensibly, cognitive theories have an advantage over non-cognitive theories, because there seems to be an intimate link between emotion and judgment. Being afraid seems to involve the recognition of danger. Being angry seems to involve the recognition of an offense. If that were not the case, the role that emotions play in our lives would be rendered unintelligible. Divorcing emotion from cognition makes it very difficult to understand why emotions perform the way they do. If emotions were mere feelings, or changes in how we process information, or internal responses to bodily states, there would be no explanation of why we run when afraid and retaliate when mad. We do not run because our hearts race, or retaliate because our focus of attention narrows. We run because we know we are in danger, and we retaliate because we know that we have been insulted.

Such considerations imply that emotions must involve cognitions. But this conclusion is threatened by various forms of evidence (Zajonc 1984). For one thing, emotions can be induced by something as simple as changing one's facial expression (Zajonc, Murphy, & Inglehart 1989; Levenson, Ekman, & Friesen 1990). If a smile brings on a feeling of happiness, there is little reason to think that the feeling is the result of an inner judgment or belief.

Another reason for resisting cognitive theories stems from work in neuroscience. It is now believed that some of our emotional responses are mediated by direct pathways from perceptual centers in temporal cortex and the thalamus to the amygdala (LeDoux 1996). Perceptual centers are in the business of recognizing perceivable features such as shapes. The amygdala is in the business of instructing other brain areas to initiate bodily responses when certain perceptual features are perceived. Often there is no need for an intervening judgment in this process. Neither perceptual centers nor the amygdala harbor the resources to reflect on something as lofty as a demeaning offense. It would even be generous to say that the amygdala harbors the concept danger. No concepts are necessary at all when the amygdala sets one's heart racing (via the hypothalamus) after one sees a snake.

These considerations provide convincing evidence that emotions do not require cognitive concomitants. This leaves the emotion researcher with a dilemma. Any theory that divorces emotions from cognitions is explanatorily anemic. Any theory that weds emotions to cognitions is subject to counterexamples. To overcome this dilemma, we must look beyond the prevailing menu of cognitive and non-cognitive theories.

The somatic appraisal theory

Prevailing theories of emotion present us with a false dichotomy. Cognitive theorists would have us believe that emotions always involve judgments, and non-cognitive theorists would have us believe that emotions carry no information at all or, at best, carry information about changes in our bodily states. If emotions are mere feelings or modes of processing, they are, strictly speaking, meaningless. They do not represent anything. If emotions are states that register changes in the body, they may be said to represent such things as heart rate or respiratory patterns rather than core relational themes. We are presented with a choice. Either emotions involve judgments representing core relational themes, or they do not involve judgments and fail to represent core relational themes. If they fail to represent core relational themes, we cannot explain the roles they play in our lives, and, if they involve judgments, we cannot explain their neural circuitry.

The solution is simple. Emotions can represent core relational themes without explicitly encoding such themes in the form of judgments. A mental state can represent a demeaning offense without being built up from the concepts *demeaning* and *offense*. To see this, it is helpful to call on work by philosophers.

Cognitive scientists often help themselves to the claim that mental states represent things without ever explaining how this is achieved. Psychologists, for example, will talk about concepts representing dogs, or tables, or screwdrivers. But what makes a state inside the head count as a representation of any of these things out in the world? Psychologists sometimes imply that the answer involves decomposition into "features". For example, a *dog* concept might be construed as a network or "frame" comprised of features such as *having fur, having a tail, barking*, and so on (e.g., Smith 1989). But this only pushes the problem back. For one must ask, what makes a mental state represent *fur* or *tails* or *barking*? The features making up one concept are concepts in their own right. On pain of regress, one cannot explain how every mental state represents by breaking it down into more basic mental states. Eventually one must explain how the most primitive features represent.

One of the most popular solutions to this problem owes to Dretske (1981; 1988; see also Fodor 1990 and Prinz 2002). Roughly, Dretske's proposal is that primitive mental representations represent that which they have the function of detecting. This definition invokes two important constructs: detection and function. An internal state *detects* some thing if it is reliably activated by that thing. My *fur* representation is reliably activated by seeing furry things. An internal state has the *function* of detecting some thing if it is created to detect that thing. Internal states can be created in two ways: by evolution or learning. My *fur* representation was probably learned during my early encounters with furry things. My fur representation has the function of detecting fur because it was created for fur detection.

The invocation of functions is important here. Suppose our primitive mental representations represented anything that reliably causes them to activate. My *fur* representation is reliably activated by seeing fur, but it is probably also activated whenever I see the word "dog". If my *fur* representation represented anything that causes it to activate, then it would represent both fur and the word "dog" (Fodor 1984). That outcome would be counter-intuitive. According to Dretske, my fur representation represents fur and only fur, because it was originally acquired for that purpose. Dretske's theory can be summarized by saying that internal states represent those things that they *set up* to be *set off* by.

Let's assume that Dretske's theory is correct. It provides us with a formula for figuring out the meaning of our internal states. If one wants to know what an internal state represents, one must ask two questions: what causes it to become active, and which of those things that cause it might it have been learned or evolved to detect.

We can apply these questions to the emotions. First, we must ask, what causes emotions to occur? I think there are two good answers to this question, associated with two traditions in emotion research. On the one hand, there is a link between emotions and bodily states. Emotions correlate well with autonomic response and changes in facial expressions (Levenson, Ekman, & Friesen 1990). With Damasio (1994) and James, I am prepared to conclude that emotions are reliably caused by changes in the body. But, they are also reliably caused by changes in core relational themes. Work by Ekman and Friesen (1971), for example, provides pan-cultural evidence that emotions can be induced by situational factors that coincide with the kind of judgments emphasized by cognitive theorists. Fear occurs when there is a danger, and anger occurs when there is an offense. If emotions are set off by both bodily states and core relational themes, there are two possible answers to the question about what emotions represent.

To adjudicate, we must ask a second question: what were emotions naturally selected for? The most plausible answer is that emotions were selected for detecting core relational themes. Fear has been passed down through the genome because of its success in detecting danger. If fear merely detected a change in heart rate without also detecting the presence of dangers, it would not have conferred the same survival advantage. Therefore, if Dretske's theory of representation is right, we have reason to believe that emotions represent core relational themes.

In sharp contrast to the assumption made on standard cognitive theories, this conclusion about what emotions represent does not require that emotions be judgments. All that matters is that they are set up and set off in a certain way. This allows us to escape the false dichotomy presented by cognitive and non-cognitive theorists. Let us suppose, with Damasio, that emotions are internal states that register changes in the body. Let us then suppose that those changes reliably occur when we encounter situations that correspond to core relational themes. If that is the case, the very states that register internal states in the body can qualify as representations of core relational themes. They are not judgments. They do not *describe* core relational themes, or deploy concepts pertaining to those themes. But they are reliably set off by those themes. On this view emotions are not cognitive states, but they carry the kind of information that cognitive states carry (Prinz, forthcoming). They represent pertinent environmental conditions.

One might think that emotions could only be reliably set off by core relational themes if judgments were involved. This is not the case. Imagine that we are born with dispositions to have automatic bodily responses to certain perceived stimuli. For example, suppose that looming objects, dark places, snakes, and loud noises are all predisposed to cause a similar pattern of autonomic changes. In particular, they cause autonomic changes that prepare us for appropriate behavioral response (e.g., flight or freezing). Suppose also that the central nervous system has states that register those changes. Those states will, on the story I have been telling, represent danger, because danger is the feature uniting looming objects, dark places, snakes, and so on. The states that register the bodily changes that prepare us for flight and freezing collectively qualify as an internal danger detector. Through learning, this danger detector comes under control of other stimuli. Sometimes the bodily changes are triggered by the perception of objects that we are not evolved to detect (e.g., guns) and sometimes they are triggered by judgments (e.g., the judgment that one is in danger). Any perception or judgment that regularly arises during dangerous situations can come to trigger the same distinctive constellation of bodily changes. The internal state that registers those bodily changes represents danger because those bodily changes are elicited by situations that have danger as a unifying theme.

In summary, emotions are internal states that register bodily changes but represent core relational themes because those bodily changes are evolved to occur in response to those themes. We represent core relational themes via the body. I call such internal representations "somatic appraisals" (Prinz, forthcoming). They count as appraisals in virtue of the fact that they represent core relational themes, but they are somatic states (states of the nervous system that detect bodily changes) rather than judgments. I conjecture that emotions are somatic appraisals.

Can emotions be unconscious?

According to the theory of emotion just sketched, emotions are information carrying states. They register bodily changes and represent core themes. I did not define emotions as feelings. For all I have said, emotions can exist unfelt. They are defined by their information-carrying role, not by the way they feel.

Some might think this is a flaw in the theory. For example, Clore (1994) argues that emotions must be conscious. He defends this claim on the grounds that emotions serve a communicative function: they draw our attention to things that concern us. Clore assumes that emotions must be conscious in order to serve this function. The argument is unconvincing. For one thing, emotions may have other functions independent of their communicative role, such as preparing our bodies for response. A state that played the preparatory role, and not the communicative role might qualify as an emotion. For another thing, there is no reason why an unconscious mechanism couldn't play a communicative role. One might find oneself mindlessly staring at a beautiful passerby, for example, as a result of an unconscious emotional attraction. When we attend to something, we become aware of that thing, but, on occasion, we may fail to become aware of the emotion that drew our attention to it.

I think a theory of emotions should proceed by determining what information emotions carry and how they contribute to behavior. Once we have identified the states that carry the right kind of information, we can be said to have identified the emotions. Then we can see whether those states are necessarily conscious. If they are not, then we will have shown that there can be unconscious emotions. To simply assume that emotions are conscious is a bit like assuming that perceptions are conscious. This was standard practice for centuries, but now just about everyone believes in unconscious perception (see, e.g., Dixon 1981). The reason is simple. States that are involved in doing what perceptions do (responding to inputs from the sense organs) can occur outside awareness. In a similar spirit, we should be open to the possibility that emotions can be unconscious. Perhaps the states that do what emotions do (detect core relational themes and initiate appropriate responses) can be unconscious as well. In fact, we might fruitfully regard emotion as a form of perception (Prinz, forthcoming). Like perceptions, emotions are often comparatively passive and they pick up information from our bodies and our world.

Of course, in embracing unconscious emotions, I do not intend to deny that emotions can be conscious. I suspect that, like perceptions, emotions are usually conscious. They may involve unconscious processes, but, ordinarily, they enter into felt experience. There may be a simple reason for this. Conscious states serve as inputs for deliberation. Unconscious processing is most likely to occur in situations where responses are very practiced or habitual. Controlled response benefits from awareness. Emotions occur in response to situations that benefit from controlled response. Dangers, insults, and other core themes bear on our survival prospects. When life is at stake, deliberation is often warranted. Therefore, emotions are likely to be consciously experienced.

Emotional consciousness is something of a puzzle. If emotions are characterized in terms of the information they carry, how do they ever come to be consciously felt? Answering this question requires a theory of consciousness. It turns out that consciousness has a great deal to do with the flow of information-bearing states.

Outline of a theory of consciousness

The mind can be described at different levels of analysis. Psychologists tend to focus their attention on large-scale systems such as memory, attention, or vision. Neurophysiologists often talk of large-scale systems too, but they also descend to finer level of detail, describing, for example, spiking patterns of individual neurons. I believe that both of these levels are important for understanding consciousness. Consciousness depends on both system-level organization and particular patterns of neuronal activity. We are not yet in a position to understand what kinds of neuronal activity correlate with consciousness, but we are in a position to offer plausible hypotheses about the large-scale systems involved. I present such an hypothesis here. An analysis of the neural underpinnings of consciousness must await further investigation. If the right large-scale systems can be identified, researchers will know where to look for details at the neural level.

Some researchers think that there can be no unified theory of consciousness. Defenders of this view say that distinct kinds of conscious states correlate with distinct kinds of systems (see Churchland 1988; Flanagan 1998). Is it really possible that all conscious feelings, from visual sensations to emotional states, arise in the same way? There is overwhelming evidence that conscious states do not arise in the same expanse of neural anatomy. There is no consciousness center in the brain (Dennett & Kinsbourne 1991). Perhaps there can be no unified theory of the systems and processes that engender conscious states.

I am more optimistic. I think that different conscious states may be underwritten by the same kind of processes. While conscious states can be quite different, they all have at least one thing in common: they feel like something. That striking commonality cries out for explanation. It is highly plausible that different conscious states involve similar processes even if they occupy different portions of neural real-estate. I believe there can be a unified account of consciousness.

The account I favor builds on the insightful work of Jackendoff (1987). Jackendoff observes that consciousness always seems to arise at an intermediate level within hierarchically organized information processing systems (see also Crick & Koch 1998). Consider visual consciousness. Vision is widely presumed to be organized into three basic levels: a low level, at which local discontinuities of luminance are detected; an intermediate level, at which those discontinuities are used to discern contours, depth, motion, and various other surface features of perceived objects and scenes; and an high level, at which invariant features of contours allow one to arrive at object recognition. Jackendoff notes that the intermediate level corresponds best to what we seem to experience consciously during vision. He argues that the intermediate level is the locus of consciousness in other sense modalities as well (such as touch and audition). If he is right, there is no single place in the brain where all conscious states reside, but there is a single level of processing at which they reside.

Elsewhere I defend Jackendoff's account and add two additional requirements (Prinz 2000, 2001). First, I argue that intermediate-level states only become conscious when we are paying attention. There is evidence that attention is necessary for consciousness. In a series of experiments, Mack and Rock (1998) asked participants to perform a task that required considerable attention. They then briefly flashed unexpected stimuli (shapes and words) in the center of the participants' visual fields. Many participants failed to notice the unexpected stimuli because their attention was consumed by task. Further evidence for the necessity of attention in consciousness comes from neurology. Patients with unilateral neglect lose awareness of things on one side due, not to a perceptual dysfunction, but to a deficit of attention (Bisiach 1992). Finally, studies of subliminal perception in healthy and brain-damaged subjects suggest that information can pass through all stages of a sensory hierarchy without conscious experience (Bisiach 1992; Dixon 1981).

Attention is essential to consciousness. If one attends to a stimulus, it is experienced. If attention is fully allocated elsewhere, not functioning properly, or not given adequate time, the stimulus is not experienced. Attention, then, is what makes perceptual states conscious. Jackendoff's theory is best construed as a theory of which perceptual states are *candidates* for consciousness. The intermediate level determines what can become conscious, and attention determines what becomes conscious. The intermediate level gives us the contents of consciousness, and attention makes those contents conscious. I call this the Attended Intermediate-level Representation (AIR) theory of consciousness (Prinz 2000).

This extension of Jackendoff's account requires further elaboration. It requires a theory of what attention is. There may be several different things that deserve to be called attention. For example, Posner and Petersen (1990) distinguish selective attention (focusing on an object or feature) from vigilance (maintaining alertness). The latter may contribute to an account of the difference between being conscious and being unconscious, but the former is, on my view, essential for producing conscious feelings.

My second addition to Jackendoff's theory involves a particular proposal about how the relevant kind of attention works. I believe that selective attention is a neuronal process that determines when systems in the brain communicate with each other (see van Essen, Anderson, & Olshausen 1994). More specifically, I believe that attention allows perceptual systems to send signals to working memory systems. When we attend to a visually detected object, for example, information flows from visual pathways in temporal cortex to centers associated with visual working memory in prefrontal cortex. Ultimately, this change in information flow might be characterized in neural terms. Distinctive patterns of activity at the cellular level allow perceptual centers to communicate with memory centers. There are a variety of proposals about how this might work. Perhaps attention works by amplifying activity in the neurons that respond to the stimulus one is attending to. Perhaps attention involves a change in the receptive fields of higher areas so that they take inputs from only the neurons in question. Perhaps attention causes those neurons to adopt a distinctive spiking pattern that is recognized by higher brain areas. A complete theory of consciousness will have to decide between these and other options.

These remarks on attention illustrate how different levels of analysis contribute to a theory of consciousness. At the highest level, one says that consciousness works when attention modulates perceptual representations at an intermediate stage in hierarchically organized sensory systems. Then one says that attention works by allowing information to flow from perceptual centers to working memory centers. To explain how this works, one must descend to the cellular level. Perhaps information is routed by altering spiking patterns. One might go on to explain this change by appeal to mechanisms at an even lower level of analysis, adverting to synapses or ion channels. Jackendoff's theory of consciousness is just a starting place. He identifies the mechanism of consciousness at a very high level of analysis, by appeal to large-scale perceptual systems. The high-level story must be supplemented by implicating other large-scale systems (i.e. attention and working memory). Then all these large-scale systems must be analyzed at lower levels. A final theory of consciousness will describe mechanisms in neural terms.

In summary, I follow Jackendoff in claiming that consciousness arises only at the intermediate level of processing within hierarchically organized perceptual systems. To this I add the conjecture that consciousness arises when and only when attention opens up the flow of information to working memory. The term "attention" refers to neural processes that we are just beginning to understand. The AIR theory must ultimately specify how those processes work. Once they are understood, we will understand the essence of conscious experience.

Emotional consciousness

Hierarchical emotion processing

I now have two pieces of theoretical machinery in place. I outlined a theory of emotion (the somatic appraisal theory) and a theory of consciousness (the AIR theory). The theory of consciousness was based on an analysis vision. My goal is to provide a theory of emotional consciousness. I must therefore show that the theory of visual consciousness can shed light on the emotions. This task faces an immediate obstacle. The AIR theory says that consciousness arises at an intermediate level of processing in hierarchically organized perceptual systems. If it applies to emotion, I must show that emotion can be regarded as an hierarchically organized perceptual system. On the somatic appraisal theory, emotions qualify as perceptual, because they are states that register changes in the body. With James (1884) and Damasio (1994; 1999), I believe that emotional feelings are feelings of changes in heart rate, respiration, and a variety of other somatic features. This only gets me half way over the obstacle. I have not provided any evidence for thinking that the systems underlying emotion are hierarchically organized. That is the goal of this section.

We are still in the early stages of understanding emotional processing systems, but current knowledge is consistent with the hypothesis that there is a three-level emotion processing hierarchy. At the lowest level, we detect local changes in bodily states, such as a racing heart. At this level, the brain has not yet determined that multiple bodily changes have occurred; each is detected independently. At the next stage in the hierarchy, the intermediate level, patterns of somatic changes are detected. Here the brain registers the co-occurrence of changes in respiratory, circulatory, endocrinal, and musculoskeletal systems. Finally, at an high level, particular patterns of somatic responses are identified as being instances of one emotion or another. The high level is the level of emotional recognition, and it can interact with systems involved in reasoning and planned response selection.

The difference between the intermediate level and the high level can be illustrated with an example. There may be several different somatic patterns associated with fear (consider the difference between fleeing and freezing). At the intermediate level, these correspond to distinct neural patterns, which map different local changes that have been detected at the lowest level of processing. At the highest level, the distinct patterns are represented in the same way. We can think of the intermediate level as harboring somatic prototypes for different emotions, each of which allows for a range of variation. When a pattern exceeds the prototype threshold, a signal is sent to the high level of processing. The somatic responses associated with both fleeing and freezing may both exceed the somatic prototype threshold for fear.

At this point, the emotion hierarchy is just an hypothesis. Support will depend, in part, on identifying neural correlates for each level. The neural correlates of emotion are not fully understood, but current understanding is consistent with an hierarchical account.

Other authors have defended the view that there is a taxonomical hierarchy of emotional states, which can be mapped on to different brain areas. According to MacLean's (1993) triune brain model, for example, emotional states involve a number of brain areas that emerged during different stages of evolution. This model postulates an hierarchy extending from more primitive emotional responses to more advanced emotional responses. Similar ideas have been defended by Damasio (1994) and Lane (2000). As remarked above, Damasio distinguishes primary emotions, which are primitive and innate, from secondary emotions, which require mediation of higher cortical areas (especially ventromedial prefrontal cortex). Lane proposes a five-level hierarchy of affective responses: there are visceral states, action tendencies, discrete emotions, blends of discrete emotions, and blends of blends. These psychological levels correspond roughly to different neuroanatomical regions: the brainstem, the diencephalon, the limbic system, paralimbic areas, and portions of prefrontal cortex.

Though important, the claim that emotions can be organized into a taxonomical hierarchy that extends from more phylogenetically primitive responses to more advanced emotions is not the claim that I am trying to defend. I claim that there is a *processing* hierarchy. All normal human emotional responses involve activity at each stage of this hierarchy. I am drawing no distinction here between different classes of emotions (though see Prinz, forthcoming). It could turn out that the earlier levels of that hierarchy are phylogenetically more primitive, but that is not essential to my story.

Some work on the neural correlates of emotion points towards a processing hierarchy. Lane and Damasio can be mentioned here as well. Lane (2000) is especially interested in the areas underlying conscious awareness. He draws a distinction between phenomenal awareness of emotions, associated with dorsal anterior cingulate cortex, and reflexive awareness of emotions, associated with rostral anterior cingulate cortex. Phenomenal awareness occurs when we are viewing an emotionally significant stimulus, and reflexive awareness occurs when we attend to the emotional significance of that stimulus. Damasio (1999) proposes an hierarchy of somatic maps underlying our emotions, beginning with the reticular formation in the brainstem, and extending to somatosensory cortex, and other areas. The somatic maps tell the brain how the body is changing.

These anatomical speculations can be appropriated within the hierarchy I have been proposing. If we combine Damasio's idea of multiple body maps, with his earlier suggestion that higher cortical areas can contribute to emotional response, we can trace out a circuit that goes from the brainstem to the frontal cortex. Lane's emphasis on anterior cingulate cortex as a locus for conscious awareness is also useful. If conscious awareness resides at the intermediate level of processing, as the AIR model suggests, and emotional consciousness arises in the anterior cingulate, then the anterior cingulate may harbor the intermediate level in the emotion hierarchy.

Putting the pieces together, I propose the following division of labor. Low-level emotional processing occurs in portions of the brainstem and somatosensory cortical areas (including the insula). In discussing the brainstem, Damasio focuses on the reticular formation, but the nucleus of the solitary tract, which contains a topographic map of the viscera, may be a key player as well (Iverson et al. 2000). Intermediate-level emotional processing occurs in select areas of cingulate cortex. Dorsal anterior cingulate, which Lane associates with emotional phenomenology, is an especially good candidate. High-level emotional processing occurs in other medial frontal areas. These probably include the rostral anterior cingulate, implicated by Lane, and the ventromedial prefrontal cortex, implicated by Damasio. All of this is extremely tentative. The proposals are likely to be revised as we learn more about the brain. It may also turn out that distinct emotions rely on distinct structures (Panksepp 2000; Damasio et al. 2000).

One might wonder where the amygdala is in this picture. The amygdala is regarded as an extremely important player in emotional response (see especially LeDoux 1996). I think the amygdala is important, but it does not play a direct role in the experience of emotions. Instead, it plays a role in generating emotions. As LeDoux has argued, the nuclei of the amygdala send messages to the hypothalamus, the central gray, and other areas that orchestrate somatic changes when we perceive emotionally significant stimuli. The amygdala mediates the link between what we perceive and how our body responds. On my view, emotions are states that characteristically occur in response to such changes. The hierarchy I have described begins to operate *after* the amygdala has done its work. There are, in other words, two processing hierarchies to distinguish. The amygdala is part of an emotion *initiation* hierarchy that characteristically begins with activity in perceptual areas and ends up with activity in somatic output centers. This hierarchy scans inputs for emotional significance (see Fulcher, this volume). When an emotionally significant object or event is detected, it initiates a constellation of somatic outputs. Once the somatic outputs occur, information propagates through an emotion *response* hierarchy, which begins in the brainstem and ends up in the frontal lobes. Both hierarchies are involves in emotion, but the emotions themselves are states in the second hierarchy.

In summary, existing neuroanatomical evidence is consistent with the supposition that emotional systems are hierarchically organized. I propose that the brain areas associated with emotion encompass a three-level emotional response system. That system begins by detecting local changes in the body, goes on to register more complex patterns of change, and ends up with a categorical representation of what emotion one happens to be undergoing. This proposal coheres with the somatic appraisal theory. Internal states that register patterned somatic responses can serve as core relational theme detectors provided those responses are induced by situations that correspond to those themes. All of these suggestions are very speculative, but they offer one way to make sense of existing evidence at this early stage of inquiry.

Emotional AIRs

If the hierarchical account of emotions is correct, then the AIR theory may explain emotional consciousness. The AIR theory situates emotional consciousness at the intermediate level of processing. According to the hierarchy I have proposed, the intermediate level in emotion processing registers patterned bodily responses, not local responses or emotional recognition. Intuitively, this intermediate level is the level at which emotions are experienced. Let's consider what's wrong with the other two levels.

Emotional experience cannot arise at the low level, because responses at that level are not sufficiently unified. When one experiences a state of terror for example, one does not experience the terror as a set of independent or discrete bodily states. Intuitively, the feel of a racing heart and strained breadth are experienced as a perceptual gestalt. Bodily symptoms must coalesce into identifiable emotional syndromes. A feeling of terror can only be analyzed into independent parts by shifting attention away from the emotion and onto its ingredients. By analogy, when we see a contour as comprising a square, we can only analyze its component corners and lines by attending away from the whole. Of course, we do see the lines that make up a square when we experience the gestalt. But the brain has a way of representing those lines as belonging together in a coherent whole. We cannot focus on the trees individually when we are looking at the forest. Likewise, we feel a racing hear when we experience terror, but the racing heart is integrated with other symptoms.

Introspective evidence also tells against the proposal that emotional experience occurs at the high level, where emotions are recognized. First, we sometimes have emotions that we cannot quite identify. Consider the mixed feelings one has when one learns that one received an award that a close friend was vying for (Greenspan 1980). Second, it seems that we can misidentify our emotions. Consider the assistant professor who mistakes her dread of an upcoming tenure review for a physical ailment (Clore 1994). Third, the categories by which we identify emotions seem to be more coarsely grained than our emotional experiences. The same emotion can feel different on different occasions. Freezing and (preparation for) fleeing feel different to us, even though they both qualify as fear responses. In this respect, the parallel between the postulated emotion hierarchy and the visual hierarchy should be obvious. The visual experience of a poodle and a rottweiler are different, even if they are both recognized as dogs.

If the AIR theory applies to emotion, then emotional feelings also depend on attention. There is considerable evidence that emotion can influence how we direct attention (e.g., McLeod & Matthews 1988), but few have investigated how attention influences emotion. Here, we must rely on anecdote and intuition. It seems very plausible that emotions require attention to become conscious. Imagine becoming temporarily distracted while feeling an emotion. For example, one might be very sad about a disturbing piece of news, but briefly lose sight of that sadness because one is distracted a telephone call, a TV commercial, or a tough question on a crossword puzzle.

As it happens, we are rarely distracted from our emotions. Emotions generally demand attention. But, on occasion, other demands on attention drown out the beckoning call of affect, and we lose sight of how we are feeling. As with vision, I think we can become inattentionally blind to our emotions. Researchers should try to determine whether anecdotal evidence can be confirmed by controlled experiments.

One paradigm that may speak to this issue makes use of emotion inducing photographs. While viewing emotion-inducing photographs, participants may be asked questions that relate to what they are feeling or they may be asked questions that are neutral. For example, participants might be asked to make emotional intensity or pleasant/unpleasant discrimination in some trials and an indoor/outdoor discrimination in others (Lane et al. 1997). It would be interesting to know whether this manipulation leads to a diminution of felt affect. The neutral condition could be made even more demanding. For example, subjects might be asked to perform difficult arithmetic problems while viewing the photographs. As these tasks consume more attention, the AIR theory predicts that affective feelings would become quite muted. Until such experiments are conducted, the AIR theory can serve only as a pointer toward future research.

Conclusions

I have argued that consciousness arises when intermediate-level perceptual states are modulated by attention. An AIR theory of emotional consciousness locates emotional consciousness at an intermediate level of emotional processing and says that states at that level become conscious when and only we are paying attention to how we are feeling. As yet, there is insufficient evidence to adequately defend this conjecture. If support can be found, it would provide evidence for the claim that different kinds of conscious states are underwritten by the same kinds of processes. It would also have significant implications for emotion research. The AIR theory points us in that direction. I believe that emotions can occur unconsciously, but that does not mean that the investigation of emotional consciousness should be postponed. It may deepen our understanding of how emotions work.

References

Arnold, M. B. (1960). *Emotion and Personality*. New York, NY: Columbia University Press.
Bisiach, E. (1992). Understanding Consciousness: Clues from Unilateral Neglect and Related Disorders. In A. D. Milner & M. D. Rugg (Eds.), *The Neuropsychology of Consciousness*. London: Academic Press.
Churchland, P. S. (1988). Reduction and the Neurobiological Basis of Consciousness. In A. J. Marcel & E. Bisiach (Eds.), *Consciousness and Contemporary Science* (pp. 273–304). Oxford: Oxford University Press.
Clore, G. (1994). Why Emotions Are Never Unconscious. In P. Ekman & R. J. Davidson (Eds.), *The Nature of Emotion: Fundamental Questions* (pp. 285–290). New York: Oxford University Press.
Crick, F. and Koch, C. (1998). Consciousness and Neuroscience. *Cerebral Cortex, 8*, 97–107.

Damasio, A. R. (1994). *Descartes' Error: Emotion Reason and the Human Brain.* New York, NY: Gossett/Putnam.
Damasio, A. R. (1999). *The Feeling of What Happens: Body and Emotion in the Making of Consciousness.* New York, NY: Harcourt Brace & Company 1999.
Damasio, A. R., Grabowski, T. J., Bechara, A., Damasio, H., Ponto, L. L. B.; Parvizi, J., & Hichwa, R. D. (2000). Subcortical and Cortical Brain Activity During the Feeling of Self-generated Emotions. *Nature Neuroscience, 3*, 1049–1056.
Dennett, D. C., & Kinsbourne, M. (1995). Time and the Observer: The Where and When of Consciousness in the Brain. *Behavioral and Brain Sciences, 15*, 183–247.
Dixon, N. F. (1981). *Preconscious Processing.* Chichester, NY: John Wiley & Sons.
Dretske, F. (1981). *Knowledge and the Flow of Information.* Cambridge, MA, MIT Press.
Dretske, F. (1988). *Explaining Behavior.* Cambridge, MA, MIT Press.
Ekman, P., & Friesen, W. V. (1971). Constants Across Cultures in the Face and Emotion. *Journal of Personality and Social Psychology, 17*, 124–129.
Ellsworth, P. C. (1994). William James and Emotion: Is a Century of Fame Worth a Century of Misunderstanding? *Psychological Review, 101*, 222–229.
Flanagan, O. (1996). Prospects for a Unified Theory of Consciousness. In J. Cohen and J. Schooler (Eds.), *Scientific Approaches to the Study of Consciousness* (pp. 405–422). Hillsdale, NJ: Erlbaum.
Fodor, J. A. (1987). *Psychosemantics.* Cambridge, MA: MIT Press.
Fodor, J. A. (1990). A Theory of Content, I & II. In *A Theory of Content and Other Essays.* Cambridge, MA: MIT Press.
Fodor, J. A. (1984). Semantics Wisconsin Style. *Synthese, 59*, 231–250.
Greenspan, P. S. (1980). A Case of Mixed Feelings; Ambivalence and the Logic of Emotions. In A. O. Rorty (Ed.), *Explaining Emotions* (pp. 223–250). Berkeley, CA: University of California Press.
Iverson, S., Iverson, L., & Saper, C. B. (2000). The Autonomic Nervous System and the Hypothalamus. In E. R. Kandel, J. H. Scwartz, & T. M. Jessell (Eds.), *Principles of Neural Science, 4th Edition* (pp. 960–981). New York: McGraw Hill.
Jackendoff, R. (1987). *Consciousness and the Computational Mind.* Cambridge, MA: MIT Press.
James, W. (1884). What is an Emotion? *Mind, 9*, 188–205.
James, W. (1894). The Physical Basis of Emotion. *Psychological Review, 1*, 516–529.
Lane, R. D. (2000). Neural Correlates of Conscious Emotional Experience. In R. D. Lane & L. Nadel (Eds.), *Cognitive Neuroscience of Emotion* (pp. 345–370). New York, NY: Oxford University Press.
Lane, R. D., Fink, G. R., Chau, P. M. L., & Dolan, R. J. (1997). Neural Activation During Selective Attention to Subjective Emotional Responses. *NeuroReport, 8*, 3969–3972.
LeDoux, J. E. (1996). *The Emotional Brain.* New York, NY: Simon & Schuster.
Mack, A., & Rock, I. (1998) *Inattentional Blindness.* Cambridge, MA: MIT Press.
MacLean, P. D. (1993). Cerebral Evolution of Emotion. In M. Lewis and J. M. Haviland (Eds.), *Handbook of Emotions, 1st Edition* (pp. 67–83). New York: Guilford Press.
McLeod, C., & Matthews, A. (1988). Anxiety and the Allocation of Attention to Threat. *Quarterly Journal of Experimental Psychology, 38*, 659–670.

Oatley, K., & Johnson-Laird, P. N. (1987). Towards a Cognitive Theory of the Emotions. *Cognition and Emotion, 1,* 29–50.

Panksepp, J. (2000). Emotions as Natural Kinds within the Mammalian Brain. In M. Lewis & J. Haviland (Eds.), *The Handbook of Emotions, 2nd Edition* (pp. 137–156). New York, NY: Guilford.

Posner, M. I., & Petersen, S. E. (1990). The Attention System of the Human Brain. *Annual Review of Neuroscience, 13,* 25–42.

Prinz, J. J. (2000). A Neurofunctional Theory of Visual Consciousness. *Consciousness and Cognition, 9,* 243–259.

Prinz, J. J. (2001). Functionalism, Dualism and the Neural Correlates of Consciousness. In W. Bechtel, P. Mandik, J. Mundale, & R. Stufflebeam (Eds.), *Philosophy and the Neurosciences: A Reader.* Oxford: Blackwell.

Prinz, J. J. (2002). *Furnishing the Mind: Concepts and Their Perceptual Basis.* Cambridge, MA: MIT Press.

Prinz, J. J. (forthcoming). *Emotional Perception.* Oxford: Oxford University Press.

Reisenzein, R. (1983). The Schachter Theory of Emotion: Two Decades Later. *Psychological Bulletin, 94,* 239–264.

Roseman I. J. (1984). Cognitive Determinants of Emotion: A Structural Theory. In P. Shaver (Ed.), *Review of Personality and Social Psychology,* Volume 5 (pp. 11–36). Beverly Hills, CA: Sage.

Schachter, S., & Singer, J. (1962). Cognitive, Social, and Physiological Determinants of Emotional State. *Psychological Review, 69,* 379–399.

Scherer, K. R. (1984). On the Nature and Function of Emotion: A Component Process Approach. In K. R. Scherer & P. Ekman (Eds.), *Approaches to Emotion* (pp. 293–318). Hillsdale, NJ: Erlbaum.

Smith, E. E. (1989). Concepts and Induction. In M. Posner (Ed.), *Foundations of Cognitive Science* (pp. 501–526). Cambridge, MA: MIT Press.

Van Essen, D. C., Anderson, C. H., & Olshausen, B. A. (1994). Dynamic Routing Strategies in Sensory, Motor, and Cognitive Processing. In C. Koch & J. L. Davis (Eds.), *Large-Scale Neuronal Theories of the Brain* (pp. 93–110). Cambridge, MA: MIT Press.

Zajonc, R. B. (1984). On the Primacy of Affect. *American Psychologist, 39,* 117–123.

Zajonc, R. B., Murphy, S. T., & Inglehart, M. (1989). Feeling and Facial Efference: Implications of the Vascular Theory of Emotion. *Psychological Review, 96,* 395–416.

CHAPTER 7

Emotion and reasoning to consistency
The case of abductive inference

Keith Oatley and P. N. Johnson-Laird
University of Toronto / Princeton University

"What is the meaning of it, Watson?" said Holmes solemnly as he laid down the paper. ... "It must tend to some end, or else our universe is ruled by chance, which is unthinkable. But what end? There is the great standing perennial problem to which human reason is as far from an answer as ever."
"The Adventure of the Cardboard Box."
A. Conan Doyle *The Strand Magazine* (1893)

... an emotion is always a simple predicate substituted by an operation of the mind for a highly complicated predicate. Now if we consider that a very complex predicate demands explanation by means of an hypothesis, that that hypothesis must be a simpler predicate substituted for that complex one; ... the analogy of the parts played by emotion and hypothesis is very striking.
C. S. Peirce *Some consequences of four incapacities* (1868)

In "The Adventure of the Cardboard Box," Sherlock Holmes investigated a case in which two human ears had been sent by mail in a cardboard box to a respectable spinster in a London suburb. Inspector Lestrade, the Scotland Yard detective, thinks it was a practical joke by some medical students. But Holmes thinks differently:

> Bodies in the dissecting rooms are injected with preservative fluid. These ears bear no sign of this. They are fresh, too. They have been cut off with a blunt instrument, which would hardly happen if a student had done it ... we are investigating a serious crime. (Conan Doyle 1930, p. 892)

Holmes always claimed that his inferences were deductions that were, "as infallible as so many propositions of Euclid." His claim was wrong. Given his observations and the truth of his premise:

> If medical students had sent the severed ears, then there would have been traces of preservatives used in the dissecting room, they wouldn't have been fresh, and the ears would have been cut off with a scalpel, not a blunt instrument,

it does follow validly that medical students had not sent the severed ears. A *valid* deduction, by definition, yields a conclusion that must be true given the truth of the premises. But his next step, from this conclusion to the claim that a serious crime had been committed, is invalid. The conclusion need not be true; for example, an undertaker might have sent the ears as a practical joke. In fact, deduction cannot resolve inconsistencies. It can establish that the evidence is inconsistent with a set of premises, but it cannot determine the premises one should abandon in the face of an inconsistency or the correct explanation to resolve the inconsistency.

What process of thought might be useful to create explanatory hypotheses? In the same story, Holmes gives an excellent answer: "The case is one where ... we have been compelled to reason backward from effects to causes" (Conan Doyle 1930, p. 895). The philosopher C. S. Peirce (1903) studied this kind of reasoning which, because of its backwards direction, he sometimes called "retroduction," though it was another of his names "abduction" that has lasted. Abduction goes beyond generalization (induction) to aim for explanation (Sebeok & Umiker-Sebeok 1983). It aims – in other words of Peirce – to explain a complex predicate by means of a simpler hypothesis and, as the second epigraph to the present paper shows, Peirce was struck by the analogy between this abductive step and the elicitation of an emotion by a complex cognition.

In this chapter, we discuss this analogy and its relation to reasoning to consistency. The first step in such reasoning is to detect an inconsistency among a set of beliefs, as Holmes detected an inconsistency between the valid consequences of Lestrade's hypothesis and the evidence. The next step is to determine what beliefs to abandon. And the final step is the abductive generation of an explanation to resolve the inconsistency. The process as a whole is not computationally tractable, that is, as the number of component beliefs increases, impossible demands are made on time and memory. In such cases, cognitive scientists turn to heuristics: procedures that have no guarantee of success but that work more frequently than would occur by chance. We argue that emotions are such heuristics – hence the analogy that Peirce drew – and that they dovetail with reasoning by means of mental models. We fancy that Holmes would have been contemptuous of the claim that emotions are much like the kind of reasoning for which he was famous, but would have accepted with equanimity that his reasoning was model-based. Peirce (1898), however, with his emphasis on diagrams as models of relations, would wonder merely why psychology has taken so long to catch up with him.

In what follows, we outline the theory of mental models and its account for the abductive process of reasoning from inconsistency to consistency (Part 1). Next, we consider how emotions are heuristics that enable human beings to deal with inconsistencies in a tractable way (Part 2). We then present some empirical studies in which inconsistencies have occurred in the expected outcomes of plans made jointly between two people (Part 3). Finally, we draw some conclusions in which we join abduction, mental models, and emotions (Part 4).

Reasoning, consistency, and mental models

Deductive reasoning is the process of trying to draw valid conclusions from premises, and much evidence suggests that naïve individuals make deductions on the basis of mental models (see e.g. Johnson-Laird 1983; Johnson-Laird & Byrne 1991). Reasoners use the meaning of assertions together with their general knowledge to construct a set of mental models of what the assertions describe. A mental model is a representation of a possibility. Hence, a central component of reasoning is the generation of possibilities. A conclusion is *necessary* if it holds in all the models of the premises. It is *possible* if it holds in at least one model of the premises; and its *probability* depends on the proportion of equiprobable models in which it holds (Johnson-Laird, Legrenzi, Girotto, Legrenzi, & Caverni 1999).

A fundamental assumption of the theory is known as the principle of *truth*: individuals represent assertions by constructing sets of mental models in which each model represents a true possibility, and each clause in the assertions (affirmative or negative) is represented in a mental model only if it is true in that possibility. The easiest way to grasp the principle is to consider an illustrative example. Suppose that the following assertion expresses an exclusive disjunction in which only one of the two clauses is true: "Either he is with his wife or else he is not happy." The mental models of the disjunction represent only the two true possibilities and, within them, they represent the two clauses in the disjunction ("he is with his wife;" "he is not happy") only when they are true within a possibility:

wife
   ¬ happy

where "wife" denotes a model of him with his wife, "¬" denotes negation, and so "¬ happy" denotes a model of him as not happy. Each row in this diagram denotes a model of a separate possibility. A second assertion:

He is not with his wife

eliminates the first model, and so one can draw the conclusion: he is not happy. This conclusion is valid because it holds in all the models – in this case the single model – in which the premises hold. Following the principle of truth, the first of the two mental models above does not represent explicitly that it is *false* that he is not happy in this possibility. Similarly, the second model does not represent explicitly that it is *false* that he is with his wife in this possibility. Reasoners make "mental footnotes" to keep track of the information about what is false, but these footnotes are ephemeral. If reasoners do keep track of the footnotes, however, then they can flesh out mental models converting them into *fully explicit* models:

wife   happy
¬ wife ¬ happy

These are also the fully explicit models of the following biconditional:

If, and only if, he is with his wife, then he is happy.

Reasoning is not always a clear-cut matter of the deduction of conclusions that follow from premises. Life often surprises you. These surprises may clash with the logical consequences of your beliefs. When you detect an inconsistency, you try to reason to consistency. Suppose that you believe, for instance:

If people are insulted, then they get angry.

and you observe that Pat has been insulted. You think to yourself: So, she'll get angry (a valid inference). Yet, to your surprise, Pat remains perfectly calm. Something has to give. You have detected an inconsistency between a valid consequence of your beliefs and a fact. You have to try to reason to consistency.

In logic, later information never invalidates earlier valid conclusions. Logic is *monotonic:* with each additional premise, further conclusions are valid, and no prior conclusion becomes invalid. And, in logic, when a set of premises is inconsistent, then anything goes: a contradiction logically implies any conclusion whatsoever. Hence, logic alone cannot tell you how to resolve an inconsistency. The process calls for a special sort of reasoning, akin to diagnosis. Unlike logical deduction, it is *nonmonotonic*. That is, you withdraw a previous valid conclusion in the light of subsequent information, with a consequent change in your beliefs. Reasoning to consistency is pervasive in everyday life, because events so often conspire to defeat valid inferences.

At the heart of reasoning to consistency is the generation of causal scenarios to explain the situation. Consider again the case of Pat and why the insult did not anger her. Your original conditional premise was: "If people are insulted, then they get angry." You are likely to try to diagnose the situation, that is, to make an *abduction* that explains why Pat did not get angry. Perhaps she knew that the apparent insult was just a joke: so you abandon your belief that Pat was insulted. Or perhaps Pat knew that the person insulting her was mentally ill: in which case, you abandon your belief in your conditional premise. Your reasoning to consistency accordingly consists in three steps: the detection of an inconsistency, the editing of beliefs, and the abduction of an explanation. We describe these steps as though they occur in a simple sequence, but it is conceivable that your attempt to explain the inconsistency itself determines which propositions you come to doubt.

The preceding analysis is due to Legrenzi, Girotto, Legrenzi, and Johnson-Laird (2001). They have also developed a computer program that implements a model-based theory of reasoning to consistency, and they have corroborated experimentally each of its three main steps. We will examine each step in turn.

The first step in reasoning to consistency is the detection of an inconsistency among a set of propositions. It is tempting to think of an inconsistency as a conflict between just two propositions, one of the form: "A," and the other its negation: "Not-A." Unfortunately, inconsistency can occur in a set of propositions where if you remove any proposition from the set the remaining propositions are consistent. For example, consider the following set of assertions:

> Either there is an arch on the table or else there is a bolt, but not both.
> Either there is a bolt on the table or else there is a cog, but not both.
> Either there is an arch on the table or else there is a cog, but not both.

They are based on based on three atomic propositions, which are propositions that contain neither negation nor connectives, such as: "There is an arch." How do individuals assess whether or not the set is consistent? The model theory proposes that they search for a single model of a possibility that satisfies all the assertions. If there is such a model, then the assertions are consistent; and if there is not such a model, then the assertions are inconsistent. Hence, as the computer program shows, reasoners can proceed by envisaging a mental model that satisfies the first assertion above:

>   arch

They continue this possibility to accommodate the second assertion:

>   arch   cog

But, this model is incompatible with the third assertion, which demands that only one of these two objects is present. They must abandon this model and can try a different way of satisfying the first two assertions with the model:

>   bolt

But, this model also fails to satisfy the third assertion, which demands either:

>   arch   bolt

which violates the first assertion, or:

>   bolt   cog

which violates the second assertion. The possibilities have been exhausted, and so the set of assertions is inconsistent. In general, the decision that a set of assertions is consistent calls only for a single possibility that satisfies the set, whereas the decision that a set of assertions is inconsistent depends on ensuring that no model can satisfy the set of assertions.

The evaluation of consistency is computationally intractable: as the number of atomic propositions in a set of beliefs increases, the demands on time and memory increase in a way that soon exceed the capacity of a computer as big as the universe running at the speed of light (see Cook 1971). The model theory similarly predicts that the more models that have to be examined the harder the search will be. In a recent experiment, the participants had to state whether or not a set of assertions could all be true at the same time, i.e., whether or not the set was consistent (Johnson-Laird, Legrenzi, Girotto, & Legrenzi 2000). The results showed that the evaluation of consistency was easier with problems based on conditionals, such as those of the form:

>   If not-A then B.
>   If B then C.
>   Not-A and C.

than with logically equivalent problems based on disjunctions :

A or B, or both.
Not-B or C, or both.
Not-A and C.

To judge the consistency of the conditionals calls only for the construction of a single model:

¬A B   C

Naïve individuals normally construct only one explicit mental model of a conditional, such as "If not-A then B:"

¬A B
...

where the ellipsis denotes a wholly implicit model representing the possibilities in which the antecedent proposition, "not-A," is false. In contrast, disjunctions call for the construction of more than one model. Thus, the disjunction: "A or B, or both," elicits the models:

A
   B
A B

Of course, there may be an alternative explanation of this result, but it has been corroborated using a variety of other sorts of assertion (see Legrenzi et al. 2001).

One phenomenon, which at present is predicted only by the model theory, is the occurrence of illusory inferences. These are compelling but invalid inferences that most individuals should draw. They are predicted on the grounds that mental models do not normally represent what is false (for illusions of consistency and illusions of inconsistency, see Johnson-Laird et al. 2000).

If an inconsistency arises from a conflict between incontrovertible evidence and a *valid* inference from propositions, then at least one of the propositions must be given up. But, which one? The simplest mismatch occurs when the evidence conflicts with just a single proposition. For example, you put some milk in the fridge, and so you believe that there is milk in the fridge. A short while later, you go to the fridge to get some milk, and you discover that there is none. Naturally, you cease to believe that there is milk in the fridge. A more complex conflict occurs when there is no single proposition with which the evidence conflicts, though it conflicts with a set of propositions as a whole. If the set includes a proposition that is more improbable or open to doubt than the others, then you should abandon this proposition. But, suppose there is no such proposition, what then? When a proposition has only mental models conflicting with the evidence, it seems to be in a direct conflict with the evidence. In fact, it isn't necessarily incompatible, but its compatibility may depend on possibilities that are not represented in the mental models. These possibilities become apparent only in the fully explicit models of the proposition. Individuals usually overlook these models, and so the theory predicts that individuals should abandon a proposition that mismatches the evidence in this way. If there is no such proposition, then they should reject a proposition because it fails to represent the evidence, given that all the other propositions in the set match the evidence. That is, these propositions have mental models that represent the evidence, and so they seem to be compatible with it. The program implementing the model theory accordingly works on the principle that individuals will reject a proposition that has only mental models conflicting with the evidence or, otherwise, that fails to represent the evidence (Legrenzi et al. 2000).

The simplest illustration of the mismatch principle is a pair of contrasting examples. Consider, first, the following example and suppose that you have no reason to doubt either informant:

> Vivien says: "If Pat was insulted then she got angry."
> Evelyn says: "Pat was insulted."
> But, you know for sure that Pat did not get angry.

Vivien's conditional assertion has the following mental models:

> insulted   angry
>   ...

where "insulted" denotes a model of Pat being insulted, "angry" denotes a model of Pat getting angry, and the ellipsis denotes a wholly implicit model representing the possibilities in which the antecedent of the conditional (Pat is insulted) is false. Evelyn's assertion has the mental model:

> insulted

The combination of the models yields the conclusion that Pat got angry. But, the incontrovertible evidence has the model:

> ¬ angry

The evidence is consistent with each premise individually, but not with both of them together. So, which premise should reasoners abandon? Because the evidence conflicts with the one explicit mental model of the conditional premise, reasoners should reject the conditional premise rather than the other premise. In the unlikely event that reasoners are able to flesh out their models of the conditional to make them fully explicit:

> insulted   angry
> ¬ insulted   angry
> ¬ insulted   ¬ angry

then the evidence matches the third model, and so now reasoners should reject Evelyn's categorical assertion because its model fails to represent the evidence.

In contrast, consider the following problem:

> Vivien says: "If Pat was insulted then she got angry."
> Evelyn says: "Pat did not get angry."
> You know for sure that Pat was insulted.

The premises have the models:

> insulted   angry
>   ...

and:

> ¬ angry

The model of the evidence is:

> insulted

Once again, the evidence is consistent with each premise, but not with both of them together. In this case, the evidence matches the one explicit mental model of the conditional premise, but it is not represented in the model of Evelyn's categorical assertion. Hence, reasoners should tend to achieve consistency by rejecting this assertion.

Elio and Pelletier (1997) carried out the pioneering psychological study of nonmonotonic reasoning. Their results confirmed the mismatch principle for the preceding pair of examples. It has also been confirmed for a variety of other sorts of problems, and these studies have shown that reasoners are computing mismatches between mental models, not merely between surface clauses in assertions (see Legrenzi et al. 2001).

The third and critical step in reasoning to consistency is to create a causal diagnosis that accounts for the inconsistency. Our culture puts the highest value on causal explanations, and so what counts as a plausible explanation should be a chain leading from a cause to an effect, in which the effect resolves the inconsistency. People know about the different causal possibilities in certain domains, i.e., they have access to explicit models of the possibilities in their *available* knowledge (see Tversky & Kahneman 1973). Hence, the abductive step, we believe, works in the following way. The inconsistent assertions trigger explicit knowledge, which takes the form of explicit models of possibilities. These explicit models then modulate the mental models of assertions, taking precedence over them in the case of contradictions. Assertions contradicted in this way are taken to represent counterfactual possibilities. The resulting *effect* in the causal chain, if one can be constructed, makes possible or necessary the facts of the matter. Hence, the chain provides an explanatory diagnosis that resolves the inconsistency.

Consider how the computer program implementing the theory deals with our earlier example:

> If individuals are insulted then they get angry.
> Pat was insulted.
> Yet Pat did not get angry.
> Why not?

The mental models of the conditional premise are as follows:

> insulted   angry
> ...

The mismatch principle predicts that individuals will cease to believe that the conditional is strictly true. It expresses a useful idealization, however, and so the program treats it as describing a counterfactual set of possibilities:

> Facts: insulted   ¬ angry
> Counterfactual possibilities: insulted   angry
> ...

In any case, the original conditional premise is no longer strictly true: it has been modulated by the facts of the matter and available knowledge. You may know that being very-calm prevents a person from getting angry. Prevention is a causal relation, and the model theory postulates that the meaning of causal assertions depends on what is possible and what is impossible in the co-occurrence of various states of affairs (Goldvarg & Johnson-Laird 2001). Hence, amongst the knowledge-base of the program are the following explicit possibilities:

> very-calm   ¬ angry
> ¬ very-calm   angry
> ¬ very-calm   ¬ angry

The factual model in the current set of mental models may trigger the relevant possibility among this available knowledge, and it serves as an explanation of the inconsistency:

> Insulted, but very-calm, and so it is not the case that angry.

This explanation in turn can elicit its own causal explanation from the knowledge-base:

> Why is the following the case: very-calm?
> Answer: Buddhist.

In other words, Buddhist practices have enabled Pat to become so calm that insults no longer elicit overt anger on her part.

The program can construct different explanations depending on which knowledge is triggered. And in human beings even the present explanation might occur as a result of a different sequence of mental processes. Indeed, human reasoners regularly fail to generate any explanatory diagnosis whatsoever.

An important feature of the model theory of causal relations is that it should be easier to infer an effect from a cause than to infer a cause from an effect. A cause is sufficient to yield, and so perhaps to infer, its effect. But, since an effect may have alternative causes, it is harder to infer its actual cause. This bias predicts a trend in the plausibility of different explanations. An assertion of a cause and an effect, in which the effect accounts for the inconsistency, should tend to be evaluated as more probable than a statement of the cause alone. The explanation, which the program can also generate:

> (1) *Pat knew that the person insulting her was mentally ill and Pat knew that the person didn't mean the insult.*   (*Cause-and-effect*)

describes a cause and its effect, which in turn explains why Pat did not get angry. Individuals know that:

> If a person is insane, then the person does not mean insults.

Hence, an explanation that states only the causal antecedent:

> (2) *Pat knew that the person insulting her was mentally ill.*   (*Cause*)

should enable reasoners to infer the consequent, and so this explanation should be judged as only slightly less probable than the explanation stating both cause and effect. A statement of the effect alone:

(3) *Pat knew that the person didn't mean the insult.*   *(Effect)*

lacks an explanation of its cause. It should be judged as less probable than the statement of the cause alone. These three causal explanations (cause-and-effect, cause, effect) are incompatible with the truth of the conditional assertion in the original problem. A different sort of explanation is one that denies the categorical premise in the original problem:

(4) *Pat wasn't really insulted.*   *(Rejection of the categorical)*

As the mismatch principle implies, however, an inconsistency between the conclusion and the facts of the matter should be resolved in this case by rejecting the conditional premise rather than the categorical premise. Hence, the three causal explanations should be rated as more probable than the rejection of the categorical premise. Only the cause-and-effect explanation is a conjunction of two propositions, and so we should consider an alternative sort of conjunction consisting of the effect paired with an antecedent that is not its cause:

(5) *The person who insulted Pat was a deadly enemy and Pat knew that the person didn't mean the insult.*   *(Non-causal conjunction)*

The effect, which resolves the inconsistency, is not caused by the antecedent. Such a non-causal assertion should be rated as the least probable of the putative explanations.

We tested this prediction of the rank-order of the five sorts of putative explanations. Each participant dealt with explanations for 20 different inconsistencies based on four problems in each of five domains (physical, mechanical, physiological, psychological, and social). For each problem, the participant ranked the five sorts of assertion and two filler items according to how probable they seemed as explanations. We carried out two such studies and the results overwhelmingly confirmed the predictions (Legrenzi et al. 2001). In both studies, all 20 participants' rankings significantly corroborated the predicted order. The greater probability of the cause-and-effect over explanations that state only the cause or only the effect is a strong instance of the conjunction fallacy (Tversky & Kahneman 1983), because the participants rated a conjunction as more probable than *either* of its constituents. Previous studies of the fallacy usually show only that a conjunction can be rated as more probable than *one* of its constituents (see Hertwig & Chase 1998).

The mismatch principle predicts that a rejection of the categorical assertion should seem more probable if the participants construct explicit models of the conditional that include the following possibilities:

insulted   angry
¬ insulted   ¬ angry

In this case, the incontrovertible evidence that Pat did not get angry matches a model of the conditional, and so reasoners should tend to reject the categorical premise. We corroborated this prediction in an experiment in which we compared the original 10 problems based on conditionals with 10 variations of them in which the conditionals were replaced by biconditionals:

If and only if Pat is insulted then she gets angry.

The model theory predicts that such biconditionals have only two fully explicit models (as shown above), and so reasoners should be more likely to succeed in constructing them. The experiment indeed showed that the participants rated the rejection of the categorical assertion as more probable when it occurred with the biconditional versions of the problems (a mean rank of 2.7 over the seven assertions, where "1" is the rank of the most probable explanation) than when it occurred in the conditional versions of the problems (a mean rank of 4.1). This result corroborates the mismatch principle.

Reasoning to consistency is in general not a tractable process. Yet, individuals are often able to abduce explanations for inconsistencies with remarkable rapidity. The model theory accounts for their performance in terms of the availability of appropriate causal knowledge, which is triggered by the inconsistent assertions. This knowledge eliminates some assertions – in the case of conditionals, it treats them as counterfactuals, and creates a plausible explanation of the facts of the matter. Yet, reasoners are not always able to come up with an explanation. Sometimes, both in life and in the laboratory, they are stumped. Such failures are not surprising, since the domain is computationally intractable. Yet, in many circumstances in life, it would be a disaster if human beings failed to react because they could not account for an inconsistency. We turn now to emotions. They are heuristics that, as Peirce foresaw, parallel abduction, but that enable us to surmount nearly all inconsistencies in daily life.

Emotions as heuristics

One of the earliest contributions to the computational theory of emotions was Simon's (1967) paper in which he argued that for any intelligent agent operating in the ordinary world, the agent's resources can not be sufficient. A human, or a robot, will have some knowledge of the world, but it is never enough to know what lies round every next corner. Humans have some powers, but they are insufficient to accomplish all the goals that they can conceive. Accordingly, to understand intelligent systems in real environments, we must postulate some mechanism or process that will manage action when the unexpected happens, when knowledge has not predicted actuality, or when physical resources have proved insufficient. This mechanism or process corresponds to what, in human experience, is called an emotion.

Let us try to make this clearer by means of a metaphor, based on De Sousa (1987) and Oatley (1992). In medieval theology God was conceived as omniscient and omnipotent. God thus knew everything and could accomplish everything. Despite the complexities of heaven and earth, the divine will would be followed by the divine deed, which would accomplish the divine end, with never a falling short. Consequently the divinity would have no emotions. Nothing would go better than expected. Nor would it go worse. There would be no longing, no sense of loneliness There would be no accidents, no threats, no losses, no frustrations.

Human perceptual and motor systems have to operate in a complex world, but it is one to which human knowledge and other resources are not fully adequate. People do contrive plans, and enact them. But human action often fails to accomplish what is willed. Outcomes occur that are not anticipated. It is at such junctures that human creatures experience emotions and their (generally) useful effects.

Though humans can and should strive for rationality, there are three classes of reason that defeat any fully rational – computationally tractable – solution to our problems of how to act in the world. First, as just discussed, we have limited knowledge and other resources, in a complex world that soon exceeds them. Second, as pointed out by Neisser (1963), we have not a single goal, as do many computational systems, but multiple goals, not all of which are compatible. Third, we have evolved a particular human adaptation that ameliorates the first of these problems: we cooperate to accomplish together more than isolated individuals ever could. We therefore need to coordinate our actions with those of other agents, but this solution sets new problems of knowledge and agency as we come to rely on other people. Each of these three problems means that computationally tractable problem solving is in general unavailable to us. Emotions are among the heuristics we have for knowing what to do when we cannot work out an optimal answer. In other species, they may play a still more important role granted still more constrained powers of reasoning.

The communicative theory of emotions

According to Oatley and Johnson-Laird (1987; 1996) and Johnson-Laird and Oatley (1992), emotional heuristics work as follows. For each goal-plan complex, there is a system that monitors the state of the world, and will emit an *emotion signal* to the rest of the brain if an event of a certain kind occurs that is relevant to it. These kinds of goal-relevant events have recurred during human evolution. Positive emotions are signalled when the event signals progress made towards a goal, and negative emotions when the event signals that progress is impeded. More specifically, according to our theory, progress better than expected prompts happiness. Goal blockage causes anger. Goal conflicts, or dangers, cause fear. Losses – when goals cannot be reinstated – cause sadness. Emotions occur, in general therefore, when consistency is increased or decreased between goals and what is known about the state of the world.

We have set our theory of emotions in relation to action and planning. The process of planning is akin to reasoning. This insight is due to Hewitt (1971) one of the pioneers of automated planning in artificial intelligence. When you reason, you derive a sequence of conclusions leading step by step from initial premises to a desired final conclusion, where each step is sanctioned by your knowledge. And when you plan, you seek to formulate a sequence of actions leading step by step from the initial circumstances to a desired final outcome, where each step is sanctioned by knowledge. In psychological terms, goal directed action depends on a form of reasoning to consistency; plans are made and enacted until the state of the world is consistent with a goal.

For humans, emotions are signals to themselves (Oatley & Johnson-Laird 1987; 1996). They allow humans, who have slender computational resources, to choose among multiple goals, and to act – despite their limited and often incorrect knowledge, and despite their limited physical powers. When new knowledge invalidates previous assumptions, they switch attention and action from one kind of goal-related action to another. You may be crossing the road with a friend, when a squeal of brakes causes a sudden fright: you stop your conversation and attend to the traffic. The fear switches your cognitive system into a mode adapted to meeting dangers. In this mode, the cognitive system is tuned to making you stop what you were doing, attend to environmental signs of safety and danger, and to prepare to avoid or escape the danger. In this mode, cognitions are simplified. The emotion prepares the system to meet the general type of unexpected contingency that has occurred.

We postulate a small number of basic emotions; each one sets the cognitive system into a mode appropriate to a recurring kind of goal-relevant event (see Table 1). Other emotions are founded upon these basic ones. (Johnson-Laird & Oatley 1989). Thus, embarrassment is founded on fear.

A typical emotion, then, consists of two parts. One is the emotion signal itself. It is not informational or propositional, i.e., it has no internal structure that has to be given an interpretation by the system: a control signal sets the cognitive system into a mode that is appropriate to certain kinds of situation that recur in relation to goals and plans (see Table 1). The second part is informational: it is a propositional message about the cause or object of the emotion. Of course, the propositional information may be slight or even mistaken. But, in structured diaries of emotions in everyday life, when people report an emotion, they generally know what caused it. When angry, for instance, they typically know who or what caused the anger, and with whom they are angry (Oatley & Duncan 1992; 1994).

Sometimes, however, emotional states can occur without the experiencer knowing why. You experience an emotion but for no apparent reason. Emotions can be, in the philosophical sense, non-intentional. In psychiatry these states are known as free floating, i.e., without an object. Thus, occasionally, people feel free-floating anxiety (the prolonged mood of fear). In diary studies, Oatley and Duncan (1992; 1994) found that about 6% of emotion episodes of happiness, sadness, anger and fear were of this kind. A corollary concerns mood-altering drugs: antidepressants, anti-anxiety drugs, and the like. These alter mood, but without any event in the outside world being responsible. Thus, although emotion signals are usually accompanied by informational messages about what happened, they can occur without such messages both naturally and after a pharmacological intervention. These phenomena tend to confirm our hypothesis that emotions have two dissociable parts. Other kinds of emotions, the varieties of love and rejection (as shown in the lower part of Table 1), always have objects.

In the case of multiple goals, reasoning to consistency can yield an appropriate plan for achieving perhaps one or a few goals. In the case of multiple beliefs, however, as their number increases, so the task of reasoning to consistency becomes computationally intractable. Emotions are heuristics that

Table 1. Nine basic emotions as postulated by Oatley & Johnson-Laird (1996), with the goal-relevant events that elicit them, the functions they perform and the transitions they accomplish. Emotions in the first group can occur without the experiencer knowing what caused them; those in the second group always have an object.

Emotion (mode)	Eliciting event or object of emotion	Actions to which transition occurs
Emotions that can occasionally be free-floating	*Goal condition*	*Adjustment of plan*
Happiness	Subgoals being achieved	Continue with plan, modifying if necessary; cooperate; show affection
Sadness	Failure of major plan or loss of active goal	Do nothing; search for new plan; seek help
Anger	Active plan frustrated	Try harder; aggress
Fear	Self-preservation goal threatened or goal conflict	Stop current plan, attend vigilantly to environment, freeze and/or escape
Emotions that always have an object	*Goal*	*Adjustment of plan*
Attachment love	Proximity to caregiver	Keep contact, talk
Caregiving love	Care for offspring	Nurture, help, support
Sexual love	Sexual partner	Engage in courtship, sexual activity
Disgust	Reject contamination	Expel substance; withdraw
Contempt	Reject outgroup person	Treat without consideration

bridge the gap created by the impossibility of complete rationality. They yield methods that are feasible for dealing with the world and that do well enough in most situations. Emotions derive from processes of the cognitive system that detect inconsistency, and act towards increasing the consistency among goals and knowledge.

Joint plans, emotions, and models of other people

In the foregoing, we have followed a common practice of cognitive scientists and concentrated on individual reasoning. Now we widen the scope of reasoning to include two people. As mentioned above, a human solution to the problem of insufficient knowledge and limited agency is cooperation. Both individual and group thinking is punctuated by emotions: success engenders optimism and trust; failure engenders frustration and distrust.

Hutchins (1991) has introduced the phrase "distributed cognition" to refer to cognition distributed between mind and the outside world, as occurs in, say, the technology of reading and writing, and to refer to cognition distributed among two or more minds. Inconsistencies can arise in joint plans arising from the distributed cognition of two individuals. Oatley and his colleagues have studied the inconsistencies that arise when such a plan fails (Oatley & Larocque 1995; Grazzani-Gavazzi & Oatley 1999; Larocque & Oatley 2001). These authors refer to this kind of inconsistency as a "joint error," and they have collected altogether a corpus of more than 500 such errors.

The general method was that participants were asked to look out for a joint error, and to complete a structured diary when one occurred. They were told that a joint plan was any explicit arrangement to perform an action involving them and another person. An error was to be recorded if the plan was not realized or was defectively realized because something went wrong, but any deliberate change of a goal or plan was not to count as an error. In their diaries, the participants recorded details of their plan, the error, and its emotional sequelae. Here is an example of a joint error in the words of a participant:

> My co-worker was measuring some circumferences of pipes, converting them to diameters and reporting them to me. I recorded the figures and used them to drill holes later. The drilled holes were incorrect for diameters. It could have been the conversion or measurement. I had to modify the holes.

When such errors occurred, they tended to elicit emotions such as anger and frustration: this participant was angry with his co-worker. In Larocque and Oatley's (2001) second study with 157 participants, 66% of them experienced anger in some form when an error occurred. The errors also elicited thoughts and attempts at repair, such as, in the case of the collaborative plan of measuring pipes and drilling holes: "I need to and want to do something about this kind of thing with him." Another general feature was the construction of mental models of the other person, and plans for the future, in this case: "My co-worker is not as careful about numbers as I am – maybe I should do this kind of task with someone else."

Emotions sometimes provide, or perhaps amplify, the first indication of an inconsistency: e.g., a pang of anxiety when a loved-one's lateness for an appointment exceeds a certain time. Similarly, the observation of someone else's emotional state can be the signal of an error. One participant had arranged to meet her mother at a shopping mall. She wrote: "I realized there was a problem when mother was cool, when she did not appear to 'recognize' me when I ran to meet her. She was angry, asked where I had been, and said: 'I've been waiting for over an hour!' "

Mental models of the other person

Oatley and Larocque (1995) found that when a joint error occurred there was a strong tendency to blame the other person for it. Participants were asked to record any thoughts that they had about the other person, and this method accordingly opened a window onto one person's mental model of the other person after the detection of an inconsistency. The reports from Larocque and Oatley's (2001) second study (N = 157) showed that in such cases nearly a third of the participants constructed mental models of their partner in which they ascribed negative personality traits to that person. The other person was described as: "unthoughtful, untrustworthy, unreliable, disrespectful, dishonest, irresponsible, inconsiderate, insensitive, incompetent, indecisive, careless, selfish, self-involved, stupid, lazy, superficial, scatterbrained, childish, an idiot, a hypocrite, a bitch." Of course, there was a large and significant tendency for participants who were angry to make such ascriptions as compared with those who were not angry. There was also very a strong correlation between a partner being held responsible for the error and being the object of negative ascriptions.

A consistent theme in these mental models was a lack of conscientiousness, which elicited an underlying emotional tone of distrust. The abductive inference in thinking about how the error came about, and about what one might do next, was twofold: the other person (a) had been the principal cause of the error by failing to play a proper part in the joint plan, and (b) was therefore not to be trusted: a matter of substantial emotional consequence.

The participants rated their planning partner in the joint error on a scale of importance of the relationship with that person. Partners rated as low or medium on this scale (i.e., 0–7 on the 11-point scale) were more likely to receive at least one negative trait ascription. Those receiving high ratings (of 8 to 10) on the relationship scale received a negative trait ascription significantly less often. Thus, a participant's tendency to make negative ascriptions of another person was modulated when the other person was someone with whom the participant had an important relationship.

When you interact with other people, you want to rely on them and to trust that they will play their part. One important sort of inconsistency is, therefore, exemplified by joint errors, which can come as nasty surprises if you perceive that someone has let you down. Larocque and Oatley found that in some circumstances, even a single inconsistency could have a large significance in one person's model of another. Trust is a fundamental aspect of interpersonal relationships, and so incidents of joint planning in which something has been accomplished or something has gone wrong are principal indications for degrees of trust. They enter your mental models of other individuals. They tell you about the suitability of these individuals for joint plans in the future. One woman, for instance, waited for a new colleague in one restaurant, while he sat for over an hour in a differently located restaurant in the same chain waiting for her. The fact that he had "stood her up", she said, would be at the back of her mind the next time she had dealings with him. Indeed, it was, even though she stated in her diary that his explanation of the error was convincing. He waited longer than she had in the restaurant, and he was the one who had to phone to find out what had gone wrong. She knew he had been no more at fault than she. Nonetheless the emotion of distrust provided a new kind of forward consistency for her in her relations with this man. This evaluation was compelling, even though she held explicit beliefs that were inconsistent with it. The emotion overruled the propositional inconsistency. It provided a kind of real-life priming that constrained her future behavior towards the other individual.

In some cases, a train of mis-managed arrangements became dominant in one partner's mental model of the other person. For example, a participant described her irritation with a friend who was often late for their meetings, and who would always compound the lapse by being annoyingly over-apologetic. With reference to the score of 6 she gave this person on the scale of importance of the relationship, she remarked: "this is why she is not a 10."

Why is it so distressing when a friend or lover, particularly a new one, forgets a lunch date? It is because you want the plan, which was important enough for you to enact your part with attention and anticipation, to hold a similar importance for the other person. Intimacy requires not only that you know the other person (have a rich mental model of this individual) but also that you both have a similar hierarchy of importance for major goals. The proper performance of a joint plan speaks louder than any declaration. It is the most sensitive index mutually available of the importance of a relationship to both parties in that relationship.

Abduction, mental models, and emotions

Like Peirce, we are struck by the analogy between making an abductive inference (to infer an hypothesis) and experiencing an emotion. More than a hundred years ago Peirce made some bald statements about the properties of abductions. "We must conquer the truth by guessing, or not at all," he said (Sebeok & Umiker-Sebeok 1983, p. 11), and he called this kind of inference "a singular salad... whose chief elements are its groundlessness, its ubiquity, and its trustworthiness" (p. 16). Nowadays we would say that abductions are not simply guesses: they are grounded in available knowledge, although some of this knowledge may be intuitive and inexplicit. Similarly Peirce overstates the trustworthiness of abductions. People often make abductions that are plausible, and then find that they were wrong. But he was right in arguing that human abductive hypotheses are correct far more frequently that would occur by chance.

Emotions, as Peirce argued, are often similar to abductive hypotheses. People detect an inconsistency, and rapidly reach a conclusion about the broad class of events that has caused it or, in some cases, about the specific cause. Consider the following from the corpus of joint errors: a participant had checked his luggage through to the final destination on an airline's route, although he planned to get off at the first stop. When he got off at the first airport, he stood waiting for his bags until everyone had left. He reported: "I did not start thinking there was a problem until I suddenly had a burning face feeling of embarrassment and thought 'Oh, s—!' " He looked at his baggage claim stub and saw that his luggage had been checked through to another state. The incident was one of a chain of mistakes that made him late for a meeting: the joint error he recorded in his diary.

The man's train of reasoning appears to have been as follows:

> *Premise:* The baggage of all the people on the flight has arrived.
> *Premise:* I was on the flight.
> *Conclusion:* My baggage has arrived.
> *Incontrovertible evidence*: My baggage has *not* arrived.
> *Abductive explanation of the inconsistency (recovered from memory)*:
> I checked my baggage on to a subsequent destination. It's still on the plane on its way to another state!
> *Corroboration of explanation*: My claim stub shows my baggage checked through to the other airport. This explanation rules out the truth of the

first of the two premises and corroborates the mismatch principle (see Part 1).

After detecting the inconsistency, the man makes the nonmonotonic leap, an abductive inference to an explanation: the reason his baggage had not appeared on the conveyor was because they were on their way to another airport. In parallel, he experiences a sequence of emotions that we discuss presently. His inference was likely to be correct. It was corroborated by his baggage claim stub. But life is sufficiently complex that even this was not certain. It is just possible that his baggage might mistakenly have been taken off the plane by the handlers at the airport where he had alighted. It might have appeared on the conveyor in front of him a few seconds later.

We are struck both by the parallel between abductive explanations and emotions, and by their typically close conjunction in time. It supports our hypothesis that abductive explanations can themselves cause emotions. Beck et al. (1979) have proposed a comparable hypothesis, and it underlies their claim that individuals can alleviate emotional disorders, such as depression, by recognizing the invalidity of certain kinds of abductive leaps. Yet, not all emotions are caused by abductions. For instance, if you are a skier of only moderate skill and you stand at the top of a very steep ski run, you feel anxious. The thought that you might fall is not an abduction, merely an induction from previous cases. Similarly, if a close friend dies, you are upset without making any abductive explanation of how this happened.

When you experience an emotion, it is usually caused by an event that does not match your expectations: an inconsistency occurs in a goal-directed sequence. The emotion makes known to you that something significant has occurred that will affect the outcome of your plans. Usually, people reach an abductive inference rapidly. Its conclusion can elicit an emotion that causes a realization that something has either gone right or gone wrong in a plan. It sets the cognitive system into a state that is broadly adapted to dealing with the class of event that has been abductively inferred: an achievement of a subgoal, a frustration, a loss, a threat, etc. The emotion lacks the ordinarily tentative qualities of a hypothesis. Instead it has a compelling quality of vivid certainty (often referred to as hot cognition) not usually shared – for instance – by recognizing an inconsistency in logic. When Pat (from Part 1 of this chapter) is insulted, it would be different if one were Pat than if one were Polly working on a logic problem to see whether some symbol "Pat" has the predicate "insulted."

In the example of the man at the baggage claim, the sequence of eliciting the emotion goes like this:

1. Detection of an inconsistency.
2. The inconsistency causes and (perhaps gradually) increases an emotion of anxiety.
3. The abductive explanation of the inconsistency impinges on consciousness. (This step doesn't always occur. It does when your baggage is missing: you figure the airline has lost it. But, in the case of the death of a friend, an abductive explanation akin to the baggage case would be to infer that the cause of the death was, say, incompetence on someone's part.)
4. The abduction causes an emotion of embarrassment.

When the detection of an inconsistency causes a sudden emotion, the sequence is as follows:

1. Detection of an inconsistency: a clash of simple predicates such as an expectation and incontrovertible evidence.
2. The inconsistency itself causes a sudden emotion.
3. If the emotion impinges on consciousness, then an attempt is usually made to abduce an explanation of the inconsistency. This is another propositional message, but it originates in conscious thought.
4. If this abduction succeeds, then it may cause a new emotion (e.g. anger at someone's incompetence causing the death of a friend).

In general, emotions are caused by conflicts (inconsistencies) between goals and states of the world that are relevant to these goals, or between incompatible goals. But because the cognitions causing emotions are simple, emotions do not seem to be caused by inconsistencies among sets of propositions, such as:

> If not A then B.
> If B then not C.
> Not-A and C.

In the corpus of errors in joint plans, typical mental processes were (a) the detection of an inconsistency between expectation and actuality: an agreed plan had gone wrong so that a goal would not be achieved, and (b) the abductive inference that its cause was the other person failing to enact his or her part properly. Most frequently the inference was of blame, the broad class of goal-related events was of frustration at the inability to accomplish the agreed goal, and the emotion was of anger at the other person who was held responsible for the error. Sometimes, however, quite different kinds of inference were made. For instance, when the participants were waiting for a loved one who did not show up, many of them reported a stab of intense anxiety triggered by the explanation that the loved person had perhaps suffered an accident and was dead.

All such emotions are what Peirce called simple predicates elicited by a complex predicate: anxiety is triggered by the thought that someone has died. The abductive explanation and the emotion flood the mind almost simultaneously. As we mentioned earlier, one is a propositional message and the other is an emotional signal. The intensity of the emotion is correlated with the importance of the inconsistency that has been discovered. The emotion confers a compelling quality to subsequent thoughts it engenders. Because almost all human goals of importance depend on other human beings, it is the relationship with the other person and the goals of *that* relationship, rather than the immediate plan, that dominates: "I'll never trust that person again," or "Something terrible has happened to her." It is the human world that we desire most intensely to be consistent.

References

Beck, A. T., Rush, A., J., Shaw, B. F., & Emery, G. (1979). *Cognitive therapy of depression*. New York: Guilford.

Conan Doyle, A. (1930). *The Complete Sherlock Holmes, Vol. II*. New York: Doubleday.

Cook, S. A. (1971). The complexity of theorem proving procedures. *Proceedings of the Third Annual Association of Computing Machinery Symposium on the Theory of Computing*, 151–158.

De Sousa, R. (1987). *The rationality of emotions*. Cambridge, MA: MIT Press.

Elio, R., & Pelletier, F. J. (1997). Belief change as propositional update. *Cognitive Science, 21*, 419–460.

Goldvarg, E., & Johnson-Laird, P. N. (2001). Naive causality: a mental model theory of causal meaning and reasoning. *Cognitive Science*, in press.

Grazzani-Gavazzi, I., & Oatley, K. (1999). The experience of emotions of interdependence and independence following interpersonal errors in Italy and Anglophone Canada. *Cognition and Emotion, 13*, 49–63.

Hertwig, R., & Chase, V. M. (1998). Many reasons or just one: How response mode affects reasoning in the conjunction problem. *Thinking and Reasoning, 4*, 319–352.

Hewitt, C. (1971). Description and theoretical analysis (using schemas) of PLANNER: a language for proving theorems and manipulating models in a robot. Unpublished PhD thesis, MIT.

Hutchins, E. (1991). The social organization of distributed cognition. In L. Resnick & J. Levine, & S. Teasley (Eds.), *Perspectives on socially shared cognition*. Washington, DC: APA Press.

Johnson-Laird, P. N. (1983). *Mental Models: Towards a Cognitive Science of Language, Inference and Consciousness.* Cambridge: Cambridge University Press; Cambridge, MA: Harvard University Press.

Johnson-Laird, P. N., & Byrne, R. M. J. (1991). *Deduction.* Hillsdale, NJ: Erlbaum.

Johnson-Laird, P. N., Legrenzi, P., Girotto, P., & Legrenzi, M. S. (2000). Illusions in reasoning about consistency. *Science, 288,* 531–532.

Johnson-Laird, P. N., Legrenzi, P., Girotto, P., Legrenzi, M. S., & Caverni, J-P. (1999). Naive Probability: A mental model theory of extensional reasoning. *Psychological Review, 106,* 62–88.

Johnson-Laird, P. N., & Oatley, K. (1989). The language of emotions: An analysis of a semantic field. *Cognition and Emotion, 3,* 81–123.

Johnson-Laird, P. N., & Oatley, K. (1992). Basic emotions, rationality, and folk theory. *Cognition and Emotion, 6,* 201–223.

Larocque, L., & Oatley, K. (2001). Trust and errors in mutual planning: face-to-face closeness and urban separation. Submitted.

Legrenzi, M. S., Legrenzi, P., Girotto, V., & Johnson-Laird, P. N. (2001). Reasoning to consistency: a theory of naïve nonmonotonic reasoning. Submitted.

Neisser, U. (1963). The imitation of man by machine. *Science, 139,* 193–197.

Oatley, K. (1992). *Best laid schemes: The psychology of emotions.* New York, NY: Cambridge University Press.

Oatley, K., & Duncan, E. (1992). Incidents of emotion in daily life. In K. T. Strongman (Ed.), *International Review of Studies on Emotion* (Vol. 2, pp. 250–293). Chichester: Wiley.

Oatley, K., & Duncan, E. (1994). The experience of emotions in everyday life. *Cognition and Emotion, 8,* 369–381.

Oatley, K., & Johnson-Laird, P. N. (1987). Towards a cognitive theory of emotions. *Cognition and Emotion, 1,* 29–50.

Oatley, K., & Johnson-Laird, P. N. (1996). The communicative theory of emotions: empirical tests, mental models, and implications for social interaction. In L. L. Martin & A. Tesser (Eds.), *Striving and feeling: Interactions among goals, affect, and self-regulation* (pp. 363–393). Mahwah, NJ: Erlbaum.

Oatley, K., & Larocque, L. (1995). Everyday concepts of emotions following every-other-day errors in joint plans. In J. Russell & J.-M. Fernandez-Dols & A. S. R. Manstead, & J. Wellenkamp (Eds.), *Everyday conceptions of Emotions: An introduction to the psychology, anthropology, and linguistics of emotion; NATO ASI Series D 81* (pp. 145–165). Dordrecht: Kluwer.

Peirce, C. S. (1868). Some consequences of four incapacities. In J. Buchler (Ed.), *Philosophical Writings of Peirce.* New York: Dover, 1955, pp. 228–250.

Peirce, C. S. (1898). *Reasoning and the Logic of Things.* (Ed.) K. Ketner, Cambridge, MA: Harvard University Press, 1992.

Peirce, C. S. (1903). Abduction and induction. In J. Buchler (Ed.), *Philosophical Writings of Peirce.* New York: Dover, 1955, pp. 150–156.

Sebeok, T. A., & Umiker-Sebeok, J. (1983). "You know my method": A juxtaposition of Charles S. Peirce and Sherlock Holmes. In U. Eco & T. A. Sebeok (Eds.), *The sign of three: Dupin, Holmes, Peirce* (pp. 11–54). Bloomington: Indiana University Press.

Simon, H. A. (1967). Motivational and emotional controls of cognition. *Psychological Review, 74*, 29–39.

Tversky, A., & Kahneman, D. (1973). Availability: a heuristic for judging frequency and probability. *Cognitive Psychology, 4*, 207–232.

Tversky, A., & Kahneman, D. (1983). Extensional versus intuitive reasoning: The conjunction fallacy in probability judgment. *Psychological Review, 90*, 292–315.

CHAPTER 8

Expected feelings about risky options

Alan Schwartz
University of Illinois at Chicago

When we face decisions, we often anticipate how we will feel about possible outcomes and use our feelings to guide choice. Winning $100 in a lottery is exciting, earning a promotion is gratifying, and losing money in the stock market is disappointing. These feelings often arise from either implicit or explicit comparisons. People assess their feelings in light of other outcomes which serve as reference points. Certainly the status quo is a reference point. Other peoples' outcomes can also serve as reference points. A number of researchers have focused on *counterfactual* reference points: outcomes which could have happened to the decision maker, but didn't (Kahneman & Miller 1986). Consider someone who wants to invest in the stock market. After careful consideration, he invests a large amount in Apple Computers. As he evaluates his investment, he may consider counterfactual outcomes: what if Apple had chosen a different strategy? What if the Federal Reserve had lowered interest rates? What if he had invested in IBM instead? Each reference point may evoke different feelings about the value of his investment.

Roese and Olson (1995) summarize recent research on counterfactual thoughts and emotions. "Upward" counterfactuals, in which outcomes are compared to better outcomes, often result in worse feelings about a given outcome; "downward" counterfactuals often produce better feelings. (Roese 1994; Markman, Gavanski, Sherman, & McMullen 1993; Medvec, Madey, & Gilovich 1995). These comparisons can have such powerful effects on feelings that *positive* outcomes can feel worse than *negative* outcomes (Boles & Messick 1995; Mellers, Schwartz, Ho, & Ritov 1997).

Can choices be predicted from emotions?

Regret theory and disappointment theory, proposed independently by Loomes and Sugden (1982; 1986) and Bell (1982; 1985) assert that utilities reflect not simply the value of an outcome, but its value relative to easily imagined counterfactual outcomes. Disappointment theory focuses on comparisons of outcomes *within* an alternative. For example, a $5 win from a lottery ticket is compared to larger or smaller prizes available from the same ticket. Regret theory highlights comparisons of outcomes *across* alternatives. For example, a $5 win from a lottery ticket is compared to larger or smaller prizes that could have been won from other lottery games.

Regret theory and disappointment theory have been proposed as both normative and descriptive theories of choice. Loomes and Sugden (1982) provide an argument for the normative and rational nature of the theories; Sugden (1993) presents an axiomatization of regret theory. Bell (1982) discusses descriptive aspects of the theories. He points out that they can predict observed violations of subjective expected utility, including the Allais paradox, the reflection effect, and preference reversals. Loomes and Sugden (1987) do a similar analysis and provide some empirical support for both theories.

In both regret theory and disappointment theory, emotions are inferred from observed choices; the feelings are never directly measured. Choices suggest that people behave "as if" they are experiencing regret or disappointment. But is that what they really experience?

Feelings about outcomes

In a recent paper, Mellers, et al. (1997) propose a model of postdecision emotional reactions to monetary outcomes of gambles called decision affect theory. They show that feelings about an outcome depend not only on the utility of the outcome, but also on counterfactual comparisons with other possible outcomes that could have occurred, but didn't. They presented participants with a series of two-outcome gambles. Participants were informed that each gamble would be played and that they would receive the sum of the outcomes, both wins and losses. After learning the outcome of each gamble, participants rated their emotional reactions on a category rating scale from −50 ("Extremely Disappointed") to 50 ("Extremely Elated").[1]

Holding all else constant, participants reported greater pleasure from larger wins and greater displeasure from larger losses. In addition, emotions depended on within-gamble counterfactual comparisons. Winning became substantially less pleasurable when one could have won more; similarly, losing became substantially less painful, and sometimes even slightly pleasurable, when one could have lost more. Losing $8 was slightly pleasurable when one could have lost $32. Finally, outcomes that were more surprising elicited more intense feelings. A surprising loss of $8 was more unpleasant than a likely loss, and a surprising win of $8 was more pleasurable than an expected win.

According to decision affect theory, people evaluate outcomes by considering both the value of the obtained outcome and the value of the obtained outcome relative to salient counterfactual outcomes. When counterfactual outcomes are worse, any given outcome is more pleasurable. Similarly, when counterfactual outcomes are better, any given outcome is less pleasurable. Furthermore, these comparisons have greater impact when the obtained outcome is surprising.

In decision affect theory, the emotional response to an outcome is assume to be the utility of the outcome plus a comparison between the outcome and other possible outcomes. This comparison is weighted by the surprisingness of the obtained outcome. For a two-outcome gamble with outcomes a and b, the emotional response to outcome a (R_a) is given by:

$$R_a = J[u_a + g(u_a - u_b)(1 - s_a)] \tag{1}$$

where u_a and u_b are the utilities of outcomes a and b and s_a is the subjective probability of outcome a. The disappointment function, g, is a function of the difference between the obtained and unobtained outcome. It is weighted by the surprisingness or unexpectedness of the obtained outcome. g is usually assumed to be a step function, with step sizes that can differ for positive and negative comparisons. Finally, the response function, J, is assumed to be linear.

Kahneman and Snell (1992) elucidated an insightful distinction between what they call experienced utilities and decision utilities. Decision affect theory can be viewed as a formal account of experienced utilities – measures of the hedonic experience of an outcome, represented by R_a in the example above. In contrast, decision utilities, represented by u_a and u_b above, are utilities inferred from choices. According to decision affect theory, experienced utilities are influenced by surprise and counterfactual comparisons. Decision utilities are typically assumed to be independent of these factors. Furthermore, experienced utilities are not necessarily a monotonic function of outcomes, but decision utilities are typically assumed to be monotonically related to monetary outcomes. Decision affect theory attempts to capture experienced utilities in terms of decision utilities, comparisons between decision utilities, and subjective probabilities.

Subjective expected emotions

Decision affect theory is a theory of postdecision experienced utilities, not a theory of choice. However, Mellers, et al. (1997) proposed that people make choices that maximize their subjective expected emotions (SEE) or long run feelings. Suppose that anticipated feelings are reasonably well-described by experienced feelings. Then, the SEE of a gamble with outcomes a and b, when only the chosen gamble's outcome will be learned, can be written:

$$SEE = s_a R_a + s_b R_b \qquad (2)$$

where R_a and R_b are the emotional responses to outcomes a and b, as predicted from decision affect theory, and s_a and s_b are the subjective probabilities of experiencing those feelings. Mellers, et al. (1997) show that, for choices between two-outcome gambles, maximizing subjective expected emotions is often similar to maximizing subjective expected utilities. However, there are some advantages to emotions over utilities. Schwartz, Mellers, and Metzger (1998) found that, for the majority of respondents, choices were better described by SEE than SEU. Furthermore, when people were explicitly asked to make choices that maximize their good feelings or minimize their bad feelings, variations of SEE outperformed simpler hedonic choice strategies, as well as SEU.

The present paper explores the nature of subjective expected emotions. Can a gamble's SEE be assessed directly – can we measure this construct in a direct judgment rather than inferring it from choice? To answer this question, participants are asked to report how they expect to feel about a gamble on average. That is, how would they typically feel about the gamble if they played it many times? The study finds that these *judged expectations* are good proxies for subjective expected emotions. In addition, when participants make choices between the gambles, subjective expected emotions could describe these choices as well as subjective expected utilities, with the additional generality of being based on a model that predicted postdecision emotions and judged expectations.

Method

Procedure

Participants performed three tasks: judged expectations about gambles, feelings associated with the outcomes of gambles, and choices between gambles. In the judged expectations task, participants were shown a series of gambles represented as pie charts on a computer screen. Outcomes were displayed as regions of the pie chart; the size of the region was proportional to the probability of the outcome. Participants were told to imagine they would play the gamble many times, sometimes receiving one outcome and sometimes the other, which might result in different feelings about their outcomes each time they played. They were asked to rate how they expected they would feel about the outcomes of the gamble on average, on a category rating scale from −50 ("Expect to be Extremely Disappointed") to 50 ("Expect to be Extremely Elated"). In this task, participants never played the gambles or learned their results.

The feelings task was similar to that used in Mellers, et al. (1997). Participants saw a series of two-outcome gambles represented as pie charts on a computer screen. When participants hit a key, a pointer appeared in the center of the gamble, spun around the gamble a number of times, slowed to stop in one region of the gamble, and displayed the outcome. Participants then rated their feelings about their outcome on a category rating scale from −50 ("Extremely Disappointed") to 50 ("Extremely Elated").

In the choice task, participants were shown a series of gamble pairs and selected the gamble they preferred to play. Tasks were counterbalanced for order in a Latin square design; no order effects were found, so analyses are pooled across orders.

Stimuli

The stimuli were 18 mixed gambles constructed from a Better Outcome x Worse Outcome x Probability of Better Outcome factorial design. Levels of Better Outcome were −$8, $8, and $32. Levels of Worse Outcome were $8, −$8, and −$32. Probabilities were 0.2, 0.5, and 0.8. In the judged expectations task, each gamble was presented once. In the feelings task, each gamble was presented twice; no gamble was presented a second time until each gamble had been presented once, and obtained outcome (better vs. worse) was randomly assigned to the first or second presentation for each gamble. In the choice task, all 36 non-dominated pairs of gambles were presented once; gamble position on the screen (left vs. right) was randomized.

Participants

Eighty-one undergraduates at the University of California, Berkeley served as participants. They were told that the computer would keep track of the results of the gambles in all three tasks. In the feelings task, participants would receive the sum of the obtained outcomes on each trial; in the judged expectations task, the computer would play each gamble and add its outcome, which participants did not see, to the total; in the choice task, the computer would play each chosen gamble and add its outcome, which participants did not see, to the total. Payments would be the grand total over all three tasks. Participants were told that the average payment would be approximately $8, but there was some chance they might earn more or less, and that in the unlikely event that they finished the experiment with a negative total, they would be required to do menial chores in the decision making laboratory to pay off their debt at the rate of $10 per hour. In fact, responses did not affect payment; each participant received $8.

Results

Postdecision feelings

Before examining the results of the judged expectation and choice tasks, it is necessary to establish that decision affect theory provided an adequate description of the responses to the feelings task; if it did not, there would be no point in considering subjective expected emotions. Postdecision emotional reactions to outcomes of gambles were qualitatively identical to those reported in Mellers, et al. (1997): there were significant effects of obtained outcomes, counterfactual comparisons between obtained and unobtained outcomes, and the surprisingness of the obtained outcome.

Decision affect theory (Equation 1) was fitted to the mean responses in the feelings task using Chandler's (1969) STEPIT subroutine, which iteratively adjusts a set of parameters to minimize the proportion of residual variance between data and model predictions. The theory had only 1% residual variance in the means; more importantly, it accurately predicted the qualitative pattern of results.[2] Decision affect theory also described individuals' feelings.

Separate fits of decision affect theory to each participant's responses in the feelings tasks alone were generally good. The median proportion of residual variance was 9%; proportions of residual variance ranged from 1% to 36%. Median parameter values were similar to parameters estimated from the mean responses.[3]

Judged expectations

Figure 1 shows judged expectations for gambles. The left panel plots judged expectations about gambles against better outcomes of gambles with separate curves for each worse outcome, averaged over probabilities; the right panel plots judged expectations about gambles against better outcomes of gambles with separate curves for each probability of better outcome, averaged over worse outcomes.

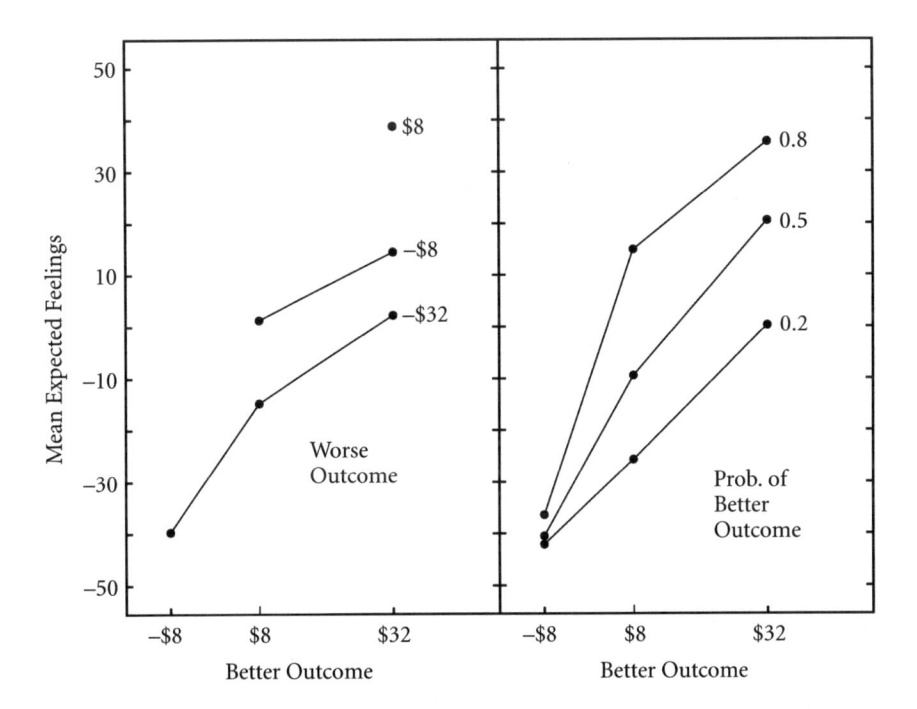

Figure 1. Judged expectations about gambles. The left panel plots judged expectations about gambles against gambles' gain amounts with separate curves for each loss amount, averaged over probabilities; the right panel plots judged expectations about gambles against gambles' gain amounts with separate curves for each probability of gain, averaged over loss amounts.

Curves show a pattern characteristic of weighted additive models. Those in the left panel suggest parallelism, consistent with an additive relationship between outcomes. Those in the right panel diverge, suggesting that outcomes and probabilities interact in a multiplicative fashion. When asked to judge how they expect to feel on average, people do not anticipate and report their feelings about the best or worst outcome alone; rather, they combine these feelings in proportion to the probability that each will be experienced. Moreover, this pattern is distinctly different than that obtained from attractiveness ratings of gambles (Mellers, Ordóñez, & Birnbaum 1992).

Fitting SEE to judged expectations

Predictions of the subjective expected emotion model were *computed* from the parameters estimated by fitting decision affect theory to the postdecision feelings. The fit of decision affect theory provided estimates of each subjective probability and predicted emotional responses to each outcome, from which each gamble's SEE was computed by Equation 2. These predictions require no additional parameter estimation or degrees of freedom.

Judged expectations should be a monotonic function of subjective expected emotions. Figure 2 presents the ranks of judged expectations as solid curves and the ranks of subjective expected emotions as dashed curves. Ranks are identical in the first panel, so dashed curves do not appear. Ranks are very similar in the other panels (Spearman's $\rho = 0.996$).

Similarly, each gamble's SEU was computed from the estimates of subjective probabilities and utilities, by Equation 3:

$$SEU = s_a u_a + s_b u_b \tag{3}$$

Subjective expected utility ranks also correlated highly with judged expectation ranks ($\rho = 0.975$). The semipartial rank correlation between SEE and judged expectations, with the effect of SEU removed, while not significant, suggests that SEE may predict some additional variance ($\rho = 0.202$).

To assess the relationship between judged expectations and SEE predictions at the level of individual participants, rank-order correlations between judged expectations and SEE were computed for each respondent. Correlations were generally good: one participant's correlation was only 0.08, but the others ranged from 0.58 to 0.98. The median individual participant correlation between ranked judged expectations and ranked SEEs was 0.88.

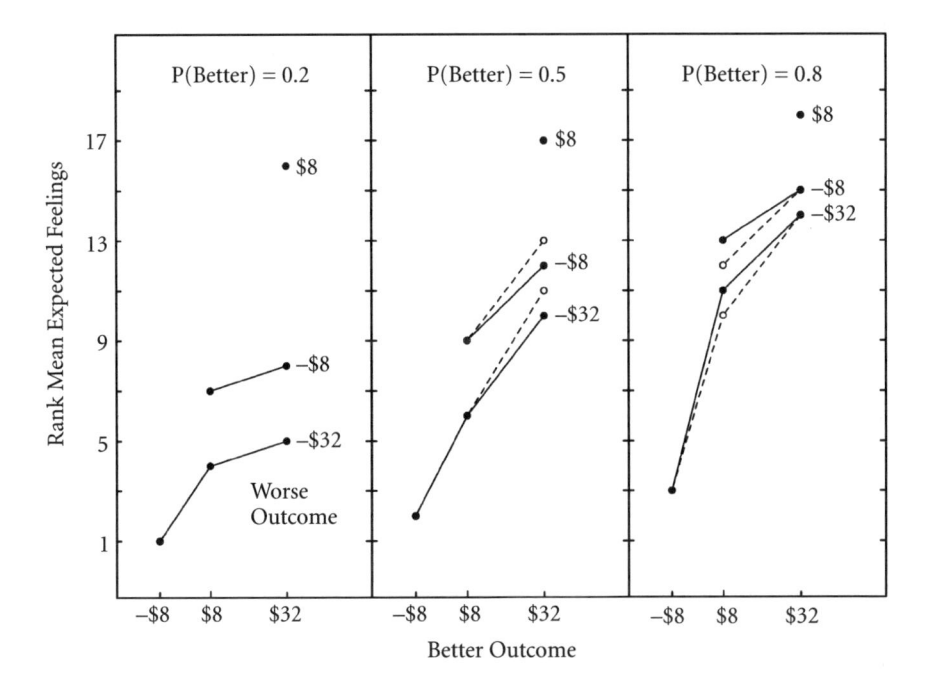

Figure 2. Ranks of mean judged expectations about gambles. Solid curves are ranks of data and dashed curves are ranks of subjective expected emotions predicted by decision affect theory. Where ranks are identical, only solid curves appear. Ranks are plotted against gambles' better outcomes with separate curves for each worse outcome in each panel. Panels plot different levels of probability of the gamble's better outcome.

Predicting choices from SEE

Do subjective expected emotions predict choices? To examine the relationship between SEE and choice, choices for each gamble pair were predicted based on the assumption that participants would choose the gamble with the higher SEE. Choice proportions were well-described by these predictions – the correlation between predictions and choice proportions was 0.87. The correlation between choice proportions and predictions based on the assumption that participants choose the gamble with the higher subjective expected utility was also 0.87. This result suggests that SEE is well-supported by these data. The rank-order correlation between the rank of the choice proportions and the rank of the difference in SEE between the two gambles, a more sensitive test that incorporates not only the direction but the magnitude of differences in the evaluation of gambles, was even higher ($\rho = 0.92$).

At the individual level, correlations between choices and individual-level predictions of SEE ranged from –0.15 to 0.85. The median individual correlation was 0.34. Two participants had nonsignificant negative correlations, 35 had nonsignificant positive correlations, and 44 had significant positive correlations.

General discussion

Mellers, et al. (1997) and Mellers, Schwartz, and Ritov (1999) showed that choices could be described as if people maximized their subjective expected emotions. This paper shows that people can judge the subjective expected emotions associated with gambles directly. Judged expectations were consistent with subjective expected emotions. Results show that people can directly and accurately evaluate their subjective expected emotions, and increase the plausibility of subjective expected emotions as a construct employed in choice.

Past research has successfully accounted for choice behavior by assuming the existence of emotions without measuring them (Bell 1982, 1985; Loomes & Sugden 1982, 1986), or has implicitly studied emotion by manipulating feedback (Boles & Messick 1995; Larrick & Boles 1995; Ritov 1996; Zeelenberg, Beattie, van der Plight, & de Vries 1996). The present research measures emotions associated with the outcomes of gambles, as well as the expected emotions associated with gambles. Decision affect theory predicts postdecision emotions directly, as a combination of utilities and surprise-weighted counterfactual comparisons. A comparison of estimated parameters in decision affect theory with disappointment and regret theories shows considerable overlap: negative counterfactual comparisons weigh more heavily than positive counterfactual comparisons, and surprising outcomes evoke more extreme feelings. In the present paper, decision affect theory accurately predicted feelings about outcomes of gambles presented individually, describing both mean and individual-level responses.

Mellers, Schwartz, and Ritov (1999) computed subjective expected emotions by fitting decision affect theory to feelings about outcomes. Results presented here provide converging evidence for subjective expected emotions by directly eliciting them from ratings of judged expectations about gambles at both the aggregate and the individual subject levels.

Decision affect theory provides a basis for a theory of choice by arguing that people may anticipate their postdecision emotions and use them to guide their choices. As the results reported here suggest, choice behavior can be described as if people maximize their subjective expected emotions, or average pleasure, when selecting gambles. Although subjective expected emotions did not describe choices or judged expectations significantly better than subjective expected utilities, it provides a parsimonious description of judged expectations, choices, and postdecision feelings simultaneously. Decision affect theory, a theory of postdecision feelings, can, with no additional degrees of freedom, be extended to describe judged expectations and choices as well as subjective expected utility theory.

The ability to assess subjective expected emotions directly through judged expectations has important implications for theories of choice, and preference assessment in general. Emotional theories of decision making provide alternatives to purely cognitive theories of choice and valuation. They can account not only for choices but also for emotional responses, and, as such, are more general than cognitive theories which, in the past, have only been applied to choices. The present paper can not answer the question of whether choice actually proceeds by computation and comparison of subjective expected emotions, but argues that decision affect theory and subjective expected emotion is a useful description of choice behavior as well as other response tasks.

Emotion-based theories of choice may be useful in applied settings. Decision analysts wish to assess utilities that conform to axioms of expected utility theories, but behavioral researchers have highlighted violations of expected utility theories that prove challenging to utility elicitation procedures. If hedonic choice strategies are similar to cognitive strategies, or if people really do prefer to maximize expected pleasure rather than expected utility, assessing emotions or expected emotions may be an appropriate tool for decision analysis, and may be easier to perform than utility assessment. Kahneman, Wakker, and Sarin's (1997) axiomatization of temporally-extended experienced utilities may be a first step toward a normative theory of hedonic judgment upon which such an assessment could be based, and decision affect theory may provide the link between experienced and decision utilities necessary to applying such an assessment to decision problems. Emotions are not simply an interesting behavioral result of our choices, but may also prove to be a powerful explanation *for* our choices.

Acknowledgements

The studies reported in this article were part of the author's doctoral dissertation in Psychology at the University of California, Berkeley. Financial support was provided by a dissertation grant from the University of California Berkeley Vice Chancellor for Research and by an NSF grant (SBR-94-09819) to Barbara Mellers. I am grateful for comments from Alan Cooke, Barbara Mellers, Ilana Ritov, Daniel Ilgen, and two anonymous reviewers. Nori Hirahara and Mona Otnaess assisted in the data collection for the studies.

Notes

1. Although "elated" and "disappointed" were (and are) used as category labels in these tasks, participants rate how they feel about outcomes, and the labels should not be confused with the theoretical constructs of elation and disappointment captured by the decision affect theory disappointment function. Labeling the scales with "happy" and "unhappy" produces the same pattern of results (Schwartz, Mellers, & Metzger 1998).

2. The theory required 8 parameters (2 utilities, 2 subjective probabilities, 2 coefficients for the J function, and 2 constants in g) to describe the 36 data points. The utilities of $-\$32$ and $\$32$ and the subjective probability of 0.5 were fixed to their objective values with no loss of generality. Estimated utilities for $\$8$ and $-\$8$ were 16.3 and -16.8, respectively. Estimated subjective probabilities of .2 and .8 were .31 and .59. Steps in the g function were 19.5 and -24.6. The intercept and slope of the J function for feelings were 2.5 and 0.85. These parameters were consistent with those found by Mellers, et al. (1997).

3. Median estimated utilities for $\$8$ and $-\$8$ were 17.5 and -15.6, respectively. Median estimated subjective probabilities of .2 and .8 were .31 and .59. Steps in the g function were 19.5 and -24.6. The intercept and slope of the J function for feelings were 2.5 and 0.85.

References

Bell, David E. (1982). Regret in decision making under uncertainty. *Operations Research, 30*, 961–981.

Bell, David E. (1985). Disappointment in decision making under uncertainty. *Operations Research, 33*, 1–27.

Boles, Terry L., & David M. Messick (1995). A reverse outcome bias: The influence of multiple reference points on the evaluation of outcomes and decisions. *Organizational Behavior and Human Decision Processes, 61*(3), 262–275.

Chandler, John P. (1969). Subroutine STEPIT: Finds local minima of a smooth function of several parameters. *Behavioral Sciences, 14*, 12067.

Kahneman, Daniel, & Dale Miller (1986). Norm theory: Comparing reality to its alternatives. *Psychological Review, 93*, 136–153.

Kahneman, Daniel, & Jackie Snell (1992). Predicting a Changing Taste: Do People Know What They Will Like? *Journal of Behavioral Decision Making, 5*, 187–200.

Kahneman, Daniel, Peter P. Wakker, & Rakesh Sarin (1997). Back to Bentham? Explorations of experienced utility. *Quarterly Journal of Economics, 122*(2), 375–405.

Larrick, Richard P., & Terry L. Boles (1995). Avoiding regret in decisions with feedback: A negotiation example. *Organizational Behavior and Human Decision Processes, 63*, 87–97.

Loomes, Graham, & Robert Sugden (1982). Regret theory: An alternative of rational choice under uncertainty. *Economic Journal, 92*, 805–824.

Loomes, Graham, & Robert Sugden (1986). Disappointment and dynamic consistency in choice under uncertainty. *Review of Economic Studies, LIII*, 271–282.

Loomes, Graham, & Robert Sugden (1987). Testing for regret and disappointment in choice under uncertainty. *Economic Journal, 97*, 118–129.

Markman, Keith, Igor Gavanski, Stephen J. Sherman, & Matthew McMullen (1993). The mental simulation of better and worse possible worlds. *Journal of Experimental Social Psychology, 29*, 87–109.

Medvec, Victoria H., Scott F. Madey, & Thomas Gilovich (1995). When less is more: Counterfactual thinking and satisfaction among Olympic medalists. *Journal of Personality and Social Psychology, 69*(4), 603–610.

Mellers, Barbara A., Lisa D. Ordóñez, & Michael H. Birnbaum (1992). A change-of-process theory for contextual effects and preference reversals in risky decision making. *Organizational Behavior and Human Decision Processes, 52*, 331–369.

Mellers, Barbara A., Alan Schwartz, Katty Ho, & Ilana Ritov (1997). Decision affect theory: Emotional Reactions to the Outcomes of Risky Options. *Psychological Science, 8*(6), 423–429.

Mellers, Barbara A., Alan Schwartz, & Ilana Ritov (1999). Emotion-based choice. *Journal of Experimental Psychology: General, 128*(3), 332–345.

Ritov, Ilana (1996). Probability of regret: Anticipation of uncertainty resolution in choice. *Organizational Behavior & Human Decision Processes, 66*(2), 228–236.

Roese, Neal. J. (1994). The functional basis of counterfactual thinking. *Journal of Personality and Social Psychology, 66*, 805–818.

Roese, Neal. J., & James M. Olson (Eds.) (1995). *What Might Have Been: The social psychology of counterfactual thinking.* New Jersey: Lawrence Erlbaum Associates.

Schwartz, Alan, Barbara A. Mellers, & Tanya Metzger (1998). Hedonic strategies in risky decisions. In J. Shanteau, B. Mellers, D. Schum (Eds.), *Decision Science and Technology: Reflections on the contributions of Ward Edwards* (pp. 65–80). Norwell, MA: Kluwer.

Sugden, Robert (1993). An axiomatic foundation for regret theory. *Journal of Economic Theory, 60*(1), 159–180.

Zeelenberg, Marcel, Jane Beattie, Joop van der Plight, & Nanne de Vries (1996). Consequences of regret aversion: Effects of expected feedback on risky decision making. *Organizational Behavior and Human Decision Processes, 65*, 148–158.

CHAPTER 9

Motivational underpinnings of utility in decision making
Decision field theory analysis of deprivation and satiation

Jerome R. Busemeyer, James T. Townsend, and Julie C. Stout
Indiana University

The concept of *utility* is central to theories of decision-making. Yet little is known about the source of the personal worth that an outcome produces. Consider a typical problem such as choosing a movie for weekend entertainment (see Table 1). According to utility theories (cf. Keeney & Raiffa 1976; Von Winterfeldt & Edwards 1982), each option (e.g., drama, comedy, or action movie) is characterized by a set of attributes (e.g., romance, humor, excitement, fearfulness). The individual assesses her subjective value or *utility* for each attribute on each option (e.g., she likes the tender romance of a drama, and she loathes the thrilling violence of an action movie). Finally, the overall evaluation of each option is based on a weighted combination of its utilities, and the option producing the greatest evaluation is chosen. The utilities that enter into these evaluations are treated as primitives – they are initially unknown and they must be estimated from a decision maker's personal judgments. For example, utility theories cannot explain why a decision maker values the romance of a drama more than the excitement of an action movie. In sum, utility theories only explain how utilities are used to make choices; the utilities themselves are left unexplained.

The purpose of this chapter is to build a theory of decision-making that attempts to identify some of the basic sources of utility. In particular, we present a theory that formally describes how needs change over time as a function of external stimulation, and internal deprivation and consummation. The remainder of the chapter is organized as follows. First we review recent research

Table 1. Multi-attribute table for movie choice problem.

Options	Romance	Humor	Excitement	Fearfulness
Drama	very high	moderate	low	low
Comedy	moderate	high	moderate	low
Action	very low	moderate	very high	high

that demonstrates the influence of need states on decision-making. Second we present a brief review of previous theoretical work on motivational mechanisms. Third, we propose a new extension of a dynamic model of decision making, called decision field theory, which incorporates a dynamic model of needs. Fourth, we apply this extension of decision field theory to research examining the influence of affect and emotion on decision-making. Finally, we present a preliminary sketch of how the psychological components of decision field theory map onto to neuro-physiological mechanisms in the brain.

Previous research on affect and decision making

Note that utility theories treat the subjective values that enter the decision rule as fixed and invariant parameters, like Platonic entities laying quietly in the mind. When asked to make a decision, it is implicitly assumed that the decision maker retrieves these entries from some fixed table of values stored permanently in memory. The process is viewed in virtually the same manner as reading off the numbers from a table printed in a consumer magazine.

Recent research has led decision theorists to change this view dramatically. It is now generally believed that utilities are constructed, at the moment and on the spot, in a manner that serves the purpose of the immediate decision context (Slovic 1995). For example, prospect theory (Kahneman & Tversky 1979) postulates that values are determined by comparing an outcome to some contextually dependent reference point. Contingent weighting theory (Tversky, Sattath, & Slovic 1988) assumes that the weight given to a dimension varies depending on the specific type of preference task. Change of process theory (Mellers, Ordóñez, & Birnbaum 1992) allows the rule for combining values to change across response measures. Adaptive decision making models (Payne, Bettman, & Johnson 1993) hypothesize that decision makers select different strategies depending on the number of attributes, options, and time pressure.

Although constructive theories allow utilities to change depending on context, if the context is held fixed, then the same construction process operates, and so the utilities remain constant across time. In this sense, constructive theories provide a *static*, as opposed to a *dynamic*, view of values. For example, it is generally thought that an elimination by aspects type of choice strategy is elicited in the context of making choices from a large set of options (Payne, Bettman, & Johnson 1993). But if the choice set is fixed, then the values of the aspects, upon which the elimination process is based, are treated as fixed parameters (cf. Tversky 1972).

According to a dynamic view, consequences are valuable only to the extent that they satisfy some demands or needs of an individual (see also Markman & Brendt 2000). Furthermore, these demands or needs change systematically over time as a function of external environmental stimulation, or internal deprivation and consummation cycles. For example, a spectacular advertisement may be used to arouse or stimulate a consumer's interest in an action movie. However, if the consumer just recently watched a series of action movies over the past few weeks, she may feel tired or satiated with that type of entertainment, and she may now feel a need for a humorous or romantic movie. After many weeks of foregoing action movies, the need for the excitement of an action movie may gradually rise to dominate once again. In this way, the individual's personal values change dynamically over time as a function of external environmental stimuli and internal deprivation-satiation mechanisms.

Empirical and experimental support for the moderating effects of need stimulation and need deprivation on decision-making has recently begun to accumulate (see Loewenstein & Lerner 2000). One notable example is a study by Goldberg, Lerner, and Tetlock (1999). Participants first viewed a stimulating anger inducing film of a violent crime, followed by a trial for the crime. For half of the viewers, the film ended with a conviction and punishment of the perpetrator; and for the other half, the film ended with the perpetrator getting off free due to a legal technicality. Subsequently, all of the participants viewed negligence cases that were completely unrelated to the earlier film, and made judgments of punishments for these cases. The justice deprived participants delivered stronger punishments in the unrelated negligence cases as compared to the participants for whom justice was satisfied. Thus the need for justice aroused by stimulation in one case spilled over into decisions on unrelated cases. Berkowitz (1993) provides many other empirical example of this type of process.

Another relevant example is study by Read and van Leeuwen (1998). Participants were asked to choose between two snacks, a healthy snack (e.g., fruits) versus an unhealthy snack (e.g., candy bars). Presumably, the former is more desirable for health reasons, and the latter satisfies hunger motivation better. Hunger deprivation was manipulated by asking participants to make this choice before lunch (high deprivation) or after lunch (low deprivation). The incentive value of the snacks was also manipulated by either delaying the snack delivery by a week, versus delivering the snack immediately after the choice. The results demonstrated a strong interaction between cognitive and motivational systems. Under the immediate choice condition, motivation always dominated, and most participants chose the unhealthy snack. When incentive was reduced by delay, healthy reasons prevailed over hunger for low deprivation participants who now preferred the health snack; however hunger still dominated the decision for high deprivation participants who continued to choose the unhealthy snack.

Shiv and Fedorikhin (1999) also found a strong interaction between cognition and motivation. Similar to the previous study, they examined choices between healthy (e.g., fruit) snacks versus unhealthy (fudge cake) snacks. They manipulated hunger stimulation by presenting the real snacks on a tray for direct inspection, versus presenting only photos of the snacks. The salience of the health rationale was also manipulated by putting half of the participants under a high memory load condition (reducing capacity to think of health reasons) and the other half was under a low memory load condition. In this case, when the health rationale was not suppressed, most participants preferred the healthy snack. However, when the high memory load suppressed reasoning, then the hunger manipulation dramatically reversed preferences: participants under high hunger stimulation preferred the unhealthy snack, whereas participants under low hunger stimulation preferred the healthy snack.

It is possible, of course, to treat needs and demands in a snapshot manner. In other words, constructive theories could include the current need state as part of the context for the computation, thus avoiding the problem of explaining the dynamics changes in need states over time. For example, some researchers have argued that strategy choice may depend on emotional states and moods (Lewinson & Mano 1993; Luce, Bettman, & Payne 1997). However, this approach fails to provide a theory that predicts how needs change over time depending on the history of past stimuli and choices. Furthermore, this snap shot approach requires specifying a construction process conditioned on each and every need state, which is far from a parsimonious solution. The present chapter takes a diametrically different approach to describing needs and their dynamic effects on decisions.

Earlier motivation theories

Identifying the source of reinforcement value was a central issue for the neo – behaviorist theories of Hull, Mower, Spence, and Tolman (see Cofer & Appley 1967, for a review). According to these earlier theories, motivational values were decomposed into two independent parts – need or drive states, and incentive magnitudes. The needs included hunger, thirst, sex, and fear; which were manipulated by hours of food and water deprivation, sexual stimulation, and shock intensity with animals. The incentive was independently manipulated by varying the amount of food, water that could be consumed, or access to sexual gratification, or escape from shock. Furthermore, it was generally assumed that these two factors multiply to determine motivational value. Thus needs moderated the effect of incentives on motivational value, and reinforcement value was derived from need or drive reduction. Although these researchers understood the importance of formulating dynamic models for these motivational mechanisms, their descriptions remained largely informal and static.

Animal behaviorists made progress toward dynamic models of motivation by using feedback control theory (see McFarland 1971, 1974; & Toates 1975, for examples). These feedback control models were built upon Walter Cannon's idea of homeostasis. The basic idea was that organisms have set points or ideal levels for various need states. Consummatory behavior acts as an error correcting control variable that feeds back and reduces the discrepancy between the current and desired states. These theories were developed to explain consummatory behavior in animals such as eating, drinking, and foraging behavior. More recently, the basic ideas of feedback control were extended and applied to social psychological theories of motivation (Carver & Scheier 1981).

Research on human motivation was advanced by the development of a motivational theory called dynamics of action (Atkinson & Birch 1970). According to this theory, each type of activity is associated with an action tendency that has some strength at any point in time. The action with the greatest strength at any moment is expressed. Actions that are not expressed grow in strength according to a linear differential equation, producing deprivation. The action that is dominant, and is thus being expressed, decreases in strength in proportion to its consummatory response, producing satiation. This theory was designed to explain the stream of behavior, that is, the changes in activities in which humans engage from moment to moment (e.g., work versus play).

Consumer researchers made progress on issues relating human motivation to consumer purchases (see Kahn, Kalwani, & Morrison 1986; & McAlister 1982, for examples). These theories incorporated dynamic models of deprivation and satiation into standard economic consumer choice models. Satiation was viewed as a household's accumulation of inventory for an attribute product, and deprivation was viewed as depleting this inventory. The value of a new purchase was determined by comparing the resulting inventory with some ideal point – value increased as the inventory approached the ideal point and it decreased as the inventory surpassed the ideal. The main purpose of these models was to explain brand switching and variety seeking observed in consumer panel data.

Most recently, Townsend (1992) incorporated mechanisms of deprivation and satiation into approach-avoidance models of movement behavior. These models generally assumed that the attraction and aversion toward a goal depended on the distance to each goal (Miller 1959; Townsend & Busemeyer 1989). Townsend's theory differs from these earlier theories by adding the assumption that the goal is partly consumed during the approach so that need for a goal also varies depending on the distance from the goal. Approach-avoidance models were designed to describe continuous changes in position and velocity of movement behavior toward competing goal objects in physical space (see McFarland & Bosser 1997).

Despite the relevance of the above motivational theories for understanding the source and dynamic nature of utilities, they have had little impact on traditional decision research. One important reason is that motivational theories and decision theories have not been systematically integrated into a common framework. The purpose of this chapter is to make some preliminary progress towards this integration.

Decision field theory

The proposed theory is an extension of a dynamic cognitive model of decision making that has been applied to a variety of traditional decision making problems including decision making under uncertainty (Busemeyer & Townsend 1993), selling prices and certainty equivalents (Townsend & Busemeyer 1995), multi-attribute decision making (Diederich 1997), and multi-alternative decision making (Roe, Busemeyer, & Townsend 2001). However, all of the previous applications of the theory treated the values entering the decision process as fixed over time. This chapter describes how these values change over time in response to external environmental stimulation, and internal deprivation-satiation mechanisms. The dynamic character of decision field theory makes it a natural candidate for incorporating these motivational mechanisms.

Figure 1 provides a diagram of the proposed cognitive-motivational network. All of these elements will be described in more detail below in a step by step manner. Here we simply outline the general idea. At the far left, the needs for an attribute (denoted N) and the quantity of need reduction produced by an action (denoted Q) combine to influence motivational values (denoted M). The motivational values and attention weights (denoted W) combine to influence valence (denoted V). The valence and previous preference state combine to generate a new preference state (denoted P). The preference state guides behavior (denoted B). Finally, past behavior, environmental goal stimulation (denoted G), and previous needs influence current needs. We begin the detailed presentation of this entire process with a description of how a decision is made.

Decision Rule. According to decision field theory, each option is associated with a preference strength, denoted P_i for option i, which could range from positive (attractive) to negative (repulsive), with zero representing a neutral state. The collection of preferences for all of the options form a preference state (a column vector) denoted **P**. Considering the movie choice example, the preference state is a three dimensional (column) vector consisting of prefer-

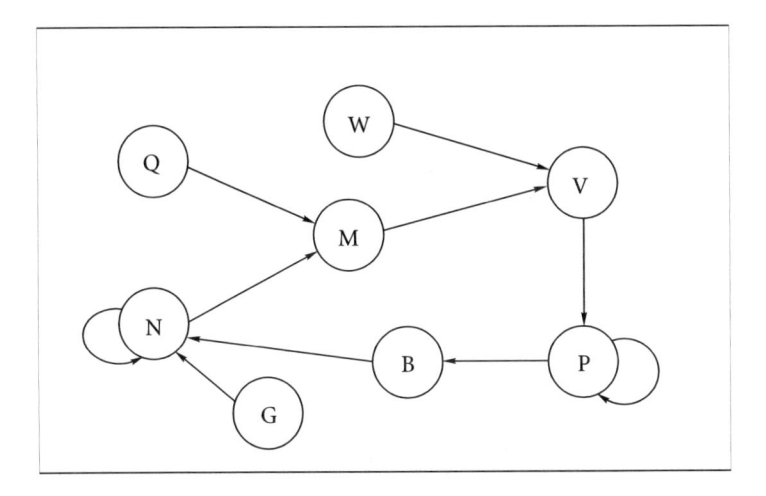

Figure 1. Cognitive-motivational network. The attribute values and needs combine to influence motivational values, the motivational values and attention weights combine to influence valence, valence and previous preference state combine to generate a new preference state, preference influences behavior, past behavior, environmental stimulation, and previous needs influence current needs. Q = attribute values, N = attribute needs, M = motivational values, W = attention weights, V = valences, P = preferences, B = behavior, G = environmental stimulation.

ence strengths for drama, comedy, and action. The preference state at the start of the decision process is denoted $P(t_0)$, the preference state at any later time point prior to making the final decision is denoted $P(t)$.

A decision is made a follows. The process starts with the initial preference state, $P(t_0)$, which may be biased by recall of preferences from past decisions. Then during the deliberation period, the preference state changes from one time moment, $P(t)$, to later time moment, $P(t+h)$, as the decision maker anticipates the consequences of each option and accumulates the anticipated affective values. This deliberation process continues until the strength of preference for one of the options exceeds a threshold bound at time T (see Figure 2). The first option to exceed the bound is chosen, and the time required for the first option to reach the bound determines the decision time, $DT = (T - t_0)$.

The choice probabilities and mean decision times are derived from the first passage time distributions of the resulting stochastic process (Busemeyer &

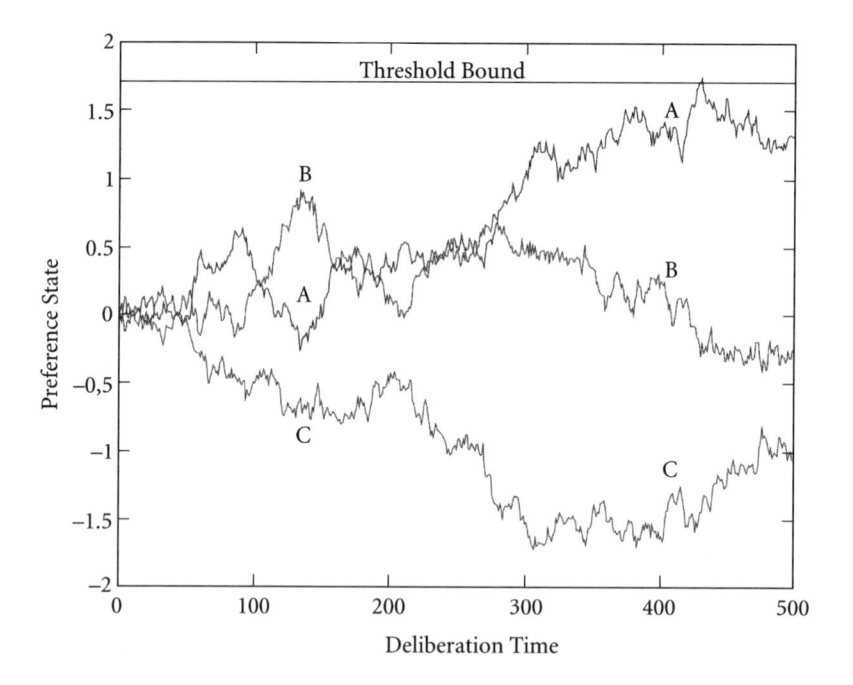

Figure 2. Stopping rule for making a decision. The horizontal axis represents decision time, and the vertical axis represents preference strength. Each trajectory represents the evolution of preference for one of the three options. In this figure, option A is the first option to reach the threshold bound (flat top line), and so this option would be chosen at time t = 425.

Townsend 1992; Busemeyer & Diederich 2001). This decision process characterizes a wide range of models for decision-making in cognitive psychology (see Link 1992; Ratcliff 1978; Smith 1995; Nosofsky & Palmeri 1997; Ashby 2000).

The threshold bound for stopping the deliberation process is a criterion that the decision maker can use to control the speed and accuracy of a decision. If the threshold is set to a very high value, then a very strong preference is required to make a decision. This high criterion will require accumulating more information, and thus generally lead to more thoughtful decisions, but at the cost of longer decision times. If the threshold bound is set to a very low criterion, then only a weak preference is required to reach a decision. This low criterion requires little information, and thus generally leads to less thoughtful decisions, but with less time. A high threshold bound is used to make important decisions entailing very high stakes, and a lower threshold bound is used for less important decisions that must be made quickly. Furthermore, prudent decision makers tend to use higher thresholds, whereas impulsive decision makers tend to use lower thresholds.

Evolution of Preferences. The preference state is assumed to change and evolve during the deliberation according to the following linear dynamic difference equation:

$$P(t+h) = S \cdot P(t) + V(t+h) \tag{1}$$

This model states that the new preference state is a linear combination of the previous preference state and the new input valence, denoted $V(t+h)$. The matrix S allows for feedback produced by the previous preference state on the new state. It serves three critical purposes in the model. First, it controls the rate of growth and decay of preferences over time during deliberation (Busemeyer & Townsend 1992). Second, it incorporates goal gradient parameters that are used to account for differences in approach-avoidance types of conflicts (Busemeyer & Townsend 1993). Third, it allows for lateral interconnections among options to produce a competitive network (Roe et al. 2001). See the previously mentioned articles for a more detailed discussion and justification for this part of the model. The present chapter is focused primarily on the important role of the second term, called the valence vector, denoted $V(t)$, described next.

Valence. The input valence vector is composed of a product that has three independent parts:

$$V(t) = C(t) \cdot M(t) \cdot W(t) \tag{2}$$

The first matrix, called the contrast matrix and denoted $C(t)$, represents the process used to compare options. If pair wise comparisons are made serially over time, then one row of $C(t)$ is used to form the current paired comparison, and the remaining rows of are set to zero. For example, setting

$$C(t_1) = \begin{bmatrix} 1 & -1 & 0 \\ 0 & 0 & 0 \\ 0 & 0 & 0 \end{bmatrix}, \quad C(t_2) = \begin{bmatrix} 0 & 0 & 0 \\ 0 & 1 & -1 \\ 0 & 0 & 0 \end{bmatrix}, \quad C(t_3) = \begin{bmatrix} 0 & 0 & 0 \\ 0 & 0 & 0 \\ -1 & 0 & 1 \end{bmatrix}$$

produces pair wise comparisons between options 1 versus 2 at time t_1, options 2 versus 3 at time t_2, and options 3 versus 1 at time t_3. In this case, $C(t)$ changes from moment to moment to represent the different pair wise comparisons across time. Alternatively, if it is assumed that all three options are processed in parallel, then each option is compared to the average of the remaining options. This is achieved by setting

$$C(t) = \begin{bmatrix} 1 & -.5 & -.5 \\ -.5 & 1 & -.5 \\ -.5 & -.5 & 1 \end{bmatrix}$$

In this second case, the contrast matrix is fixed across time. (Note that the parallel contrast matrix is the expectation over all the possible serial contrast matrices).

The second matrix, called the motivational value matrix denoted $M(t)$, represents the motivational values of each option on each attribute. Considering the movie choice example, the motivational value matrix would consist of three rows and four columns, each row representing an option (drama, comedy, action), and each column representing an attribute (romance, humor, excitement, fearfulness). Each cell, $m_{ij}(t)$, of this matrix represents the value of an option on an attribute (e.g., the motivational value of drama on romance). This is similar to a multi-attribute table posited in utility theories, except that these values may change dynamically over time. This is the major innovation to be introduced in the present chapter, and we will return to a detailed description of this component after describing the last term in Equation 2.

The last matrix, called the weight vector denoted $W(t)$, represents the amount of attention allocated to each attribute at each moment. Considering the movie choice example, then $W(t)$ is column vector with four elements, with each element representing the amount of attention allocated to one of the attributes (attention to the romantic, humorous, exciting, and fearful aspects of each movie). Again this is similar to the importance weights posited in utility theories, except that these weights change dynamically over time. At one moment at time t, the decision maker may focus on the romantic aspects of each movie (e.g., $w_1(t) = 1$ and other weights zero), but at another moment, $t + h$, attention may switch to the exciting aspects of each movie (e.g., $w_2(t + h) = 1$

and all other weights zero). Thus the weight vector changes from moment to moment reflecting the momentary changes in attention to each attribute. Formally, the weight vector is assumed to be a stationary stochastic process. The mean of the weight vector represents the average amount of attention allocated to each attribute, and this is assumed to be a function of the importance or probability of each attribute.

Motivational Values. It is now time to return to the specifications for the sources of the motivational value matrix, $M(t)$. First it is assumed that each individual has accumulated some experience with each attribute to produce a current degree of attainment (level of satisfaction or dissatisfaction) with each attribute, denoted $a_j(t)$ for attribute j. The attribute state vector, denoted $A(t)$, represents the collection of all of these attainment levels for all the attributes. Considering the movie choice example, $A(t)$ is a four dimensional vector representing an individual's cumulative experience with movies regarding romance, humor, excitement, and fear attributes. For example, the individual may have watched too many action movies lately, and may feel tired of the mindless excitement produced by that type of movie.

Second, it is also assumed that each individual has an ideal level for each attribute, denoted L_j, for attribute j. Collecting these ideal levels across attributes produces an ideal point, denoted L, in the attribute space. For the movie choice example, L is a four dimensional vector representing an individual's ideal levels for experiencing romance, humor, excitement, and fear when watching movies.

Third, it is assumed that there exists a need state, denoted $N(t)$, which is a vector representing the needs on each of the attributes. Each element, $n_j(t)$, of the vector $N(t)$ represents the need for a particular attribute. For example, an individual's current level of excitement may lie below his ideal level, and thus she feels a need to experience more excitement. The needs may be positively or negatively signed, depending on whether or not the current state is below or above the desired state. For example, an individual's current level of experienced fear may be higher than her ideal level, and so she may wish to walk out to avoid watching the rest of a horror movie. The needs are updated according to the linear dynamic system

$$N(t+h) = L \cdot N(t) + G(t+h) - A(t+h) \tag{3}$$

The last term in the above equation, $G(t+h)$, represents the change in goals produced by environmental stimulation (e.g., stress from losing a job, enticements by advertisements).

The fourth assumption concerns the quantity of change in attribute state that is consumed by choosing an option. The parameter, q_{ij}, denotes the quantity of change in attribute j produced by choosing option i. For example, watching an intense action movie may produce a big increase in an individual's current state of excitement; avoiding a terrorizing horror movie may produce a big reduction in fear. The matrix Q represents the quantities for each option on each attribute. Finally, the motivational values are determined from the matrix product

$$M(t) = Q \cdot \text{Diag}[N(t)] \qquad (4)$$

In other words, the motivation value produced by an option on an attribute equals the product of the attribute need and the quantity produced by the option, $m_{ij}(t) = n_j(t) \cdot q_{ij}$.

There are several properties to note about Equation 3. First, it reproduces the multiplicative model for need and incentives, adopted by the early neobehaviorists. Second, the motivational values move the decision maker in the direction of need reduction, reducing the distance between the current and ideal states, and so Equation 3 also serves as a feedback control loop. Third, the need state can also be interpreted as differences between the current and desired inventory levels in a household for some product attribute, consistent with the earlier consumer choice models. Finally, note that if the needs are equal in magnitude and constant across time, then the motivational values are fixed and static quantities like those assumed by classic utility theories.

The last remaining theoretical issue is the problem of specifying how the attribute states change across time. Three factors are assumed to influence the new attribute state: the previous attribute state, new changes in state produced by past behavior, and new environmental stimulation. The attribute state is assumed to change across time according to the following linear dynamic model:

$$A(t+h) = F \cdot A(t) + Q' \cdot B(t) \qquad (5)$$

The last term of Equation 5 represents the effect of past actions on the current attribute state. The vector, $B(t)$, indicates which, if any, choice occurred in the previous moment. For example, if the first option, say drama, was chosen at time t_1, then $b_1(t_1) = 1$ and all the other elements of $B(t_1)$ are zero. Alternatively, if the third option, say the action movie, was chosen at time t_2, then $b_3(t_2) = 1$ and other elements of $B(t_2)$ are zero. The product, $Q' \cdot B(t)$, simply selects the row of quantitative changes in attributes produced by the behavior that occurred at time t.

The feedback matrix F in the first term of Equation 4 determines how the previous attribute state affects the new attribute state. For example, if F is set equal to an identity matrix, $F = I$, then the new state would simply equal the previous state plus the adjustments from the environment and behavior. However, in this case all past environmental events and behaviors have equal impact on the current state, independent of when they occurred. In other words, this simple case produces perfect memory for past outcomes. If F is proportional to the identity matrix, $F = \alpha I$ with $0 < \alpha < 1$, then the impact of a past outcome decays exponentially with the age of its experience, producing recency effects and limited memory for past outcomes. Finally, if F is a symmetric matrix with non-zero off diagonal entries, $f_{jk} = f_{kj}, j \neq k$, then these off diagonal entries allow for substitution effects: f_{jk} represents the partial fulfillment of attribute j indirectly gained by satisfying attribute k. For example, experiencing an exciting action movie could lead to a reduced need for watching a fearful horror movie and visa-versa.

The dynamic model expressed in Equation 4 shares properties with the earlier dynamics of action theory. Both use linear dynamic systems to describe growth of states over time and consummation of states produced by actions. Furthermore, both allow for substitution effects so that consummation of one attribute may also reduce the need for other related attributes. The main differences between the theories are the mechanisms for making decisions. Decision field theory postulates two integrated dynamical systems for making choices – a dynamical evolution for preference state, and a dynamic process for need state. In contrast, dynamics of action theory postulates only one dynamical system – action tendencies (which correspond most closely to our need states). Excluding the preference state dynamics makes applications to decision research difficult for the dynamics of action theory.

Theoretical Derivations. Now we consider how the two interlinked dynamic processes – preference states driven by motivational values, and motivational values driven by needs – work altogether to influence choice (see Figure 1). We will restrict our analysis to the evolution of the mean preference state over time. Although the choice probabilities are partly dependent on the means, they also are partly dependent on the covariance matrix for preferences (see, Busemeyer & Townsend 1993; Roe, et al. 2001). However, deriving the latter involves technical derivations that go beyond the intended scope of this chapter. Derivations regarding the mean preference state are fairly straightforward. First we derive the asymptotic mean preference state for the current choice. Then we examine how the dynamic properties of the needs moderate the asymptotic mean preference for the current choice. In all of the following derivations, the expression $E[X]$ symbolizes the expectation of the random vector X.

First we derive from Equation 1 the asymptotic mean preference state for a choice that starts at time t_0, allowing the needs to be changing dynamically before that point in time, but fixed during the deliberation period. The expectation for the last term in Equation 1 is:

$$E[V(t+h)] = E[C(t) \cdot M(t) \cdot W(t)] = E[C(t) \cdot Q \cdot \text{Diag}[N(t)] \cdot W(t)].$$

The comparison process, $C(t)$, is assumed to be a stationary process with a mean equal to $E[C(t)] = C$, which is statistically independent of the other processes. This allows us to factor it out of the expectation and rewrite the above equation as

$$E[V(t+h)] = C \cdot Q \cdot E[\text{Diag}[N(t_0)] \cdot W(t)].$$

Note that $N(t_0)$ is assumed to be fixed after time t_0, so it can also be factored out of the expectation to yield:

$$E[V(t+h)] = C \cdot Q \cdot \text{Diag}[N(t_0)] \cdot E[W(t)].$$

The attention weights are assumed to fluctuate according to a stationary stochastic process with a mean equal to $E[W(t)] = w$, and replacing this in the above equation yields:

$$E[V(t+h)] = C \cdot Q \cdot \text{Diag}[N(t_0)] \cdot w.$$

Returning to Equation 1, the mean preference state now can be expressed as

$$E[P(t+h)] = S \cdot E[P(t)] + E[V(t+h)] = S \cdot E[P(t)] + C \cdot Q \cdot \text{Diag}[N(t_0)] \cdot w.$$

The asymptotic solution to this vector difference equation is

$$E[P(\infty)] = (I - S)^{-1} \cdot C \cdot Q \cdot \text{Diag}[N(t_0)] \cdot w. \tag{5a}$$

To simplify this expression a bit, suppose that $S = (1-s) \cdot I$, so that Equation 5 reduces to

$$E[P(\infty)] = (s^{-1}) \cdot C \cdot Q \cdot \{\text{Diag}[N(t_0)] \cdot w\}. \tag{5b}$$

In this case, Equation 5b implies the following simple expression for the preference strength of option i:

$$E[P_i(\infty)] = (3/2) \cdot (s^{-1}) \cdot (v_i - \mu) \tag{5c}$$

where

$$v_i = \Sigma_j n_j(t_0) \cdot w_j \cdot q_{ij} \quad \text{and} \quad \mu = (v_1 + v_2 + v_3)/3. \tag{5d}$$

In short, the asymptotic mean preference for option i is linearly related to the weighted average of the attribute values for that option, denoted v_i in Equation 5d. But the weights of each attribute are modified by the needs, which change depending on the timing of past environmental stimuli and past consummatory behaviors (governed by Equation 4). The idea of shifting importance weights depending on the emotional needs involved in the decision is consistent with earlier research (Luce, Payne, & Bettman 1999) and theories on affect and decision making (Loewenstein 1986).

Applications to research on affect and decision making

Rage and Reason (Goldberg et al. 1999). There are two purposes for this application. One is to illustrate how the theory works with a concrete example that is made a simple as possible. The second reason is to illustrate some of the dynamic properties of the model that could be used for future tests. The reported experiment did not empirically evaluate the dynamic properties needed to test the theory, and so this application is not intended to provide evidence for the present theory.

Recall that in this experiment, the decision maker first witnessed a violent crime for which the perpetrator was convicted or not convicted, and this was followed by a decision about an independent negligence case. To model this experiment, denote t_v as the time point marking the end of the presentation of the violent crime film, and denote $t_0 > t_v$ as the later time point when a penalty decision about a negligence case was presented.

Suppose the decision regarding the penalty for the negligence case is based on two attributes, one is the level of punishment (needed for crime prevention), and the second is compassion (needed for human nature). For simplicity, we assume equal attention weight ($w_p = w_c = .50$) allocated to each attribute, and also for concreteness, the quantities shown in Table 2 are used to measure the effects of the three options on the two attributes. These particular weights and quantities are not at all critical – the main requirement is to make the medium penalty most preferred when the needs are equated. Inserting these parameters into Equation 5d yields:

$$v_{\text{low}} = (.5)(10)n_p(t) + (.5)(90)n_c(t), \tag{6}$$
$$v_{\text{med}} = (.5)(40)n_p(t) + (.5)(70)n_c(t),$$
$$v_{\text{high}} = (.5)(50)n_p(t) + (.5)(10)n_c(t).$$

The ideal levels for compassion and punishment are both set equal to $L_1 = L_2 = 1$, however, this simply changes the levels of the prediction curves, and any positive value will produce the same qualitative pattern of results. The experimental condition in which the perpetrator goes unpunished for the violent crime produces an environmental stimulant, $G(t_v) = [-g\ 0]'$, that reduces the attribute level for punishment, thus arousing a need for punishment. Thus g is a parameter representing the magnitude of the stimulation produced by the violent film. The need for punishment and need for compassion are assumed to be inversely related, and this is modeled by setting $f_{11} = f_{22} = \alpha$, and $f_{21} = f_{12} = -\alpha$ in the feedback matrix F in Equation 4 (however, setting $F = \alpha I$ produces virtually the same result). The parameter α determines the rate of decay of the stimulation. We will examine the model predictions for a range of parameters values corresponding to g (the magnitude of stimulation) and α (the decay rate).

Inserting these assumptions into Equation 4 and Equation 5d produces the predictions from the model shown in Figure 3. The horizontal axis in the figure represents the time delay between presentation of the violent film and the penalty decision $(t_0 - t_v)$, and the vertical axis represents the preference strength for a severe penalty (as compared to preferences for moderate or weak). Each curve represents a different magnitude of stimulation, and each panel represents a different rate of decay. As can be seen in the figure, the model predicts that soon after stimulation, the severe penalty is preferred, but this effect exponentially decreases as a function of the delay. Furthermore, the severe penalty is preferred only when the stimulation is large in magnitude. Increasing the magnitude of the stimulation increases the persistence, but eventually all these effects decay away in time. These results are in general accord with Goldberg et al. (1999), however they did not examine the time course of the effect that they observed. This temporal manipulation would provide stronger tests of the present theory.

Cognitive-Motivational Conflicts (Read & van Leeuwen 1998; Shiv & Fedorikhin 1999). The purpose of this application is to show how the theory accounts for the cognitive and motivational interactions that result in preference reversals. Recall that in these experiments, decision makers chose between unhealthy (e.g., fudge cake) versus healthy (e.g. fruit) snacks under different

Table 2. Multiattribute table for the penalty decision for negligence.

	Attributes	
Options	Punishment	Compassion
Low Penalty	10	90
Medium Penalty	40	70
High Penalty	50	10

hunger states. This decision can be analyzed on the basis of two attributes – one is hunger craving and the other is a concern for health. According to Equation 5d, the asymptotic mean preference for this decision will be determined by the difference

$$v_{\text{Unhealthy Snack}} - v_{\text{Healthy Snack}} \tag{7}$$
$$= w_{\text{Hunger}} \cdot (q_{\text{High Taste}} - q_{\text{Low Taste}}) \cdot n_{\text{Hunger}} - w_{\text{Health}} \cdot (q_{\text{High Health}} - q_{\text{Low Health}}) \cdot n_{\text{Health}}.$$

where $(w_{\text{Hunger}}, w_{\text{Health}})$ represent the average attention weights for the hunger craving and health reasons attributes, $(n_{\text{Hunger}}, n_{\text{Health}})$ represent the needs for

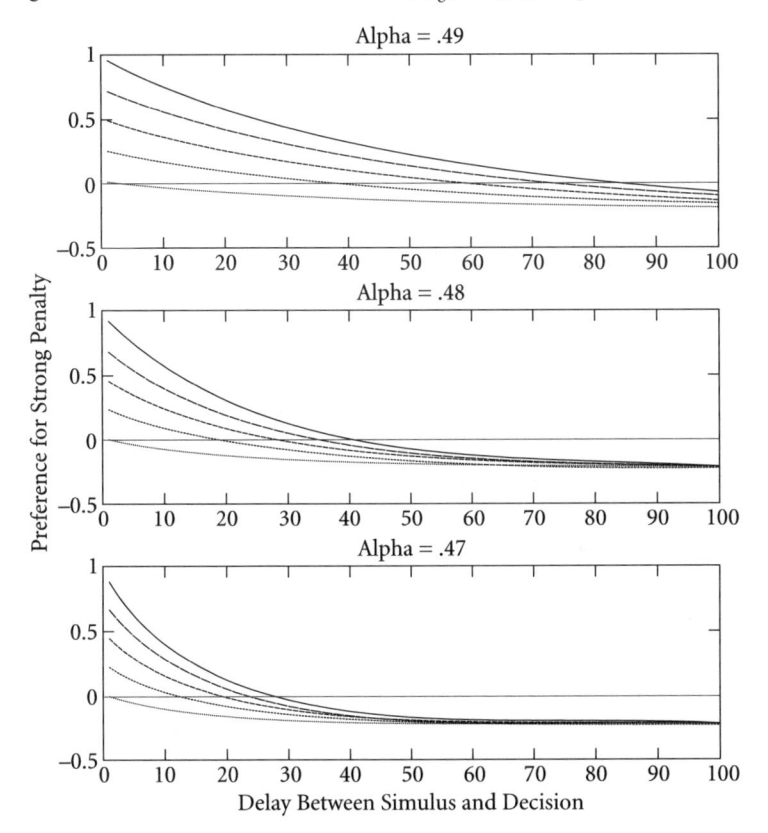

Figure 3. Predictions for the Goldberg et al. (1999) experiment. The horizontal axis represents the time delay between the stimulation and the penalty decision. The vertical axis represents preference for the most severe penalty. Each curve is produced by a different magnitude of stimulation, and each panel is produced by a different decay rate. The horizontal line represents the average preference, averaged across all three penalty choices.

these attributes, and the q's represent the quantitative changes produced by each option on each attribute.

The results of Read and van Leeuwen (1998) are explained as follows. The immediate versus delayed consumption of the snacks manipulates the reward value of the unhealthy snack, $q_{\text{High Taste}}$ – its value is much reduced under the delay condition. The timing of the decision (before versus after lunch) manipulates the need state for hunger, n_{Hunger}. When the snack is immediately available, then reward value for the snack, $q_{\text{High Taste}}$, is so large that it is generally preferred, even under low need for hunger. When the reward value is reduced by delay, but the hunger need, n_{Hunger}, is high, then the latter compensates for the former, producing a preference for the unhealthy snack. When both the hunger need and the reward value are low, then there is no motivational value for choosing the unhealthy snack, and the healthy snack is preferred.

The results of Shiv and Fedorikhin (1999) require a slightly different explanation. The presentation of the snacks (displaying real snacks versus only showing a photo) manipulates the stimulation of the hunger need, n_{Hunger}. The memory load (low versus high load) manipulates the amount of attention, w_{Health}, given to the reasons for the healthy snack – more attention can be given to thinking of health related reasons under the low memory load condition. When the memory load is low, sufficient attention can be given to health related reasons, the large weight, w_{Health}, causes the healthy snack to be generally preferred. When the memory load is high, lowering the weight w_{Health} for health reasons, then hunger stimulation has a major effect. High stimulation produces a high hunger need, n_{Hunger}, producing a preference for the unhealthy snack; low stimulation produces a low hunger need, producing a preference for the healthy snack.

In sum, according to Equation 7, the manipulations of the need for hunger shift the weight given to the hunger attribute, which causes the reversal of preference. The above analyses generally agree those provided by Read and van Leeuwen's (1998) and Shiv and Fedorikhin (1999). The purpose of this presentation is to make linkages between this previous research and the present theory.

Variety Seeking Consumer researchers have long been interested in the problem of variability in consumer choice including brand switching, switching among product variants, switching among services, and switching among activities. Although there are many reasons for this variation (including probabilistic choice, curiosity, and product learning), one of the main explanations is the mechanism of deprivation-satiation (see McAlister & Pessemier 1982, for a review). Rigorous quantitative comparisons of the proposed motivational

Motivational underpinnings of utility 215

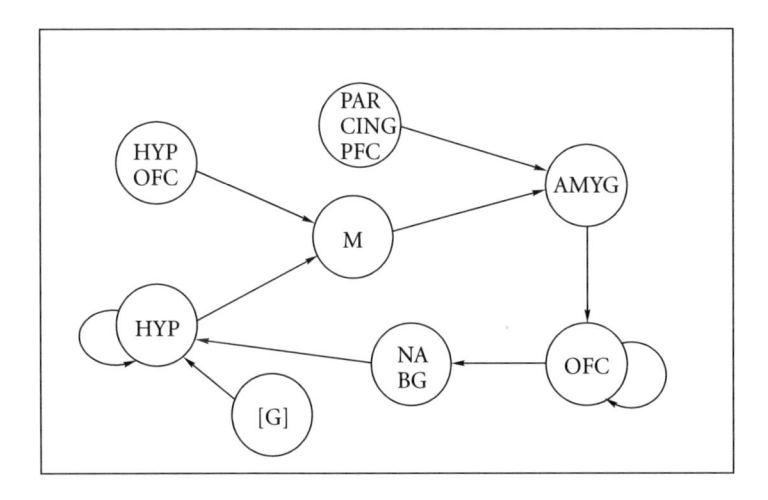

Figure 4. Suggestions for the neurophysiological basis of Figure 1. HYP = hypothalamus, OFC = orbitofrontal cortex, BF = basal forebrain, CING = cingulated cortex, PAR = parietal cortex, PFC = prefrontal cortex, AMYG = amygdala, NA = nucleus accumbens, BG = basal forbrain. [G], not part of the physiological basis of Figure 1, but retained from Figure 1 itself, refers to the environmental need stimuluation.

theory with earlier theories of variety seeking are planned using consumer purchases from scanner data in future research.

Neurophysiological basis

We would like to conclude this chapter with some suggestions concerning the neuro-physiological mechanisms corresponding to the cognitive – motivational network shown in Figure 1. Our initial guesses are shown in Figure 4, although these must be treated in a very tentative manner. Some of these ideas are based on previous theorizing and integrations of neurophysiological studies by Rolls (1999).

In general, the cognitive – motivational network would be implemented in distributed brain circuitry, and single nodes in the network would correspond to integrated neural systems rather than to specific brain regions. At the cortical level, this circuitry would include the orbitofrontal cortex as well as other prefrontal regions, cingulate cortex, temporal cortex, and at subcortical levels, the hypothalamus, basal forebrain, neostriatum (basal ganglia) and the archistriatal nucleus accumbens. Some candidate regions are identified below, although it should be borne in mind that these regions are not meant to be considered in isolation, but as part of the neural circuits with which they are imbedded.

The hypothalamus is one candidate for basic physiological homeostatic mechanisms such as hunger that correspond to the attribute needs (denoted N in Figure 1), although other systems would be involved in higher or more abstract level needs. For example, the frontal and temporal cortexes would be involved in more long term and abstract needs (i.e., achievement, intellectual satisfaction, social stimulation), which would rest on rational linguistic and memory systems. The hypothalamus and orbitofrontal cortex may implement some aspect of the reward value of an action (denoted Q in Figure 1) – with various regions of the hypothalamus being important for specific physiological needs, and the orbitofrontal cortex representing the rewarding properties of primary reinforcers and connecting these to action selection. The motivational value of a stimulus (denoted M in Figure 1) may be realized by a hypothalamus and the basal forebrain memory system. These influences would combine with attention weights (denoted A in Figure 1) perhaps perhaps put into action by the ascending noradrenergic attentional system including in the cingulated, parietal, and frontal cortexes. The combination of the motivational value and attention weights would then determine the valence (denoted V in Figure 1) implemented neurophysiologically in the amydala, and then in turn leading to a new preference state (denoted P in Figure 1), an idea similar to the preference ranking functions of the orbitofrontal cortex, which can modify stimulus-reinforcement relationships as conditions change. Finally, behavior (denoted B in Figure 1) would be influenced by and ultimately selected via the output systems of the brain regions mentioned above, including the ventral striatum (nucleus accumbens), which is an output structure for the amygdala and orbitofrontal cortex essential allowing rewarding properties of stimuli to influence action, and by the neostriatum, including the caudate nucleus and putamen, which are output structures for neocortical regions such as the sensorimotor cortexes and association cortex. The selection of behaviors via these striatal systems would then lead to implementation of behavioral goals via the decending voluntary motor control system which influences and coordinates specific muscle activity for movement.

Concluding comments

The purpose of this chapter was to outline the beginnings of a theory of decision-making that identifies some of the sources of subjective value or utility. The sources that we identified are the external environmental stimulation of needs, and the internal deprivation and satiation of needs. At this point the theory is tentative, and further experimental testing is required. Nevertheless, new tests cannot be designed without first putting down some formal hypotheses. The main contribution of this work will be to provide hypotheses for future research.

References

Ashby, F. G. (2000). A stochastic version of general recognition theory. *Journal of Mathematical Psychology, 44*, 310–329.
Atkinson, J. W., & Birch, D. (1970). *The Dynamics of action*. NY: Wiley.
Berkowitz, L. (1993). Towards a general theory of anger and emotional aggression: Implications of the Cognitive-neoassoaciationistic perspective for the analysis of anger and other emotions. In R. S. Wyer & T. K. Srull (Eds.), *Advances in Social Cognition*, Vol. 6 (pp. 1–46). Hillsdale NJ: Erlbaum.
Busemeyer, J. R., & Townsend, J. T. (1992). Fundamental derivations from decision field theory *Mathematical Social Sciences, 23*, 255–282.
Busemeyer, J. R., & Townsend, J. T. (1993). Decision Field Theory: A dynamic cognition approach to decision making. *Psychological Review, 100*, 432–459.
Busemeyer, J. R., & Diederich, A. (2001). Survey of decision field theory. Manuscript under review for *Mathematical Social Sciences*.
Carver, C. S., & Sheier, M. F. (1981). Attention and self – regulation: A control theory approach to human behavior. NY: Springer.
Cofer, C. N., & Appley, M. H. (1967). Motivation: Theory and Research. NY: Wiley.
Diederich, A. (1997). Dynamic stochastic models for decision making under time constraints. *Journal of Mathematical Psychology, 41*(3), 260–274.
Goldberg, J. H., Lerner, J. S., & Tetlock, P. E. (1999). Rage and reason: The psychology of the intuitive prosecutor. *European Journal of Social Psychology, 29*, 781–795.
Kahn, M., Kalwani, U., & Morrison, D. (1986). Measuring variety seeking and reinforcement behaviors using panel data. *Journal of Marketing Research, 23*, 89–100.
Kahneman, D., & Tversky, A. (1979). Prospect theory: An analysis of decision under risk. *Econometrica, 47*, 363–391.
Keeney, R. L., & Raiffa, H. (1976). *Decisions with multiple objectives: Preference and value tradeoffs*. New York: John Wiley & Sons.
Lewinsohn, A., & Mano, H. (1993). Multiattribute choice and affect: The influence of naturally occurring and manipulated mood on choice processes. *Journal of Behavioral Decision Making, 6*, 33–52.
Link, S.W. (1992). *The wave theory of difference and similarity*. Hillsdale, NJ: Lawrence Erlbaum Associates
Loewenstein, G., & Lerner, J. S. (2000). Emotions and decision making. In R. Davidson, K. Sherer, & H. Goldsmith (Eds.), *Handbook of affective science*. NY: Oxford University Press.

Loewenstein, G. (1986). Out of control: Visceral influences on behavior. *Organizational Behavior and Human Decision Processes, 65,* 272–292.

Luce, M. F., Bettman, J. R., & Payne, J. W. (1997). Choice processing in emotionally difficult decisions. *Journal of Experimental Psychology: Learning, Memory, & Cognition, 23,* 384–405.

Luce, M. F., Payne, J. W., & Bettman, J. R. (1999). Emotional trade-off difficulty and choice. *Journal of Marketing Research, 36,* 143–159.

Markman, A. B., & Brendt, C. M. (2000). The influence of goals on value and choice. In D. L. Medin (Ed.), *The psychology of learning and motivation,* Vol. 39 (pp. 97–139). San Diego, CA: Academic Press.

McAlister, L. (1982). A dynamic attribute satiation model of variety behavior. *Journal of Consumer Research, 9,* 141–150.

McAlister, L., & Pessemier, E. (1982). Variety seeking behavior: An interdisciplinary review. *Journal of Consumer Research, 9,* 311–322.

McFarland, D. J. (1971). *Feedback mechanisms in animal behavior.* NY: Academic Press.

McFarland, D. J. (1974). *Motivational control systems.* Academic Press.

McFarland, D. J., & Bosser, T. (1997). *Intelligent behavior in animals and robots.* Cambridge: MIT Press.

Mellers, B. A., Ordonez, L. D., & Birnbaum, M. H. (1992). A change-of-process theory for contextual effects and preference reversals in risky decision making. *Organizational-Behavior-and-Human-Decision-Processes 1992, 52,* 331–369.

Miller, N. E. (1959). Liberalization of basic S-R concepts: Extensions to conflict behavior, motivation and social learning. In S. Koch (Ed.), *Psychology: A study of science,* Vol. 2 (pp. 196–292). NY: McGraw - Hill,

Nosofsky, R. M., & Palmeri, T. J. (1997). An exemplar based random walk model of speeded classification. *Psychological Review, 104,* 266–300.

Payne, J. W., Bettman, J. R., & Johnson, E. J. (1993). *The adaptive decision maker.* NY: Cambridge University Press.

Ratcliff, R. (1978). A theory of memory retrieval. *Psychological Review, 85,* 59–108.

Read, D., & van Leeuwen, B. (1998). Predicting hunger: The effects of appetite and delay on choice. *Organizational Behavior and Human Decision Processes, 76,* 189–205.

Roe, R., Busemeyer, J. R., & Townsend, J. T. (2001). Multi-Alternative Decision Field Theory: A Dynamic Connectionist Model of Decision-Making. *Psychological Review, 108,* 370–392.

Rolls, Edmund T. (1999). *The Brain and Emotion.* Oxford: Oxford University Press.

Shiv, B., & Fedorikhin, A. (1999). Heart and mind in conflict: The interplay of affect and cognition in consumer decision making. *Journal of Consumer Research, 26,* 278–292.

Slovic, P. (1995). The construction of preference. *American Psychologist, 50,* 364–371.

Smith, P. L. (1995). Psychophysically principled models of visual simple reaction time. *Psychological Review, 102*(3), 567–593.

Townsend, J. T. (1992). Don't be phased by PHASER: Beginning exploration of a cyclic motivational system. *Behavioral Research Methods, Instrumentation, & Computers, 24,* 219–227.

Townsend, J. T., & Busemeyer, J. R. (1989). Approach-avoidance: Return to dynamic decision behavior. In C. Izawa (Ed.), *Current issues in cognitive processes: Tulane Flowerree Symposium on cognition* (pp. 107–133). Hillsdale, NJ: Erlbaum.

Townsend, J. T., & Busemeyer, J. R. (1995). Dynamic representation of decision-making. In R. F. Port and T. van Gelder (Eds.), Mind as Motion. MIT press.

Toates, F. M. (1975). *Control theory in biology and experimental psychology.* London: Hutchinson Educational.

Tversky, A. (1972). Elimination by aspects: A theory of choice. *Psychological Review, 79*(4), 281–299.

Tverksy, A., Sattath, S., & Slovic, P. (1988). Contingent weighting in judgment and choice. *Psychological Review, 95*, 371–384.

Von Winterfeldt, D., & Edwards, W. (1986). Decision analysis and behavioral research. Cambridge: Cambridge University Press.

CHAPTER 10

An informational value for mood
Negative mood biases attention to global information in a probabilistic classification task

Simon C. Moore and Mike Oaksford
Cardiff University

It is well documented that emotion affects visual attention. For example, objects that invoke fear (e.g. lions and snakes) 'grab' ones attention. However, these attentional effects are closely tied to the informational content of the emotions experienced and the objects that elicit them. For example, a lion grabs attention because it is fearful and fear has clearly defined consequences for the well being of the person experiencing it. Although mood has generally been assumed to have no informational content (Schwarz & Bless 1991), Moore and Oaksford (in press) have presented data suggesting that mild positive and negative moods modulate visual attention. In this chapter we present empirical research designed to test the attentional biases associated with varying moods states and how these biases may affect classification choices. If mood effects how people classify stimuli then it may be reasonable to assume that mood does have informational content under certain conditions.

Moore and Oaksford (in press) presented participants with a simple visual discrimination task. Participants were presented with an array of similar shapes and they were asked to judge whether one of those shapes was inverted. The experiment was originally designed to assess how mood affected skill acquisition: participants completed similar visual discrimination tasks across a two week period and before each session they were placed in either a positive, a negative or a neutral mood using standard techniques (Velten 1968). Initially, participants in the negative condition performed significantly slower than those in the positive condition. However, over time, and as performance improved with practice, the difference between the positive and negative groups decayed to the point where the two groups performed comparably (Moore & Oaksford, in press).

Moore and Oaksford (in press) suggested that the initial effects of mood in the visual discrimination task might be due to mood modulating attention to one or other end of the visual spatial frequency spectrum. The stimuli used in the task resembled a Navon stimulus (Navon 1977; see Figure 1), which has previously been used in research into the attentional aspects of visual spatial frequency. Generally, referring to Figure 1, the global T presents information at a low visual spatial frequency and the local Hs present information at a high visual spatial frequency. Due to the similarity between Navon stimuli and the stimuli used in Moore and Oaksford's study, they concluded that negative mood biased attention towards information at the global, low visual spatial frequency, level.

```
HHHHHHH
   H
   H
   H
   H
   H
   H
```

Figure 1. An example of a Navon stimulus.

Cognitive and neuroscientific accounts of processing Navon stimuli

Exploring some of the neuropsychological aspects of how information at high and low visual spatial frequencies is processed suggests a possible locus of interaction between mood and visual attention. Shulman and Wilson (1987) argued that identifying the global letter in a Navon stimulus is associated with processing of low visual spatial frequency information, whereas identifying the local letters is associated with processing of high visual spatial frequencies. Moreover, Fink, Halligan, Marshall, Frith, Frackowiak, and Dolan (1996) demonstrated laterality effects using the Navon stimuli. In this study, processing the global features of a stimulus appeared to be associated with greater activation of the right hemisphere (right extrastriate cortex), whereas the local details were more associated with activation of the left hemisphere (left extrastriate cortex). Furthermore, Fink, Marshall, Halligan, and Dolan (1999) presented data suggesting that this lateralised effect may be due to hemispheric specialisation for relatively high and low spatial frequencies. The right hemisphere specialises in relatively low visual spatial frequencies, and the left hemisphere specialises in relatively high visual spatial frequencies. Different visual spatial frequencies appear to be associated with one or other hemisphere, a finding that suggests a possible sight where the effects of mood may interact with attention to different ends of the visual spatial frequency spectrum.

In a series of studies employing EEG, positive mood has been associated with greater relative activation of the left mid-prefrontal region, whereas negative mood has been associated with greater relative activation of the right mid-prefrontal region of the cerebral cortex (Davidson 1998). These results suggest a relatively direct relationship between mood and biases towards one or other end of the visual spatial frequency spectrum. However, such a hypothesis needs to take account of observations made by Mayberg and colleagues (Mayberg et al. 1999). They presented neuroimaging data suggesting that both depression and negative mood are associated with an increase in activation in the hippocampus and a decrease in activation in the dorsolateral prefrontal cortex (DLPFC). Both Davidson's and Mayberg et al.'s work suggests that the frontal cortices are differentially activated depending on mood, although they may disagree on how this is mediated. Nevertheless the frontal cortex is strongly associated with visual attention and how that visual information is integrated (e.g. Dias, Robbins, & Roberts 1996; Rao, Rainer, & Miller 1997).

Not only is the prefrontal cortex associated with the integration of information processed as distinct streams in the cortex (Rao et al. 1997) this region also appears to be involved in what visual information is selected for further processing (Dias et al. 1996). Dias et al. suggested that the ability to "shift attention between the features of visual stimuli, such as their perceptual dimensions" is a central function of the prefrontal cortex.

These considerations suggest that a negative mood state may bias visual processing and Davidson's work suggests a bias towards low visual spatial frequencies in a negative mood. Importantly, there are behavioural data that supports this view (Otto & Hanze 1994; Klauer, Siemer, & Stober 1991). An induced positive mood state leads to a better performance on visual discrimination tasks relative to induced negative mood state in the laboratory (Klauer et al. 1991) and with naturally occurring moods (Otto & Hanze 1994). As in Moore and Oaksford's (in press) study, visual discrimination tasks seem to require attention to high visual spatial frequency information.

There are several studies showing mood related cognitive biases with visually presented material that may be interpretable from a visual spatial frequency framework. For example, in the left hemispheric word association task used by

Davidson and colleagues (Davidson, Chapman, Chapman, & Henriques 1990), participants were asked to select the closest associate to a previously seen cue word from an array of words. In this task, participants were presented with an array of words. Of these words, one was the target word, the rest were eight distracter words and participants were required to find the target word as quickly as possible. There were as many as eight distracter words surrounding the target word. If positive mood biases visual processing towards high visual spatial frequencies, then positive mood may facilitate performance on this task relative to negative mood. That is, reading the words in a complex array will be facilitated if early visual processing were biased towards high visual spatial frequencies, and this is what was found. Participants in the positive mood group performed comparably better than participants in the negative mood group. Thus, this study may provide further support for the hypothesis that mood biases attention along a visual spatial frequency spectrum in the manner discussed above. In summary, we suggest that in a negative mood state participants are biased towards low visual spatial frequencies.

Navon stimuli, uncertainty and visual perception

Further attention to the literature on Navon stimuli and visual spatial frequency suggests *why* mood may bias attention in this way. In this section we argue that information located at a low visual spatial frequency is information associated with an objects position and movement. As negative mood is generally associated with loss to ones well being, attending to the low visual spatial frequencies may assist in *avoiding* potential dangers in the future.

In a series of experiments, Cutting (Cutting 1978) demonstrated that considerable information could be inferred from lights attached to a person in the dark. With as few as six moving lights, participants are able to accurately state whether the person is carrying a heavy or light load. Thus movement can be inferred from a relatively limited amount of information.

Marr (Marr 1982) presented a model that allows an interpretation of Cutting's data, and suggests why mood may bias attention in the way we have suggested. Marr argued that most shapes could be 'hierarchically' decomposed. Under some circumstances parts of an object, for example its surface texture, may serve to allow identification. Alternatively, the overall shape of an object may allow identification (Marr 1982; Kosslyn 1994). For example, a hand is in part composed of fingers and fingers are in part composed of nails. This hierarchical approach to understanding human object identification has been studied extensively, in particular by Navon himself (Navon 1977).

When asked to identify either the local or global letters Navon (1977) demonstrated that participants would respond to the global letter faster than the local letters. In one version of this task, participants heard the name of a letter and were then required to judge if it was present at either the local or global level, responding with a 'yes' if the letter was present, and a 'no' if it was not.

Navon demonstrated that if the response to the large and small letters were in conflict, then there was interference from the global letter when judging the smaller letter, but not vice versa. For example, looking at Figure 1, if participants were asked to judge whether there was 'H' at the local level, then an interference effect is observed. However, if participants were asked to judge whether there was a 'T' at the global level no interference effect was observed.

This *global precedence* effect and the selective pattern of interference suggest that, in terms of Marr's hierarchy, the global level is available before the local, fine detail. The global shape 'T' (see Figure 1) is equivalent to the perceptual grouping of the lights attached to a person in Cutting's experiment (Cutting 1978). That is, shape and movement are levels of information coded at the low frequency end of the visual spatial frequency spectrum.

In sum, it seems plausible that mood provides information on where in the visual scene mood relevant information may be found. For example, and assuming that negative mood is a consequence of loss or harm, then further loss may be averted if attention is paid to information at a low visual spatial frequency as it is here that information about the location of potentially harmful objects is found. However, mood is not the only potential factor that may serve to bias attention to one or other end of the visual spatial frequency spectrum. Consequently, in exploring whether mood biases attention, it is necessary to control for these other factors.

Factors affecting attention to high and low visual spatial frequencies

Visual Angle. Kinchla and Wolfe (1979) presented data that suggests that when the Navon stimulus is very large, the global precedence effect is reduced. In their study, when the global stimulus subtends a sufficiently large visual angle, participants were unable to perceive the global dimension in its entirety. Navon and Norman (1983) suggested that this mitigating effect of stimulus size might be caused by eccentricity. For example, it would not be possible to identify an elephant based upon the visual input available if you were standing only twelve inches away from it.

Volitional Control. Other effects have been shown to effect the global precedence effect: spatial uncertainty, familiarity and stimulus presentation duration (Kimchi 1992). Moreover, Earhard (1990) demonstrated that participants have some control over what dimension is encoded. If the task is oriented so that the local level is more likely to provide the information relevant to the solution a local precedence effect is observed (Earhard 1990). For example, participants may be given the name of a letter and asked whether or not it is present at either the local or global level. The task can be arranged so that the majority of positive responses occur when the target letter matches the local level letters. After a period of time participants will come to expect the match to occur at the local level. When this occurred, Earhard (1990) argued that participants override the more general global precedence of stimuli and initially focus on the local level. Under these circumstances, a local precedence effect may occur.

There is interplay between local and global precedence effects. If all other things are equal, in terms of task demands, then a global precedence may emerge. In other words, where prior experience with the task does not aid its solution visual processing appears to default to focus initially on the global level of detail for a visually presented object. However, participants' expectations can be manipulated by task demands. Under these circumstances, prior experience may aid the solution on any given trial, and visual processing will adjust to a strategy that offers the most likely solution. This interplay between local and global precedence effects and prior knowledge will be used in the experiment reported here.

Time. Where prior knowledge does not aid the solution on a given trial, the duration a stimulus is presented may effect the global precedence effect. Loftus, Nelson and Kallman (1983) initially presented participants with a simple picture. Having studied the picture, participants were presented, simultaneously, with two further pictures. One picture was identical to the first the other was slightly different. The picture that was slightly different was presented in one of two forms. In one condition, the change involved a small detail, such as swapping a tape measure with a pack of cigarettes. In the other condition, a more holistic component was changed, for example the scene was photographed from a slightly different perspective.

Participants were then required to spot which of the two pictures differed from the first. By altering the time the initial picture was presented, Loftus et al. (1983) demonstrated that at low presentation times (250 ms), participants were more accurate at discriminating pictures at the holistic, or global level.

At longer presentation intervals (1,500 ms), however, participants were more accurate discriminating the differences at the local, fine detail, level.

Loftus et al.'s (1983) data are consistent with the view that participants encode global details first *followed* by local details. Loftus and Mackworth (1978) provided further evidence for this view. They tracked participants eye movements while they examined pictures. They found that later eye movements appeared to seek out the finer detail of these pictures. In the case of a face, participants initially engaged the general shape of the face, then later focused on the fine detail around the eyes. Moreover, their data suggest that stimulus presentation duration also affects the global precedence effect: the longer the Navon stimuli are presented the more likely participants encode both the local and global elements of the stimulus (Loftus & Mackworth 1978).

The experiment presented in this chapter assumed participants' classification choice for Navon stimuli would be effected by their mood state. Negative mood was hypothesised to bias attention to the global dimension of the Navon stimulus resulting in a bias in participants' classification choices (the details of this hypothesis are discussed below). However, the literature we just discussed also suggested that stimulus presentation duration affects the accessibility of the local level of visual information. If mood biases classification responses, then it may be that mood affects the time spent examining the Navon stimuli, rather than biasing attention directly. In order to examine this possible confound participants reaction times were collected and analysed.

Summary

In sum, this discussion leads to the following hypothesis: negative mood biases visual processing to low spatial frequencies. Positive mood biases visual processing towards high spatial frequencies. However, a requirement of local processing (discussed above) is that the global characteristics of the stimulus are processed first. Therefore, it is unlikely that positive mood will bias processing towards high spatial frequencies, per se. Rather, relative to negative mood, there will be facilitation for high spatial frequencies, having already encoded the low visual spatial frequency information.

If mood biases attention to different spatial frequencies, mood should modulate participants' choices in a classification task where the features of the to-be-classified stimuli are at different spatial frequencies. Mood should bias the classification choice when information presented at a high spatial frequency suggests membership of one category and information presented at a low spatial frequency suggests membership of a different category. To test this hypothesis Navon stimuli were used as the to-be-classified stimuli in a probabilistic classification task (see below).

The probabilistic classification task

The task was based on one used by Gluck and Bower (1988b). There are two reasons why this task was chosen. First, the task is implicit in nature: although the probabilistic classification task (PCT) can be mastered, participants are generally unable to explicitly state what the classification rule is (Gluck & Bower 1988b). It may be that using mood induction procedures lead participants to conform to the expected behaviour of someone in a given mood state. Therefore, it may not be their mood state that is influencing behaviour. The implicit nature of the PCT will help reduce this possible confound, as it is hard to see how participants may alter their behaviour in such a task, especially when they have no idea what they are doing in the first place.

Second, Gluck and Bower (1988b) showed that participants do not show the normative behaviour of matching their probability of classification to the objective probabilities with each cue predicts each category (i.e., "probability matching"). This suggests that we can not assess whether participants have learnt the task simply by checking that at asymptote their probability of classifying a stimulus matches the objective task probabilities. Gluck and Bower modelled the PCT using a simple neural network. This model provided a reasonable fit to the group data (Gluck & Bower 1988a) and explains why participants behaviour may diverge from normative predictions. Consequently, in this experiment, we used the Gluck and Bower model the to assess whether participant had adequately learnt the task.

Structure of the probabilistic classification task

In the PCT, Navon stimuli were used as the stimuli to be classified. These stimuli present two items of information: the local and the global letter. This section describes how the Navon stimuli were used in the PCT.

The PCT related each stimulus to one of two categories in a probabilistic manner. The task was structured so that each stimulus was presented a number of times. Initially participants did not know how each stimulus relates to each of the two categories. However, they were instructed that via feedback they would learn how each stimulus is related to each category. Participants therefore began the task by guessing.

Feedback was given according to the probabilistic relationship between the stimulus presented and the category selected. For example, if participants were presented with a large L composed of smaller Js and they select category A there was a 0.20 probability of receiving correct feedback and a 0.80 probability of receiving incorrect feedback. Whereas, if they selected category B there was a 0.80 probability of receiving correct feedback and a 0.20 probability of receiving incorrect feedback. According to normative standards, by presenting the full stimulus set over a series of trials participants should eventually probability match. That is, at asymptote, they should place a large L composed of smaller Js in category A twenty percent of the time. Of course, this behaviour may be modulated according to Gluck and Bower's (1988) model, as we discussed above. Further details on how the PCT was implemented are presented in the Methods section.

To check that participants were able to acquire the probabilistic structure of the task used several versions were piloted. As we now discuss, these pilot data motivated several important changes to the PCT.

Revision of the probabilistic classification task

Pilot data demonstrated several aspects of the task that required revision prior to implementing the PCT. First, it was noted in debriefing that some participants developed rather unusual classification strategies. Although most participants were unable to report what the classification rule was, some reported that the classification rule was related to the shape of the stimulus. For example, if the large letter were curved, such as a letter J, then it would be in category A, whereas if it were angular, as with the letter T, then it would be in category B. The origin of these classification heuristics is unknown.

Two modifications to the task were made in order to prevent the development of these heuristics affecting the data. First, the instructions were altered to read:

> Initially you will be given no clue on how each stimulus relates to the two available choices. However, after you have made your choice you will be told whether that choice is correct or incorrect. Therefore, although you will feel that you are at first just guessing, your performance will gradually improve.

> This is a difficult task. Because it is difficult, it will not be possible to work out the precise relationship between each stimulus and each category. Therefore, rather than waste time trying to work out the rule, just put each stimulus into the category you think it is most likely to be in.

Second, two versions of the PCT were constructed. Each version was identical to the other, only the probability rules were different: each was a mirror image of the other. This allowed stimulus properties to be counter-balanced between-subjects. For example, in task one a global 'J' composed of local 't' letters would be related to category A at the 90% level, whereas for task two the same stimulus would be associated with category A at the 10% level. This aspect will be covered more fully in the methodology section.

A second problem that was encountered involved task difficulty. If the relationship between the stimuli and the categories approaches 0.50 for all stimuli, the task becomes too difficult. This is because when all stimuli are associated with the categories at the 0.50 level there is no structure in the task to learn! To provide a measure of the discriminability of the two categories we used Shannon Entropy (Attneave 1957). The closer the stimuli were to the 0.50 level the higher the level of entropy (H) in the task as a whole, as

$$H = \sum_i p_i \log_2 \left(\frac{1}{p_i}\right) \tag{1}$$

where p_i is the subjective probability of some event, i, occurring within a given context. For example, if a stimulus is associated with category A at the 0.80 level, and so with category B at the 0.20 level then:

$$H_i = 0.80 \log_2 \left(\frac{1}{0.80}\right) + 0.20 \log_2 \left(\frac{1}{0.20}\right) = 0.722 \tag{2}$$

Summing across all stimuli within that context provided an overall measure of entropy. We further divided this total value by the total number of stimuli to provide the mean entropy per stimulus, H hereafter. As H increases the difficulty of the PCT as a whole increases. When H is at the maximum value of 1, then all stimuli in the PCT are related to the two categories at the 0.50 level. Clearly there is no reason to assess how mood modulates classification behaviour where participants cannot learn the task in the first place. Thus, the PCT was extensively piloted using different probabilistic relationships between the stimuli and the categories. Of these pilot tasks, the task with the highest level of entropy that could be learnt was one where $H = 0.84$. Tasks where H is greater than this value proved to be very difficult to learn whereas tasks with lower values of H were learnable.

Predicting performance on the probabilistic classification task

Although probability-matching behaviour is the assumed optimal performance when the PCT has been learnt, Gluck and Bower have argued that there are systematic differences between performance and this ideal (Gluck & Bower 1988a; Gluck & Bower 1988b; see above). Gluck and Bower used a least means squared (LMS) model of probabilistic classification learning, embodied in a two layer neural network based on Rescorla and Wagner's (Rescorla & Wagner 1972) associative learning model (Gluck & Bower 1988a; Gluck & Bower 1988b).

To predict participants' performance, the structure of the model used here was in the form of a simple two-layer neural network. The stimuli were composed of four letters (J, L, T and Y) at two levels (local or global) and with no stimulus constructed with the same letter at both local and global levels. Making the local and global dimensions explicit in the model gives an eight-node input array (see Figure 2). Eight input nodes, four for each level of information, feed forward to one output node.

The asymptotic weights of the network are derived from the probabilistic structure of the task (Gluck & Bower 1988a) and a logistic function is then used

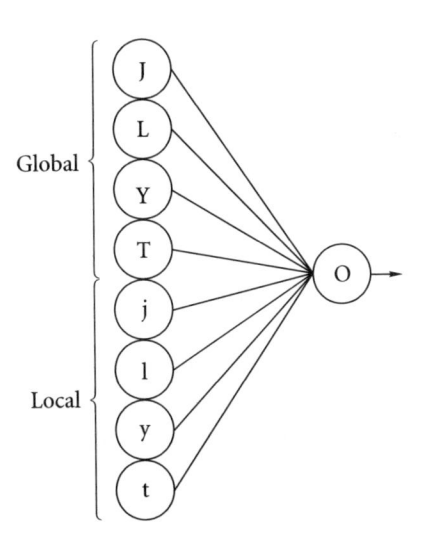

Figure 2. A representation of the network model used in the current research.

to convert these weights to the predicted probability of a given stimulus being categorised into one or other category:

$$P_k = P(A|S_k) = \frac{1}{1 + e^{-\theta(O_k)}} \quad (3)$$

where $P(A|S_k)$ is the probability of responding Category A given the stimulus pattern S_k, O_k denotes the activation in the output node resulting from the presentation of S_k to the input nodes, and θ is a (positive) scaling parameter. O_k is calculated from:

$$O_k = \sum_{i=1}^{n} a_i w_i \quad (4)$$

where a_i is the activation on input node i, w_i is the weight between the input node i and the output node, and the summation is over the n input nodes. As each stimulus activates one local and one global input node, these dimensions can be made explicit giving,

$$O_k = a_l w_l + a_g w_g \quad (5)$$

where a_l is the activation on the local input node (assumed to 1 for on and 0 for off), w_l is the weight between the local input node and the output node and a_g is the activation on the global input node, w_g is the weight between the global input node and the output node. Equation 5 was used to examine participant performance on the classification task. The model incorporates a free parameter, θ, when calculating predicted choice probabilities. As the empirical data examines performance between subject groups, it was important this parameter is kept constant across the analyses. Otherwise, any notable differences maybe consequent on changes in this parameter and not reflected in the data. Therefore, θ was assigned a value prior to the analyses, and kept at this value throughout.

The value of θ was determined by finding the value that minimises the residual sum of squared error between model and data by fitting the model to the pooled data (i.e. positive, neutral and negative mood groups combined). It was then kept constant when defining performance for each of the sub-groups and thus the model is used to provide a normative prediction for participants' choice probabilities.

Methodology

Participants

Forty-eight healthy volunteers, twenty-four men and twenty-four women, participated in return for payment (£4 per hour), these subjects were recruited through a poster displayed at a central location in the School of Psychology, Cardiff University. All subjects had English as their first language, were right handed, were between the ages of 18 and 25 years and had normal or corrected to normal eyesight.

Materials

The materials consisted of a probabilistic classification task, a transfer task and a mood induction procedure.

Probabilistic classification task

The initial learning task was a probability classification task. For the category-learning task, participants are presented with 8 stimuli over a series of trials. Each stimulus was in the form of a Navon stimulus composed of one of two letters: J, L, T and Y using the Geneva font, with the exception that the local and global letters were not the same. These letters were specifically chosen for this study as each could be adequately constructed from eleven constituent letters ensuring that the complexity of each stimulus at the local level was the same across the stimulus set.

Global level letters measured 3.2 cm wide and 6.7 cm high. At the local level each letter measured 0.3 cm wide and 0.7 cm high. These dimensions provided roughly the same height to width ratio for both the global and local stimulus letters. The size of the stimulus insured participants encoded the global information in its entirety. For very large stimuli, a local precedence effect may be observed (Kinchla & Wolfe 1979) where the global shape does not fit into the visual field in its entirety.

On each trial, there was an inter-trial interval (a blank screen) of 250 ms followed by a centrally presented fixation point (500 ms). The stimulus was then presented for 400 ms followed by a blank screen. If the stimulus SOA is sufficiently brief then participants may not base their classification choice on both the local and global dimensions of the stimuli. The literature suggests an SOA at or below 180 ms may lead to a global precedence effect. In a replication of Navon's (Navon 1977) original study using the stimuli used in this task, an SOA of 400 ms allowed both dimensions to be identifiable and yielded no significant difference in either reaction time or error rate by dimension.

Participants were instructed to assign each Navon stimulus to one of two categories (A or B). Following each response, feedback was given through a centrally presented character (a 'x' for incorrect and a '✓' for correct) together with a short tone (a low tone for incorrect and a high tone for correct). The trial terminated when a response was made at which point the programme moved to the next trial. 240 learning trials were presented and the relationship between participant response and task feedback followed a probabilistic rule. The relationship between the stimuli and the categories were also organised so that, assuming participants learnt to probability match, the four removed stimuli predicted each category at the 0.50 level. Two tasks were constructed. The second task was a mirror image of the one just presented. Using these two tasks allowed any stimulus effects to be balanced.

The probabilistic relations between the stimuli and the two categories were organised so that each component letter strongly predicted either category A or category B (see Table 1), but also so that each category was equally represented in the task and each dimension equally predicted categories A and B.

The experimental trials were grouped into sections of 8 trials. For each section each stimulus was presented once. With a fully random presentation of stimuli there was the risk that some stimuli may become randomly grouped together, thus resulting in a skewed distribution of stimuli in the task. As some exemplar models of category learning assume that the strength of a memory trace for an exemplar degrades over time (Nosofsky 1998) a random grouping may affect asymptotic performance. Specifically, the information gained from learning trials presented at the beginning of the learning task would have

Table 1. The probabilistic relationship between stimuli and category A, showing the probability that a given Navon stimulus with global letter I and local letter i, is in category A, $P(A|Ii)$.

	$P(A	Ii)$	\multicolumn{4}{c	}{Local}	
		J	L	T	Y	Mean
Global	J		0.20		0.30	0.25
	L	0.90		0.70		0.80
	T		0.30		0.10	0.20
	Y	0.60		0.90		0.75
	Mean	0.75	0.25	0.80	0.20	0.50

less influence on the later transfer task classification behaviour as this information is more likely to have been forgotten. Following one section of eight trials, an exclamation mark was presented. Participants were instructed to press the space bar when they were prepared to complete the next eight trials.

Transfer task

The transfer task was identical to the learning task. However, four additional stimuli (Jt, Ly, Tj and Yl; lowercase denotes the local level of the Navon stimulus) were added to the stimulus set. To ensure participants did not begin to learn the relationship between the new stimulus set and the two categories, no feedback was provided. The transfer task consisted of sixty trials.

All tasks were presented on a Power Macintosh computer (4400/200) with the keys '<' and '>' marked 'A' and 'B' to allow participants to assign a category to each stimulus. The Psyscope programme (Cohen, MacWhinney, Flatt, & Provost 1993) was used to control stimulus delivery and to record responses and response times.

Mood induction procedure

Positive, neutral, and negative mood states were induced by an amalgamation of three well-used procedures. Subjects first underwent an adapted version of the Velten mood induction procedure (Velten 1968). While performing the task they also listened to music (Positive: Mozart's Eine kleine Nachtmusik first, third & fourth movement; Neutral: Brahms 2nd movement from the first symphony, 2nd and 3rd movement from the 3rd symphony; Negative: Barber's Adagio for Strings & Mahler's 5th Symphony Adagietto). Finally, participants were specifically asked to co-operate by using the mood induction procedures' to actively enter the required mood-state (Slyker & McNally 1991). Previous research has documented the effectiveness of these tasks in inducing the required mood states (Westermann, Spies, Stahl, & Hesse 1995) and that employing these mood induction procedures in conjunction has greater effect (Martin 1990).

Mood induction check

Likert scales have proven to be good indicators of overall affective state and to provide consistent results (Isen & Gorglione 1983). They are therefore employed throughout this study. Each scale was arranged along a line with two statements at each end. Each pair of statements were opposites and affectively salient. The affectively positive adjectives (refreshed, calm, alert, positive and amused) were presented to the right. The affectively negative adjectives (tired, anxious, unaware, negative and sober, respectively) were presented to the left. All scales were presented on a Macintosh computer and seven keys on the computer keyboard (3 to 9) were marked −3 to +3 to allow participants to respond accordingly. One mood induction check was completed directly after each mood induction procedure. Furthermore, each participant completed a second paper and pencil version of the Mood Induction Check (MIC) before leaving the laboratory to insure that each participant left in not too negative a mood state.

Procedure

Before testing, approval was sought, and given, by the Ethics Committee, School of Psychology, University of Wales, Cardiff, for all aspects of this research. Before testing, the tasks were piloted to ensure validity. Participants involved at the piloting stage were not allowed to participate in the experimental stage.

Upon entering the laboratory, participants were asked to sit in a small testing cubicle. A statement of informed consent, which briefly outlined the structure of the experiment, possible risks and discomforts and that each participant's right to withdraw from the study would be respected, was read and signed by each participant. The experiment was then begun. Participants first completed the learning trials, followed by the mood induction procedure and then the transfer task.

Data reduction and analysis

It was hypothesised that negative mood would bias participants to make a classification choice based upon information at the low visual spatial frequency. In order to examine the effect of mood on early visual processing the classification choice for the novel stimuli, those stimuli not seen in the learning trials, were analysed. Participants must either classify the stimulus into either category A or category B. Therefore, from the element category relationships presented in Table 1, it is possible to calculate whether participants are classifying the stimulus according to the local or the global element. On the one hand, if participants probability-match, then across the transfer trials the local and global elements should be equally represented in their choices. On the other hand, if mood biases early visual processing towards either the high or low visual spatial frequencies, then the classification choice will be biased to the local or global level.

Results

The hypothesis this experiment tests, concerning how mood biases visual attention to the different levels in a Navon stimulus, relies on the underlying assumption that participants were able to acquire the probabilistic classification task. To examine whether participants had acquired the task, asymptotic behaviour on the learning trials was collected from the last 72 trials for each participant. Table 2 shows the objective task probability (P(A)), the behaviour predicted by the LMS model (P_k), and participants pooled asymptotic behaviour calculated from the 72 trials of the PCT learning task (*Actual*). Comparing the participant's data with the objective task probabilities yielded a significant correlation ($r(6) = 0.94, p < 0.0005$; see Table 2). Fitting the eight node model to the participants data by minimising the residual sum of squared error yielded a value of $\theta = 0.44$. Comparing participant data with the model's predictions yielded a significant correlation ($r(6) = 0.81, p < 0.025$). These data confirm that participants have learnt the task and that the model does predict their performance.

The correlation coefficients seem to indicate that the objective task probabilities predict participant performance, at the group level, better than the LMS model. However, this is very misleading. The correlation co-efficient only reveals how well the model or the objective task probabilities capture the trend

Table 2. The probabilistic relationships between the stimuli and category A, in the data (Actual), in the objective task probabilities (P(A)), and predicted by the LMS rule (P_k). SEM = standard error of the mean for the observed (Actual) probabilities.

Global	Local	Actual	SEM	P_k	P(A)
J	L	0.36	0.050	0.32	0.20
J	Y	0.40	0.045	0.47	0.30
L	J	0.68	0.047	0.66	0.90
L	T	0.61	0.044	0.63	0.70
T	L	0.42	0.042	0.42	0.30
T	Y	0.38	0.044	0.58	0.10
Y	J	0.63	0.045	0.62	0.60
Y	T	0.61	0.0410	0.59	0.90

in the data. It does not provide an indication of fit to exact location. Using the standard errors for the data means, we computed the root mean squared scaled deviation (RMSSD), which provides a scale invariant estimate of the fit to exact location in standard error units. For the LMS model RMSSD = 1.76, whereas for the objective task probabilities, RMSSD = 4.21. That is, on average, the LMS model deviated from the observed means by only 1.76 standard error units, whereas probability matching deviated by 4.21 standard error units. That is, the LMS rule provided a much better fit to exact location than the objective task probabilities. Indeed, a χ^2 goodness of fit test (with $N = 8 \times 48 = 384$) showed that although the LMS model could not be rejected, $\chi^2(7) = 9.45, p > .20$, as a model for these data, probability matching could be rejected, $\chi^2(7) = 127.77$, $p < .00001$. Consequently, the results of this experiment are consistent with past results on the PCT, which demonstrates that the use of Navon stimuli has not altered the way that the task is learnt.

For the mood induction check, a one-way between subjects (positive, neutral and negative) ANOVA on the mood ratings yielded a significant effect ($F(2, 45) = 23.07, p < 0.01$). Planned contrasts showed that the positive group (positive mean = 1.63, SD = 0.96) rated themselves as more positive than the neutral group (neutral mean = 0.41, SD = 0.69; $F(1, 45) = 15.05, p < 0.01$) and that the negative group rated themselves as more negative than the neutral group (negative mean = –0.491, SD = 0.97; $F(1, 45) = 8.35, p < 0.01$).

The model was then used to assess participant performance on the transfer tasks. Following the mood induction procedure, participants continued to perform according to the LMS rule on the original eight stimuli (Positive: $r(6) = 0.75, p < 0.05$; Neutral: $r(6) = 0.76, p < 0.05$; Negative: $r(6) = 0.82, p < 0.05$).

It was hypothesised that negative mood would bias participants to make a classification choice based upon information at the low visual spatial frequency, with no hypothesised difference between positive and neutral groups. If the negative group use both local and global information equally then the local level will predict classification choices for 50% of the choices made.

One-way between subjects ANOVAs were conducted with mood group as the between subjects factor and the proportion of the novel stimuli classified according to the local dimension as the dependent variable. Planned contrasts revealed that for the positive and neutral groups there was no significant difference between the groups (positive mean = 0.49, SD = 0.21; neutral mean = 0.52, SD = 0.21; $F(1, 30) < 1$). These two groups attended to both local and global dimension equally, i.e., the proportion of novel stimuli classified according to the local dimension ≈ .5. Planned contrasts further revealed a near significant difference between the positive and negative groups (negative mean

= 0.35, SD = 0.19; F(1, 30) = 3.85, p = 0.059). That is, in a negative mood, significantly fewer of the novel stimuli were classified at the local level, and so more were classified at the global level. Further planned contrasts revealed a significant difference between the negative and neutral groups (F(1, 30) = 5.97, $p < 0.05$). Collapsing across the positive and neutral groups (mean = 0.50, SD = 0.21) and comparing these data with the negative group (mean = 0.35, SD = 0.19) yielded a significant effect (F(1, 46) = 6.34, MSE = 0.04, p = 0.015). Consistent with the hypothesis, the negative group was biased towards the global dimension of the Navon stimulus when making their classification choice for the novel stimuli.

An alternative explanation of these results is that participants in a negative mood state did not study the novel Navon stimuli long enough to encode the local dimension. We have already argued that the SOA for a Navon stimulus could determine the discriminability of local level information. For shorter SOAs the local level is harder to discern. It may be that participants in the negative group did not study the stimuli long enough to encode the local level of information so suggesting that mood-state has speeded decision-making rather than biasing early visual processing directly. However, an analysis of the reaction times does not support this alternative account. On the transfer task there was no significant difference in reaction time between mood groups (positive, neutral and negative), F(2, 45) < 1, in a one-way ANOVA. Moreover, a the planned contrast between the combined positive and neutral group vs. the negative group was also not significant (F(1, 46) < 1).

Debriefing

In debriefing, consistent with the implicit nature of the task, no participant indicated any awareness of the experimental hypothesis or was explicitly aware of any classification rule. Moreover, the inclusion of the additional stimuli in the transfer task went unnoticed. Participants in the positive and negative mood groups indicated that the mood induction procedure was effective and that they experienced the intended mood-state.

Discussion

For the task as a whole, participants learnt to classify the initial eight stimuli according to the LMS model's predictions and continued to do so following the mood induction procedure. Thus, it is reasonable to suggest that participants had some representation, although not explicit, of how the stimulus elements predicted category membership. The effects of mood on the novel stimuli in the transfer task suggest that negative mood leads to more attention to the global, low visual spatial frequency, level of information when participants made their classification choice.

These data also suggest that mood may have some informational value. The classification task was arranged so that the participants had no prior information on how to classify the novel stimuli introduced in the transfer task. Although the component parts of the stimuli, the local and global letters, suggested one or other category, taken together the whole stimulus was equidistant between the two categories. The situation participants confront in the classification experiment is analogous to the situation confronted by Burridan's Ass. Burridan's Ass was placed equidistant between two equally attractive carrots and, not being able to break the symmetry between these two options, died of starvation. Fortunately none of the participants in the classification task met the same fate. Participants in the positive and neutral group presumably made a random choice. That is, they broke the symmetry by a simple randomisation procedure. However, participants in the negative group could use their mood state to inform the decision, because their mood biases their attention towards one or other dimension. Consequently, whether saving an Ass or biasing a classification choice, it seems that mood may have some informational content.

One way of explaining these results may be in terms of mood acting as a dimension in multidimensional models of classification choice. Nosofsky's (Nosofsky 1998; Nosofsky & Palmeri 1997) generalised context model treats classification choices as based on information described along a series of dimensions. For example, when classifying animals into *dog* or *cat* categories one might attend to information based along the dimensions of height, shape and so forth. Niedenthal and her colleagues (Niedenthal, Halberstadt, & Innes-Ker 1999; Niedenthal, Halberstadt, & Setterlund 1997) have proposed that mood can be understood within a dimensional account of classification. She presented participants with a cue word followed by two target words. Participants judged which of the two target words was most closely related to the cue word. Under differing mood states participants appeared to select target words based upon their current mood. For example, for the cue word *trophy* and the target words *ring* and *metal*, participants in a positive emotional state tended to select *ring* more often than participants in a negative mood state. Niedenthal argues that this effect is due to mood biasing judgements of similarity along an emotion dimension. A *ring* and a *trophy* are related by positive emotional events (weddings and winning competitions), whereas *metal* is not.

Our results seem to suggest another role for emotion or mood. Rather than representing another dimension in multidimensional space, our results suggest that mood is better regarded as a modulating factor, or weight, in dimensional accounts of classification behaviour. The stimuli in our experiment are classified along two dimensions: local and global letters. Negative mood weights the global dimension more heavily than the local dimension. In Nosofsky's GCM model, such an increase in the weighting has the effect of stretching the dimension, making stimuli classified along that dimension seem more dissimilar. Consequently, the similarity of the novel stimuli to one or other category (convex region of multidimensional space) will be more marked along the global dimension than the local. We are currently exploring models of emotionally modulated classification choice along these lines.

References

Attneave, F. (1957). Physical determinants of the judged complexity of shapes. *Journal of Experimental Psychology, 53*(4), 221–227.

Cohen, J. D., MacWhinney, B., Flatt, M., & Provost, J. (1993). A new graphic interactive environment for designing psychology experiments. *Behavioral Research Methods, Instruments and Computers, 25*(2), 257–271.

Cutting, J. E. (1978). Generation of synthetic male and female walkers through manipulation of a biomechanical invariant. *Perception, 1*, 393–405.

Davidson, R. J. (1998). Affective style and affective disorders: Perspectives from affective neuroscience. *Cognition and Emotion, 12*(3), 307–330.

Davidson, R. J., Chapman, J. P., Chapman, L. J., & Henriques, J. B. (1990). Assymetrical brain electrical-activity discriminates between psychometrically-matched verbal and spatial cognitive tasks. *Psychophysiology, 27*(5), 528–543.

Dewey, J. (1894). The theory of emotions: Emotional attitudes. *Psychological Review, 1*, 553–569.

Dias, R., Robbins, T. W., & Roberts, A. C. (1996). Dissociation in prefrontal cortex of affective and attentional shifts. *Nature, 380*, 69–72.

Earhard, B. (1990). The generality of outside-in processing routines in the analysis of form. *Canadian Journal of Psychology, 44*, 14–29.

Fink, G. R., Halligan, P. W., Marshall, J. C., Frith, C. D., Frackowiak, R. S. J., & Dolan, R. J. (1996). Where in the brain does visual attention select the forest from the trees? *Nature, 382*, 626–628.

Fink, G. R., Marshall, J. C., Halligan, P. W., & Dolan, R. J. (1999). Hemispheric asymmetries in globa/local processing are modulated by perceptual salience. *Neuropsychologia, 37*, 31–40.

Gluck, M. A., & Bower, G. H. (1988a). Evaluating an adaptive network model of human learning. *Journal of Memory and Language, 27*, 166–195.

Gluck, M. A., & Bower, G. H. (1988b). From conditioning to category learning: An adaptive network model. *Journal of Experimental Psychology: General, 117*(3), 227–247.

Isen, A. M., & Gorglione, J. M. (1983). Some specific effects of four affect-induction procedures. *Personality and Social Psychology Bulletin, 9*(1), 136–143.

Kimchi, R. (1992). Primacy of wholistic processing and the global/local paradigm: A critical review. *Psychological Bulletin, 112*, 24–38.

Kinchla, R. A., & Wolfe, J. (1979). The order of visual processing: "Top down", "bottom up" or "middle out". *Perception and Psychophysics, 25*, 225–231.

Klauer, K. C., Siemer, M., & Stober, J. (1991). Stimmung und leistungsniveau bei einfachen aufgaben. *Zeitschrift Fur Experimentelle Und Angewandte Psychologie, 38*(3), 379–393.

Kosslyn, S. M. (1994). *Image and Brain: The Resolution of the Imagery Debate*. Cambridge, MA: MIT Press.

Loftus, G. R., & Mackworth, N. H. (1978). Cognitive determinants of fixation location during picture viewing. *Journal of Experimental Psychology: Human Perception and Performance, 4*, 565–572.

Loftus, G. R., Nelson, W., & Kallman, H. J. (1983). Differential acquisition rates for different types of information frm pictures. *Quarterly Journal of Experimental Psychology, 35A*, 187–198.

Marr, D. (1982). *Vision: A Computational Investigation into the Human Representation and Processing of Visual Information*. New York: Freeman.

Martin, M. (1990). On the induction of mood. *Clinical Psychology Review, 10*, 669–697.

Mayberg, H. S., Liotti, M., Brannan, S. K., McGinnis, S., Mahurin, R. K., Jerabek, P. A., Silva, J. A., Tekell, J. L., Martin, C. C., Lancaster, J. L., & Fox, P. T. (1999). Reciprocal limbic-cortical function and negative mood: Converging PET findings in depression and normal sadness. *American Journal of Psychiatry, 156*, 675–682.

Moore, S. C., & Oaksford, M. (in press). Some long-term effects of emotion on cognition. *British Journal of Psychology*.

Navon, D. (1977). Forest before the trees: The precedence of global features in visual perception. *Cognitive Psychology, 9*, 353–383.

Navon, D., & Norman, J. (1983). Does global precedence really depend on visual angle? *Journal of Experimental Psychology: Human Perception and Performance, 9*, 955–965.

Niedenthal, P. M., Halberstadt, J. B., & Innes-Ker, A. H. (1999). Emotional response categorization. *Psychological Review, 106*(2), 337–361.

Niedenthal, P. M., Halberstadt, J. B., & Setterlund, M. B. (1997). Being happy and seeing "happy": Emotional state mediates visual word recognition. *Cognition and Emotion, 11*(4), 403–432.

Nosofsky, R. M. (1998). Optimal performance and exemplar models of classification. M. R. Oaksford, & N. Chater (Eds), *Rational Models of Cognition* (pp. 218–247). Oxford: Oxford University Press.

Nosofsky, R. M., & Palmeri, T. J. (1997). An exemplar-based random walk model of speeded classification. *Psychological Review, 104*(2), 266–300.

Otto, J. H., & Hanze, M. (1994). Effekte naturlicher stimmungsveranderungen auf diskriminationsleistung und antworttendenz bei der mustererkennung. *Zeitschrift Fur Experimentelle Und Angewandte Psychologie, 41*(4), 566–583.

Rao, S. C., Rainer, G., & Miller, E. K. (1997). Integration of what and where in the primate prefrontal cortex. *Science, 276*, 821–823.

Rescorla, R. A., & Wagner, A. R. (1972). A theory of Pavlovian conditioning: Variations in the effectiveness of reinforcement and non-reinforcement. Black, A. H., & Prokasy, W. F. *Classical Conditioning II: Current Research and Theory* (pp. 64–99). New York: Appleton-Century-Crofts.

Rueckl, J. G., Cave, K. R., & Kosslyn, S. M. (1989). Why are "what" and "where" processed by separate cortical visual systems? *Journal of Cognitive Neuroscience, 1*(2), 171–186.

Schwarz, N., & Bless, H. (1991). Happy and mindless, but sad and smart? The impact of affective states on analytic reasoning. J. P. Forgas (Ed.), *Emotion and Social Judgements* (pp. 55–71). Oxford: Pergamon Press.

Shulman, G. L., & Wilson, J. (1987). Spatial frequency and selective attention to local and global information. *Perception, 16*, 89–101.

Slyker, J. P., & McNally, R. J. (1991). Experimental induction of anxious and depressed moods – are Velten and musical procedures necessary? *Cognitive Therapy and Research, 15*, 33–45.

Velten, E. (1968). A laboratory task for the induction of mood states. *Behaviour Research and Therapy, 6*, 473–482.

Westermann, R., Spies, K., Stahl, G., & Hesse, F. W. (1995). Relative effectiveness and validity of mood induction procedures: A meta-analysis. *European Journal of Social Psychology, 26*, 557–580.

CHAPTER 11

The effects of positive affect and arousal on working memory and executive attention
Neurobiology and computational models

F. Gregory Ashby, Vivian V. Valentin and And U. Turken
University of California at Santa Barbara / Stanford University

There is now overwhelming evidence that moderate fluctuations in feelings can systematically affect cognitive processing (for reviews, see Ashby, Isen, & Turken 1999; Isen 1993). For example, Isen and others have shown that mild positive affect, of the sort that people could experience every day, improves creative problem solving (e.g., Isen, Daubman, & Nowicki 1987; Isen, Johnson, Mertz, & Robinson 1985), facilitates recall of neutral and positive material (Isen, Shalker, Clark, & Karp 1978; Nasby & Yando 1982; Teasdale & Fogarty 1979), and systematically changes strategies in decision-making tasks (Carnevale & Isen 1986; Isen & Geva 1987; Isen & Means 1983; Isen, Nygren, & Ashby 1988; Isen, Rosenzweig, & Young 1991).

Recently, Ashby et al. (1999) proposed a neuropsychological theory of many of these results. Specifically, they assumed that some of the cognitive influences of positive mood are due to increased levels of dopamine in frontal cortical areas that result from the events eliciting the elevation in mood. The starting point for this theory is the huge literature on the neurobiology of reward (for reviews, see Beninger 1983; Liebeman & Cooper 1989; Wise 1982; Wise & Rompré 1989), which in humans, often induces positive affect. In fact, one of the most common methods of inducing positive affect in subjects is to administer an unexpected noncontingent reward (i.e., by giving an unanticipated gift), and there is consensus in the neuroscience literature that unexpected reward causes dopamine release from brain stem sites (for reviews, see, e.g., Beninger 1991; Bozarth 1991; Philips, Blaha, Pfaus, & Blackburn 1992; Schultz 1992).

The theory developed by Ashby et al. (1999) was purely neuropsychological. It described some of the neural pathways and structures (and neurotransmitter systems) that might participate in mediating the neural effects of positive affect and its influence on cognition – with special emphasis on creative problem solving. In this chapter we describe a computational extension of that theory. The computational version is a connectionist network that successfully accounts for the effects of positive feelings on three creative problem solving tasks (i.e., word association, the Remote Associates Test, and the Duncker candle task). Although these include verbal and performance tasks and have different surface features, for each task the connectionist network we describe has the same architecture. In addition, the same parameter values are used to represent the mood effects of the control and positive affect groups in all three applications. The network also successfully accounts for the effects of amphetamines on a two-choice guessing task. This demonstration is important because amphetamines directly increase brain dopamine levels, and therefore, we postulate that in low doses, amphetamines should have some of the same effects as positive affect. On the other hand, amphetamines stimulate other neurotransmitter systems in addition to dopamine (e.g., norepinephrine), and so some important differences between amphetamines and positive affect are expected in some tasks and conditions.

A second goal of this chapter is to explore more fully the concept of *arousal*, which is closely related to positive affect, both empirically and theoretically. Generally, conditions that induce positive affect are also likely to increase arousal, and as we will see, like positive affect, arousal is thought to increase the level of certain neuromodulators in frontal cortical areas. Thus, a major challenge to understanding the neural effects of positive affect is to disambiguate its effects from those of arousal.

The next section briefly reviews the literature on the influences of positive affect on cognition, with a focus on its effects on creative problem solving. The third section reviews the dopaminergic theory of positive affect that was developed by Ashby et al. (1999). The fourth section presents and tests a computational model that was inspired by this theory. Next, we examine arousal, focusing on its neuropsychological underpinnings, its effects on cognition, and on how it is related to positive affect. Finally, we close with some brief conclusions.

Positive affect and creative problem solving

It is now well-recognized that positive affect leads to greater cognitive flexibility and facilitates creative problem solving across a broad range of settings (e.g., Aspinwall & Taylor 1997; Carnevale & Isen 1986; Estrada, Isen, & Young 1995; Estrada, Young, & Isen 1994; Fiske & Taylor 1991; George & Brief 1996; Greene & Noice 1988; Hirt, Melton, McDonald, & Harackiewicz 1996; Isen 1987, 1993; Isen & Baron 1991; Isen et al. 1985, 1987; Kahn & Isen 1993; Mano 1997; Showers & Cantor 1985; Staw & Barsade 1993; Staw, Sutton, & Pelled 1994; Taylor & Aspinwall 1996). This work suggests that positive affect increases a person's ability to organize ideas in multiple ways and to access alternative cognitive perspectives. In dozens of experiments supporting this conclusion, subjects were assigned randomly to either a neutral or positive affect condition, and positive affect was induced in a variety of simple ways, such as receiving a small unanticipated gift, watching a few minutes of a comedy film, reading funny cartoons, or experiencing success on an ambiguous task. This indicates that the effects can be prompted readily, by small things in people's lives.

A detailed examination of this literature is beyond the scope of this chapter. The interested reader should consult Ashby et al. (1999). Instead, we will focus only on those empirical results that will be modeled below. First, in word association, positive affect subjects have been shown to respond to neutral words (but not to negative words) with a broader range of first associates than control subjects (Isen et al. 1985). Similarly, in a study with young adolescents, positive affect increased verbal fluency, and children in the positive affect condition gave more category words and more unusual examples of the category than children in the neutral affect control condition (Greene & Noice 1988). A similar finding, with adult subjects, was obtained recently by Hirt et al. (1996).

Second, positive affect has been shown to improve performance in several tasks that typically are used as indicators of creativity or innovative problem solving (Isen et al. 1987). In one of these, called Duncker's (1945) candle task, a person is given a candle, a box of tacks, and a book of matches, and is asked to attach the candle to the wall in such a way that it will burn without dripping wax on the floor or table. To solve the problem, the person can empty the box of tacks, tack the box to the wall, and then use the box as a platform for the candle. Thus, the person must use one of the items (the box) in an unaccustomed way – a classic criterion of creativity (e.g., Koestler 1964). This type of cognitive flexibility has also been referred to as "breaking set" or overcoming "functional fixedness" (Duncker 1945; Wertheimer 1945). A number of studies have shown that positive affect subjects perform significantly better than controls on Duncker's candle task (Greene & Noice 1988; Isen et al. 1987).

A third task that has been used to study the influence of positive affect on cognitive flexibility or creativity is based on the Remote Associates Test (Mednick, Mednick, & Mednick 1964), which was designed in accord with S. Mednick's (1962) theory of creativity. In this test, which in its full form was designed to measure individual differences in creativity, subjects are presented with three words and a blank line and are asked to respond with a word that relates to each of the three words given in the problem. An example is the following:

MOWER ATOMIC FOREIGN _____.

(The correct answer is POWER.) Seven items of moderate difficulty from the Remote Associates Test have been used in the research on the influence of affect. Several studies have found that positive affect improves accuracy in this test, not only in college students, but also in a sample of practicing physicians (Estrada et al. 1994; Isen et al. 1987).

Note that we are not claiming that positive affect will improve performance on all cognitive tasks. In fact, there are reports that positive affect impairs performance on some tasks (Oaksford, Morris, Grainger, & Williams 1996). For this reason, we focus on creative problem solving, where the data have been remarkably consistent.

The dopamine hypothesis of positive affect

Ashby et al. (1999) proposed that many of the cognitive effects of positive mood are due to increases in brain dopamine levels that co-occur with mild elevations in mood. There is much evidence supporting this hypothesis. First, of course, is the already mentioned fact that dopamine is released after an animal encounters an unexpected reward (e.g., Mirenowicz & Schultz 1994; Schultz 1992), and reward is closely associated with positive affect, at least in humans. Second, drugs that mimic the effects of dopamine (i.e., dopamine agonists) or that enhance dopaminergic activity, elevate feelings (e.g., apomorphine, cocaine, and amphetamines) (e.g., Beatty 1995). Third, dopamine antagonists (i.e., neuroleptics), which block the effects of dopamine, flatten affect (e.g., Hyman & Nestler 1993). Fourth, dopamine release and positive affect are both associated with increased motor activity (e.g., Hale & Strickland 1976; Kelly, Sevior, & Iversen 1975; Protais, Bonnet, & Costentin 1983; Strickland, Hale, & Anderson 1975).

Although Ashby et al. (1999) proposed that dopamine mediates the cognitive effects (or some of the cognitive effects) of pleasant feelings, several lines of evidence suggest that it does not mediate the pleasant feelings associated with positive affect. First, dopamine cells in the ventral tegmental area (VTA) of cats have been shown to fire to loud clicks and bright flashes of light that have never been paired with a reward (Horvitz, Stewart, & Jacobs 1997). Second, stressful or anxiety-provoking events, which presumably would produce negative affect in humans, actually appear to increase dopamine levels in certain brain regions (i.e., prefrontal cortex) (Abercrombie et al. 1989; Cenci et al. 1992; Imperato et al. 1991; Sorg & Kalivas 1993; Zacharko & Anisman 1991). Finally, many researchers have argued that a primary function of dopamine is to serve as the reward signal in reward-mediated learning (e.g., Beninger 1983; Miller 1981; Montague, Dayan, & Sejnowski 1996; White 1989; Wickens 1993). Thus, one possibility is that at least some of the results that purportedly link dopamine and reward are actually due to a failure of learning. Although these results do not disconfirm the hypothesis that dopamine release occurs during periods of positive affect, they do argue against the stronger hypothesis that dopamine release is responsible for initiating the pleasant feelings associated with positive affect.

Ashby et al. (1999) were also careful to point out that in addition to dopamine, other neurotransmitters and neuromodulators are known to influence mood and emotion. For example, theories of depression have long focused on norepinephrine and serotonin (e.g., Schildkraut 1965). As a result, a complete theory of mood, and probably also a complete theory of positive affect, must consider many neurochemicals. Even so, Ashby et al. (1999) argued that to account for the influences of positive affect on cognition, the most important place to begin is with dopamine.

Ashby et al. (1999) developed the dopaminergic theory of positive affect in considerably more detail in the case of frontal cortical functioning. They postulated that during positive affect conditions, dopamine is released from the VTA into the prefrontal cortex and anterior cingulate. They further proposed that the dopamine projection into prefrontal cortex facilitates working memory, whereas the projection into anterior cingulate facilitates executive attention and the selection of cognitive perspective. There is growing consensus that prefrontal cortex is the key cortical substrate of working memory (a review is beyond the scope of this chapter; see, e.g., Fuster 1989; Goldman-Rakic 1987, 1995). There is also strong evidence that reductions in dopamine levels in prefrontal cortex cause working memory deficits (Brozoski, Brown, Rosvold, & Goldman 1979; Gotham, Brown, & Marsden 1988; Levin, Labre, &

Weiner 1989; Roberts et al. 1994; Williams & Goldman-Rakic 1995). Data on the effects of increases in prefrontal cortex dopamine levels suggest that moderate increases facilitate working memory, but large increases cause deficits – in other words, working memory performance is optimized at some intermediate dopamine level (Lange et al. 1992; Luciano, Depue, Arbisi, & Leon 1992; Williams & Goldman-Rakic 1995). Based on these data, Ashby et al. (1999) hypothesized that moderate, but not extreme levels of positive affect might improve working memory.

Posner and Petersen (1990; see, also Posner & Raichle 1994) proposed that the anterior cingulate cortex is a key structural component of the anterior (i.e., executive) attentional system. Specifically, they hypothesized that the (dorsal) anterior cingulate is involved in the selection of cognitive perspective and in the conscious directing of executive attention. Ashby et al. (1999) reviewed evidence supporting this general model, and also that dopamine enhances these abilities. For example, dopamine antagonists impair cognitive set shifting (Berger et al. 1989), and patients with Parkinson's disease, which reduces brain dopamine levels, are impaired in tasks that require selection or set shifting (e.g., Brown & Marsden 1988; Cools et al. 1984).

Ashby and his colleagues argued that the act of switching attention from one cognitive set to another involves two separate operations – first, a new cognitive set must be selected, and second, attention must be switched from the old set to the new one (Ashby, Alfonso-Reese, Turken, & Waldron 1998; Ashby et al. 1999). They also proposed, and presented evidence in support of the hypothesis that the selection operation is mediated cortically, by the anterior cingulate and possibly also by the prefrontal cortex, and that switching is mediated by the head of the caudate nucleus. A complete review of this evidence is beyond the scope of this chapter (i.e., see Ashby et al. 1998, 1999). However, we will briefly mention a few results supporting this general model of executive attention. First, a recent neuroimaging study identified the (dorsal) anterior cingulate as the site of hypothesis generation in a rule-based category-learning task (Elliott, Rees, & Dolan 1999). Second, lesion studies in rats implicate the dorsal caudate nucleus in rule switching (Winocur & Eskes 1998). Third, injections of a glutamate agonist directly into the striatum increase the frequency with which cats switch from one motor activity to another in a task where food rewards are delivered for such switching behaviors (Jaspers, De Vries, & Cools 1990a, 1990b).

Finally, lesioning the dopamine fibers that project from VTA into the prefrontal cortex *improves* the performance of monkeys in an analogue of the Wisconsin card sorting test, even though it impairs their spatial working memory

(Roberts et al. 1994). If switching occurs in the prefrontal cortex, then such lesions should impair switching performance (as seen, e.g., in Parkinson's patients). If the switching occurs in the basal ganglia, then one's first thought might be that lesioning dopamine fibers in the prefrontal cortex should have no direct effect on switching. However, it turns out that such lesions increase dopamine levels in the basal ganglia (Roberts et al. 1994). Therefore, if the basal ganglia are responsible for switching, and if switching is enhanced by dopamine, then lesioning dopamine fibers in prefrontal cortex should improve switching, which is exactly what Roberts et al. (1994) found.

Ashby et al. (1999) proposed that much of the improvement in creative problem solving that is observed under conditions of positive affect is due to the facilitation of the executive attention system that occurs with increased dopamine release into the anterior cingulate cortex. We will next test this hypothesis more rigorously by implementing it within a connectionist model of some common creative problem solving tasks, and ask whether the model can account for the known effects of positive affect on performance in these tasks.

A connectionist model of creative problem solving

In this section we describe and test a general connectionist model of mental flexibility in creative problem solving tasks that makes specific predictions about any experimental manipulation that increases brain dopamine levels, including positive affect. We focus on three tasks that were described in an earlier section, and that are known to be affected by positive feelings. The first is word association, in which the subject is presented with a stimulus word and then responds with the first word that comes to mind. As described above, Isen et al. (1985) found that positive affect subjects were more likely to respond with unusual first associates (54% of total responses) compared to neutral affect subjects (39% of responses), where unusualness was defined by the Palermo and Jenkins (1964) word association norms. In addition, subjects in the positive affect condition showed greater diversity in their responses than did those in the control group.

The second task is the Remote Associates Test (Mednick et al. 1964), in which subjects are presented with three cue words and are asked to find a fourth word that is related in some way to each of the three cue words. For example, one set of cue words is *gown*, *club*, and *mare*. In this case, the correct response is *night* (i.e., *nightgown*, *nightclub*, and *nightmare*). As mentioned previously, Isen et al. (1987) found that positive affect subjects were significantly more accurate on a subset of moderately difficult items from the Remote Associates Test than neutral affect subjects (63% correct versus 50% correct).

The third task is Duncker's (1945) candle problem, in which subjects are given a box of tacks, a book of matches, and a candle, and are asked to attach the candle to the wall and light it in such a way that no wax drips on the floor. Isen et al. (1987) found that positive affect subjects were significantly more accurate (58% correct) on the candle problem than neutral affect controls (13% correct).

In the candle task, success is more likely if the subject overcomes the dominant cognitive set (viewing the box as a container) and selects a set that is less typical (viewing the box as a platform). If dopamine enhances the ability of the executive attention system to select more flexibly, then it seems reasonable to expect positive affect to improve performance in the candle task. We hypothesize that such selection effects could also influence performance in the word association and remote associates tasks. For example, in the Remote Associates Test, to produce the word *night* when presented with the cue words *club, gown,* and *mare,* the subject must overcome the dominant cognitive set that the correct response is semantically related to the cue words. Instead, the subject must consider alternative ways in which the words may be related, such as by being part of a compound word.

It is also easy to imagine situations in which the selection of unusual or nondominant cognitive sets would lead to unusual responses in the word association task. For example, consider a trial on which the stimulus word is *pen*. To respond, the subject must select among the various meanings of this word. The dominant interpretation (or set) is of *pen* as a writing implement. In this case, the subject is likely to respond with a high frequency associate, such as *pencil* or *paper*. A more unusual interpretation is of *pen* as a fenced enclosure. A subject who selects this interpretation is likely to respond with a low frequency associate, such as *barn* or *pig*. Thus, it is possible that the effects of positive feelings on the word association, remote associates, and candle tasks are all due to a common phenomenon – namely, that positive affect is associated with increased dopamine release into anterior cingulate, which increases the flexibility of the executive attention system.

A connectionist model that instantiates this hypothesis is shown in Figure 1. This model was proposed by Ashby, Turken, and Isen (1996), who called it the creative problem solver. The alternative cognitive sets are represented by the units P1 and P2 in prefrontal cortex. For example, in the word association task when the stimulus word is *pen*, P1 might represent *pen as a writing implement* and P2, *pen as a fenced enclosure*. The anterior cingulate selects one of

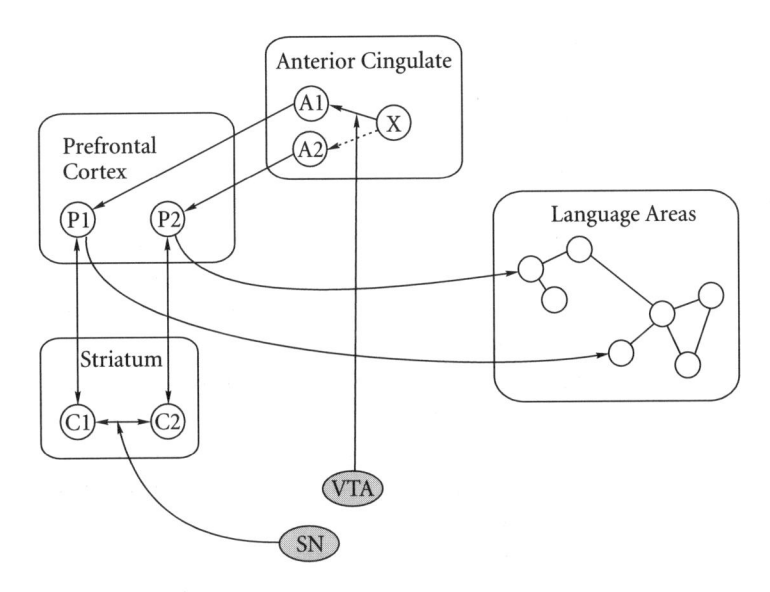

Figure 1. Computational architecture of the creative problem solver connectionist network (SN = Substantia Nigra, VTA = Ventral Tegmental Area).

the cognitive sets via the units X, A1, and A2. If P1 is the dominant set and the anterior cingulate is able to overcome this dominance and select P2, then the switching is accomplished via lateral inhibition in the caudate nucleus between units C1 and C2. Next, each of the cognitive set units (i.e., P1 and P2) projects back to a different semantic network in some cortical language area (presumably in the temporal lobe). For example, P1 presumably projects to a network that includes the words *paper* and *pencil* and P2 to a network that includes *barn* and *pig*.

Neuroimaging data support this general model. For example, Frith, Friston, Liddle, and Frackowiak (1991a) used PET scanning to examine cortical activity in normal adults during word fluency and lexical decision tasks, as well as a number of control tasks. Relative to the control tasks, they found increased activation in anterior cingulate and (dorsal lateral) prefrontal cortex in the semantic tasks, and either increased or decreased activation in the temporal language areas, depending on the type of semantic task. Based on these results, Friston, Frith, Liddle, and Frackowiak (1991) postulated that in semantic tasks involving selection or generation, the prefrontal cortex modulates activity in temporal language areas via (glutaminergic) cortico-cortical projections. Frith, Friston, Liddle, and Frackowiak (1991b) generalized this hypothesis to nonsemantic tasks. Specifically, they proposed that in many tasks requiring "willed action", the prefrontal cortex modulates activity in remote, but task relevant, cortical areas. We adopt the Frith et al. (1991b) assumption here. Later in this section, we simulate the performance of the creative problem solver in two nonsemantic performance tasks (i.e., the Duncker candle task and a two-choice guessing task). In these cases, we assume the relevant cortico-cortical projections are from the cognitive set units in prefrontal cortex (e.g., P1 and P2 in Figure 1) to specific motor units in premotor or motor cortex.

We assume the dopamine projection from VTA into cingulate enhances the ability of the cingulate to overcome the dominant set, but in a connectionist network we must be precise about the effect of increasing dopamine levels in the cingulate. Some dopamine is present even in the neutral affect conditions, so the effect of positive mood must be to alter activation patterns in the anterior cingulate, rather than to initiate any new processing. The question then, is how might dopamine modulate activation functions in a connectionist network? The next section proposes an answer to this question.

A dopamine modulated activation function

After studying data on the firing rates of striatal cells, Servan-Schreiber, Printz, and Cohen (1990) proposed that dopamine in the prefrontal cortex increases the gain of a standard logistic activation function. Let A_k represent the output activation of unit k and let a_i represent the activation of the ith unit that feeds into unit k. Then the logistic activation function (e.g., Rumelhart & McClelland 1986) assumes

$$A_k = \frac{1}{1 + e^{-(\alpha_k \sum_i w_{ik} a_i) + \beta_k}} \qquad (1)$$

where w_{ik} is the weight connecting units i and k, and α_k and β_k are the gain and bias on unit k, respectively. Servan-Schreiber et al. (1990) assumed that increasing the amount of dopamine into unit k increases the gain α_k. Figure 2 illustrates this model for two different dopamine levels. In this model, dopamine has two effects on activation. First, when dopamine levels are increased, the slope of the activation function increases. Second, activation functions associated with different dopamine levels cross. Thus, when the net input to unit k is small (i.e., when there is little overall stimulation), dopamine has an inhibitory effect on output activation. However, when the net input is large (as when there are many sources of stimulation or the stimulation is intense), the effects of dopamine are excitatory. Cohen and Servan-Schreiber (1992) used

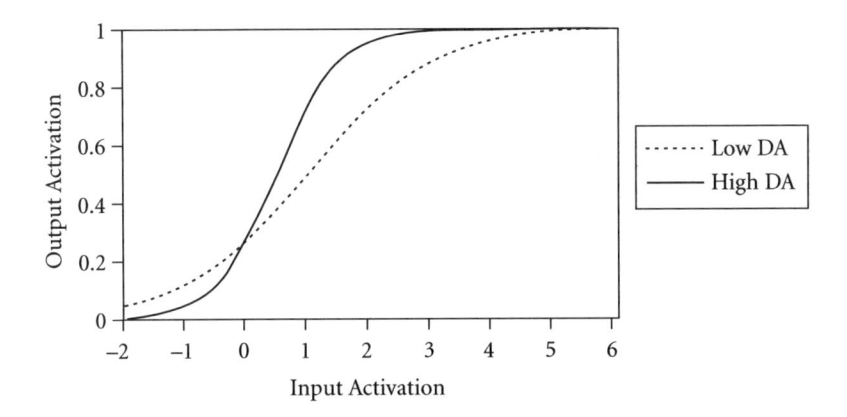

Figure 2. Activation functions assumed by Servan-Schreiber, Printz, and Cohen (1990). The effect of dopamine is to increase the slope of the activation function.

this model to construct connectionist networks to account for the behavioral deficits of schizophrenics in several different cognitive tasks.

A somewhat different model was proposed by Ashby and Casale (under review), who derived their model from standard pharmacological techniques. The two most important assumptions of this technique are that the magnitude of the tissue response is proportional to the concentration of the final product of the chemical reaction, and that the tissue response is determined after chemical equilibrium is reached. The nature of the final product depends on whether the drug (e.g., the neurotransmitter) activates a second messenger system. If it does (e.g., as is the case with dopamine) then the final product is the concentration of activated second messenger.

There are two classes of dopamine receptors. The D_1 class includes the D_1 and D_5 receptors, and the D_2 class includes the D_2, D_3, and D_4 receptors (e.g., Seeman & Van Tol 1994; Sibley, Monsma, Jr., & Shen 1993). Of these, the D_1 and D_2 receptors are, by far, the most common, and in frontal cortical areas, there are approximately ten times as many D_1 as D_2 receptors (Lidow, Goldman-Rakic, Gallagher, & Rakic 1991). For this reason, Ashby and Casale focused on the D_1 receptor, which is a so-called Class II (i.e., slow acting) receptor that is linked to a G protein that acts to increase intracellular levels of cAMP (e.g., Cooper, Bloom, & Roth 1991; Strange 1988).

There is now substantial evidence that dopamine modulates the effects of glutamate through the D_1 receptor (e.g., Cepeda, Radisavljevic, Peacock, Levine, & Buchwald 1992; Smiley, Levey, Ciliax, & Goldman-Rakic 1994). Glutamate is an excitatory neurotransmitter with two classes of receptors – NMDA and non-NMDA (e.g., Hyman & Nestler 1993). At low levels of stimulation, the glutamate response is dominated by activity at non-NMDA (e.g., AMPA) receptors. At high levels of stimulation, the glutamate response is dominated by activity at NMDA receptors. Recent evidence indicates that dopamine increases the efficacy of glutamate by prolonging the action of the Ca^{2+} second messenger that is activated when glutamate binds to the NMDA receptor (Hemmings, Walaas, Ouimet, & Greengard 1987; Pessin et al. 1994; Wickens 1990, 1993).

Cepeda et al. (1992) applied selective NMDA and non-NMDA glutamate agonists *in vitro* to human cortical tissue, both in the presence and absence of dopamine. As predicted, they found that dopamine enhanced the tissue response to NMDA agonists. However, they also found that dopamine depressed the tissue response to non-NMDA agonists. The mechanism through which dopamine inhibits the glutamate response through non-NMDA (e.g., AMPA) receptors is unknown. When deriving the activation function, however, the nature of this mechanism is relatively unimportant. Therefore, Ashby and Casale assumed that dopamine decreases the affinity of glutamate for non-NMDA receptors.

Let A_k denote the overall output activation of unit k, and let $A_{k,AMPA}$ and $A_{k,NMDA}$ denote the activations produced through the AMPA (i.e., non-NMDA) and NMDA channels, respectively. Then from the assumptions described above, Ashby and Casale proposed that:

$$A_k = e^{-\theta(A_{k,AMPA} + A_{k,NMDA})} A_{k,AMPA} + [1 - e^{-\theta(A_{k,AMPA} + A_{k,NMDA})}] A_{k,NMDA}, \quad (2)$$

for some positive constant θ. The two channel activation functions are defined as

$$A_{k,AMPA} = \frac{\sum_i w_{ik} a_i}{\sum_i w_{ik} a_i + K_{AMPA}(DA)} \quad (3)$$

and

$$A_{k,NMDA} = \frac{1}{1 + K_E(DA)\left(1 + \frac{K_{NMDA}}{\sum_i w_{ik} a_i}\right)}. \quad (4)$$

$K_{AMPA}^{-1}(DA)$ is the affinity of glutamate for the AMPA receptor. As mentioned above, dopamine inhibits the action of glutamate through non-NMDA receptors, so $K_{AMPA}(DA)$ is assumed to increase with dopamine level. On the other hand, $K_E^{-1}(DA)$ is proportional to the efficacy of the glutamate response through the NMDA channel. Since dopamine facilitates this glutamate response, $K_E(DA)$ is assumed to decrease with dopamine level. Finally, K_{NMDA}^{-1} is the affinity of glutamate for the NMDA receptor.

Figure 3 shows plots of the activation function defined by Equations 2–4 for two different dopamine levels. Note that the Ashby and Casale (under review) model confirms the intuition of Servan-Schreiber et al. (1990) about two key properties of the effects of dopamine on activation functions. First, the activation functions in Figures 2 and 3 both show steeper slopes with increasing dopamine levels. Second, the activation functions in both figures cross. In both cases, dopamine is inhibitory at low levels of input activation and excitatory at high levels. The most striking difference between the two functions is in asymptotic activation levels. The Servan-Schreiber et al. model assumes that large input activations drive the unit to saturation for all dopamine levels. In contrast, the Figure 3 model assumes saturation is virtually never reached and that increasing dopamine levels substantially increases asymptotic activation. According to the pharmacological theory used by Ashby and Casale, saturation occurs only when every receptor molecule and every second messenger molecule in the tissue are activated. These conditions are virtually impossible to meet, so saturation is essentially impossible.

Tests of the model

The Ashby et al. (1996) general connectionist model of cognitive set selection and switching (i.e., the creative problem solver) is illustrated in Figure 1, and the effects of dopamine on activation produced within the anterior cingulate (and prefrontal cortex) are modeled by Equations 2–4. Before determining whether this model could account for the influence of positive affect

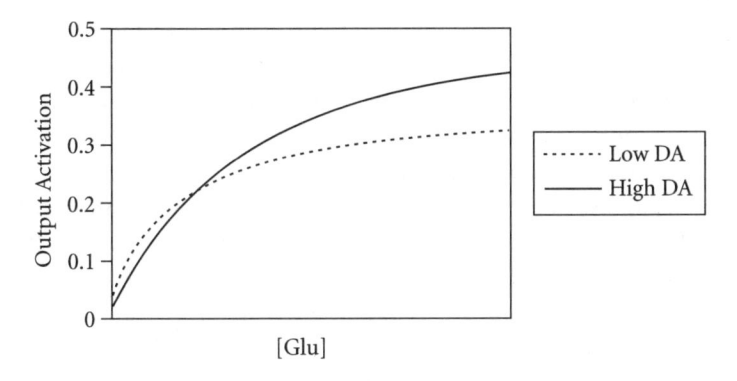

Figure 3. Activation functions assumed by Ashby and Casale (under review).

on creative problem solving, Ashby et al. (1996) applied it to data from an experiment where brain dopamine levels were directly manipulated. Specifically, this application asked whether the model could account for the effects of amphetamines (which, among other effects, increase dopamine release) on a probability learning task reported by Ridley et al. (1988). Amphetamines are known to stimulate other neurotransmitters as well as dopamine (e.g., norepinephrine), and thus the model described in this section does not provide a complete description of the effects of amphetamines on cognition. Also, we do not expect positive affect to have the same effects as amphetamines in all cognitive tasks, even though they may have some of the same effects because of the dopamine release associated with each.

Two-Choice Guessing. Ridley et al. (1988) had two groups of normal (human) adults participate in a standard probability learning task (e.g., see, Estes 1976). Prior to the task, one group was administered amphetamines and the second control group was given a saline solution. On each trial, two identical boxes appeared and the subjects were asked to guess which one contained a target. The target was equally likely to appear in either the right (R) or the left (L) box, so there is no strategy that guarantees greater than chance accuracy. Ridley et al. arbitrarily defined a perseveration as guessing the same box four times in a row (i.e., either responding *RRRR* or *LLLL*) and an alternation as successively switching on four consecutive trials (i.e., either responding *RLRL* or *LRLR*). The results are summarized in Figure 4a (averaged across subjects). With the Ridley et al. design, completely random responding leads to an average of 5 perseverations and 5 alternations. These data are characterized by the following three qualitative properties: (1) both groups showed more perseverations than expected by chance, (2) both groups showed fewer alternations than expected by chance, and (3) the amphetamine group had significantly more alternations than the control group, which caused an interaction between condition (saline versus amphetamine) and response type (perseveration versus alternation).

A similar increase in alternation responses has been reported under positive affect conditions, as one component of a more general increase in variety seeking (Kahn & Isen 1993, Experiment 1). Amphetamines are well known to have similar effects on a wide variety of behaviors. Evenden and Robbins (1983) summarized the effects of amphetamines as follows: "responses occurring with a high probability ... are reduced by the drug, whereas responses occurring with a lower probability may be increased" (p. 72). Of course, one consequence of such an effect is that under amphetamines, subjects should be more likely to adopt an unusual or nondominant cognitive perspective (or

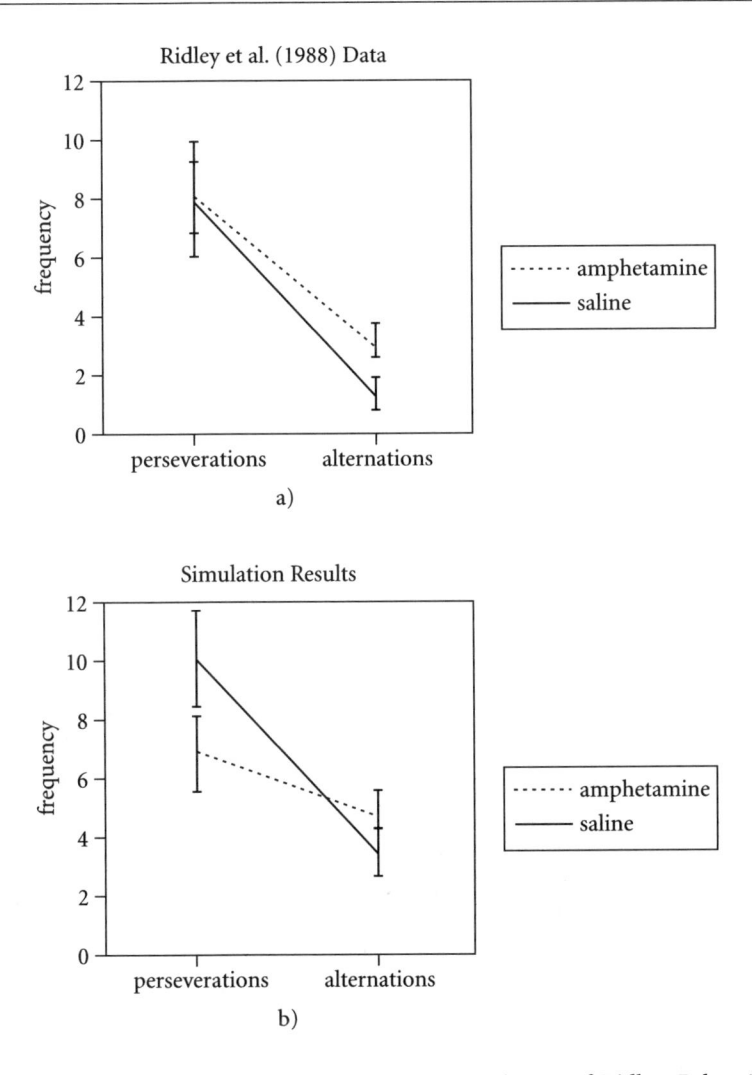

Figure 4. Results from the two-choice guessing experiment of Ridley, Baker, Frith, Dowdy, and Crow (1988) (Figure 4a) and from simulations of this experiment by the creative problem solver connectionist network (Figure 4b).

set). This result supports the hypothesis that amphetamines do not simply increase arousal, since arousal has long been known to facilitate dominant, not innovative responding.

On the surface, this experiment appears quite different from the tasks for which the creative problem solver (i.e., the Figure 1 connectionist network) was developed. Even so, only minor modifications need to be made to the

Figure 1 network to account for the Ridley et al. (1988) results. In particular, Ashby et al. (1996) assumed the units A1 and P1 correspond to one response (say, response R) and units A2 and P2 correspond to the other (response L). Rather than project to temporal language areas, they assumed units P1 and P2 project directly to the relevant motor areas in premotor and motor cortex (the cortico-striatal-pallidal-thalamic loops could still be operative). Given this slight modification, the behavior of the creative problem solver in the Ridley et al. (1988) task was simulated. Subjects were assumed to have no initial bias toward either response. After a correct guess, the habit strength associated with that particular response was increased, which raised the probability that the same response would be chosen on the next trial. Following an error, the habit strength associated with the incorrect response was decreased. Technical details of all simulations are described in the Appendix.

The results of the simulations are shown in Figure 4b. The predicted values were obtained by averaging across 1000 replicated simulations of the experiment. Figure 4b also shows predicted error bars. These were generated by computing the standard deviation in the predicted frequencies over the 1000 replications. The resulting standard deviations were then divided by $\sqrt{12}$, since Ridley et al. (1988) used 12 subjects in each experimental condition. The creative problem solver displayed all three qualitative properties seen in the human data. Specifically, both simulated groups showed more perseverations than expected by chance and fewer alternations, and there was an interaction between condition and response type. In addition, the predicted error bars were close to the error bars observed by Ridley et al. (1988). The only real deviation between the model and the data was that the creative problem solver predicted a few more perseverations for the saline group than were observed by Ridley et al. (1988). Overall, the model was quite successful at accounting for the effects of amphetamine on two-choice guessing (especially given that no real attempt was made to maximize goodness-of-fit).

Word Association. Next, consider the ability of the model to account for the influence of positive affect on creative problem solving. Ashby et al. (1996) simulated the performance of the creative problem solver in the word association task, the Remote Associates Test, and the Duncker candle task. Across the three tasks they assumed one dopamine level for the neutral affect control condition and another higher level for the positive affect condition[1].

Recall that Isen et al. (1985) found that positive affect subjects were more likely to respond with unusual associates in a word association task than neutral affect subjects (54% versus 39%). Ashby et al. (1996) simulated the performance of the creative problem solver in a word association task in which the stimulus word was *palm*. For illustrative purposes, they assumed the most common response of a neutral affect control subject to be *hand*, followed in order of decreasing frequency by *finger, sweaty, tree, Hawaii, reader, steal, lift*, and *basketball*. The creative problem solver model for this particular example is shown in Figure 5. In this example, the cognitive set units in prefrontal cortex correspond to the alternative interpretations of *palm*, as a *part of the hand*, as a verb describing a *use of the hand*, or as a component of a *compound word*. Each of these units then projects back to a different semantic network in the temporal language area.

The performance of the creative problem solver in this task is illustrated in Figure 6. There are no published data that allow us to specify the semantic networks associated with the various alternative interpretations of *palm* (i.e., including the architecture and the numerical values of all weights between nodes). Therefore, when constructing the version of the creative problem solver shown in Figure 5, Ashby et al. (1996) chose the various weights so the network

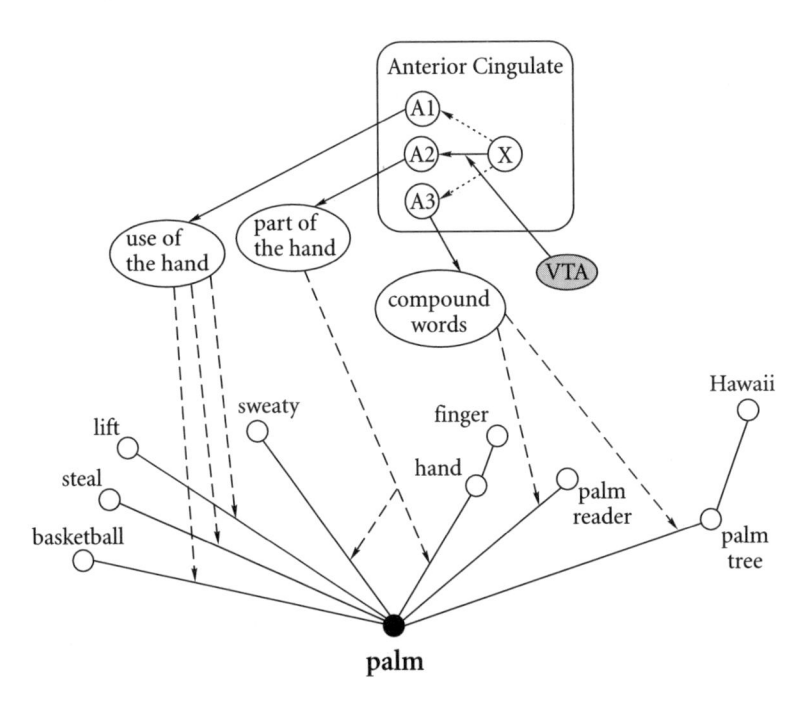

Figure 5. The computational architecture assumed by the creative problem solver connectionist network for a trial of the word association task in which the stimulus word is *palm*.

would reproduce the ordinal relations among the responses assumed in our illustration. As a result, the network could mimic any set of data that could be collected in the neutral affect control condition. However, once the weights are fixed in this manner, the predictions for the positive affect condition are also fixed[2]. Therefore, the true test of the model is not whether it can account for the data from the control condition, but whether it correctly predicts the relation between the control and positive affect data.

In agreement with the Isen et al. (1985) results, note that the creative problem solver correctly predicts that the first-associate response proportions for the positive affect subjects are higher for all unusual associates (and therefore, necessarily lower for the most common response). The Isen et al. (1985) data and the creative problem solver both agree that the most common associate is not necessarily lost or unavailable to the positive affect subjects. Instead, both the data and the model suggest that other responses are also cued, so that the dominant response becomes somewhat less dominant than it is under neutral affect conditions, and less typical responses become relatively more accessible.

Remote Associates Test. Among the most reliable effects of positive mood is that it improves performance in the Remote Associates Test (e.g., Estrada et al. 1994; Isen et al. 1987). For example, Isen et al. (1987) found that positive affect improved performance in that test by 13% (from 50% to 63%) when the test items were of moderate difficulty. On one trial of this study, subjects were

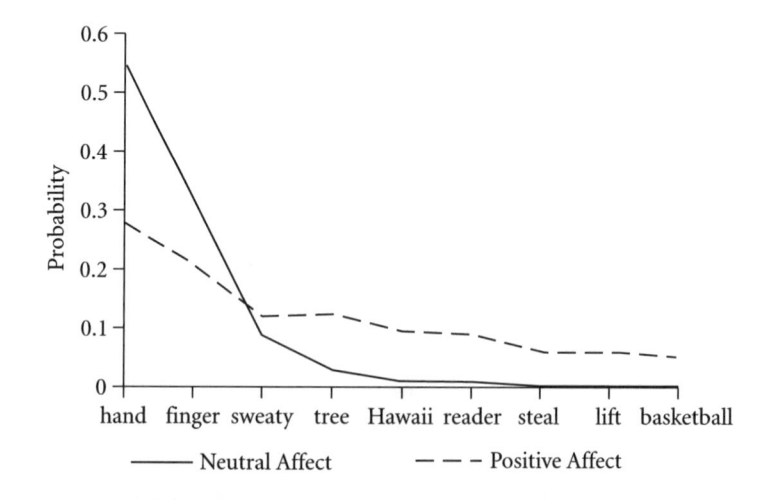

Figure 6. Simulated data from the creative problem solver connectionist network for a trial of the word association task in which the stimulus word is *palm*.

presented with the cue words *gown*, *club*, and *mare*. In this case, the correct response is *night*. Ashby et al. (1996) simulated the performance of the creative problem solver on this trial of the Remote Associates Test by using the architecture shown in Figure 7. Here two relevant cognitive sets are that the correct response is a word that is *semantically* related to the cue words, or that it might be part of a compound word with each of the cue words. In the former case, likely responses are words like *dance* or *party*, but the correct response will be discovered only if the latter cognitive set is adopted. The results of the simulations are illustrated in Figure 8. Note that in agreement with the empirical literature, accuracy is substantially higher in the positive affect condition (since the correct response is *night*).

This version of the model is overly simple for at least two different reasons. First, it almost surely oversimplifies the representation of alternative cognitive sets or perspectives for this problem. A more realistic model would show many more alternative perspectives. Nevertheless, the performance of a version with more alternative cognitive sets would be qualitatively similar to the performance of the Figure 7 version. Second, the model shown in Figure 7 is a feedforward connectionist network. As such, it ignores the temporal dynamics

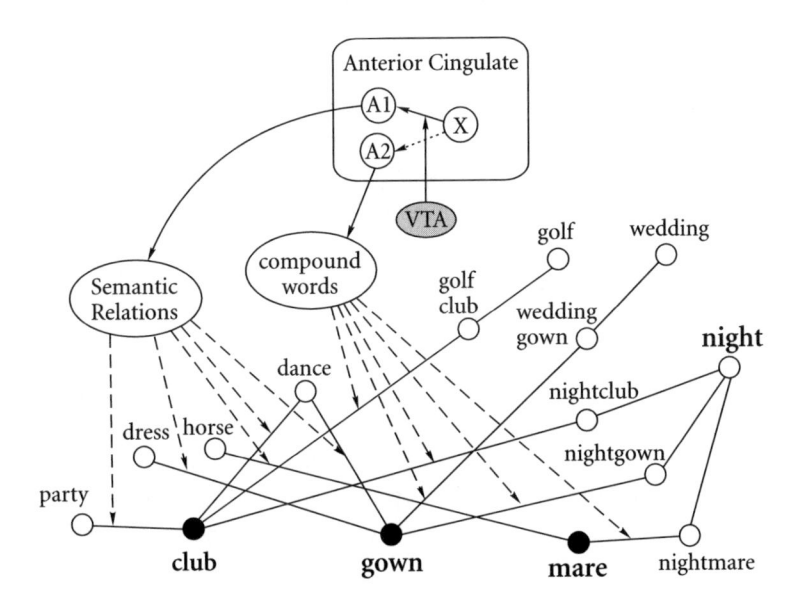

Figure 7. The computational architecture assumed by the creative problem solver connectionist network for a trial of the remote associates task in which the stimulus words are *gown*, *club*, and *mare*.

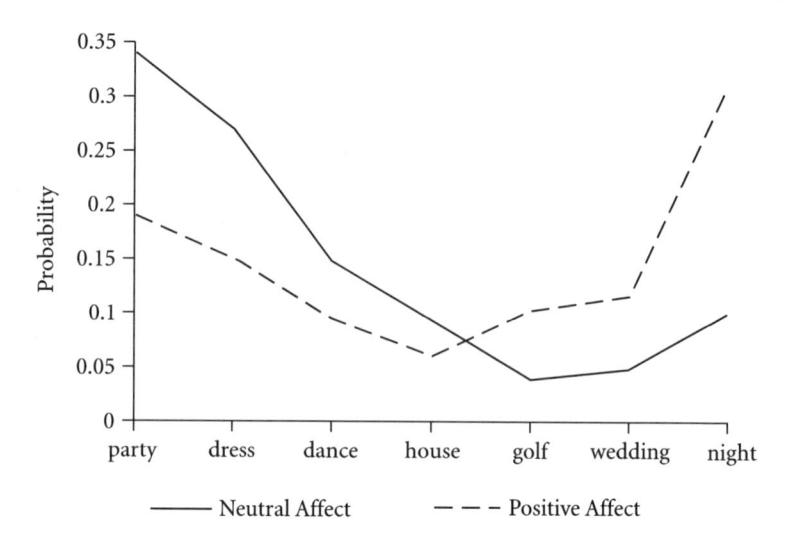

[Figure 8: graph with Probability on y-axis (0 to 0.35) and words on x-axis: party, dress, dance, house, golf, wedding, night. Two lines: Neutral Affect (solid) and Positive Affect (dashed).]

Figure 8. Simulated data from the creative problem solver connectionist network for a trial of the remote associates task in which the stimulus words are *gown*, *club*, and *mare*.

of the problem solving process. A human subject who failed initially to solve the problem might try again. It is straightforward to generalize the network in this fashion; that is, to make it recurrent. In fact, the version of the creative problem solver that Ashby et al. (1996) applied to the Duncker candle task is recurrent (see the next subsection). However, because of the uncertainty as to the true nature of the semantic networks that are accessed during the Remote Associates Test, little is gained by making the Figure 7 network recurrent.

Duncker Candle Task. Isen et al. (1987) found that a positive affect group was successful in the Duncker candle task much more frequently than the neutral affect control group (58% versus 13% correct). The network architecture of the creative problem solver when applied to the candle task is shown in Figure 9. Here the dominant cognitive set is to view the box as a container for the tacks. To solve the problem, the subject must switch away from the dominant set and view the box as an independent object that might serve as a potential platform for the candle. Once a set or perspective is selected, the motor actions that follow are predetermined. Thus, in the creative problem solver, the cognitive set units project to units in the premotor and motor cortices that are associated with specific motor actions. To this point, then, the network is identical to the version of the creative problem solver that Ashby et al. (1996) used to model the Ridley et al. (1988) two-choice guessing task. In the candle task, however, a

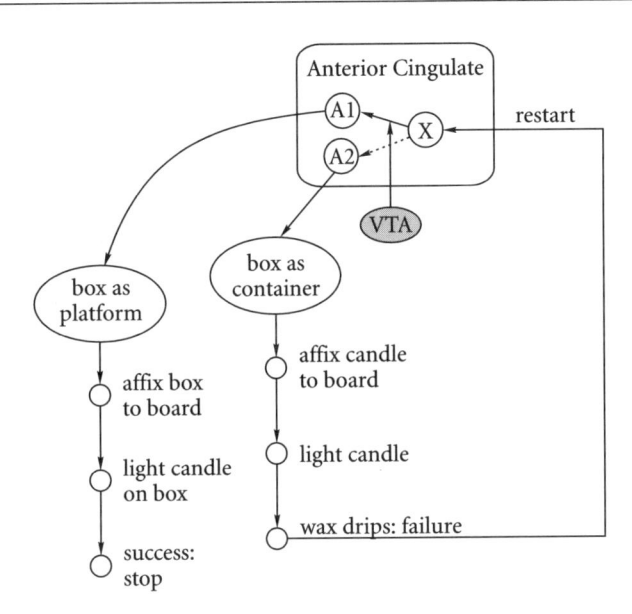

Figure 9. The computational architecture assumed by the creative problem solver connectionist network for the Duncker (1945) candle task.

subject who fails might try to solve the problem again. So, the Figure 9 network allows multiple attempts at a solution. It was assumed that if the subject failed to solve the problem after five attempts, then he or she would either give up or run out of time.

Ashby et al. (1996) simulated the performance of this version of the creative problem solver in the candle task – again, using the same dopamine levels for the control and positive affect conditions as in the simulations of the word association and remote associates tasks. The results are shown in Figure 10. The success rates of the creative problem solver (65% correct in the positive affect condition and 22% in the control condition) were comparable to the success rates found in the Isen et al. (1987) study (i.e., 58% correct in the positive affect condition and 13% correct in the control condition). On trials when the creative problem solver was ultimately successful, it invariably had some initial failures and succeeded only because it tried something different on a subsequent attempt (i.e., it selected more than one cognitive perspective). This same pattern characterized the positive affect human subjects in the study by Isen et al. (1987). In contrast, the control subjects were much more likely to adopt repeatedly the same perspective throughout the task, thereby attempting the same incorrect solution over and over.

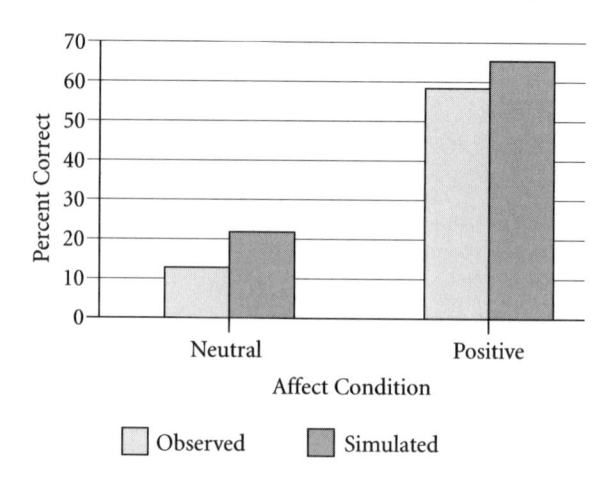

Figure 10. Success rates in the Duncker (1945) candle task observed by Isen, Daubman, and Nowicki (1987) and as simulated by the creative problem solver.

Discussion

Using the same general architecture and the same dopamine levels for all positive and neutral affect conditions, the creative problem solver mimicked the qualitative influences of positive affect on word association, the Remote Associates Test, and the Duncker's candle task. In addition, the same network successfully accounted for the effects of amphetamine on two-choice guessing.

In the applications to the three creative problem solving tasks, it should be stressed once again that the specific versions of the creative problem solver that were tested are considerable simplifications. More realistic versions would postulate the existence or potential existence of many more alternative cognitive sets or perspectives. It is also important to note that the creative problem solver makes no assumptions about whether these alternative perspectives pre-exist or whether they are constructed as the task progresses.

It should also be stressed that the present modeling attempts are limited because the data on the effects of feelings on cognition do not sufficiently constrain the model. When the creative problem solving data modeled in this section were collected, there were no theories that made specific quantitative predictions about how positive affect would influence performance in these tasks. Instead, the major interest was on *whether* there would be effects. It is possible that a number of different models could account for the word association, remote associates, and Duncker candle task data considered in this section just as well as the creative problem solver. Thus, the fact that the creative problem solver was able to account for the major ordinal properties of these data should be considered more a demonstration of the potential of the dopaminergic theory of positive affect rather than as a rigorous test of that theory. Also, since there now is a theory that makes rigorous quantitative predictions, future experiments can collect and report data in such a way that allows more rigorous testing.

Positive affect versus arousal

Environmental conditions that induce positive affect are also likely to increase arousal. This brings to mind a number of questions. 1) Is there any difference between arousal and affect? 2) What is the neurobiological basis of arousal and how does it differ from positive affect? 3) How does arousal affect frontal cortex? 4) What are the cognitive effects of increased arousal and how do these differ from the effects caused by improved affect? This section attempts to answer these questions.

Do arousal and positive affect differ?

Early theorists defined arousal as a general state of central nervous system activity (see, e.g., Trevor 1997). There are two common ideas about how to manipulate arousal. One is through exercise (e.g., Zillmann 1979), and the other is by inducing an emotional state (e.g., LeDoux 1996). Typically, this involves negative affect such as fear or anger, but according to some views, arousal increases with either positive or negative affect. Thus, if the cognitive effects of positive affect are due simply to increases in arousal, then exercise and induced negative affect should have similar effects on cognition.

Some studies have tried to test this hypothesis. For example, in two sets of experiments, positive affect subjects reported more positive affect, but not more arousal or alertness, than neutral affect control subjects, on a manipulation-check questionnaire that followed the affect induction (Isen & Daubman 1984; Isen & Gorgoglione 1983). In addition, the results of these experiments correlated better with the affect-induction treatments than with the reported levels of arousal. In another series of studies, Isen et al. (1987) asked four groups of subjects to solve the candle problem and to complete a subset of items taken from the Remote Associates Test. One group served as neutral affect controls. Positive affect was induced in a second group. In a third, exercise group, subjects stepped up and down on a cinderblock for 2 minutes before the test, which increased heart rate by about 60%. Finally, the fourth, negative affect group viewed a few minutes of a depressing film (i.e., *Night and Fog*, a French documentary of the World War II German death camps). As expected, the positive affect subjects performed better than the control subjects on both the candle test and on the Remote Associates Test items. Equally important, people in the exercise and negative affect groups performed no better than the control subjects on either test. Thus, again, Isen et al. (1987) found evidence that, unlike positive affect, arousal does not improve creative problem solving.

There is other evidence against the hypothesis that the effects of positive affect on creative problem solving are due to arousal. First, current theories do not predict that arousal increases creativity, because arousal is thought to increase the likelihood of the *dominant* response, rather than of an innovative response (Berlyne 1967; Easterbrook 1959). Second, several authors have suggested that arousal is not a unitary construct and may need to be investigated differently from the way it has been addressed in the past (e.g., Lacey 1967, 1975; Neiss 1990; Venables 1984). Third, other researchers have recently argued that arousal and pleasantness form orthogonal dimensions (e.g., Lewinsohn & Mano 1993; Mano 1997). On the other hand, even though they may be logically independent, pleasantness and arousal may be empirically correlated. Even so, as we will see in the next section, there is considerable evidence that arousal is associated with increased activity in neurotransmitter systems other than dopamine (e.g., norepinephrine). And, as noted, the empirical effects of arousal or negative affect are different from those of positive affect. Thus, in sum, there is substantial reason to believe that the effects of positive affect and arousal are not identical, as was once proposed (e.g., Duffy 1934, 1941), and that the well-documented improvements in creative problem solving that occur under positive affect conditions are indeed due to the induced positive affect, and not simply to increases in arousal.

What is the neurobiological basis of arousal?

Arousal is associated with stimulation of the brain stem reticular formation (e.g., Carlson 2001). At least four different neurotransmitters are involved, including norephinephrine (NE), acetylcholine, serotonin, and histamine (e.g., Marrocco, Witte, & Davidson 1994; McCormick 1992; Wada et al. 1991). Of these, probably the most attention has been given to NE.

The locus coeruleus, located in the brain stem, is the largest NE producing nucleus within the ascending reticular activating system and it releases NE to a surprisingly diverse area of the brain. The densest projections are to the hippocampus and neocortex (Ungerstedt 1971), but it also projects throughout the cerebral cortex, thalamus, midbrain, brainstem, cerebellum, and spinal cord (Aston-Jones et al. 1982; Foote et al. 1983). In fact, this small nucleus innervates a greater variety of brain areas than any other single nucleus yet described. Brain areas that are associated with attentional processing (e.g., parietal cortex, pulvinar nucleus, superior colliculus) receive a particularly dense NE innervation from the locus coeruleus (Morrison & Foote 1986).

Spontaneous activity of NE cells in the locus coeruleus change dramatically depending on the animal's stage of sleep and waking, with the highest firing rates occurring when the animal is awake and the lowest during sleep (Aston-Jones & Bloom 1981; Foote et al. 1983; Jacobs 1987). NE cells in the locus coeruleus also respond phasically to novel or noxious stimuli, including conditioned stimuli, and they may also be mildly responsive to appetitive events (Aston-Jones & Bloom 1981; Jacobs 1987). Repeated presentation of an initially novel stimulus causes the firing rate of NE cells to decline gradually (Aston-Jones & Bloom 1981; Jacobs 1987). A simple way to summarize these results is that NE cells in the locus coeruleus generally will fire to any stimulus that elicits an orienting response from the animal. If the same stimulus is presented in other conditions that do not elicit such a response (e.g., because of repeated presentation), then the locus coeruleus response will be small (Aston-Jones & Bloom 1981; Foote et al. 1980; Grant et al. 1988).

Because of these results, Aston-Jones and his colleagues proposed that the primary function of cortical NE is to mediate vigilance (Aston-Jones & Bloom 1981a, 1981b; Aston-Jones, Rajkowski, & Cohen 1999). In support of this hypothesis, Aston-Jones et al. (1994) recorded from NE cells in the locus coeruleus of monkeys while they performed a vigilance task, and found that performance was best when firing rate of the NE cells was high, and that performance deteriorated when the firing rate decreased. Note that according to this hypothesis, the primary action of NE is attentional.

A similar hypothesis was put forth by Robbins (1984), who proposed that NE helps focus attention on task relevant behaviors by attenuating the influence of distracting stimuli, particularly under conditions of elevated arousal. In support of this, Carli et al. (1983) found that lesions that resulted in severely depleted levels of NE in prefrontal cortex, impaired discriminative abilities and reaction times when, and only when, bursts of loud white noise occurred during the delay period. Similar impairment was shown by Cole and Robbins (1992) when the inter-trial interval was made unpredictable in a 5-choice reaction time task. Loud noise and signal unpredictability both tend to increase arousal, thereby suggesting that NE is necessary for accurate attentional performance under arousing conditions. Related results have been found in human studies. For example, Tafalla et al. (1997) reported that in an arithmetic task (Lundberg & Frankenhaeuser 1976), distracting noise increased NE levels in urine during a high effort condition, but not in a low effort condition. This result also suggests that NE helps focus attention during an aroused state, so that a demanding task can be adequately performed, whereas NE is not recruited for tasks requiring low attention, so arousal can affect level of performance. Understanding the interaction between arousal, attention, and NE is thus a fundamental stepping stone to formulating neurochemical theories of attention (Coull 1997).

How does arousal affect the function of frontal cortex?

Whether the overall effect of NE in prefrontal cortex is facilitative or disruptive depends on dose. High doses of NE applied to sensory neurons suppress neural activity (Armstrong-James & Fox 1987; Hoffer, Siggins & Bloom 1971; Stone 1973), whereas low doses enhance both excitatory and inhibitory synaptic inputs (Foote, Freedman, & Oliver 1975; Kossl & Vater 1989; Waterhouse & Woodward 1980; Woodward 1979). An *in vitro* study found an inverted U-shaped dose response of NE on glutamate-evoked discharges in sensory cortical neurons (Devilbliss & Waterhouse 1996). This U-shape corresponds to behavioral data in which locus coeruleus NE discharge was measured during a sustained attention task. The level of NE correlated with performance, such that performance was poor at low and high levels of NE, and good at intermediate levels (Rajkowski et al. 1992).

One explanation of the nonmonotonic effect of NE dose on performance comes from studies of specific NE receptor types. There are two distinct classes of NE receptors, called α and β receptors. Suppressant effects of NE have been shown to be mediated by β receptors, although this inhibitory effect has not been tied to working memory performance. On the other hand, the α receptors seem most important for arousal's effect on prefrontal cortex. Within the class of α receptors, there are two different subtypes, denoted α_1 and α_2, and there is now good evidence that they have opposing effects on prefrontal cortical function. In particular, activation of α_2 receptors appears to have a facilitative effect, whereas activation of α_1 receptors seems to impair prefrontal cortical function.

A variety of studies support the hypothesis that α_2 receptor activation facilitates prefrontal cortical functioning. For example, in both rats and monkeys, α_2 agonists improve performance on a variety of working memory related tasks that are known to depend on the prefrontal cortex, including delayed response (Arnsten et al. 1988), delayed match-to-sample (Jackson & Buccafusco 1991), and delayed alternation (Arnsten & Goldman-Rakic 1985; Carlson et al. 1992). Such results are even more pronounced in elderly animals, which is especially significant because NE levels in prefrontal cortex decrease dramatically with age (Arnsten 1997; Gaspar et al. 1989, 1991). On the other hand, these same α_2 agonists have little effect on memory tasks that are primarily mediated outside of prefrontal cortex (PFC), including recognition memory and reference memory (Arnsten & Goldman-Rakic 1985, 1990).

Arnsten and Contant (1992) hypothesized that α_2 agonists benefit delayed response performance by reducing interference from distracting stimuli. A selective α_2 agonist (i.e., clonidine) improved performance in a delayed response task when the delay period was free of distractors, but the drug was most effective when distracting noise was present (Jackson & Buccafuso 1991; Arnten & Contant 1992). These findings are consistent with NE depletion increasing distractability (Roberts et al. 1976; Carli et al. 1983) emphasizing the importance of NE mechanisms in attention regulation.

Although α_2 agonists have a generally beneficial effect on prefrontal cortical function, the story is quite different for α_1 agonists. A number of recent studies have shown that low doses of α_1 agonists (e.g., cirazoline, phenylephrine) impair spatial working memory in rats and monkeys (Arnsten & Jentsch 1996; Steere et al. 1996).

If NE binds to both α_1 and α_2 receptors and the actions through these two receptor types have conflicting effects, then why don't these opposite effects just cancel out? One possible answer to this important question comes from pharmacological studies of NE binding. Such studies show that NE has a higher affinity for α_2 receptors than for α_1 receptors (Arnsten 1997). Therefore, for small increases in NE, the effects of α_2 activation will dominate the effects of α_1 activation, and the overall effect of NE in prefrontal cortex will be facilitative. As NE levels increase, the effects of α_1 receptor activation will also increase, and eventually the overall effect of NE will be to impair prefrontal cortical function. Of course, these effects perfectly mimic the well-known Yerkes-Dodson (1908) effect, in which small and moderate increases in arousal improve performance but large increases have a detrimental effect.

As discussed above, α_2 receptor activation appears to facilitate prefrontal cortical function. Given this, the next important question is to ask how this facilitation occurs. As with dopamine, the action of NE on prefrontal cortex is thought mainly to be modulatory. In particular, many results suggest that NE does not transmit specific moment-to-moment details. Rather, it appears to alter the efficacy of the major excitatory and inhibitory neurotransmitters (glutamate and GABA, respectively) (e.g., Jiang et al. 1996; Kasamatsu & Heggelund 1982; Kossl & Vater 1989; McLean & Waterhouse 1994; Waterhouse et al. 1990).

Perhaps the most popular model of the neuromodulatory effects of NE is that a constant low level administration of NE increases the signal-to-noise ratio of synaptically mediated responses (e.g., Foote, Freedman, & Oliver 1975; Waterhouse, Moises, & Woodward 1980; Waterhouse & Woodward 1980). Such relative enhancement of responses to strong inputs relative to low-level or basal activity has been found in several locus coeruleus target areas including cerebral cortex, hippocampus, midbrain, thalamus, and spinal cord (for a review see Aston-Jones et al. 1991; Foote et al. 1983), and is consistent with recent neural modeling work hypothesizing that NE acts to enhance signal-to-noise ratios in target systems (Servan-Schreiber et al. 1990).

The contribution of other neurotransmitters to arousal

As mentioned above, in addition to NE, other neurotransmitters have been implicated in the control of arousal, especially acetylcholine (ACh), serotonin (5-HT), and histamine. The release of all three of these neurotransmitters is closely tied to the sleep-wake cycle, with release increasing as the animal becomes more active (e.g., Day, Damsma, & Fibiger 1991; Steininger et al. 1996; Trulson & Jacobs 1979).

ACh has some of the same effects as (low doses of) NE on prefrontal cortical function. In particular, working memory is facilitated by drugs that enhance cholinergic activity and impaired by drugs that block the action of ACh (Dawson & Iverson 1993; Glasky et al. 1994; Robbins et al. 1997). Also, like NE, ACh increases the signal-to-noise ratio of individual cortical neurons (Drachman & Sahakian 1979; Hasselmo 1995; Sato, Hata, Masui, & Tsumoto 1987), and some recent evidence suggests it does this both by boosting the signal and decreasing the noise (Furey, Pietrini, & Haxby 2000). The basal forebrain cholinergic cells seem to be particularly influenced by conditioned visual stimuli and by reinforcers, but also by aversive air-puffs (Wilson & Rolls 1990; Richardson & De Long 1990).

What are the cognitive effects of increased arousal and how do these differ from the effects caused by improved affect?

We have already discussed evidence that in the case of creative problem solving, positive affect and arousal seem to make contrasting predictions. First, we reviewed much data suggesting that positive affect improves creative problem solving. We also discussed a more restricted set of data that failed to find any effect of arousal on creative problem solving (Isen et al. 1987). This latter result is consistent with theories of arousal that predict arousal increases the likelihood of the *dominant* response, rather than of an innovative response (Berlyne 1967; Easterbrook 1959). If one is attacked by a predator, then the dominant response (e.g., to flee) is frequently adaptive, but in tests of creative problem solving, an innovative response is usually more likely to succeed.

On the other hand, it appears that in the case of working memory, positive affect and arousal make similar predictions. In particular, dopamine, NE, and ACh released into prefrontal cortex all have similar effects on performance in working memory tasks – at low or moderate doses they are facilitative, but at high doses they impair performance. Thus, if positive affect leads to increased dopamine release in frontal cortex and arousal is associated with increased release of NE and ACh, then mild to moderate levels of positive affect and arousal should both improve working memory. In contrast, extreme levels of positive affect or arousal should impair working memory. To our knowledge, these predictions are largely untested.

It is difficult to make specific predictions about how the effects of arousal and positive affect might differ in other cognitive tasks. From a theoretical perspective, one of the problems is that many of the neural effects appear to be similar (e.g., increasing signal-to-noise ratio). In addition, positive affect and arousal often co-occur. It is not difficult to predict that before much progress occurs in this area, a much more extensive data-base must be collected (especially behavioral data).

Conclusions

The dopaminergic theory of positive affect that was proposed by Ashby et al. (1999) assumes that during periods of mild positive affect, there is a concomitant increased dopamine release, primarily in the mesocorticolimbic system. The theory further assumes that the resulting elevated dopamine levels in anterior cingulate increase cognitive flexibility and facilitate the selection of cognitive perspective or set, thereby improving creative problem solving ability. Note that this theory does not assume that positive affect simply turns dopamine on or off. Instead, it is assumed that moderate levels of dopamine are present even under neutral affect conditions. The induction of mild positive affect is assumed only to increase slightly these normal dopamine levels.

A computational version of the theory was described that takes the form of a connectionist network called the creative problem solver. Standard pharmacological techniques were used to derive the theoretical effects of dopamine on the activation function of units in the portion of the network that corresponds to the anterior cingulate. The network successfully accounted for the effects of amphetamines on a two-choice guessing task and it accounted for the effects of positive feelings on three creative problem solving tasks (word association, the Remote Associates Test, and Duncker's candle task). Although the focus of this chapter was primarily on positive affect, the creative problem solver provides a general model of creative problem solving that could be used to model data from many different experimental tasks and collected from a variety of different subject populations. In addition, the model makes specific predictions about the effects on creative problem solving of any experimental factor that systematically alters cortical dopamine levels. Thus, the potential contribution of the model is considerably greater than the rather narrow applications considered here.

We also briefly discussed the neurobiological basis of arousal. This is important because arousal often seems to co-occur with states of positive affect. Because of this empirical correlation, a complete understanding of the cognitive effects of positive mood requires an accurate theory of arousal.

Acknowledgements

This research was supported by grants SBR-9514427 and BCS99-75037 from the National Science Foundation. We thank Alice Isen for her helpful comments.

Notes

1. These were not the same dopamine levels as assumed in the simulations of the saline and amphetamine conditions of the two-choice guessing task. There is no reason to expect a 10 mg dose of amphetamine to cause the same increase in brain dopamine levels as the giving of a small unanticipated gift. Also, intravenous infusion of saline could alter mood, especially since the Ridley et al. (1988) experiment was double blind. Thus, it seemed reasonable to assume that the dopamine levels in the Ridley et al. saline group might differ from the dopamine levels in the neutral affect groups of the Isen creative problem solving studies.

2. At this point, the only free parameter is the dopamine level associated with the positive affect group. However, manipulating this parameter confers little flexibility since the same

dopamine level was assumed for the positive affect conditions in all three creative problem solving applications (i.e., word association, the Remote Associates Test, and the Duncker candle task).

References

Abercrombie, E. D., Keefe, K. A., DiFrischia, D. S., & Zigmond, M. J. (1989). Differential effect of stress on in vivo dopamine release in striatum, nucleus accumbens, and medial frontal cortex. *Journal of Neurochemistry, 52*, 1655–1658.

Armstrong-James, M., & Fox, K. (1987). Effects of iontophoresed noradrenaline on the spontaneous activity of neurones in rat primary somatosensory cortex. *Journal of Comparative Neurology, 263*, 265–281.

Arnsten, A. F. T. (1997). Catecholamine regulation of prefrontal cortex. *Journal of Psychopharmocology, 11*, 151–162.

Arnsten, A. F. T., Cai, J. X., & Goldman-Rakic, P. S. (1988). The alpha-2 adrenergic agonist guanfacine improves memory in aged monkeys without sedative or hypotensive side effects: Evidence for alpha-2 receptor sybtypes. *Journal of Neuroscience, 8*, 4287–4298.

Arnsten, A. F. T., & Contant, T. A. (1992). Alpha-2 adrenergic agonists decrease distractibility in aged monkeys performing the delayed response task. *Psychopharmacology, 108*, 159–169.

Arnsten, A. F. T., & Goldman-Rakic, P. S. (1985). Alpha-2 adrenergic mechanisms in prefrontal cortex associated with cognitive decline in aged nonhuman primates. *Science, 230*, 1273–1276.

Arnsten, A. F. T., & Goldman-Rakic, P. S. (1990b). Analysis of alpha-2 adrenergic agonist effects on the delayed nonmatch-to-sample performance of aged rhesus monkeys. *Neurobiology of Aging, 11*, 583–590.

Arnsten, A. F. T., Steere, J. C., & Hunt, R. D. (1996). The contribution of alpha-2 noradrenergic mechanisms to prefrontal cortical cognitive function: Potential significance to attention deficit hyperactivity disorder. *Archives of General Psychiatry, 53*, 448–455.

Ashby, F. G., Alfonso-Reese, L. A., Turken, A. U., & Waldron, E. M. (1998). A neuropsychological theory of multiple systems in category learning. *Psychological Review, 105*, 442–481.

Ashby, F. G., Casale, M. (under review). A model of dopamine-modulated cortical activation.

Ashby, F. G., Isen, A. M., & Turken, A. U. (1999). A neuropsychological theory of positive affect and its influence on cognition. *Psychological Review, 106*, 529–550.

Ashby, F. G., Turken, A. U., & Isen, A. M. (1996, November). *Positive affect and creative problem solving: A dopaminergic hypothesis.* Paper presented at the 37th Annual Meeting of the Psychonomic Society, Chicago.

Aspinwall, L. G., & Taylor, S. E. (1997). A stitch in time: Self-regulation and proactive coping. *Psychological Bulletin, 121*, 417–436.

Aston-Jones, G., & Bloom, F. E. (1981a). Activity of norepinephrine-containing locus coeruleus neurons in behaving rats anticipates fluctuations in the sleep-waking cycle. *Journal of Neuroscience, 1*, 876–886.

Aston-Jones, G., & Bloom, F. E. (1981b). Norepinephrine-containing locus coeruleus neurons in behaving rats exhibit pronounced responses to non-noxious environmental stimuli. *Journal of Neuroscience, 1*, 897–900.

Aston-Jones, G., Chiang, C., & Alexinsky, T. (1991). Discharge of noradrenergic locus coeruleus neurons in behaving rats and monkeys suggests a role in vigilance. *Progress in Brain Research, 88*, 501–520.

Aston-Jones, G., Foote, S. L., & Bloom F. E. (1984). Anatomy and physiology of locus coeruleus neurons: functional implications. In Ziegler, M. & Lake, C. R. (Eds.), *Norepinephrine (Frontiers of Clinical Neuroscience*. Baltimore: Williams and Wilkins, 2, 92–116.

Aston-Jones, G., Rajkowski, J., Kubiak, P., & Alexinsky, T. (1994). Locus coeruleus neurons in monkey are selectively activated by attended cues in a vigilance task. *Journal of Neuroscience, 14*, 4467–4480.

Aston-Jones, G., Rajkowski, J., & Cohen, J. (1999). Role of locus coeruleus in attention and behavioral flexibility. *Biological Psychiatry, 46*, 1309–1320.

Beatty, J. (1995). *Principles of behavioral neuroscience*. Dubuque: Brown & Benchmark.

Beninger, R. J. (1983). The role of dopamine in locomotor activity and learning. *Brain Research, 287*, 173–196.

Beninger, R. J. (1991). Receptor subtype-specific dopamine agonists and antagonists and conditioned behavior. In P. Wiener & J. Scheol-Kroger (Eds.), *The mesolimbic dopamine system: From motivation to action* (pp. 273–300). New York: John Wiley & Sons.

Berlyne, D. E. (1967). Arousal and reinforcement. *Nebraska Symposium on Motivation, 15*, 1–110.

Berger, H. J. C., van Hoof, J. J. M., van Spaendonck, K. P. M., Horstink, M. W. I., van den Bercken, J. H. L., Jaspers, R., & Cools, A. R. (1989). Haloperidol and cognitive shifting. *Neuropsychologia, 27*, 629–639.

Bozarth, M. A. (1991). The mesolimbic dopamine system as a model reward system. In P. Willner & J. Scheol-Kroger (Eds.), *The mesolimbic dopamine system: From motivation to action* (pp. 301–330). New York: John Wiley & Sons.

Brown, R. G., & Marsden, C. D. (1988). Internal versus external cues and the control of attention in Parkinson's disease. *Brain, 111*, 323–345.

Brozoski, T., Brown, R. M., Rosvold, H. E., & Goldman, P. S. (1979). Cognitive deficit caused by regional depletion of dopamine in prefrontal cortex of rhesus monkey. *Science, 205*, 929–932.

Carli, M., Robbins, T. W., Evenden, J. L., & Everitt, B. J. (1983). Effects of lesions to ascending noradrenergic neurones on performance of a 5-choice serial reaction time task; implications for theories of dorsl noradrenergic bunle function based on selective attention and arousal. *Behavioural Brain Research, 9*, 361–380.

Carlson, N. R. (2001). *Physiology of behavior* (7th Ed.). Boston: Allyn and Bacon.

Carlson, S., Tanila, H., Rama, P., Mecke, E., & Pertovaara, A. (1992). Effects of medetomidine, an alpha-2 adrenoreceptor agonist, and atipamezole, an alpha-2 antagonist, on spatial memory performance in adult aged rats. *Behavioral and Neural Biology, 58*, 113–119.

Carnevale, P. J. D., & Isen, A. M. (1986). The influence of positive affect and visual access on the discovery of integrative solutions in bilateral negotiation. *Organizational Behavior and Human Decision Processes, 37*, 1–13.

Cenci, M. A., Kalen, P., Mandel, R. J., & Bjoerklund, A. (1992). Regional differences in the regulation of dopamine and noradrenaline release in medial frontal cortex, nucleus accumbens and caudate-putamen: A microdialysis study in the rat. *Brain Research, 581*, 217–228.

Cepeda, C., Radisavljevic, Z., Peacock, W., Levine, M. S., & Buchwald, N. A. (1992). Differential modulation by dopamine of responses evoked by excitatory amino acids in human cortex. *Synapse, 111*, 330–341.

Cohen, J. D., & Servan-Schreiber, D. (1992). Context, cortex, and dopamine: A connectionist approach to behavior and biology in schizophrenia. *Psychological Review, 99*, 45–77.

Cole, B. J., & Robbins, T. W. (1992). Forebrain norepinephrine: Role in controlled information processing in the rat. *Neuropsychopharmacology, 7*, 129–141.

Cooper, J. R., Bloom, F. E., & Roth, R. H. (1991). *The biochemical basis of neuropharmacology* (6th Edition). New York: Oxford University Press.

Cools, A. R., van den Bercken, J. H. L., Horstink, M. W. I., van Spaendock, K. P. M., & Berger, H. J. C. (1984). Cognitive and motor shifting aptitude disorder in Parkinson's disease. *Journal of Neurology, Neurosurgery and Psychiatry, 47*, 443–453.

Coull, J. T. (1998). Neural correlates of attention and arousal: Insights from electrophysiology, functional neuroimaging and psychopharmacology. *Progress in Neurobiology, 55*, 343–361.

Dawson, G. R., & Iverson, S. D. (1993). The effects of novel cholinesterase inhibitors and selective muscarinic receptor agonists in tests of reference and working memory. *Behavioural Brain Research, 57*, 143–153.

Day, J., Damsma, G., & Fibiger, H. C. (1991). Cholinergic activity in the rat hippocampus, cortex and striatum correlates with locomotor activity: An in vivo microdialysis study. *Pharmacology, Biochemistry, and Behavior, 38*, 723–729.

Devilbliss, D. M., & Waterhouse, B. D. (1996). Effect of increasing tonic levels of norepinephrine on glutamate evoked discharge of single neurons in layers II/III and V of rat barrel field cortex. *Society of Neuroscience Abstracts, 240.10*, 601.

Drachman, D. R., & Sahakian, B. J. (1979). The effects of cholinergic agents on human learning and memory. In A. Barbeau, J. H. Growden & R. J. Wurtman (Eds.), *Nutrition in the Brain* (pp. 351–366). New York, NY: Raven Press.

Duffy, E. (1934). Emotion: An example of the need for reorientation in psychology. *Psychological Review, 41*, 184–198.

Duffy, E. (1941). An explanation of "emotional" phenomena without the use of the concept of "emotion." *Journal of General Psychology, 25*, 282–293.

Duncker, K. (1945). On problem solving. *Psychological Monographs, 58*(5).

Easterbrook, J. A. (1959). The effect of emotion on cue utilization and the organization of behavior. *Psychological Review, 66*, 183–201.

Elliott, R., Rees, G., & Dolan, R. J. (1999). Ventromedial prefrontal cortex mediates guessing. *Neuropsychologia, 37*, 403–411.

Estes, W. K. (1976). The cognitive side of probability learning. *Psychological Review, 83*, 37–64.

Estrada, C. A., Isen, A. M., & Young, M. J. (1995). Positive affect facilitates integration of information and decreases anchoring in reasoning among physicians. Paper presented at the annual meeting of the Society for Medical Decision-Making, Tempe, AZ, October.

Estrada, C., Young, M., & Isen, A. M. (1994). Positive affect influences creative problem solving and reported source of practice satisfaction in physicians. *Motivation and Emotion, 18*, 285–299.

Evenden, J. L., & Robbins, T. W. (1983). Increased response switching, persereation and perseverative switching following *d*-amphetamine in the rat. *Psychopharmacology, 80*, 67–73.

Fiske, S. T., & Taylor, S. E. (1991). *Social Cognition*, 2nd edition. Reading, MA: Addison-Wesley.

Foote, S. L., Aston-Jones, G., & Bloom, F. E. (1980). Impulse activity of locus coeruleus neurons in awake rats and monkeys is a function of sensory stimulation and arousal. *Proceedings of the National Academy of Sciences of the United States of America, 77*, 3033–3037.

Foote, S. L., Bloom, F. E., & Aston-Jones, G. (1983). Nucleus locus ceruelus: new evidence of anatomical and physiological specificity. *Physiological Review, 63*, 844–914.

Foote, S. L., Freedman, R., & Oliver, A. P. (1975). Effects of putative neurotransmitters on neuronal activity in monkey auditory cortex. *Brain Research, 86*, 229–242.

Frith, C. D., Friston, K. J., Liddle, P. F., & Frackowiak, R. S. J. (1991a). A PET study of word finding. *Neuropsychologia, 29*, 1137–1148.

Frith, C. D., Friston, K. J., Liddle, P. F., & Frackowiak, R. S. J. (1991b). Willed action and the prefrontal cortex in man: A study with PET. *Proceedings of the Royal Society of London (B), 244*, 241–246.

Friston, K. J., Frith, C. D., Liddle, P. F., & Frackowiak, R. S. J. (1991). Investigating a network model of word generation with positron emission tomography. *Proceedings of the Royal Society of London (B), 244*, 101–106.

Fuster, J. M. (1989). *The prefrontal cortex* (2nd Edition). New York: Raven Press.

Gaspar, P., Berger, B., Febvret, A., Vigny, A., & Henry, J. P. (1989). Catecholamine innervation of the human cerebral cortex as revealed by comparative immunohistochemistry of tyrosine hydroxylase and dopamine-beta-hydroxylase. *Journal of Comparative Neurology, 279*, 249–271.

Gaspar, P., Duyckaerts, C., Alvarez, C., Javoy-Agid, F., & Berger, B. (1991). Alterations of dopaminergic and noradrenergic innervations in motor cortex in Parkinson's disease. *Annual Neurology, 30*, 365–374.

George, J. M., & Brief, A. P. (1996). Motivational agendas in the workplace: The effects of feelings on focus of attention and work motivation. In L. L. Cummings & B. M. Staw (Eds.), *Research in Organizational Behavior, 18*, 75–109. Greenwich, CT: J Press.

Glasky, A. J., Melchior, C. L., Pirzadeh, B., Heydari, N., & Ritzmann, R. F. (1994). Effect of AIT-082, a purine analog, on working memory in normal and aged mice. *Pharmacology, Biochemistry and Behavior, 47*, 325–329.

Goldman-Rakic, P. S. (1987). Circuitry of the prefrontal cortex and the regulation of behavior by representational knowledge. In F. Plum & V. Mountcastle (Eds.), *Handbook of physiology* (pp. 373–417). Bethesda, Maryland: American Physiological Society.

Goldman-Rakic, P. S. (1995). Cellular basis of working memory. *Neuron, 14*, 477–485.

Gotham, A. M., Brown, R. G., & Marsden, C. P. (1988). "Frontal" cognitive function in patients with Parkinson's disease "on" and "off" levodopa. *Brain, 111*, 299–321.

Grant, S. J., Aston-Jones, G., & Redmond, D. E. J. (1988). Responses of primate locus coeruleus neurons to simple and complex sensory stimuli. *Brain Research Bulletin, 21*, 401–411.

Greene, T. R., & Noice, H. (1988). Influence of positive affect upon creative thinking and problem solving in children. *Psychological Reports, 63*, 895–898.

Hale, W. D., & Strickland, B. (1976). Induction of mood states and their effect on cognitive and social behaviors. *Journal of Consulting and Clinical Psychology, 44*, 155.

Hasselmo, M. E. (1995). Neuromodulation and cortical function: modeling the physiological basis of behavior. *Behavioral Brain Research, 67*, 1–27.

Hemmings, H. C., Walaas, S. I., Ouimet, C. C., & Greengard, P. (1987). Dopaminergic regulation of protein phosphorylation in the striatum: DARRP-32, *Trends in Neuroscience, 10*, 377–383.

Hirt, E. R., Melton, R. J., McDonald, H. E., & Harackiewicz, J. M. (1996). Processing goals, task interest, and the mood-performance relationship: A mediational analysis. *Journal of Personality and Social Psychology, 71*, 245–261.

Hoffer, B. J., Siggins, G. R., & Bloom, F. E. (1971). Studies on norepinephrine-containing afferents of Purkinje cells of rat cerebellum: II. Sensitivity of Purkinje cells to norepinephrine and related substances administered by microiontophoresis, *Brain Research, 25*, 523–534.

Horvitz, J. C., Stewart, T., & Jacobs, B. L. (1997). Burst activity of ventral tegmental dopamine neurons is elicited by sensory stimuli in the awake cat. *Brain Research, 759*, 251–258.

Hyman, S. E., & Nestler, E. J. (1993). *The molecular foundations of psychiatry*. Washington, DC: American Psychiatric Press.

Imperato, A., Puglisi-Allegra, S., Casolini, P., & Angelucci, L. (1991). Changes in brain dopamine and acetylcholine release during and following stress are independent of the pituitary-adrenocortical axis. *Brain Research, 538*, 111–117.

Isen, A. M. (1987). Positive affect, cognitive processes, and social behavior. In L. Berkowitz (Ed.), *Advances in Experimental Social Psychology* (Vol. 20, pp. 203–253). San Diego, CA: Academic Press.

Isen, A. M. (1993). Positive affect and decision making. In M. Lewis & J. Haviland (Eds.), *Handbook of Emotion* (p. 261–277). NY: Guilford.

Isen, A. M., & Baron, R. A. (1991). Positive affect in organizations. In L. Cummings & B. Staw (Eds.), *Research in Organizational Behavior*. Greenwich, CT: JAI, 1–52.

Isen, A. M., & Daubman, K. A. (1984). The influence of affect on categorization. *Journal of Personality and Social Psychology, 47*, 1206–1217.

Isen, A. M., Daubman, K. A., & Nowicki, G. P. (1987). Positive affect facilitates creative problem solving. *Journal of Personality and Social Psychology, 52*, 1122–1131.

Isen, A. M., & Geva, N. (1987). The influence of positive affect on acceptable level of risk: The person with a large canoe has a large worry. *Organization Behavior and Human Decision Processes, 39*, 145–154.

Isen, A. M., & Gorgoglione, J. M. (1983). Some specific effects of four affect-induction procedures. *Personality and Social Psychology Bulletin, 9*, 136–143.

Isen, A. M., Johnson, M. S., Mertz, E., & Robinson, G. F. (1985). The influence of positive affect on the unusualness of word associations. *Journal of Personality and Social Psychology, 48*, 1413–1426.

Isen, A. M., & Means, B. (1983). The influence of positive affect on decision-making strategy. *Social Cognition, 2*, 18–31.

Isen, A. M., Nygren, T. E., & Ashby, F. G. (1988). The influence of positive affect on the subjective utility of gains and losses: It's just not worth the risk. *Journal of Personality and Social Psychology, 55*, 710–717.

Isen, A. M., Rosenzweig, A. S., & Young, M. J. (1991). The influence of positive affect on clinical problem solving. *Medical Decision Making, 11*, 221–227.

Isen, A. M., Shalker, T. E., Clark, M., & Karp L. (1978). Affect, accessibility of material in memory, and behavior: A cognitive loop? *Journal of Personality and Social Psychology, 36*, 1–12.

Jackson, W. J., & Buccafusco, J. J. (1991). Clonidine enhances delayed matching-to-sample performance by young and aged monkeys. *Pharmacology, Biochemistry and Behavior, 39*, 79–84.

Jacobs, B. L. (1987). Brain monoaminergic activity in behaving animals. In A. N. Epstein & A. R. Morrison (Eds.), *Progress in Psychobiology and Physiological Psychology* Vol. 12 (pp. 171–206). New York, NY: Academic Press.

Jaspers, R. M. A., De Vries, T. J., & Cools, A. R. (1990a). Effect of intrastriatal apomorphine on changes in switching behavior induced by the glutamate agonists AMPA injected into the cat caudate nucleus. *Behavioral Brain Research, 37*, 247–254.

Jaspers, R. M. A., De Vries, T. J., & Cools, A. R. (1990b). Enhancement in switching motor patterns following local application of the glutamate agonist AMPA into the cat caudate nucleus. *Behavioral Brain Research, 37*, 237–246.

Jiang, M., Griff, E. R., Ennis, M., Zimmer, L. A., & Shipley, M. T. (1996). Activation of locus coeruleus enhances the responses of olfactory bulb mitral cells to weak but not strong olfactory nerve input. *Journal of Neuroscience, 16*, 6319–6329.

Kahn, B. E., & Isen, A. M. (1993). Variety seeking among safe, enjoyable products. *Journal of Consumer Research, 20*, 257–270.

Kasamatsu, T., & Heggelund, P. (1982). Single cell responses in cat visual cortex to visual stimulation during iontophoresis of noradrenaline. *Experimental Brain Research, 45*, 317–327.

Kelly, P. H., Sevior, P. W., & Iversen, S. D. (1975). Amphetamine and apomorphine responses in the rat following 6-OHDA lesions of the nucleus accumbens septi and corpus striatum. *Brain Research, 94*, 507–522.

Koestler, A. (1964). *The act of creation*. New York: Macmillan.

Kossl, M., & Vater, M. (1989). Noradrenaline enhances temporal auditory contrast and neuronal timing precision in the cochlear nucleus of the mustached bat. *Journal of Neuroscience, 9*, 4169–4178.

Lacey, J. I. (1967). Somatic response patterning and stress: Some revisions of activation theory. In M. H. Appley & R. Trumball (Eds.), *Psychological stress: Issues in research* (pp. 14–44). New York: Appleton-Century-Crofts.

Lacey, J. I. (1975). Psychophysiology of the autonomic nervous system. In J. R. Nazarrow (Ed.), *Master lectures on physiological psychology*. Washington, DC: American Psychological Association. (Audiotape).

Lange, K. W., Robbins, T. W., Marsden, C. D., James, M., Owen, A. M., & Paul, G. M. (1992). L-DOPA withdrawal in Parkinson's disease selectively impairs cognitive performance. *Psychopharmacology, 107*, 394–404.

LeDoux, J. E. (1993). Emotional memory systems in the brain. *Behavioural Brain Research, 58*, 69–79.

Levin, B. E., Labre, M. M., & Weiner, W. J. (1989). Cognitive impairments associated with early Parkinson's disease. *Neurology, 39*, 557–561.

Lewinsohn, S., & Mano, H. (1993). Multiattribute choice and affect: The influence of naturally-occurring and manipulated moods on choice processes. *Journal of Behavioral Decision Making, 6*, 33–51.

Liebeman, J. M., & Cooper, S. J. (Eds.) (1989). *The neuropharmacological basis of reward*. New York: Clarendon Press.

Luciano, M., Depue, R. A., Arbisi, P., Leon, A. (1992). Facilitation of working memory in humans by a D_2 Dopamine receptor agonist. *Journal of Cognitive Neuroscience, 4*, 58–68.

Lundberg, U., & Frankenhaeuser, M. (1976). Adjustment to noise stress. *Reports from the Department of Psychology, U. Stockholm, 484*, 16.

Mano, H. (1997). Affect and persuasion: The influence of pleasantness and arousal on attitude formation and message elaboration. *Psychology & Marketing, 14*, 315–335.

Marrocco, R. T., Witte, E. A., & Davidson, M. C. (1994). Arousal systems. *Current Opinion in Neurobiology, 4*, 166–170.

McCormick, D. A. (1992). Neurotransmitter actions in the thalamus and cerebral cortex. *Journal of Clinical Neurophysiology, 9*, 212–223.

McLean, J., & Waterhouse, B. D. (1994). Noradrenergic modulation of cat area 17 neuronal responses to moving visual stimuli. *Brain Research, 667*, 83–97.

Mednick, M. T., Mednick, S. A., & Mednick, E. V. (1964). Incubation of creative performance and specific associative priming. *Journal of Abnormal and Social Psychology, 69*, 84–88.

Mednick, S. A. (1962). The associative basis of the creative process. *Psychological Review, 69*, 220–232.

Miller, F. E., Heffner, T. G., & Seiden, L. S. (1981). Magnitude and duration of hyperactivity following neonatal 6-hydroxydopamine is related to the extent of brain dopamine depletion. *Brain Research, 229*(1), 123–132.

Mirenowicz, J., & Schultz, W. (1994). Importance of unpredictability for reward responses in primate dopamine neurons. *Journal of Neurophysiology, 72*, 1024–1027.

Montague, P. R., Dayan, P., & Sejnowski, T. J. (1996). A framework for mesencephalic dopamine systems based on predictive Hebbian learning. *Journal of Neuroscience, 16*(5), 1936–1947.

Morrison, J., & Foote, S. (1986). Noradrenergic and serotonergic innervation of cortical, thalamic and tectal visual structures in old and new world monkeys. *Journal of Comparative Neurology, 243,* 117–128.

Neiss, R. (1990). Ending arousal's reign of error: A reply to Anderson. *Psychological Bulletin, 107,* 1010–1050.

Oaksford, M., Morris, F., Grainger, B., & Williams, J. M. G. (1996). Mood, reasoning, and central executive processes. *Journal of Experimental Psychology: Learning, Memory, & Cognition, 22,* 476–492.

Owen, A. M., Roberts, A. C., Hodges, J. R., Summers, B. A., Polkey, C. E., & Robbins, T. W. (1993). Contrasting mechanisms of impaired attentional set-shifting in patients with frontal lobe damage or Parkinsons's disease. *Brain, 116,* 1159–1175.

Palermo, D. S., & Jenkins, J. J. (1964). *Word association norms: Grade school through college.* Minneapolis, MN: University of Minnesota Press.

Pessin, M. S., Snyder, G. L., Halpain, S., Girault, J. -A., Aperia, A., & Greengard, P. (1994). DARPP-32/Protein Phosphatase-1/Na+/K+ ATPase System: A mechanism for bidirectional control of cell function. In K. Fuxe, L. F. Agnati, B. Bjelke, & D. Ottoson (Eds.), *Trophic regulation of basal ganglia* (pp. 43–57). New York: Elsevier Science.

Phillips, A. G., Blaha, C. D., Pfaus, J. G., & Blackburn, J. R. (1992). Neurobiological correlates of positive emotional states: Dopamine, anticipation and reward. In K. T. Strongman (Ed.), *International review of studies on emotion* (Vol. 2, pp. 31–49). John Wiley & Sons Ltd.

Posner, M. I., & Petersen, S. E. (1990). The attention system of the human brain. *Annual Reviews of Neuroscience, 13,* 25–42.

Posner, M. I., & Raichle, M. E. (1994). *Images of mind.* New York: Scientific American Library.

Protais, P., Bonnet, J. J., & Costentin, J. (1983). Pharmacological characterization of the receptors involved in the apomorphine induced polyphasic modifications of locomotor activity in mice. *Psychopharmacology, 81,* 126–134.

Rajkowski, J., Kubiak, P., & Aston-Jones, G. (1992). Activity of locus coeruleus neurones in behaving monkeys varies with forcused attention: short- and long-term changes. *Society of Neuroscience Abstracts, 18,* 538.

Richardson, R. T., & De Long, M. R. (1990). Responses of primate nucleus basalis neurons to water rewards and related stimuli. In M. Steriade, & D. Biesold (Eds.), *Brain Cholinergic Systems* (pp. 282–293). Oxford, Oxford University Press.

Ridley, R. M., Baker, H. F., Frith, C. D., Dowdy, J., & Crow, T. (1988). Stereotyped responding on a two-choice guessing task by marmosets and humans treated with amphetamine. *Psychopharmacology, 95,* 560–564.

Robbins, T. W. (1984). Cortical noradrenaline, attention and arousal. *Psychological Medicine, 14,* 13–21.

Robbins, T. W., & Everitt, B. J. (1996). Neurobehavioural mechanisms of reward and motivation. *Current Opinion in Neurobiology, 6,* 228–236.

Robbins, T. W., Semple, J., Kumar, R., Truman, M. I., Shorter, J., Ferraro, A., Fox, B., McKay, G., & Matthews, K. (1997). Effects of scopolamine on delayed-matching-to-sample and paired associates tests of visual memory and learning in human subjects: comparison with diazepam and implications for dementia. *Psychopharmacology, 134,* 95–106.

Roberts, A. C., De Salvia, M. A., Wilkinson, L. S., Collins, P., Muir, J. L., Everitt, B. J., & Robbins, T. W. (1994). 6-hydroxydopamine lesions of the prefrontal cortex in monkeys enhance performance on an analog of the Wisconsin card sort test: Possible interactions with subcortical dopamine. *The Journal of Neuroscience, 14,* 2531–2544.

Roberts, D. C. S., Price, M. T. C., & Fibiger, H. C. (1976). The dorsal tegmental noradrenergic projection: an analysis of its role in maze learning. *Journal of Comparative Physiological Psychology, 90,* 363–372.

Rumelhart, D. E., & McClelland, J. L. (Eds.) (1986). *Parallel distributed processing* (Vol. 1). Cambridge, MA: Bradford.

Sato, H., Hata, Y., Masui, H., & Tsumoto, T. (1987). A functional role of cholinergic innervation to neurons in cat visual cortex. *Journal of Neurophysiology, 58,* 765–780.

Schultz, W. (1992). Activity of dopamine neurons in the behaving primate. *Seminars in Neuroscience, 4,* 129–138.

Schildkraut, J. J. (1965). The catecholamine hypothesis of affective disorders: A review of supporting evidence. *American Journal of Psychiatry, 12,* 509–522.

Seeman, P., & Van Tol, H. H. (1994). Dopamine receptor pharmacology. *Trends in Pharmacological Sciences, 17,* 264–270.

Servan-Schreiber, D., Printz, H. W., & Cohen, J. D. (1990). A network model of catecholamine effects: Gain, singal-to-noise ratio and behavior. *Science, 249,* 892–895.

Shepherd, G. M. (1994). *Neurobiology* (3rd Edition). New York: Oxford University Press.

Showers, C., & Cantor, N. (1985). Social cognition: A look at motivated strategies. *Annual Review of Psychology, 36,* 275–305.

Sibley, D. R., Monsma Jr., F. J., & Shen, Y. (1993). Molecular neurobiology of dopaminergic receptors. *International Review of Neurobiology, 35,* 391–415.

Smiley, J. F., Levey, A. I., Ciliax, B. J., & Goldman-Rakic, P. S. (1994). D_1 dopamine receptor immunoreactivity in human and monkey cerebral cortex: Predominant and extrasynaptic localization in dendritic spines. *Proceedings of the National Academy of Sciences, 91,* 5720–5724.

Sorg, B. A., & Kalivas, P. W. (1993). Effects of cocaine and footshock stress on extracellular dopamine levels in medial prefrontal cortex. *Neuroscience, 53,* 695–703.

Staw, B. M., & Barsade, S. G. (1993). Affect and managerial performance: A test of the sadder-but-wiser vs. happier-and smarter hypotheses. *Administrative Science Quarterly, 38,* 304–331.

Staw, B. M., Sutton, R. I., & Pelled, L. H. (1994). Employee positive emotion and favorable outcomes at the workplace. *Organizational Science, 5,* 51–71.

Steere, J. C., Li, B. M., Jentsch, J. D., Mathew, R., Taylor, J. R., & Arnsten, A. F. T. (1996). Alpha-1 noradrenergic stimulation impairs, while alpha-2 stimulation improves, prefrontal cortex spatial working memory function. *Society of Neuroscience Abstracts, 22,* 1126.

Steininger, R. L., Alam, M. N, , Szymusiak, R., and McGinty, D. (1996). State dependent discharge of tuberomammillary neurons in the rat hypothalamus. *Sleep Research, 25*, 28.

Stone, T. W. (1973). Pharmocology of pyramidal tract cells in the cerebral cortex, Naunyn-Schmiedeberg. *Pharmacology, 278*, 333–346.

Strange, P. G. (1988). The structure and mechanism of neurotransmitter receptors. *Biochemical Journal, 249*, 309–318.

Strickland, B. R., Hale, W. D., & Anderson, L. K. (1975). Effect of induced mood states on activity and self-reported affect. *Journal of Consulting and Clinical Psychology, 43*, 587.

Tafalla, R. J., & Evans, G. W. (1997). Noise, physiology, and human performance: the potential role of effort. *Journal of Occupational Health Psychology, 2*, 148–155.

Taylor, S. E., & Aspinwall, L. G. (1996). Mediating and moderating processes in psychosocial stress: Appraisal, coping, resistance and vulnerability. In H. B. Kaplan (Ed.), *Psychosocial stress: Perspectives on structure, theory, life-course, and methods* (pp. 71–110). San Diego: Academic Press.

Trevor, R. W. (1997). Arousal systems and attentional processes. *Biological Psychology, 45*, 57–71.

Trulson, M. E., & Jacobs, B. L. (1979). Raphe unit activity in freely moving cats: Correlation with level of behavioral arousal. *Brain Research, 163*, 135–150.

Ungerstedt, U. (1971). Stereotaxic mapping of the monoamine pathways in the rat brain. *Acta Physiologica Scandinavica. Supplementum, 367*, 1–48.

Venables, P. H. (1984). Arousal: An examination of its status as a concept. In M. G. H. Coles, J. R. Jennings, & J. A. Stern (Eds.), *Psychophysiological perspectives: Festschrift for Beatrice and John Lacey* (pp. 134–142). New York: Van Nostrand Reinhold.

Wada, H., Inagaki, N., Itowi, N., & Yamatodani, A. (1991). Histaminergic neuron systems in the brain: distribution and possible functions. *Brain Research Bulletin, 27*, 367–370.

Waterhouse, B. D., Azizi, S. A., Burne, R. A., & Woodward, D. J. (1990). Modulation of rat cortical area 17 neuronal responses to moving visual stimuli during norepinephrine and serotonin microiontophoresis. *Brain Research, 514*, 276–292.

Waterhouse, B. D., Moises, H. C., & Woodward, D. J. (1980). Noradrenergic modulation of somatosensory cortical neuronal responses to ionophoretically applied putative neurotransmitters, *Experimental Neurology, 69*, 30–49.

Waterhouse, B. D., & Woodward, D. J. (1980). Interaction of norepinephrine with cerebrocortical activity evoked by stimulation of somatosensory afferent pathways in the rat. *Experimental Neurology, 67*, 11–34.

Wertheimer, M. (1945). *Productive thinking*. New York: Harper & Row.

White, N. M. (1989). Reward or reinforcement: what's the difference? *Neuroscience and Biobehavioral Reviews, 13*, 181–186.

Wickens, J. R. (1990). Striatal dopamine in motor activation and reward-mediated learning: Steps towards a unifying model. *Journal of Neural Transmission, 80*, 9–31.

Wickens, J. (1993). *A theory of the striatum*. New York: Pergamon Press.

Williams, G. V., & Goldman-Rakic, P. S. (1995). Modulation of memory fields by dopamine D1 receptors in prefrontal cortex. *Nature, 376*, 572–575.

Wilson, F. A. W., & Rolls, E. T. (1990). Learning and memory is reflected in the responses of reinforcement-related neurons in the primate basal forebrain. *Journal of Neuroscience, 10*, 1254–1267.

Winocur, G., & Eskes, G. (1998). Prefrontal cortex and caudate nucleus in conditional associative learning: Dissociated effects of selective brain lesions in rats. *Behavioral Neuroscience, 112*, 89–101.

Wise, R. A. (1982). Neuroleptics and operant behavior: The anhedonia hypothesis. *Behavioral Brain Science, 5*, 39–88.

Wise, R. A., & Rompré, P. P. (1989). Brain dopamine and reward. *Annual Review of Psychology, 40*, 191–225.

Woodward, D., Moises, H., Waterhouse, B., Hoffer, R., & Freedman R. (1979). Modulatory actions of norepinephrine in the central nervous system. *Federation Proceedings, 38*, 2109–2116.

Yerkes, R. M., & Dodson, J. D. (1908). The relationship of strength of stimulus to rapidity of habit formation. *Journal of Comparative and Neurological Psychology, 18*, 459–482.

Zacharko, R. M., & Anisman, H. (1991). Stressor-provoked alterations of intracranial self-stimulation in the mesocorticolimbic system: An animal model of depression. In P. Willner & J. Scheel-Krüger (Eds.), *The mesolimbic dopamine system: From motivation to action* (pp. 411–442). New York: Wiley.

Zillmann, D. (1979). *Hostility and aggression*. Hillsdale, NJ: Erlbaum.

Appendix

The creative problem solver connectionist network

This appendix describes the details of the Ashby et al. (1996) simulations of the creative problem solver under high and low dopamine level conditions in the four tasks described in the chapter. In each simulation, the two experimental conditions were assumed to differ only in dopamine level, and this difference was instantiated via the activation function described in Equations 2–4. The activation function parameters, K_{NMDA} and θ were fixed at the values 1 and 2, respectively. The parameters $K_E(DA)$ and $K_{AMPA}(DA)$ were assumed to vary with dopamine level. Numerical values for these parameters were selected via trial-and-error. A single value of $K_E(DA)$ was chosen for the word association, remote associates, and the candle tasks, since the experimental manipulation was identical in all three (i.e., $K_E(DA) = 1.25$ for the positive affect conditions, and $K_E(DA) = 5$ for the neutral affect conditions). The value of $K_{AMPA}(DA)$ was set arbitrarily to $1/K_E(DA)$ in all simulations (i.e., therefore, $K_{AMPA}(DA) = 0.8$ for the positive affect conditions, and $K_{AMPA}(DA) = 0.2$ for the neutral affect conditions). For the two choice guessing task, in which dopamine levels were manipulated by amphetamine administration, different values were used

(K_E(DA) = K_{AMPA}(DA) = 1.0 for the amphetamine group, and K_E(DA) = 2.5 and K_{AMPA}(DA) = 0.4 for the saline group).

The weights between all nodes in the semantic networks (i.e., see Figures 5 and 7) were chosen so that the performance of the creative problem solver matched the performance of the neutral affect control subjects (see text for more details). Each cognitive set unit (e.g., P1 and P2 in Figure 1) was assigned an initial bias or salience. Let B_i denote the salience of cognitive set Pi. For example, in Figure 7, the set or perspective *Semantic Relations* was assigned a higher salience than the set *Compound Words*.

The selection operation performed by the anterior cingulate was modeled in the following way. First, one of the anterior cingulate units Ai (where $i = 1$ or 2 in all simulations except word association, where $i = 1, 2,$ or 3; i.e., see Figures 5, 7, and 9) was selected randomly (according to a uniform distribution). Second, unit X generated a value of random magnitude (denoted by X and normally distributed with a mean of 2 and a variance of 1). The connections between node X and nodes Ai are modulated by dopamine (i.e., see Figure 1), so the third step was to treat X as the input to the activation function shown in Equations 2–4 (i.e., so $\sum w_{ik} a_i = X$). Call this output activation value $act(X)$. Fourth, the net input activation of cognitive set unit Pi was:

$$act(Pi) = B_i + act(X)$$

if unit Ai was selected in step 1. Otherwise,

$$act(Pi) = B_i.$$

Finally, unit Pi became the active cognitive set if

$$act(Pi) = max[act(P1), act(P2), \ldots, act(Pn)],$$

(where n is the total number of alternative cognitive set units). Each cognitive set unit projected to a different semantic network (i.e., see Figures 5, 7, and 9). The weights between every pair of nodes in semantic networks associated with inactive cognitive sets were all set to zero. To generate model predictions, 100 simulations were run for each condition of each task.

For the two-choice guessing task, the initial values for the salience parameters were set to 0 for each response (i.e., $B_1 = B_2 = 0$). At the end of each trial, the salience for the emitted response was updated. If the response was reinforced (i.e., correct), the salience was increased by 0.35, otherwise it was decreased by the same amount. If this method produced a negative value, the salience was set to 0. Stimulus generation procedures were the same as used by Ridley et al. (1988).

The word association and remote associates tasks were simulated using the architectures shown in Figures 5 and 7. For the word association network, the initial salience of the cognitive set *part of the hand* was set to 0.15, the salience of *use of the hand* was set to 0, and the salience of *compound words* was set to 0.35. For the remote associates network, the initial salience of the cognitive set *semantic relations* was set to 0.55, and the salience of *compound words* was set to 0.2. For both networks, the weights between every pair of nodes in the semantic network is shown in Table 1. In both tasks, the activation values of the nodes representing the stimulus words were set at 1 on each trial, and the activation function for each node in the semantic networks was linear. The probability that the word represented by any given node would be chosen for that trial was determined by dividing the activation level of that node by the sum of the activations of all words in the semantic network.

For the candle task, the architecture shown in Figure 9 was used. The initial salience of the cognitive set *box as a container* was 0.3 and the initial salience of *box as a platform* was 0. As described in the text, a trial was considered a failure only if the network failed to solve the problem on five successive attempts.

Table 1. Weights between word nodes in the semantic network portion of the Creative Problem Solver Network.

		NETWORK	
Word Association Word Pair	Weight	Remote Associates Word Pair	Weight
palm-basketball	0.3	club-party	1.1
palm-steal	0.6	gown-dress	0.6
palm-lift	0.5	mare-horse	0.1
palm-sweaty	0.2	club-dance	0.2
palm-hand	0.7	gown-dance	0.2
hand-finger	0.4	club-golf club	0.5
palm-palm reader	0.9	golf club-golf	1.0
palm-palm tree	0.3	gown-wedding gown	1.0
palm tree-Hawaii	0.2	wedding gown-wedding	1.0
		club-nightclub	0.6
		nightclub-night	1.0
		gown-nightgown	0.6
		nightgown-night	1.0
		mare-nightmare	0.6
		nightmare-night	1.0

CHAPTER 12

Integration of emotion and cognitive control
A neurocomputational hypothesis of dynamic goal regulation

Jeremy R. Gray and Todd S. Braver
Harvard University / Washington University

This chapter sketches how one aspect of a theory of cognitive-emotional interactions might develop, with a particular emphasis on computational constraints. In general, the prefrontal cortex (PFC) might serve as a neurocomputational substrate for integrating information about goal-related emotional states with the cognitive control of behavior by actively maintained goals. The specific possibility we consider in detail concerns the relation between emotional and cognitive information processing: that these processes are likely to interact in a selective or functionally integrated rather than non-selective manner. In particular, goal management in a dynamic environment in which there are unpredictable threats and rewards is an important self-regulatory problem that might have been solved computationally, in part, through an integration of cognitive and affective processes in lateral PFC (Gray in press; Gray 2001; Gray, Braver, & Raichle 2002; Tomarken & Keener 1998).

The *cognitive control* of behavior refers to an important set of psychological functions (see Braver & Cohen 2000; Norman & Shallice 1986; Posner & Snyder 1975): the ability to develop and carry out temporally extended plans of action, especially novel ones, to do so in the absence of sensory cues, to resist distraction or interference, and to update goals and subgoals in a flexible manner. Cognitive control is clearly not a unitary process; rather, many subfunctions contribute in a coordinated manner. Working memory, or maintaining and manipulating information actively in mind (Baddeley & Hitch 1974), is an important aspect of cognitive control, and itself has component processes.

Emotional states might modulate components of cognitive control to allow for the temporary, adaptive enhancement of some subfunctions over others (Gray 2001, in press). In the hypothesis presented, we focus on mechanisms for updating goals in a flexible manner, viewing unpredicted threats and rewards as critical events which require flexibility and efficiency in goal management. The proposed role of emotion is to exert a "bottom-up" influence on the functioning of the PFC (especially WM subsystems), thereby modulating the efficacy of active goals in guiding behavior. The key aspect we highlight concerns the ability of such regulation to be both context-dependent and yet require only a bottom-up mechanism. Such a computational architecture could support the adaptive prioritization of goals in environments having unpredictable threats and rewards.

To our knowledge, selective effects of emotion on cognitive control have been little considered with reference to a theoretical basis (but see Gray in press; Gray 2001; Gray et al. 2002; Tomarken & Keener 1998). That is, models in which emotional selectivity is implicit have typically described patterns of association rather than emphasized how psychologically adaptive, functional relations among components might give rise to the observed associations. The model we present in this chapter is based in part on connectionist neural network models of brain function. In such models, implementing different kinds of processes typically requires some computational specialization, which in turn promotes specialization within neural systems (O'Reilly, Braver, & Cohen 1999; Rueckl, Cave, & Kosslyn 1989). That is, when there are inherent computational tradeoffs, different brain regions tend to become specialized for handling incompatible aspects of the overall problem. Applying this logic to emotion suggests that there might be a functional reason for hemispheric specialization for approach- and withdrawal-related emotion. Specifically, asymmetries for both emotion and cognitive control might enable selective effects of emotion on cognitive control, thereby allowing for context-dependent regulation of cognitive control by emotion.

The existence of prefrontal brain asymmetries for both emotion and cognition separately are consistent with the idea that emotional states might modulate cognitive control on a hemispheric basis (Heller 1990; Heller & Nitschke 1997; Tomarken & Keener 1998), thereby supporting selective effects of emotion on higher cognition (Gray, in press; Gray 2001; Gray, Braver, & Raichle 2002). In humans, lateral PFC is somewhat specialized by hemisphere for aspects of cognitive control, e.g., domains of working memory (D'Esposito et al. 1998; Smith & Jonides 1999), sustained attention (Cabeza & Nyberg 2000; Pardo, Fox, & Raichle 1991), and other functions (Banich 1997; Hellige

1993). A largely separate line of work has suggested that the PFC is also somewhat specialized by hemisphere for aspects of subjectively experienced emotion (namely, approach- and withdrawal-related emotional states: Davidson 1995; Fox 1991; Sutton & Davidson 1997). This has been supported by a recent meta-analysis of neuroimaging studies of emotion (Murphy & Lawrence 2001), and by direct recordings from neurons using depth electrodes in humans during induced emotional states (Kaufman et al. 2001). Approach states tend to be associated with greater neural activation in left anterior areas relative to right, and withdrawal states with greater right activation relative to left. Given evidence for asymmetries, hemispheric differences are a possible mechanism supporting selective effects, although need not be the only one (e.g., dorsal-ventral distinctions are also important, Liotti & Tucker 1995).

Our larger argument depends on the existence of selective effects of emotion on cognitive control. There are two empirical issues: whether selective effects are possible, and whether a hemispheric basis is responsible. In our work (Gray 2001; Gray et al. 2002), selectivity is of primary interest while hemispheric differences are secondary (providing a possible mechanism for selectivity). In related work, hemispheric differences have been emphasized (Bartolic, Basso, Schefft, Glauser, & Titanic-Schefft 1999; Heller 1990; Heller & Nitschke 1997). Asymmetries might make sense computationally, and we elaborate this possibility in some detail to help make the discussion of a goal-regulation architecture more concrete. However, the hemispheric hypothesis about the mechanism supporting selectivity should be understood as empirically separable from and secondary to our main interest in selectivity.

We first present evidence for emotional-cognitive integration, focusing on selective effects of emotion on cognitive control, and then a neurocomputational hypothesis in which this form of integration holds a pivotal role.

Selective effects of emotion on cognitive control: Evidence for integration

Are the effects of emotion on cognitive control diffuse, general, or otherwise non-specific, or can they be selective, in the sense of influencing some processes and not others? Selectivity implies a more complex functional organization, as it necessitates the existence of a mechanism whose input includes information about emotional state and cognitive demands, and whose output is not determined exclusively by one or the other, nor by main effects of one on the other, but also by both conjointly (i.e., their interaction). The clearest evidence for a selective effect would be a double dissociation in which cognitive control depends on the emotional context. Such a selective effect would logically imply a true interaction at some point of processing (cf. Sternberg 1969). An interaction means that, at some point, cognitive and emotional information must be integrated to permit a contextual dependence of one on the other. In this section, we briefly present data from experiments designed to test the hypothesis that selective influences of induced emotion on cognitive control are possible.

In three experiments (Gray 1999; Gray 2001), participants had a standard emotion induction (watching 9–10 minute video) and then performed a verbal or nonverbal (spatial) version of a computerized cognitive control task (n-back tasks: Braver et al. 1997) likely to recruit lateralized working memory systems (D'Esposito et al. 1998; Smith & Jonides 1999). All three experiments showed the predicted effect: a significant two-way interaction on performance between the type of task (verbal, nonverbal) and the type of video preceding it (approach, withdrawal). The results are illustrated in Figure 1. Spatial performance was impaired by an approach state relative to the withdrawal state, and the opposite held for the verbal task. Self-reported ratings confirmed the emotion induction and showed that the emotional videos were matched for arousal. Moreover, the crossover interaction was significantly stronger for participants finding the tasks more difficult than for those finding them less difficult. This is of note because individual differences in performance on working memory tasks reflect mainly differences in controlled attention (for a review, see Engle, Kane, & Tuholski 1999), suggesting the effect of emotion was specific to cognitive control. These behavioral data are strong evidence for a selective effect,

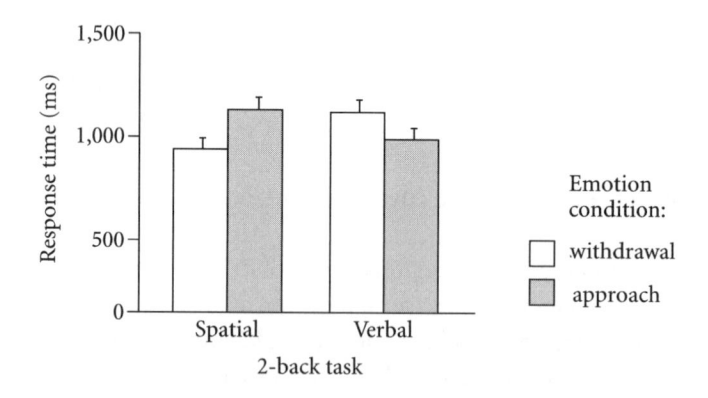

Figure 1. Response times during n-back working memory tasks: spatial or verbal task following approach or withdrawal emotion induction. From Experiment 2, Gray (2001); redrawn with permission, ©American Psychological Association.

and imply the existence of cognitive-emotional integration at some point of processing.

A limitation of these studies was relying on individual differences in overall performance to suggest that the effect was specific to cognitive control. However, Moore and Oaksford (in press) found that induced emotion had the opposite effects on verbal and nonverbal tasks not strongly requiring working memory (visual search, word association). Visual search was enhanced by a positive mood, and word association enhanced by a depressed mood, a crossover interaction in the opposite direction. These results further suggest specificity of the effect of emotion on the n-back tasks to cognitive control.

The selective effect may have been mediated on a hemispheric basis (Gray 2001; Heller 1990). That is, numerous other studies have shown hemispheric differences in processing during verbal versus spatial tasks (see Smith & Jonides 1999) and approach versus withdrawal emotions (see Davidson 1995). We have recently found evidence consistent with this hypothesis using functional magnetic resonance imaging (fMRI, Gray et al. 2002). In an initial behavioral study using verbal (word) and nonverbal (face) versions of an n-back task, the expected crossover interaction in performance was found to hold with these stimuli, again consistent with a hemisphere-based interpretation. In the fMRI study, 14 participants were scanned while they were performing the n-back tasks immediately after having viewed one of the emotional videos. The same behavioral effect held for these participants. Dorsolateral PFC (DLPFC), which is known to be critical for cognitive control, showed the expected hemispheric asymmetry for stimulus type, with words leading to greater left activity and faces to greater right activity. DLPFC also showed hemispheric asymmetry for emotion. Most critically, a third area in DLPFC showed a crossover Stimulus x Emotion interaction, with the pattern of activity related to behavioral performance. The crossover interaction is further evidence for integration of emotion and cognition. Thus lateral PFC is sensitive to the conjunction of emotional state and cognitive task demands (as has been suggested for medial PFC: Bechara, Damasio, Damasio, & Anderson 1994; Damasio 1994; Luu, Collins, & Tucker 2000; Simpson, Drevets, Snyder, Gusnard, & Raichle 2001a; Simpson, Snyder, Gusnard, & Raichle 2001b). The separate hemispheric asymmetries for stimuli and emotion that were also found in PFC suggest that the integration is in fact computed in lateral PFC. Whatever the mechanism may be that computes the interaction for a particular cognitive control function, it effectively integrates information about on-going emotional state with the demand for cognitive control in order to do so.

In sum, behavioral and neuroimaging evidence suggests that selective effects of emotion on cognitive control are possible. An integration of emotional and cognitive information appears to be computed and represented in lateral PFC. A hemispheric basis for these effects is a possible explanation, although has not been definitively shown and other explanations are possible. What is critical for the following argument is that selective effects occur, because this implies some integration of emotional state and cognitive control processes at some point of processing. We next focus on the question of why such selectivity and integration might be useful.

Dynamic goal management: A need for integration?

In this section, we argue that the integration of emotional state with cognitive control is likely to be adaptive. Adaptive is meant in the psychological sense of promoting function. It might also be evolutionarily adaptive, but for pragmatic reasons the hypothesis concerns only computational efficiency. This of itself will be a somewhat speculative argument because not all aspects of the model are instantiated in a computer program. Some aspects have been instantiated: those related to the active maintenance of context information that guides behavior (Braver & Cohen 2000). Goal representations are an important kind of context information. While we believe that hemispheric specialization and selective modulation by emotional state could be incorporated into this model and would bear out the general conclusions, this awaits demonstration.

The argument concerns the computational requirements of goal management in a dynamic environment. Not all goals are appropriate in all situations, and in particular, a good goal in the wrong context can be disastrous (e.g., continuing to forage for food despite the sudden appearance of a predator). When conditions change and so alter the balance of impending reward and threat, the appropriateness of active goals is likely to change as well. For this reason, the ability of goals to control behavior should depend in part on the context. At times, the relevant context may be strongly emotional in nature, signaling the presence of unexpected reward or threat. This analysis suggests a computational need for a mechanism that can provide an emotional-context-dependent regulation of active goals. The idea that one function of emotion is to help mediate priorities is widely held, but to our knowledge it has not been elaborated in detail commensurate with its probable complexity and importance for self-regulation (see Carver & Scheier 1990; Carver, Sutton, & Scheier 2000; Ekman

& Davidson 1994; Gray 1990; Gray 1999b; Lang 1995; Lazarus 1991; Simon 1967; Tomarken & Keener 1998).

Goals can be considered a kind of mental representation that engage cognition and action in the service of making a particular, motivated state of affairs more likely to come about through one's own efforts. For goals to bias behavior adaptively, suitable representations need to be maintained in a manner that can influence self-regulatory behavior. The influence that goals have on behavior can be diverse, e.g., manifesting as selective attention, sustained attention, inhibitory control, and so on, although this does not necessarily imply separate mechanisms (see Braver & Cohen 2000). Because goals need to exert a powerful influence on cognitive control, there must also be some way to ensure that they are appropriate given other aspects of a situation. That is, some mechanism is necessary to effect dynamic adjustments in goal priority in response to changes in external conditions.

We focus on one possible way that dynamic prioritization could be instantiated: the active maintenance of goal representations in working memory subsystems, plus a selective modulation of these subsystems (and hence the active representations within them) by approach-withdrawal emotional states. The relative strength of an active goal's representation would determine how effectively that goal could influence behavior. The key idea is that a dynamic goal management system would benefit from separating the active maintenance of approach and withdrawal goal representations, and from the selective regulation of these active maintenance systems by emotional states. To achieve selectivity, such a system would benefit from or even require a computational architecture that integrates emotional state with active maintenance to provide situationally appropriate regulation.

The term *goal* is intended to denote a motivationally-relevant representation that, when actively maintained, constrains or otherwise coordinates the control of cognition and behavior to fulfill the corresponding motivation. Goals are representations that help configure the rest of the overall perceptual-cognitive-behavioral control system. A goal constrains what part of that system is most relevant for further processing. For example, in the Stroop task, the participant's goal (set up by the task instructions) is to report the color of printed words regardless of the semantic content of the words. The semantic content can refer to colors, thereby creating response conflict between the goal (report the color) and a prepotent response (read the word). As used here, goals need not be recognized explicitly as goals, nor need be conscious (cf. Bargh & Chartrand 1999), although can be. Rather, goals direct or guide the focus of attention, and are not usually the object of attention. Goals are an important kind of context information that bias other on-going processing (Braver & Cohen 2000). Multiple goals can be active simultaneously, many more can be activated by retrieval cues (Gollwitzer 1999), and complex or higher-order goals typically require the implementation of subgoals. Such goal hierarchies are very important, but beyond the scope of the current model (see Carver & Scheier 1990; Koechlin, Basso, Pietrini, Panzer, & Grafman 1999).

To a first approximation, most and perhaps all goals can be considered to be associated with approach- or withdrawal-related motivations (for a more nuanced discussion, including the possibility of the same goal having conflicting motivational implications at different levels in a hierarchy, see Carver & Scheier 1990). It is possible to distinguish between what might be termed explicit or pure approach goals (e.g., "take two steps forward") versus implicit or approach-consistent goals in which a pure approach component would be a necessary subgoal (e.g., "oooh, jelly donut... must have", leading to a first subgoal "take two steps forward" followed by "pick up donut" and "ingest donut"). To simplify the discussion we do not elaborate this distinction, although it could be useful in further refinements of the model. For withdrawal-related motivation, the term goal may seem inappropriate, but the intended sense applies equally for approach and withdrawal motivation.

The core argument is that approach and withdrawal emotional states might differentially modulate WM subsystems in order to regulate the strength of approach- and withdrawal-related goal representations held within them. Stronger active representation in working memory should afford greater influence over behavior. There are six key points, each elaborated in a separate section:

1. Approach and withdrawal are two important dimensions of motivation. The motivational implications of on-going interactions with the environment can come to be reflected in approach- and withdrawal-related emotional states.
2. Active goals are maintained in working memory, allowing them to coordinate thought, affect, and behavior by serving as context information, with approach goals in one subsystem and withdrawal goals in another subsystem.
3. Approach-withdrawal states can have selective effects on working memory subsystems in order to selectively regulate the active goals within the different subsystems.
4. Multiple goals can be simultaneously active, even inherently conflicting ones, and so co-exist in some balance. A critical function of approach-

withdrawal emotion is to tip the balance in favor of one or the other class of goals when it is important to do so.
5. Approach and withdrawal goals are incompatible in terms of their regulation by emotion. Physical segregation of active approach-withdrawal goal representations would make a physiological mechanism for their selective regulation more simple.
6. Lateral PFC is a plausible neural and computational substrate for the active maintenance and regulation of goals by emotional state, given (a) lateral PFC involvement in WM, goal-directed behavior, and emotion; (b) hemispheric specialization in PFC for both emotion and WM; and (c) integration of emotion and WM in lateral PFC.

Approach and withdrawal emotion

In general terms, emotions are brief, relatively strong states that are triggered by specific events having significance for the organism (see Ekman & Davidson 1994; Lazarus 1991). The pervasiveness of approach and withdrawal motivation across species (Lima & Dill 1990; Schneirla 1959) forms part of the theoretical basis for postulating approach and withdrawal as two major classes of emotion (Davidson, Ekman, Saron, Senulis, & Friesen 1990; Fox 1991; Lang, Bradley, & Cuthbert 1990). Such emotions are strongly goal-directed.

The events that trigger an emotion can be real and on-going, anticipated, reconstructed from memory, or even the product of fantasy. In Figure 2, these triggering events are denoted collectively as the Situation. When a stimulus or event suggests a threat, the resulting state is unpleasant and withdrawal motivated (e.g., fear, anxiety). If the event is expected to be favorable or rewarding, the resulting state is pleasant and approach motivated (e.g., desire, enthusiasm). Pleasant but post-goal attainment states (e.g., satiation) are not approach related despite positive emotional valence, because they lack goal-directedness (Davidson 1998a). Similarly, some unpleasant states are not goal-directed (e.g., disappointment, sadness) and so are not withdrawal related. This article is concerned only with emotional states that involve pleasant-approach motivation or unpleasant-withdrawal motivation, and is agnostic about emotions that are not goal directed, e.g., contentment, fulfillment, sadness, or disappointment.

Regulation of goals by emotional state

It is impossible for an organism to simultaneously approach and withdraw from something. The incompatibility of approach and withdrawal behavior

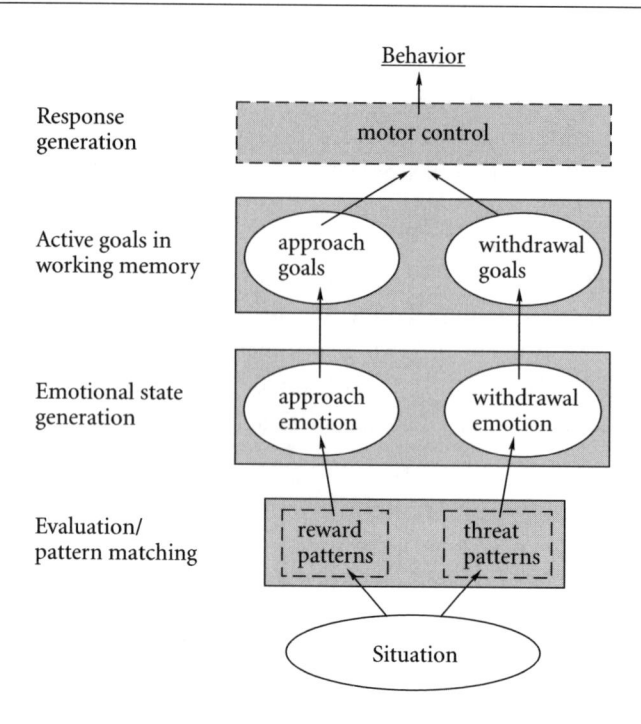

Figure 2. Schematic outline of emotion-related processing stages. These stages are intended only to help illustrate points important for the present argument, rather than describe a general or complete architecture of emotional cognition. The stage most relevant to the proposed architecture is that of active goals in working memory. This stage allows for both active maintenance in attractor states (via recurrent connections), and bottom-up, situation-dependent regulation (via emotional states).

in no way eliminates the potential for motivational conflict: Strong motivations to approach and withdraw can be held simultaneously (Carver & Scheier 1990; Miller 1944). For this reason, a dilemma faced repeatedly in both individual and evolutionary history is: given the current situation, are the advantages to be had from approach behavior greater than those from withdrawal? Once Evaluation processes (Figure 2) settle in favor of one alternative, the motivational conflict is reduced. Cognitive, affective, and motor control should be coordinated and come to reflect and implement the assessment of the course of action that appears better (regardless of whether the assessment is objectively correct). Emotional states are well suited to play a modulatory role that can bring about such prioritization, coordinating multiple systems in parallel. Selectivity would be useful for enhancing some functions but not others, depending on the particular emotional state.

Evaluations of potential rewards and threats in the environment are routinely computed (Figure 2, Evaluation stage). Simple pattern matching or feature detection could suffice at the earliest stages, even operating outside of awareness (LeDoux 1996; Morris, Ohman, & Dolan 1998; Whalen et al. 1998b). If some relevant aspect of the situation is novel, anomalous, or ambiguous (Whalen 1998), it is likely to trigger further processing, including evaluations that are focused, elaborated, and potentially conscious especially as more information is sought and obtained from the environment and associative memory. Given ambiguity, both withdrawal and approach motor programs are primed for subsequent activation. If the outcome of the Evaluation process is that the situation is interpreted as a threat, withdrawal motor programs are activated and approach programs inhibited. The resulting modulation of the brain-plus-body state profile constitutes a withdrawal-motivated emotional state (Figure 2, Emotion Generation stage; motor priming is not illustrated).

In almost any situation, multiple goals are active to varying degrees, and so there is typically some on-going conflict or tension between goals (Figure 2, Active Goals stage). In a withdrawal state, withdrawal goals need greater access to high-level control and approach goals less access. Previously active approach goals should be dampened, whereas withdrawal goals including those activated by the withdrawal program should be strengthened. The strengthening or weakening of goal representations is postulated to bring about adaptive cognitive and behavioral responses by modulating the ability of an actively maintained goal to influence motor control. Similarly, approach states are postulated to prioritize approach goals and dampen withdrawal goals. Although we expect considerable similarity, the symmetry is not perfect. For example, the strength of withdrawal-related motivation falls off more quickly than approach-motivation with increasing distance (Miller 1944). This steeper slope for withdrawal holds quite generally, and strongly suggests two underlying systems (Cacioppo, Gardner, & Berntson 1999). Moreover, there are large individual differences in the strength of threat and reward systems (Carver et al. 2000; Gray 1991; Kagan, Reznick, & Snidman 1988; Sutton & Davidson 1997).

A function of emotional states is to bias the on-going tension between approach and withdrawal classes of goals when the situation is sufficiently critical. Further prioritization of different specific goals within the same motivational class would also be useful, but is beyond the scope of the current model. Many theoretical views concerning the function(s) of the more basic emotions hold that, as almost inherent in the definition of emotion, prioritization occurs in some form (Ekman & Davidson 1994; Gray 1990; Gray 1999b; Lang et al. 1990; Lazarus 1991; Schwarz 1990; Simon 1967). However, there are few empirical investigations. This widely held assumption might be tractable in terms of specific effects of emotional states on working memory.

Representation of goals in working memory

WM is the process for holding and manipulating information actively in mind, and is well suited to hold representations of goals. In the sense of the term goal used here (Braver & Cohen 2000), a hard distinction between goals and other forms of information to be maintained actively is likely a false dichotomy (see also Gallese & Goldman 1998). In Braver and Cohen's (2000) model, PFC actively maintains context information — mental representations that can perform a general biasing function by providing top-down support, e.g., for encoding information from one perceptual dimension rather than another (e.g., in the Stroop task), for task-relevant information in the face of competing distractors (e.g., for the item seen two trials ago in a 2-back task, rather than the item seen either one or three trials previously). Braver and Cohen explicitly point out that goals have this function, and note that other kinds of context information can as well. A WM subsystem dedicated for goal maintenance but not context information is unlikely.

The original model of human WM (Baddeley & Hitch 1974) posited three distinct systems for actively maintaining and manipulating information. Two subsystems provide segregated maintenance of phonological and visuospatial information, with overall coordination by a modality-independent central executive. The central executive component of working memory is specifically conceptualized as being independent of storage modality, being involved in planning and the coordination of action (see Norman & Shallice 1986). A recognized limitation of this influential model concerns the mechanisms that implement the control functions ascribed to the central executive (for discussion, see Baddeley 1996).

The inclusion of context information as a component of WM (Cohen & Servan-Schreiber 1992) suggests a mechanistic way to model how cognitive control might be regulated by bottom-up processes, avoiding the need to posit a central executive (Braver & Cohen 2000; Braver, Cohen, & Servan-Schreiber 1995). Braver and Cohen's theory is instantiated as a gated-attractor (neural network) model. The computationally realized mechanism can a) learn to appropriately select which items need to be maintained using a reward-like mechanism for feedback about performance (modeled on dopamine function); b) hold active for arbitrary periods of time the items that are critical for constraining responses to other events (i.e., the information that acts as contextual constraint on subsequent actions); c) protect such information against interference during the delay period; and d) update such information as needed (Braver & Cohen 2000). The model is neurobiologically plausible, as shown by converging evidence from normal aging, brain imaging, schizophrenia, and amphetamine challenge (Braver 1997), and studies of dopamine and reward prediction (see Schultz, Dayan, & Montague 1997) and dopamine-WM interactions (e.g., Luciana, Depue, Arbisi, & Leon 1992; Sawaguchi & Goldman-Rakic 1994). In the model, transient fluctuations in dopamine signals (which are biologically realistic, modeled on responses to unpredicted reward) provide overall, bottom-up control of network dynamics.

Because other evidence suggests a relationship between dopamine and positive emotion (Ashby, Isen, & Turken 1999; Depue, Luciana, Arbisi, Collins, & Leon 1994; Luciana et al. 1992), it might be possible to incorporate emotional modulation into the Braver and Cohen model. Specifically, neuromodulators might carry information about emotional states, setting attractor dynamics that prioritize some high-level functions over others. Small changes in the neural firing of brainstem neuromodulator nuclei that project diffusely could lead to global, sustained effects on information processing dynamics in cortical networks critical for higher cognition and goal-directed behavior (cf. Hasselmo & Bower 1993; Hobson & Stickgold 1995). To speculate boldly, diffuse-projecting neuromodulators might suffice as a bottom-up mechanism able to selectively regulate cognitive control. Dopamine (Luciana, Collins, & Depue 1998; Luciana et al. 1992), norepinephrine (Arnsten & Goldman-Rakic 1987), serotonin (Luciana et al. 1998), corticosteroids (Lupien, Gillin, & Hauger 1999), and acetylcholine (Furey, Pietrini, & Haxby 2000; Robbins et al. 1997) have been shown to modulate WM performance in human participants. Computational models have suggested a link between dopamine, pleasant emotions, and modulation of higher cognitive functions (Ashby et al. 1999).

Separate representation to facilitate regulation

A physical separation of mechanisms for approach and withdrawal information processing could be beneficial for computational reasons. Different benefits might accrue at each of three stages of approach-withdrawal processing shown in Figure 2: Evaluation, Emotion Generation, and Active Goals.

First, at the Evaluation stage, we posit separate subsystems for the initial processing or pattern matching of approach cues (potential reward) and withdrawal cues (potential threat). Two subsystems are likely to be more accurate and useful than a single combined system that is sensitive only to the difference or relative balance between reward and threat. The reason is that there is an important difference between a high-conflict choice, with high reward but also high threat, and a trivial choice, with low reward and low threat. For a high-conflict choice, gathering more information, and so on, would be important, but would be unimportant and even wasteful for a trivial choice. Consider a 2-dimensional space with an approach dimension orthogonal to a withdrawal dimension, with the strength of motivation going from low to high on each dimension. A high-conflict choice involves high approach and high withdrawal, whereas a trivial choice involves low approach and low withdrawal. Representation as one dimension (a continuum of the approach-withdrawal difference) would not allow an easy recovery of the degree of conflict. Separate initial representations of approach and withdrawal (two dimensional) would allow an extraction of conflict information.

In previous work, we have proposed a hypothesis relating conflict monitoring to cognitive control (Botvinick, Braver, Carter, Barch, & Cohen 1998; Carter et al. 1998). In particular, the anterior cingulate cortex (ACC) is postulated to evaluate the demand for cognitive control by monitoring for the occurrence of conflict in on-going information processing. By conflict, we mean interference or interactions between different information processing pathways. In a series of computer simulation studies, we provide a detailed examination the theoretical consequences of this hypothesis (Botvinick et al. 1998). One of the predictions that arises from such a theoretical position is that the ACC should be engaged whenever two or more incompatible responses are simultaneously activated. Recent neuroimaging studies of cognitive tasks have provided direct empirical support for this prediction (Barch et al. 2001; Barch, Braver, Sabb, & Noll 2000; Botvinick, Nystrom, Fissel, Carter, & Cohen 2001; Braver, Barch, Gray, Molfese, & Snyder 2001; Carter et al. 2000; Casey et al. 2000; MacDonald, Cohen, Stenger, & Carter 2000). In this context, it is interesting that some areas of ACC are related to emotion (Bush, Luu, & Posner 2000; Devinsky, Morrell, & Vogt 1995; Whalen et al. 1998a). A possibility is that ACC might be particularly sensitive to emotional conflict, as much or perhaps even more so than to emotion. Emotional conflict might be ubiquitous in experiments in which participants are asked to voluntarily engage with negatively valenced stimuli or in difficult tasks, which are often subjectively unpleasant and provoke performance anxiety. This novel hypothesis (see also Gray & Braver, in press) has yet to be tested, but if supported could potentially provide a unifying conceptual basis of anterior cingulate function.

To better preserve information about the degree of emotional conflict, the initial evaluation of the benefits of approach and withdrawal should not cancel each other out or otherwise interfere before the two have been computed. Representations of each separately would be more informative than a single representation of the difference (a relative representation). Thus in terms of initial evaluation, approach and withdrawal are more usefully computed as two dimensions, each ranging from low activation to high activation. Considerable evidence suggests two underlying systems (see Cacioppo et al. 1999; Carver et al. 2000; Miller 1944).

Splitting a network by reducing the connections between subsystems reduces interference between computationally incompatible functions that process the same input. Such splitting can yield a measurable computational advantage (Rueckl et al. 1989). For example, in computing *where* something is and computing *what* something is from visual input, the information critical to one computation is irrelevant to the other. The key idea, supported by the simulations, is that splitting a network removes connections that can only cause interference – those that cannot contribute to performing the computation needed, but could contribute irrelevant information. These considerations suggest that implementing two subsystems for the extraction of approach and withdrawal information would be more efficient computationally. The what-where distinction is found not only in dorsal versus ventral visual streams (Ungerleider & Mishkin 1982), but is also maintained in WM (Ungerleider, Courtney, & Haxby 1998).

Second, segregation of approach-withdrawal processing would also be useful during an Emotion Generation stage (Figure 2) because it would permit reciprocal inhibition between two systems. Reciprocal inhibition provides more flexibility and precision in the degree of control that a system can achieve. Reciprocal inhibition necessitates having more than one subsystem. In principle, one subsystem that computed a single dimension (from high approach to neutral to high withdrawal) cannot provide as much flexibility and precision as two subsystems that are mutually inhibitory. These are inherent benefits of reciprocal inhibition in control systems, and there is evidence for reciprocal inhibition between approach and withdrawal emotion subsystems (Lang et al. 1990; Solomon & Corbit 1974).

Third, and most critically, separate representation of approach and withdrawal classes at the Active Goals stage (Figure 2) would simplify the selective regulation of active goals by emotional states. The physiological mechanism for regulation could be simpler to implement given representations separated physically on the basis of motivational class. Non-specific modulation would be sufficient to influence the entire class. Having systems that are enmeshed physically would require considerable specificity and therefore complexity in the regulatory mechanism. The reason is that, at the stage of active maintenance, there is not likely to be a functional distinction between approach or withdrawal goals – they are both simply information that has to be maintained actively. WM performs a general holding function, effectively blind to its own contents; response generation subsystems are posited to operate differentially depending on the contents of WM. Because the function of WM is the same regardless of the functional implications of the contents, a mechanism for the regulation of that content would be complex to implement if it depended on the specific content. Physical segregation is likely a simpler (and therefore more robust) mechanism for selective, bottom-up regulation on the basis of the motivational class of the emotion (approach, withdrawal). Complex mechanisms are probably possible, but a compelling reason would be needed to justify the additional physiological complexity and greater proneness to errors that this would likely entail.

To recap this section of the argument, segregation of approach-withdrawal processing would be useful at three stages of processing (Figure 2). Computational efficiency would be enhanced in Evaluation stages, because two orthogonal dimensions can carry more information about conflict. Control would be enhanced in the Emotion Generation stage, because reciprocal inhibition between two subsystems is more flexible and precise than a single system acting alone. These two kinds of segregation are likely to be reflected in the Active Goals stage. Most critically, approach and withdrawal goals are strongly incompatible in terms of regulation by emotional state, given the incompatibility of approach and withdrawal behavior. When approach goals are prioritized, withdrawal goals should be dampened, and vice versa. Which class of goals is prioritized at any one time should be situation dependent, and should be amenable to flexible updating. These three considerations provide a theoretical basis for expecting a physically separate maintenance of approach versus withdrawal representations of active goals.

Lateral prefrontal cortex as a substrate

The aim of this section is to suggest on empirical grounds that hemispheric specialization in PFC provides a suitable, two-part neural substrate for the active representation and regulation of goals. Although hemispheric specialization is not the only possible way to achieve physical separation between subsystems for either emotion or WM, to our knowledge it is the one that is the most consistent with constraints provided by neurobiology. This section therefore reviews evidence for hemispheric specialization of emotion and WM in PFC.

In humans, lateral PFC is critical for cognitive control. These functions include planning, reasoning, voluntary action, and decision making – all of which involve goal directed activity. PFC is large and many functions have been proposed for all or part of it: working memory (Goldman-Rakic 1987; Smith & Jonides 1999), context and cognitive control (Braver & Cohen 2000; Cohen & Servan-Schreiber 1992), the cross-temporal organization of behavior (Fuster 1997), the voluntary control of behavior (Passingham 1993), and aspects of personal and social decision making (Damasio 1994; Tucker, Luu, & Pribram 1995). As shown by neuroimaging studies in humans (see Braver et al. 1997; D'Esposito et al. 1998; Smith & Jonides 1999), critical areas for WM include dorsal PFC (Brodmann's Areas [BA] 46, 9) and ventral PFC (BA 44, 45, 47).

Lateralization of experienced emotion. Diverse evidence suggests a prefrontal asymmetry related to subjectively experienced approach and withdrawal emotion (see Davidson 1995; Fox 1991; Gray, in press). Patients with damage to left PFC more easily become depressed, whereas those with right damage tend to display inappropriately indifferent or even positive affect (Robinson, Kubos, Starr, Rao, & Price 1984). As shown in normal participants by electroencephalogram (EEG) recordings, relatively greater left prefrontal activity is associated with approach states and traits; relatively greater right activity is associated with withdrawal states and traits. Induced (state) changes are deflections away from a baseline, trait-like asymmetry, which is stable within individuals yet quite variable across individuals (Sutton & Davidson 1997; Tomarken, Davidson, Wheeler, & Doss 1992). Phasic asymmetry from induced emotion is superimposed upon large individual differences in the baseline degree of asymmetry. The anterior asymmetry is found for induced emotional states not only in adults but also in neonates, 10 month olds, and non-human primates. A functional neuroimaging study specifically tested for the emotion asymmetry using fMRI and controlled for arousal (Canli, Desmond, Zhao, Glover, & Gabrieli 1998). The asymmetry was present as shown by the numbers of activation clusters and the extent of activation.

The evidence suggesting an asymmetry is generally reliable. However, there are also exceptions (see Gray, in press; Heller & Nitschke 1998), including findings of no asymmetry (Hagemann, Nauman, Becker, Maier, & Bartussek 1998; Reid, Duke, & Allen 1998) or asymmetries in the opposite direction (Chua, Krams, Toni, Passingham, & Dolan 1999; Shin et al. 1997). Conceptual and methodological considerations are likely to be important (Davidson 1998b), as well as moderating factors (Heller & Nitschke 1998; Reid et al. 1998) and greater understanding of what the asymmetry reflects mechanistically (Gray 2002; Gray, in press; Tomarken & Keener 1998).

Lateralization of working memory. Some WM subsystems are lateralized in PFC. One review of human WM concluded that spatial WM is more right lateralized and verbal WM left lateralized (Smith & Jonides 1997): "different neural circuits mediate verbal, spatial, and object working memory, with spatial memory being right lateralized and verbal ... memory typically being left lateralized. The difference in lateralization is likely quantitative rather than qualitative" (p. 38). More specifically, ventral PFC dissociates by content, with verbal left and spatial right, whereas dorsal PFC typically activates bilaterally and shows only weak evidence of dissociating by content (D'Esposito et al. 1998; Smith & Jonides 1999). It is possible that PFC lateralization exists for other information processing dimensions as well.

Interactions of emotion and working memory. Hemispheric specialization for both emotion and WM separately is, by itself, hardly evidence for an interaction. However, considerable indirect evidence supports an interaction (see Heller 1990; Heller & Nitschke 1997). There are only two functional neuroimaging studies we are aware of, and both suggest that interactions might occur in areas critical for WM. Induced emotional states modulated the degree to which left PFC was activated by a verbal fluency task (Baker, Frith, & Dolan 1997). In an fMRI study described above (Gray et al. 2002) activity in lateral PFC depended conjointly on the task stimulus and the induced emotion, with the crossover pattern in activity related to behavioral performance providing strong evidence.

Summary

Approach and withdrawal emotional states might differentially modulate WM subsystems in order to differentially prioritize representations of approach and withdrawal goals, strengthening or weakening their influence over cognition and behavior. The neural system for the active maintenance and manipulation of information (WM) meets the computational requirements for both the representation of active goals and selective regulation according to the motivational class (approach, withdrawal) of the emotional states. Lateralization of goal representations would allow a separate maintenance of approach and withdrawal goals in WM subsystems, and therefore allow a relatively simple (bottom-up) regulatory mechanism to selectively prioritize one class of goals over the other in a situationally appropriate manner.

How might the goal-regulation architecture explain the evidence for selectivity?

In this final section we speculate on how the proposed goal-regulation architecture could account for the empirical data with which this chapter began: the double dissociation between verbal and nonverbal n-back task performance revealed by induced emotion (Gray 2001) and the related effect in dorsolateral PFC brain activity (Gray et al. 2002). (Note: in this discussion, nonverbal refers only to spatial and face WM, not object WM or other modalities.) Considerably more data is needed for any interpretation of these first findings to be fully satisfactory. However, a consideration of several possibilities suggests testable hypotheses.

A conceptual comparison between the n-back task and the goal-regulation architecture is facilitated by describing both in terms of the active maintenance of context information, that is, information that constrains or otherwise biases on-going processing and behavior (Braver & Cohen 2000). In the n-back task, to comply with the instructions on a given trial, participants have to extract the relevant stimulus-based information (verbal, nonverbal) from the current percept, compare it against stimulus information held in mind from a specific previous trial, report a match or mismatch, and then update the set of stimulus items held in mind in preparation for the next trial. In the n-back task, a verbal or nonverbal stimulus serves as context information; in the goal-regulation architecture, an approach or withdrawal goal serves as context information.

In the n-back task, emotional states did not simply enhance or impair the ability to comply with task instructions, but rather had a selective effect depending on the stimulus type. Similarly, in the goal-regulation architecture, an overall or general effect (e.g., on the ability to implement any goal) would probably be deleterious. What is needed is a selective enhancement and impairment of goals depending on their motivational class (approach, withdrawal). This suggests some parallel between stimulus type in the n-back task and motivational class of goals in the goal-regulation architecture. Specifically, we posit that there exist associations between verbal and approach-related context information, and between nonverbal and withdrawal-related context information. One kind of association we consider is that of a common physiological substrate for active maintenance that is specialized by hemisphere.

In this view, approach-related states improve verbal n-back task performance because a) approach-related emotion enhances the function of a left-lateralized WM subsystem that handles the maintenance of approach-goals; and b) verbal WM depends more on that same subsystem for the active maintenance of verbal stimulus information. Withdrawal states should correspondingly impair verbal WM for dampening that subsystem (i.e., the one that is left-lateralized) in order to dampen approach goals. In contrast, to regulate withdrawal goals, approach states should impair the function of a right-lateralized substrate for the active maintenance of nonverbal information whereas withdrawal states should enhance it. That is, the association we posit is physiological: a shared substrate for the active maintenance of context information.

The hypothesis as presented so far is agnostic about whether verbal WM should be associated with approach goals and nonverbal WM with withdrawal goals. That is, the hypothesis could be the same even if lateralization was the opposite of observed (verbal right lateralized, nonverbal left lateralized). The assumption is that there are two lateralized subsystems (left, right) which support four kinds of information (approach and withdrawal goals, verbal and nonverbal information). Thus there are two possible associations: approach-verbal and withdrawal-nonverbal, or approach-nonverbal and withdrawal-verbal. The empirical pattern (left lateralization of both verbal processing and approach emotion) could be accidental.

Nonetheless, meaningful associations are also possible and potentially interesting. These would probably take the form of weak biases on computational efficiency. Having some component functions be co-lateralized so that they can be regulated by emotional states could provide a slight advantage, a positive bias in favor of such an architecture. Several such weak biases acting together could give rise to an overall and perhaps even substantial computational advantage. This argument rests on relative computational advantage, rather than computational necessity: There are considerable individual differences in the degree of lateralization, and these differences are not catastrophic.

Sustained attention might be more critical in withdrawal-related than approach-related states to facilitate temporally extended processing of a particular problem or potential threat. Nearly all creatures face the threat of predation (Lima & Dill 1990). A failure of sustained attention or vigilance in the context of a predator could be disastrous. Although sustained attention would be useful in approach-related states, it is unlikely to be as critical for approach as it is for withdrawal states. Sustained attention and attentional orienting are relatively right lateralized (Cabeza & Nyberg 2000; Pardo et al. 1991). Some evidence suggests an enhancement of sustained attention in withdrawal states:

Negative moods promote more systematic processing, whereas positive moods promote heuristic processing (see Bless & Schwarz 1999). Systematic processing probably requires more sustained attention to a problem than heuristic processing requires.

Fine versus gross movement control could be more important in approach versus withdrawal states, respectively, and there is evidence for left lateralization of fine motor control (e.g., left hemisphere control of the right hand Hellige 1993). Fine control would be more important in approach (e.g., precise grasping), whereas coordination of large muscles groups would be more critical for escape (e.g., running). Fine motor control is critical for speech production, which is one of the few functions to be completely left lateralized in almost all people (Hellige 1993).

Finally, the action of grasping an object is approach motivated. In humans, viewing objects being grasped versus viewing objects alone activates left but not right PFC (inferior frontal gyrus, BA 45) (Rizzolatti et al. 1996). In non-human primates, neurophysiological studies of grasping have revealed a class of PFC neurons, called mirror neurons, that respond to specific kinds of grasping actions regardless of whether the actions are observed or executed (Gallese & Goldman 1998). These cells are located in area F5, an analog of Broca's area in humans, crucial for language production.

In sum, a number of weak biases acting collectively could produce an overall computational advantage for co-lateralization of cognitive control functions to enable selective regulation by approach-withdrawal states. These extrapolations from the behavioral and fMRI data (Gray 2001; Gray et al. 2002) are speculative but, in principle, are empirically testable in terms of explicit computational models (e.g., Braver & Cohen 2000).

Summary

Evidence suggests that an integration of emotional state information with cognitive control can occur and comes to be represented in lateral PFC. This claim rests on evidence for selective effects of induced emotion on behavioral performance and brain activity (Gray 2001; Gray et al. 2002). How such integration comes about has not been definitively shown, although available evidence is consistent with a hemispheric basis. An integration of emotion and cognition might play an important computational role in human self-regulation. The active maintenance of goals is likely to be subserved by working memory systems. The regulation of active goals could be subserved in part by emotional states.

A mechanism for integration would allow for selective regulation that depends on emotional state, which in turn depends on appraisals or evaluations of the situation. Approach-withdrawal states could differentially modulate working memory subsystems in order to selectively prioritize entire classes of goals in a manner sensitive to on-going events. For this reason, architectures of emotional cognition that include integration could be adaptive for allowing the prioritization of goals dynamically in response to changing conditions.

Author Note

The preparation of this article was supported by a grant from the National Science Foundation, BCS 0001908, and the McDonnell Center for Higher Brain Function, Washington University. We thank Dr.'s Stephen M. Kosslyn, Daniel Simons, Richard J. McNally, Michelle Leichtman, and Ken Nakayama for discussion and comments on a previous draft.

References

Arnsten, A. F. T., & Goldman-Rakic, P. S. (1987). Noradrenergic mechanisms in age-related cognitive decline. *Journal of Neural Transmission, 24*, 317–324.

Ashby, F. G., Isen, A. M., & Turken, A. U. (1999). A neuropsychological theory of positive affect and its influence on cognition. *Psychological Review, 106*, 529–550.

Baddeley, A. (1996). Exploring the central executive. *Quarterly Journal of Experimental Psychology, 49*(A), 5–28.

Baddeley, A., & Hitch, G. (1974). Working memory. In G. H. Bower (Ed.), *The psychology of learning and motivation* (Vol. 8, pp. 47–89). New York: Academic Press.

Baker, S. C., Frith, C. D., & Dolan, R. J. (1997). The interaction between mood and cognitive function studied with PET. *Psychological Medicine, 27*(3), 565–578.

Banich, M. T. (1997). *Neuropsychology.* Boston: Houghton Mifflin.

Barch, D. M., Braver, T. S., Akbudak, E., Conturo, T., Ollinger, J., & Snyder, A. V. (2001). Anterior cingulate cortex and response conflict: Effects of response modality and processing domain. *Cerebral Cortex, 11*, 837–848.

Barch, D. M., Braver, T. S., Sabb, F. W., & Noll, D. C. (2000). The anterior cingulate cortex and response competition: Evidence from an fMRI study of overt verb generation. *Journal of Cognitive Neuroscience, 12*, 298–305.

Bargh, J. A., & Chartrand, T. L. (1999). The unbearable automaticity of being. *American Psychologist, 54*(7), 462–479.

Bartolic, E. I., Basso, M. R., Schefft, B. K., Glauser, T., & Titanic-Schefft, M. (1999). Effects of experimentally-induced emotional states on frontal lobe cognitive task performance. *Neuropsychologia, 37*, 677–683.

Bechara, A., Damasio, A. R., Damasio, H., & Anderson, H. W. (1994). Insensitivity to future consequences following damage to human prefrontal cortex. *Cognition, 50*, 7–15.
Bless, H., & Schwarz, N. (1999). Sufficient and necessary conditions in dual-process models: The case of mood and information processing. In S. Chaiken & Y. Trope (Eds.), *Dual-process theories in social psychology* (pp. 423–440). New York: Guilford.
Botvinick, M. M., Braver, T. S., Barch, D. M., Carter, C. S., & Cohen, J. C. (2001). Conflict monitoring and cognitive control. *Psychological Review, 108*, 624–652.
Botvinick, M. M., Nystrom, L., Fissel, K., Carter, C. S., & Cohen, J. D. (1999). Conflict monitoring versus selection-for-action in anterior cingulate cortex. *Nature, 402*(6758), 179–181.
Braver, T. S. (1997). *Mechanisms of cognitive control: A neurocomputational model.* Unpublished Ph.D. dissertation, Carnegie Mellon University, Pittsburg, PA.
Braver, T. S., Barch, D. M., Gray, J. R., Molfese, D. L., & Snyder, A. (2001). Anterior cingulate cortex and response conflict: Effects of frequency, inhibition, and errors. *Cerebral Cortex, 11*, 825–836.
Braver, T. S., & Cohen, J. D. (2000). On the control of control: The role of dopamine in regulating prefrontal function and working memory. In S. Monsell & J. Driver (Eds.), *Control of cognitive processes: Attention and Performance XVIII* (pp. 713–737). Cambridge, MA: MIT Press.
Braver, T. S., Cohen, J. D., Nystrom, L. E., Jonides, J., Smith, E. E., & Noll, D. C. (1997). A parametric study of prefrontal cortex involvement in human working memory. *Neuroimage, 5*, 49–62.
Braver, T. S., Cohen, J. D., & Servan-Schreiber, D. (1995). A computational model of prefrontal cortex function. In D. S. Touretzky, G. Tesauro, & T. K. Leen (Eds.), *Advances in neural information processing systems* (Vol. 7, pp. 141–148). Cambridge, MA: MIT Press.
Bush, G., Luu, P., & Posner, M. I. (2000). Cognitive and emotional influences in anterior cingulate. *Trends in Cognitive Sciences, 4*, 215–222.
Cabeza, R., & Nyberg, L. (2000). Imaging cognition II: An empirical review of 275 PET and fMRI studies. *Journal of Cognitive Neuroscience, 12*, 1–47.
Cacioppo, J. T., Gardner, W. L., & Berntson, G. G. (1999). The affect system has parallel and integrative processing components: Form follows function. *Journal of Personality and Social Psychology, 76*, 839–855.
Canli, T., Desmond, J. E., Zhao, Z., Glover, G., & Gabrieli, J. D. (1998). Hemispheric asymmetry for emotional stimuli detected with fMRI. *Neuroreport, 9*(14), 3233–3239.
Carter, C. S., Braver, T. S., Barch, D. M., Botvinick, M. M., Noll, D., & Cohen, J. D. (1998). Anterior cingulate cortex, error detection, and the online monitoring of performance. *Science, 280*(5364), 747–749.
Carter, C. S., Macdonald, A. M., Botvinick, M., Ross, L. L., Stenger, A., Noll, D., & Cohen, J. D. (2000). Parsing executive processes: Strategic versus evaluative functions of the anterior cingulate cortex. *Proceedings of the National Academy of Sciences, USA, 97*, 1944–1948.
Carver, C. S., & Scheier, M. F. (1990). Origins and functions of positive and negative affect: A control-process view. *Psychological Review, 97*(1), 19–35.

Carver, C. S., Sutton, S. K., & Scheier, M. F. (2000). Action, emotion, and personality: Emerging conceptual integration. *Personality and Social Psychology Bulletin, 26*, 741–751.

Casey, B. J., Thomas, K. M., Welsh, T. F., Badgaiyan, R., Eccard, C. H., Jennings, J. R., & Crone, E. A. (2000). Dissociation of response conflict, attentional selection, and expectancy with functional magnetic resonance imaging (fMRI). *Proceedings of the National Academy of Sciences, 97*(15), 8728–8733.

Chua, P., Krams, M., Toni, I., Passingham, R., & Dolan, R. (1999). A functional anatomy of anticipatory anxiety. *Neuroimage, 9*, 563–571.

Cohen, J. D., & Servan-Schreiber, D. (1992). Context, cortex, and dopamine: A connectionist approach to behavior and biology in schizophrenia. *Psychological Review, 99*, 45–77.

D'Esposito, M., Aguirre, G. K., Zarahn, E., Ballard, D., Shin, R. K., & Lease, J. (1998). Functional MRI studies of spatial and nonspatial working memory. *Brain Research Cognitive Brain Research, 7*(1), 1–13.

Damasio, A. R. (1994). *Descartes' error*. New York: Grosset/Putnam.

Davidson, R. J. (1995). Cerebral asymmetry, emotion, and affective style. In R. J. Davidson & K. H. Hugdahl (Eds.), *Brain asymmetry* (pp. 361–387). Cambridge, MA: MIT Press.

Davidson, R. J. (1998a). Affective style and affective disorders: Perspectives from affective neuroscience. *Cognition and Emotion, 12*, 307–330.

Davidson, R. J. (1998b). Anterior electrophysiological asymmetries, emotion, and depression: conceptual and methodological conundrums. *Psychophysiology, 35*(5), 607–614.

Davidson, R. J., Ekman, P., Saron, C. D., Senulis, J. A., & Friesen, W. V. (1990). Approach/withdrawal and cerebral asymmetry: Emotional expression and brain physiology: I. *Journal of Personality and Social Psychology, 58*, 330–341.

Depue, R. A., Luciana, M., Arbisi, P., Collins, P., & Leon, A. (1994). Dopamine and the structure of personality: Relation of agonist-induced dopamine activity to positive emotionality. *Journal of Personality and Social Psychology, 67*, 485–498.

Devinsky, O., Morrell, M. J., & Vogt, B. (1995). Contributions of anterior cingulate cortex to behavior. *Brain, 118*, 279–306.

Ekman, P., & Davidson, R. J. (Eds.). (1994). *The nature of emotion*. New York: Oxford.

Engle, R. W., Kane, M. J., & Tuholski, S. W. (1999). Individual differences in working memory capacity and what they tell us about controlled attention, general fluid intelligence, and functions of the prefrontal cortex. In A. Miyake & P. Shah (Eds.), *Models of working memory* (pp. 102–134). New York: Cambridge University Press.

Fox, N. A. (1991). If it's not left, it's right: Electroencephalographic asymmetry and the development of emotion. *American Psychologist, 46*, 863–872.

Furey, M. L., Pietrini, P., & Haxby, J. V. (2000). Cholinergic enhancement and increased selectivity of perceptual processing during working memory. *Science, 290*, 2315–2319.

Fuster, J. (1997). *The prefrontal cortex*. (3rd ed.). New York: Lippincott-Raven.

Gallese, V., & Goldman, A. (1998). Mirror neurons and the simulation theory of mind-reading. *Trends in Cognitive Sciences, 2*, 493–501.

Goldman-Rakic, P. S. (1987). Circuitry of primate prefrontal cortex and regulation of behavior by representational memory. In V. B. Mountcastle, F. Plum, & S. R. Geiger (Eds.), *Handbook of physiology* (Vol. 1, Sec. 1, pp. 373–417). New York: Oxford.

Gollwitzer, P. M. (1999). Implementation intentions: Strong effects of simple plans. *American Psychologist, 54*(7), 493–503.

Gray, J. A. (1990). Brain systems that mediate both emotion and cognition. *Cognition and Emotion, 4*(2), 269–288.

Gray, J. A. (1991). Neural systems, emotion, and personality. In J. Madden (Ed.), *Neurobiology of learning, emotion, and affect*. New York: Raven Press.

Gray, J. R. (1999-a). *Emotional modulation of working memory*. Unpublished Ph. D. dissertation, Harvard University, Cambridge, MA.

Gray, J. R. (1999-b). A bias toward short-term thinking in threat-related negative emotional states. *Personality and Social Psychology Bulletin, 25*, 65–75.

Gray, J. R. (2001). Emotional modulation of cognitive control: Approach-withdrawal states double-dissociate spatial from verbal two-back task performance. *Journal of Experimental Psychology: General, 130*, 436–452.

Gray, J. R. (2002). Frontal brain asymmetries in emotion may not be purely emotional: Behavioral evidence for verbal activation in anxious apprehension. *Manuscript submitted for publication.*

Gray, J. R. (in press). Does a prosocial-selfish distinction help explain the biological affects? Comment on Buck (1999). *Psychological Review.*

Gray, J. R., & Braver, T. S. (in press). Personality predicts working memory related activation in the caudal anterior cingulate cortex. *Cognitive, Affective, and Behavioral Neuroscience.*

Gray, J. R., Braver, T. S., & Raichle, M. E. (2002). Integration of emotion and cognition in the lateral prefrontal cortex. *Proceedings of the National Academy of Sciences USA, 99*, 4115–4120.

Hagemann, D., Nauman, E., Becker, G., Maier, S., & Bartussek, D. (1998). Frontal brain asymmetry and affective style: A conceptual replication. *Psychophysiology, 35*, 372–388.

Hasselmo, M. E., & Bower, J. M. (1993). Acetylcholine and memory. *Trends in Neurosciences, 16*, 218–222.

Heller, W. (1990). The neuropsychology of emotion: Developmental patterns and implications for psychopathology. In N. Stein, B. L. Leventhal, & T. Trabasso (Eds.), *Psychological and biological approaches to emotion* (pp. 167–211). Hillsdale, NJ: Erlbaum.

Heller, W., & Nitschke, J. B. (1997). Regional brain activity in emotion: A framework for understanding cognition in depression. *Cognition and Emotion, 11*, 637–661.

Heller, W., & Nitschke, J. B. (1998). The puzzle of regional brain activity in depression and anxiety: The importance of subtypes and comorbidity. *Cognition and Emotion, 12*, 421–447.

Hellige, J. B. (1993). *Hemispheric asymmetry*. Cambridge, MA: Harvard University Press.

Hobson, J. A., & Stickgold, R. (1995). The conscious state paradigm: A neurocognitive approach to waking, sleeping, and dreaming. In M. S. Gazzaniga (Ed.), *The cognitive neurosciences* (pp. 1373–1389). Cambridge, MA: MIT Press.

Kagan, J., Reznick, J. S., & Snidman, N. (1988). Biological bases of childhood shyness. *Science, 240*, 167–171.

Kaufman, O., Howard III, M., Kawasaki, H., Damasio, H., Granner, M., & Adolphs, R. (2001, March 25–27). *Lateralized processing of pleasant and unpleasant emotions from single-unit recordings in human prefrontal cortex and amygdala.* Paper presented at the 8th Annual Meeting of the Cognitive Neuroscience Society, New York.

Koechlin, E., Basso, G., Pietrini, P., Panzer, S., & Grafman, J. (1999). The role of the anterior prefrontal cortex in human cognition. *Nature, 399,* 148–151.

Lang, P. J. (1995). The emotion probe: Studies of motivation and attention. *American Psychologist, 50*(5), 372–385.

Lang, P. J., Bradley, M. M., & Cuthbert, B. N. (1990). Emotion, attention and the startle reflex. *Psychological Review, 97,* 377–398.

Lazarus, R. S. (1991). *Emotion and adaptation.* New York: Oxford.

LeDoux, J. E. (1996). *The emotional brain.* New York: Simon and Schuster.

Lima, S. L., & Dill, L. M. (1990). Behavioral decisions made under risk of predation: A review and prospectus. *Canadian Journal of Zoology, 68,* 619–640.

Liotti, M., & Tucker, D. M. (1995). Emotion in asymmetric corticolimbic networks. In R. J. Davidson & K. H. Hugdahl (Eds.), *Brain asymmetry* (pp. 389–423). Cambridge, MA: MIT Press.

Luciana, M., Collins, P. F., & Depue, R. A. (1998). Opposing roles for dopamine and serotonin in the modulation of human spatial working memory functions. *Cerebral Cortex, 8*(3), 218–226.

Luciana, M., Depue, R. A., Arbisi, P., & Leon, A. (1992). Facilitation of working memory in humans by a D_2 dopamine receptor agonist. *Journal of Cognitive Neuroscience, 4*(1), 58–68.

Lupien, S. J., Gillin, C. J., & Hauger, R. L. (1999). Working memory is more sensitive than declarative memory to acute effects of corticosteroids: A dose-response study in humans. *Behavioral Neuroscience, 113*(3), 420–430.

Luu, P., Collins, P., & Tucker, D. M. (2000). Mood, personality, and self-monitoring: negative affect and emotionality in relation to frontal lobe mechanisms of error monitoring. *Journal of Experimental Psychology: General, 129,* 43–60.

MacDonald, A. W., Cohen, J. D., Stenger, V. A., & Carter, C. S. (2000). Dissociating the role of the dorsolateral prefrontal cortex and anterior cingulate cortex in cognitive control. *Science, 288,* 1835–1838.

Miller, N. E. (1944). Experimental studies of conflict. In J. McV. Hunt (Ed.), *Personality and the behavior disorders* (Vol. 1, pp. 431–465). New York: Ronald.

Moore, S. C., & Oaksford, M. R. (in press). Some long-term effects of emotion on cognition. *British Journal of Psychology.*

Morris, J. S., Ohman, A., & Dolan, R. J. (1998). Conscious and unconscious emotional learning in the human amygdala. *Nature, 393,* 467–470.

Murphy, F. C., & Lawrence, A. D. (2001, March 25–27). *A role for frontal asymmetry in positive and negative emotion? A view from functional neuroimaging.* Paper presented at the 8th Annual Meeting of the Cognitive Neuroscience Society, New York.

Norman, D. A., & Shallice, T. (1986). Attention to action: Willed and automatic control of behavior. In G. E. Schwartz & D. Shapiro (Eds.), *Consciousness and self-regulation* (Vol. 4, pp. 1–18). New York: Plenum.

O'Reilly, R. C., Braver, T. S., & Cohen, J. D. (1999). A biologically based computational model of working memory. In A. Miyake & P. Shah (Eds.), *Models of working memory: Mechanisms of active maintenance and executive control.* New York: Cambridge University Press.

Pardo, J. V., Fox, P. T., & Raichle, M. E. (1991). Localization of a human system for sustained attention by positron emission tomography. *Nature, 349,* 61–64.

Passingham, R. (1993). *The frontal lobes and voluntary action.* New York: Oxford.

Posner, M. I., & Snyder, C. R. R. (1975). Attention and cognitive control. In R. L. Solso (Ed.), *Information processing and cognition* (pp. 55–85). Hillsdale, N.J.: Erlbaum.

Reid, S. A., Duke, L. M., & Allen, J. J. B. (1998). Resting frontal electroencephalographic asymmetry in depression: Inconsistencies suggest the need to identify mediating factors. *Psychophysiology, 35,* 389–404.

Rizzolatti, G., Fadiga, L., Matelli, M., Bettinardi, V., Paulesu, E., Perani, D., & Fazio, F. (1996). Localization of grasp representations in humans by PET: 1. Observation versus execution. *Experimental Brain Research, 111*(2), 246–252.

Robbins, T. W., Semple, J., Kumar, R., Truman, M. I., Shorter, J., Ferraro, A., Fox, B., McKay, G., & Matthews, K. (1997). Effects of scopolamine on delayed-matching-to-sample and paired associates tests of visual memory and learning in human subjects: comparison with diazepam and implications for dementia. *Psychopharmacology (Berl), 134*(1), 95–106.

Robinson, R. G., Kubos, K. L., Starr, L. B., Rao, K., & Price, T. R. (1984). Mood disorders in stroke patients. Importance of location of lesion. *Brain, 107,* 81–93.

Rueckl, J. G., Cave, K. R., & Kosslyn, S. M. (1989). Why are "what" and "where" processed by separate cortical visual systems? A computational investigation. *Journal of Cognitive Neuroscience, 1*(2), 171–186.

Sawaguchi, T., & Goldman-Rakic, P. S. (1994). The role of D1-dopamine receptor in working memory: Local injections of dopamine antagonists into the prefrontal cortex of rhesus monkeys performing an oculomotor delayed-response task. *Journal of Neurophysiology, 71*(2), 515–528.

Schneirla, T. C. (1959). An evolutionary and developmental theory of biphasic processes underlying approach and withdrawal. In M. R. Jones (Ed.), *Nebraska symposium on motivation: 1959* (pp. 1–42). Lincoln, NB: University of Nebraska Press.

Schultz, W., Dayan, P., & Montague, P. R. (1997). A neural substrate of prediction and reward. *Science, 275,* 1593–1599.

Schwarz, N. (1990). Happy but mindless? Mood effects on problem solving and persuasion. In R. M. Sorrentino & E. T. Higgins (Eds.), *Handbook of motivation* (Vol. 2, pp. 527–561). New York: Guilford.

Shin, L. M., Kosslyn, S. M., McNally, R. J., Alpert, N. M., Thompson, W. L., Rauch, S. L., Macklin, M. L., & Pitman, R. K. (1997). Visual imagery and perception in post-traumatic stress disorder. A positron emission tomographic investigation. *Archives of General Psychiatry, 54,* 233–241.

Simon, H. A. (1967). Motivational and emotional controls of cognition. *Psychological Review, 74,* 29–39.

Simpson, J. R., Drevets, W. C., Snyder, A. Z., Gusnard, D. A., & Raichle, M. E. (2001a). Emotion-induced changes in human medial prefrontal cortex: II. During anticipatory anxiety. *Proceedings of the National Academy of Science USA, 98,* 688–693.

Simpson, J. R., Snyder, A. Z., Gusnard, D. A., & Raichle, M. E. (2001b). Emotion-induced changes in human medial prefrontal cortex: I. During cognitive task performance. *Proceedings of the National Academy of Science USA, 98,* 683–687.

Smith, E. E., & Jonides, J. (1997). Working memory: A view from neuroimaging. *Cognitive Psychology, 33,* 5–42.

Smith, E. E., & Jonides, J. (1999). Storage and executive processes in the frontal lobes. *Science, 283,* 1657–1661.

Solomon, R. L., & Corbit, J. D. (1974). An opponent-process theory of motivation: I. Temporal dynamics of affect. *Psychological Review, 81,* 119–145.

Sternberg, S. (1969). The discovery of processing stages: Extensions of Donders' method. In W. G. Koster (Ed.), *Attention and performance II*. Amsterdam: North-Holland.

Sutton, S. K., & Davidson, R. J. (1997). Prefrontal brain asymmetry: A biological substrate of the behavioral approach and inhibition systems. *Psychological Science, 8,* 204–210.

Tomarken, A. J., Davidson, R. J., Wheeler, R. E., & Doss, R. C. (1992). Individual differences in anterior brain asymmetry and fundamental dimensions of emotion. *Journal of Personality and Social Psychology, 62,* 676–687.

Tomarken, A. J., & Keener, A. D. (1998). Frontal brain asymmetry and depression: A self-regulatory perspective. *Cognition and Emotion, 12,* 387–420.

Tucker, D. M., Luu, P., & Pribram, K. H. (1995). Social and emotional self-regulation. In Grafman, Holyoak, & Boller (Eds.), *Structure and functions of the human prefrontal cortex* (pp. 213–239). New York: New York Academy of Sciences.

Ungerleider, L. G., Courtney, S. M., & Haxby, J. V. (1998). A neural system for human visual working memory. *Proceedings of the National Academy of Science USA, 95*(3), 883–890.

Ungerleider, L. G., & Mishkin, M. (1982). Two cortical visual systems. In D. J. Ingle, M. A. Goodale, & R. J. W. Mansfield (Eds.), *Analysis of visual behavior* (pp. 549–586). Cambridge, MA: MIT Press.

Whalen, P. J. (1998). Fear, vigilance, and ambiguity: Initial neuroimaging studies of the human amygdala. *Current Directions In Psychological Science, 7,* 177–188.

Whalen, P. J., Bush, G., McNally, R. J., Wilhelm, S., McInerney, S. C., Jenike, M. A., & Rauch, S. L. (1998a). The emotional counting Stroop paradigm: a functional magnetic resonance imaging probe of the anterior cingulate affective division. *Biological Psychiatry, 44,* 1219–1228.

Whalen, P. J., Rauch, S. L., Etcoff, N. L., McInerney, S. C., Lee, M. B., & Jenike, M. A. (1998b). Masked presentations of emotional facial expressions modulate amygdala activity without explicit knowledge. *Journal of Neuroscience, 18*(1), 411–418.

Name index*

A
Abe, K.   29
Abercrombie, E.D.   249
Adams, C.D.   38, 53
Adolphs, R.   3, 4, **9–33**, 9, 16, 17, 19, 43, 105
Ajzen, I.   111, 112
Akerman, C.   21
Alderson, H.L.   59
Alfonso-Reese, L.A.   250
Alheid, G.F.   41
Alkire, M.T.   20
Allan, L.G.   113
Allen, J.J.B.   118, 119, 305
Allport, D.A.   83
Alvarez-Royo, P.   13
Amaral, D.G.   13, 27, 28, 35
American Psychological Association   292
Amorapanth, P.   45
Anderson, C.H.   147
Anderson, L.K.   248
Anderson, N.H.   111, 112
Anderson, H.W.   293
Anisman, H.   249
Appley, M.H.   201
Arak, A.   125
Arbisi, P.   250
Armstrong-James, M.   270
Arnold, M.B.   138
Arnsten, A.F.T.   271

Ashby, F.G.   6, 205, **245–87**, 245, 246, 247, 248, 249, 250, 251, 252, 255, 256, 257, 258, 260, 261, 263, 264, 265, 273, 285
Aspinwall, L.G.   247
Aston-Jones, G.   269, 272
Atkinson, J.W.   201
Attneave, F.   230

B
Babinsky, R.   *17*
Baeyens, F.   76, 77, 79, 87
Baker, H.F.   *259*
Baker, S.C.   306
Ball, J.   53, 62
Balleine, B.W.   38, 39, 47, 48, 49, 53, 54, 56, 57, 60, 61, 62, *63*, 64, 66, 67
Banich, M.T.   290
Bar, M.   114
Barch, D.M.   302
Bargh, J.A.   111, 295
Baron, R.A.   247
Barron, K.E.   120
Barron, K.W.   29
Barsade, S.G.   247
Barto, A.G.   60
Bartolic, E.I.   291
Bartussek, D.   305
Basso, G.   291, 296
Baylis, G.C.   123
Beattie, J.   192

---

* Page numbers in *italics* refer to figures and tables
  Page numbers in **bold** refer to chapters

318 Name index

Beatty, J. 248
Bechara, A. 15, 105, 293
Beck, A.T. 178
Becker, G. 305
Beeman, M. 121
Bell, D.E. 184, 192
Beninger, R.J. 245, 249
Berger, H.J.C. 250
Berkowitz, L. 199
Berlyne, D.E. 125, 268, 273
Bermudez-Rattoni, F. 29
Berntson, G.G. 116, 117, 299
Berridge, K.C. 53, 56, 57, 60, 67
Bettman, J.R. 198, 199, 200, 211
Betz, A.L. 79
Biederman, I. 114
Binder, N. 116
Birch, D. 201
Bird, C. 102
Birley, A.R. 1
Birnbaum, M.H. 198
Birnbaum, M.H. 190
Bisiach, E. 146
Blackburn, J.R. 245
Blaha, C.D. 245
Bless, H. 221, 309
Bloom, F.E. 255, 269, 270
Blundell, P.J. 4, 35–73, 47
Boakes, R.A. 36, 53, 60, 64, 67
Bohbot, V. 105
Boiton, F. 5
Boles, T.L. 183, 192
Bonanno, G.A. 115
Bonke, B. 87, 88
Bonnet, J.J. 248
Bornstein, R.F. 113, 115, 126, 127
Boss, M. 87, 88
Bosser, T. 202
Botvinick, M.M. 302
Bouton, M.E. 85
Bower, G.H. 228, 229, 231
Bozarth, M.A. 245
Bradley, M.M. 2, 10, 11, 28, 101, 104, 297
Brandon, S.E. 37, 38, 53, 56

Braver, T.S. 6, **289–316**, 289, 290, 292, 294, 295, 296, 302, 305, 307, 309
Brendt, C.M. 199
Brewer, J. 21, *22*
Brief, A.P. 247
Brody, N. 113, 115, 123
Brown, R. 10, 249, 250
Browning, R.A. 30
Brozowski, T. 249
Buccafusco, J.J. 271
Buchanan, S.L. 53
Buchanan, T.W. 3, 4, **9–33**, 19, 24, 25, *26*
Buchel, C. 28
Bucy, P.C. 44
Buffalo, E.A. 10
Bullock, M. 10, 11
Burns, L.H. 59
Burton, M. 60
Busemeyer, J.R. 5, 6, **197–219**, 202, 204, 205, 209
Bush, G. 302
Bush, L.K. 117
Byrne, R.M.J. 159

C
Cabeza, R. 290
Cacioppo, J.T. 116, 117, 118, 120, 299, 303
Cador, M. 59
Cahill, L. 11, 12, 13, 16, *17*, 19, 20, 21, 23, 24, 28
Canli, T. 20, 21, *22*, 23, 305
Canon, W. 201
Cantor, N. 247
Carli, M. 269, 271
Carlson, N.R. 268
Carlson, S. 271
Carmichael, S.T. 27
Carnevale, P.J.D. 245, 247
Carter, C.S. 302
Carver, C.S. 120, 128, 201, 294, 296, 298, 299, 303
Casale, M. 255, 256, 257

Casey, B.J.   302
Cave, K.R.   290
Caverni, J.-P.   159
Cenci, M.A.   249
Cepeda, C.   255, 256
Chandler, D.P.   188
Chapman, J.P.   and L.J.   224
Chappell, M.   123
Chartrand, T.L.   295
Chase, V.M.   168
Checkosky, S.F.   114, 125
Chelazzi, L.   123
Christianson, S.A.   4
Chua, P.   21, 305
Churchland, P.S.   145
Cimatti, D.   4
Clark, K.B.   30
Clark, M.   245
Cleland, G.G.   47, 64
Clore, G.L.   112, 113, 127, 128, 143, 152
Clower, R.P.   13
Cocks, R.P.   77, 97, 104
Cofer, C.N.   201
Cohen, J.C.   289, 290, 295, 296, 305, 307, 309
Cohen, J.D.   235, 254, *255*, 269, 302
Cohen, N.J.   28
Cole, B.J.   269
Cole, R.P.   89
Collins, A.   112
Collins, P.F.   293
Colwill, R.   38, 39
Conan Doyle, A.   157, 158
Contant, T.A.   271
Cook, S.A.   162
Cools, A.R.   250
Cooper, J.R.   255
Cooper, S.J.   245
Corbit, J.D.   303
Corbit, L.H.   67
Costentin, J.   248
Coull, J.T.   270
Courtney, S.M.   303
Crick, F.   145

Crombez, G.   77, 79, 87
Crow, T.   *259*
Curran, T.   119
Cuthbert, B.N.   28, 101, 297
Cutting, J.E.   224, 225

D
D'Agostino, P.R.   113, 115, 127
Dallas, M.   113
Damasio, A.R.   3, 9, 43, 105, 111, 139, 142, 148, 149, 150, 293, 305
Damasio, H.   105, 293
Damsma, G.   272
Darwin, C.R.   1, 5
Daubman, K.A.   245, *266*, 267
Davey, G.C.L.   47, 64, 78
Davidson, M.C.   268
Davidson, R.J.   106, 223, 224, 291, 293, 295, 297, 299, 305
Davis, M.   29
Davis, M.   38
Dawson, G.R.   272
Day, J.   272
Dayan, P.   249
De Houwer, J.   77, 79, 90
De Long, M.R.   272
De Sousa, R.   170
de Vries, N.   192
De Vries, T.J.   250
Dearing, M.F.   37, 56, 57, 63
Del Pesce, M.   4
Delamater, A.   67
Denberg, N.L.   17, 19
Dennett, D.C.   145
Depue, R.A.   250
Derryberry, D.   120
Desimone, R.   123
Desmond, J.E.   20, 305
D'Esposito, M.   290, 292, 305, 306
Devilbliss, D.M.   270
Devine, P.   120
Devinsky, O.   302
Dias, R.   223

Dickinson, A. 36, 37, 38, 39, 47, 48, 49, 53, 56, 57, 60, 61, 62, *63*, 66, 67, 78
Diederich, A. 202, 205
Dill, L.M. 297, 308
Dimberg, U. 117
Dixon, N.F. 144, 146
Dolan, R.J. 21, 23, 28, 44, 222, 250, 299, 305, 306
Doss, R.C. 305
Dowdy, J. *259*
Drachman, D.R. 272
Dretske, F. 141, 142
Drevets, W.C. 293
Drogosz, M. 123, 124
Drysdale, E. 24
Duffy, E. 268
Duke, L.M. 305
Duncan, E. 172
Duncker, K. 246, 247, 252, 254, 260, 264–65, *265*, *266*, 267, 268, 274, 275
Dunn, L.T. 57
Dywan, J. 113, 115

E
Earhard, B. 226
Easterbrook, J.A. 10, 268, 273
Ebmeier, K.P. 24
Edwards, W. 197
Eelen, P. 76, 77, 79, 87
Eichbaum, H. 28
Ekman, P. 2, 5, 140, 142, 294, 297, 299
Elio, R. 165
Elliot, A.J. 120
Elliott, R. 250
Ellsworth, P.C. 139
Elmehed, K. 117
Ely, T.D. 20
Engle, R.W. 87, 292
Enquist, M. 125
Escobar, M.L. 29
Eskes, G. 250
Estes, W.K. 258
Estrada, C.A. 247, 248, 262
Etcoff, N. 125
Euclid 157
Evenden, J.L. 258
Everaerd, W. 24
Everitt, B.J. 57, 59
Eysenck, M. 105

F
Fallon, J.H. 20
Fanselow, M.S. 13
Fazio, R.H. 83, 100
Fedorikhin, A. 200, 212, 214
Fernandez-Duque, D. 120
Fibiger, H.C. 272
Field, A.P. 78
Fink, G.R. 222
Fishbein, M. 111, 112
Fiske, S.T. 247
Fissel, K. 302
Fitchett, H. 104
Flanagan, O. 145
Flatt, M. 235
Fletcher, P. 21
Flykt, A. 112
Fodor, J.A. 141
Foote, S.L. 269, 270, 272
Fox, K. 270
Fox, N.A. 291, 297, 305
Fox, P.T. 290
Frackowiak, R.S.J. 222, 253
Frankenhaeuser, M. 270
Freedman, R. 270, 272
Freeman, W.J. 123
French, C.C. 105
Friesen, W.V. 2, 140, 142, 297
Frijda, N.H. 28, 112
Friston, K.J. 28, 253
Frith, C.D. 222, 253, 254, *259*, 306
Fulcher, E.P. 4, **75–109**, 77, 78, 90, 92, 93, 97, 101, 104, 105, 151
Furey, M.L. 272
Fuster, J.M. 249, 305

G

Gabrieli, J.D.   20, 21, *22*, 305
Gallese, V.   309
Galverna, O.G.   67
Gangstead, S.W.   125
Garcia, J.   56
Garcia-Marques, T.   120
Gardner, W.L.   116, 299
Garner, C.   53, 62, 66
Gaspar, P.   271
Gatenby, J.C.   28
Gavanski, I.   183
Geva, N.   245
George, J.M.   247
Gigerenzer, G.   5
Gilovich, T.   183
Girard, K.   113
Girotto, P.   159, 161, 162
Glasky, A.J.   272
Glauser, T.   291
Glover, G.   20, 305
Gluck, M.A.   228, 229, 231
Goldberg, J.H.   199, 211, 212, *213*
Goldman, A.   309
Goldman, P.S.   249
Goldman-Rakic, P.S.   249, 250, 255, 271, 305
Goldstein, D.G.   5
Goldvarg, E.   166
Goleman, D.   1
Gollwitzer, P.M.   296
Gonzalez, F.   53, 62, 66, 67
Gooren, L.J.   24
Gore, J.C.   28
Gorglione, J.M.   235, 267
Gotham, A.M.   249
Grabitz, H.-J.   76, 77, 88
Grady, J.M.   125
Grafman, J.   296
Grafton, S.T.   20
Grainger, B.   248
Grant, S.J.   269
Gray, J.R.   6, **289–316**, 289, 290, 291, 292, 293, 295, 299, 302, 305, 306, 307, 309

Grazzani-Gavazzi, I.   174
Greene, T.R.   247, 248
Greengard, P.   256
Greenspan, P.S.   152
Greenwald, A.G.   115
Greenwald, M.K.   2, 10, 11, 104
Gusnard, D.A.   293

H

Haber, R.N.   113
Hagemann, D.   305
Haier, R.J.   20
Halberstadt, J.   125
Halberstadt, J.B.   240
Hale, W.D.   248
Halligan, P.W.   222
Hamann, S.B.   11, 17, 20, 23, 29
Hamm, A.O.   10, 104
Hammerl, M.   76, 77, 88, 92, 93
Hanze, M.   223
Harackiewicz, J.M.   247
Harley, T.A.   101, 105
Harmon-Jones, E.   118, 119, 120
Hasselmo, M.E.   123, 272
Hata, Y.   272
Hatfield, T.   46, 56, 57, 58
Haxby, J.B.   272, 303
Heggelund, P.   272
Heller, W.   290, 291, 293, 305, 306
Hellige, J.B.   290, 309
Hemmings, H.C.   256
Hendrickx, H.   77
Henriques, J.B.   224
Herkenham, M.   41
Hernandez, L.   53
Hershenson, M.   113
Hertwig, R.   168
Hesse, F.W.   235
Heuer, F.   11, 12, 16
Hewitt, C.   171
Higgins, E.T.   113
Hirstein, W.   120
Hirt, E.R.   247
Ho, K.   183
Hoffer, B.J.   270

Holland, P.C.   36, 37, 56, 58, 62, 64,
    65, 78
Holmes, Sherlock   157, 158
Honkaniemi, J.   29
Hopfield, J.J.   121, 122, 124
Horvitz, J.C.   249
Huber, D.E.   121
Hutchins, E.   174
Hyman, B.T.   15
Hyman, S.E.   248, 256

I

Ikegaya, Y.   29
Imperato, A.   249
Inglehart, M.   140
Innes-Ker, A.H.   240
Irwin, W.   106
Isen, A.M.   6, 235, 245, 247, 248,
    251, 252, 258, 260, 262, 264, 265,
    266, 267, 268, 273, 274
Iversen, S.D.   248, 272
Iverson, S.   150
Izquierdo, I.   14, 24, 29

J

Jackendoff, R.   145, 146, 147
Jackson, W.J.   271
Jacobs, B.L.   249, 269, 272
Jacoby, L.L.   92, 113, 115, 119
James, W.   2, 139, 142, 148
Jaspers, R.M.A.   250
Jenkins, J.J.   251
Jensen, R.A.   30
Jiang, M.   272
Johnson, M.S.   245
Johnson, E.J.   198, 199
Johnston, J.B.   40
Johnson-Laird, P.N.   5, 120, 139,
    157–82, 159, 161, 162, 163, 166,
    171, 172
Johnstone, R.A.   125
Johnsrude, I.S.   105
Jonides, J.   7, 290, 292, 305, 306

Joordens, S.   92
Jussim, L.J.   79

K

Kagan, J.   299
Kahn, M.   201
Kahn, B.E.   247, 258
Kahneman, D.   86, 166, 168, 183,
    185, 193, 198
Kalivas, P.W.   249
Kallman, H.J.   226
Kalwani, U.   201
Kane, M.J.   292
Kardes, F.R.   83
Karp, L.   245
Kasamatsu, T.   272
Kauff, D.M.   113, 115
Kaufman, O.   291
Keele, S.W.   125
Keener, A.D.   289, 290, 295
Keeney, R.L.   197
Kelley, C.M.   113, 115, 119
Kelly, P.H.   248
Kety, S.   6
Killcross, S.   4, **35–73**, 40, 45, 47, 48,
    49, 53, 57, 59
Kilts, C.D.   20
Kimchi, R.   226
Kinchla, R.A.   225, 233
Kinsbourne, M.   145
Klauer, K.C.   223
Klinger, M.R.   115
Kluver, H.   44
Koch, C.   145
Koechlin, E.   296
Koestler, A.   247
Konorski, J.   36, 37, 53, 56, 63
Koriat, A.   119
Kossl, M.   270, 272
Kosslyn, S.M.   224, 290
Krahl, S.E.   30
Krams, M.   305
Krosnick, J.A.   79
Kruse, J.M.   54
Kubos, K.L.   305

Kulick, J. 10
Kunst-Wilson, W.R. 124

L
LaBar, K.S. 18, 28
Labre, M.M. 249
Lacey, J.I. 268
Ladavas, E. 4
Lane, R. 21
Lane, R.D. 120, 149, 150
Lang, P.J. 1, 10, 11, 28, 101, 104, 295, 297, 299, 303
Lange, C.G. 2
Lange, K.W. 250
Langlois, J.H. 125
Larocque, L. 174, 175, 176
Larrick, R.P. 192
Law, S. 77
Lawrence, A.D. 291
Lazarus, R.S. 76, 138, 295, 297, 299
LeDoux, J.E. 3, 4, 13, 27, 28, 30, 40, 106, 111, 112, 140, 150, 267, 299
Legrenzi, P. 159, 161, 162, 163, 164, 165, 168
Legrenzi, M.S. 159, 161, 162
Lennartz, R.C. 53
Leon, A. 250
Lerner, J.S. 199
Levenson, R.W. 2, 140, 142
Levey, A.B. 76, 79, 89
Levin, B.E. 249
Levine, M.S. 255
Lewenstein, M. 121, 122, 123, 129
Lewicka, M. 10
Lewinsohn, S. 268
Lewinson, A. 200
Liddle, P.F. 253
Liebeman, J.M. 245
Lima, S.L. 297, 308
Link, S.W. 205
Liotti, m. 291
Lipp, O.V. 104
Loewenstein, G. 199, 211
Loftus, E. 10, 11
Loftus, G.R. 226, 227

Loomes, G. 184, 192
Losch, M.E. 120
Lovallo, W.R. 24, 25, *26*
Lovibond, P.F. 78, 95
Luce, M.F. 200, 211
Lueschow, A. 123
Lundberg, U. 270
Lundqvist, D. 112
Lupien, S.J. 25
Luu, P. 293, 302, 305
Lynn, A.R. 79

M
McAlister, L. 201, 214
McClelland, J.L. 121, 123, 125
McCormick, D.A. 268
Macdonald, A.W. 302
McDonald, H.E. 247
McEwen, B.S. 25
McFarland, D.J. 201, 202
McGaugh, J.L. 11, 12, 13, 14, 16, 23, 24, 28, 29, 30
McGlone, M.S. 126
Macgreggor-Morris, R. 102
Mack, A. 146
McKenna, P.A. 116
Mackie, D.M. 120
Mackintosh, B. 77
Mackintosh, N.J. 36
Mackworth, J.F. 114
Mackworth, N.H. 227
McLean, J. 272
MacLean, P.D. 149
McClelland, J.L. 254
MacLeod, C. 100, 102, 152
McMullen, M. 183
McNally, R.J. 235
MacWhinney, B. 235
Madey, S.F. 183
Maier, S. 305
Malkova, L. 45, 59
Mandler, G. 115, 116, 117
Mano, H. 200, 247, 268
Maren, S. 13
Markman, A.B. 199

Markman, K.   183
Markowitsch, H.J.   15
Marr, D.   3, 224, 225
Marrocco, R.T.   268
Marsden, C.D.   249, 250
Marsh, R.L.   123
Marshall, J.C.   222
Martin, I.   76, 79, 89
Martin, M.   235
Martindale, C.   125
Masui, H.   272
Mathews, A.   77, 100, 101, 102, 105, 152
Mayberg, H.S.   223
Mazzoni, G.   119
Means, B.   245
Mednick, E.V.   248, 251
Mednick, M.T.   248, 251
Mednick, S.A.   248, 251
Medvec, V.H.   183
Mellers, B.A.   183, 184, 186, 187, 188, 190, 192, 194, 198
Melton, R.J.   247
Merickle, P.M.   92
Mertz, E.   245
Messick, D.M.   183, 192
Metcalfe, J.   119
Metzger, T.   186, 194
Miller, D.   183
Miller, E.K.   123, 223
Miller, F.E.   249
Miller, N.E.   202, 298, 299, 303
Miller, R.R.   89
Mineka, S.   104
Mirenowicz, J.   248
Mishkin, M.   303
Mogg, K.   102
Moises, H.C.   272
Molfese, D.L.   302
Monahan, J.L.   118, 119
Monsma, Jr.   F.J.   255
Montague, P.R.   249
Monti, L.A.   121
Moore, B.R.   38
Moore, K.   125

Moore, S.C   1–8, 6, **221–43**, 221, 222, 223, 293
Morrell, M.J.   302
Morris, F.   248
Morris, J.S.   28, 44, 299
Morrison, D.   201
Morrison, J.   269
Mowrer, O.H.   53
Munakata, Y.   121, 124
Murphy, S.T.   90, 93, 94, 118, 140
Murphy, F.C.   291
Murray, E.A.   13
Murre, J.M.J.   121
Myers, D.A.   29

N
Nader, K.   28, 40
Nakanishi, K.   29
Nakamura, Y.   115
Nalwa, V.   123
Naritoku, D.K.   30
Nauman, E.   305
Navon, D.   222, 224, 225, 234
Neiss, R.   268
Neisser, U.   170
Nelson, T.O.   119
Nelson, W.   226
Nestler, E.J.   248, 256
Niedenthal, P.M.   240
Niit, T.   10
Nitschke, J.B.   290, 291, 305, 306
Noice, H.   247, 248
Noll, D.C.   302
Norman, D.A.   289
Norman, J.   225
Norman, K.A.   121, 123
Nosofsky, R.M.   205, 234, 240, 241
Nowak, A.   4, **111–35**, 120, 121, 122, 123, 124, 129
Nowicki, G.P.   245, *266*
Nyberg, L.   290
Nygren, T.E.   245
Nystrom, L.   302

O

Oaksford, M. 1–8, 6, **221–43**, 221, 222, 223, 248, 293
Oatley, K. 5, 120, 139, **157–82**, 170, 171, 172, 174, 175, 176
O'Carroll, R.E. 24
Oehman, A. 112
Öhman, A. 44, 77, 299
Oliver, A.P. 270, 272
Olshausen, B.A. 147
Olson, J.M. 183
Ordóñez, L.D. 190, 198
O'Reilly, R.C. 121, 124, 290
Ortony, A. 112, 121
Osgood, C.E. 76
Otto, J.H. 223
Ouimet, C.C. 256
Overmier, J.B. 57
Owen, A.M. 105

P

Packard, M.G. 13, 14
Palermo, D.S. 251
Palmer, S.E. 125, 129
Palmeri, T.J. 205, 240
Panskepp, J. 150
Panzer, S. 296
Pardo, J.V. 290
Parker, A. 21
Passingham, R. 305
Pavlov, I.P. 38; see also Pavlovian conditioning
Payne, J.W. 198, 199, 200, 211
Peacock, W. 255
Peirce, C.S. 157, 158, 159, 169, 177, 180
Pelled, L.H. 247
Pelletier, F.J. 165
Pessemier, E. 214
Pessin, M.S. 256
Petersen, S.E. 146, 250
Petrovitch, G. 40, 41
Petry, M.C. 11
Pfaus, J.G. 245
Phaf, R.H. 120, 121
Phelps, E.A. 18, 28
Philips, A.G. 245
Pietrini, P. 272, 296
Pinker, S. 125
Pitkänen, A. 27, 41
Port, R.T. 121
Posner, M.I. 125, 146, 250, 289, 302
Powell, D.A. 53
Powell, M.C. 83
Pribram, K.H. 305
Price, J.L. 27
Price, T.R. 305
Prins, B. 11
Printz, H.W. 254, *255*
Prinz, J.J. 5, **137–55**, 141, 142, 146, 149
Proffitt, F. 125
Protais, P. 248
Provost, J. 235

Q

Quirarte, G.L. 29

R

Radisavljevic, Z. 255
Raichle, M.E. 250, 289, 290, 293
Raiffa, H. 197
Rainer, G. 223
Rajkowski, J. 269, 270
Ramachandran, V.S. 120
Rao, K. 305
Rao, S.C. 223
Rashotte, M.E. 58
Ratcliff, R. 205
Read, D. 199, 212, 214
Reber, R. 113, 114, 115, 116, 126
Rees, G. 250
Reid, S.A. 305
Reisberg, D. 10, 11, 12, 16
Reisenzein, R. 116, 120, 138
Rescorla, R.A. 36, 37, 38, 39, 54, 57, 58, 62, 64, 231
Reznick, J.S. 299
Rhodes, G. 125

Richards, A.   105
Richardson, R.T.   272
Ridgeway, V.   100
Ridley, R.M.   258, *259*, 260, 264, 274
Ritov, I.   183, 192
Rizley, R.C.   58
Rizzolatti, G.   309
Robbins, T.W.   223, 258, 269
Roberts, A.C.   223, 250, 251, 271
Robinson, G.F.   245
Robinson, R.G.   305
Robinson, T.E.   53
Robledo, P.   67
Rock, I.   146
Rockland, C.   105
Roe, R.   202, 205, 209
Roediger, H.L.   126
Roese, N.J.   183
Roggman, L.A.   125
Rolls, E.T.   123, 215, 272
Rompré, P.P.   245
Roozendaal, B.   13, 14, 24, 25, 29
Roseman, I.J.   138
Rosen, J.B.   106
Rosenzweig, A.S.   245
Roskos-Ewoldson, D.R.   100
Ross, R.T.   58
Rosvold, H.E.   249
Roth, R.H.   255
Rotteveel, M.   120
Rueckl, J.G.   290, 303
Rumelhart, D.E.   121, 125
Rumelhart, D.E.   254
Russell, J.A.   10, 11

S
Sahakian, B.J.   272
St. John, M.F.   77, 78
Saito, H.   29
Sanbonmatsu, D.M.   83
Sara, S.J.   28
Sarin, R.   193
Saron, C.D.   297
Sato, H.   272
Sattah, S.   198

Schacter, D.L.   126
Schacter, S.E.   115, 116, 138
Schafe, G.E.   28
Schefft, B.K.   291
Scheier, M.F.   120, 128, 294, 296, 298
Scherer, K.R.   138
Schildkraut, J.J.   6, 249
Schmolck, H.   10
Schneiderman, N.   53
Schneirla, T.C.   297
Schul, R.   *17*
Schulkin, J.   106
Schultz, W.   245, 248
Schwartz, A.   **183–95**, 183, 186, 192, 194
Schwartz, B.   10
Schwarz, N.   4, 5, 90, **111–35**, 111, 113, 126, 127, 128, 221, 399, 309
Seamon, J.G.   113, 115, 116, 123
Sebeok, T.A.   158, 177
Seeman, P.   255
Sejnowski, T.J.   249
Senulis, J.A.   297
Servan-Schreiber, D.   254, *255*, 257, 272, 305
Setterlund, M.B.   240
Sevior, P.W.   248
Shajahan, P.   24
Shalker, T.E.   245
Shallice, T.   289
Shanks, D.R.   77, 78, 95
Sheier, M.F.   201
Shen, Y.   255
Shepard, J.D.   29
Sherman, S.J.   183
Shimamura, A.P.   119
Shimp, T.A.   87
Shin, L.M.   305
Shiv, B.   200, 212, 214
Showers, C.   247
Shulman, G.L.   222
Sibley, D.R.   255
Siddle, D.A.T.   104
Siemer, M.   223
Siggins, G.R.   270

Simbayi, L.C. 60
Simon, H.A. 120, 170, 295, 299
Simpson, J.R. 293
Singer, J. 115, 116, 138
Skarda, C.A. 123
Skinner, B.F. 38
Skurnik, I. 127
Slovic, P. 198
Slyker, J.P. 235
Smith, D.C. 30
Smith, E.E. 7, 141, 290, 292, 305, 306
Smith, E.R. 115, 121
Smith, P.L. 205
Snell, J. 185
Snidman, N. 299
Snyder, A.Z. 289, 293, 302
Soares, J.F. 77
Sokolov, E.N. 123
Solomon, R.L. 36, 54, 303
Sorg, B.A. 249
Spencer, D.D. 18
Spies, K. 235
Spijksma, F.P. 120
Squire, L.R. 10, 11, 13, 120
Stahl, G. 235
Starr, L.B. 305
Staw, B.M. 247
Steere, J.C. 271
Steininger, R.L. 272
Stenger, V.A. 302
Sternberg, S. 292
Stewart, T. 249
Stillings, N.A. 115
Stober, J. 223
Stolz, J.A. 92
Stone, T.W. 270
Stout, J.C. 5, **197–219**
Strange, P.G. 255
Straub, J.J. 36, 65
Strickland, B.R. 248
Stuart, E.W. 87, 88
Suci, G.L. 76
Sugden, R. 184, 192
Sumich, A. 125

Sutton, R.I. 247
Sutton, R.S. 60
Sutton, S.K. 291, 294, 299, 305
Swanson, L.W. 40, 41

T
Tafalla, R.J. 270
Tannenbaum, P.H. 76
Tassinary, L.G. 117
Tata, P. 100
Tauer, J.M. 120
Taylor, S.F. 21
Taylor, S.E. 247
Teather, L.A. 13, 14
Tetlock, P.E. 199
Thomas, K.M.
Thompson, R.F. 53
Thorndike, E.L. 38
Thornhill, R. 125
Thunberg, M. 117
Titanic-Schefft, M. 291
Toates, F.M. 201
Tofighbakhsh, J. 126
Tolman, E.C. 38, 201
Tomarken, A.J. 289, 290, 295, 305
Toni, I. 305
Townsend, J.T. 5, 6, **197–219**, 202, 205, 209
Tranel, D. 15, 17, 19, 43, 105
Trapold, M.A. 50, 57
Tremewan, T. 125
Trevor, R.W. 267
Trulson, M.E. 272
Tsumoto, T. 272
Tucker, D.M. 120, 291, 293, 305
Tuholski, S.W. 292
Tuozzi, G. 4
Turken, A.U. 6, **245–87**, 245, 250, 252
Turner, B.H. 41
Tversky, A. 86, 166, 168, 198, 199

U
Umiker-Sebeok, J. 158, 177
Ungerleider, L.G. 303

Ungerstadt, U.   269

V
Valentin, V.V.   6, **245–87**
Vallacher, R.R.   120, 121
van den Bergh, O.   76, 77, 79, 87
van der Plight, Z.   192
van Essen, D.C.   147
van Gelder, T.   121
van Leeuwen, B.   199, 212, 214
van Tol, H.H.   255
van Zandt, B.J.   115
van Stegeren, A.H.   24
Vandercar, D.H.   53
Vater, M.   270, 272
Velten, E.   221, 235
Venables, P.H.   268
Vogt, B.   302
Von Winterfeldt, D.   197

W
Wada, H.   268
Wagner, A.R.   37, 38, 53, 56, 231
Walaas, S.I.   256
Waterhouse, B.D.   270, 272
Wertheimer, M.   247
Whalen, P.J.   302
Wickens, J.   256
Wise, R.A.   245
Wakker, P.P.   193
Waterhouse, B.D.   270
Watt, A.   67
Weber, M.   11
Weiner, W.J.   250
Weinberger, N.M.   13, 53
Welch, T.F.   312
Westermann, R.   235
Whalen, P.J.   299
Wheeler, R.E.   305

White, N.M.   105, 249
Whitlock, D.   114, 125
Whittlesea, B.W.A.   113, 119, 120, 126, 127, 129
Wickens, J.R.   249, 256
Wilding, E.   21
Wilensky, A.E.   28
Williams, G.V.   248, 250
Williams, J.M.G.   100
Williams, L.D.   119, 127, 129
Williamson, D.A.   100
Willoughby, P.J.   47, 57
Wilson, F.A.W.   272
Wilson, J.   222
Winkielman, P.   4, 90, 92, **111–35**, 111, 113, 115, 116, 117, 118, 120, 126, 127
Winocur, G.   250
Witherspoon, D.   113
Witte, E.A.   268
Wolfe, J.   225, 233
Wolters, G.   121
Woodward, D.J.   270, 272
Wyvell, C.L.   53

Y
Young, M.J.   245, 247

Z
Zacharko, R.M.   249
Zajonc, R.B.   90, 93, 94, 111, 112, 113, 114, 118, 120, 124, 138, 139, 140
Zeelenberg, M.   192
Zhao, W.V.   105
Zhao, Z.   20, 21, *22*, 305
Zillmann, D.   267
Zochowski, M.   129
Zola-Morgan, S.   13

Subject index[*]

A

abductive inference   161, 165, 166–169, 177
   and consciousness   179
   and emotion   157, 158, 159, 177–180
   and expectation   178
   see also reasoning
ACC *see* anterior cingulate cortex
acetylcholine (ACh)   268, 272, 273; *see also* neurotransmitters
action discrimination   49, *50*, 57
action dispositions   138
action theory   209
activation-based priming   124
adaptive conservatism   104
adrenaline, bodily responses to   138
adrenergic: attentional system   216
   beta blockade   24
   function, and memory   24, 25, 29
   see also norepinephrine
aesthetic judgments   127
   see also evaluations; judgments
affective priming   90, 92, 93, 94
affective response   123, 124
   measuring   117, 118
Allais paradox   184
amnesia, diencephalic/hippocampal   17
amphetamines   246, 248

effect on probability learning tasks   258–260, 274
effect on two-choice guessing task   258–260, *259*, 266, 274
amygdala   27, 40–43
   animal research studies   13, 14, 21, 23, 24, 28, 29, 30, 44, 45; *see also* lesion studies
   basolateral nuclei   40, 41, 42; *see also* lesion studies
   central nuclei   42, 59, 67
   and cognition   140
   hormonal output   29
   hyperexcitability in anxiety   106
   lateralized activity   19, 23, 28, 44
   medial nuclei   43
   neural connectivity   41, 42, 43, 67, 120, 140, 150
   neuroimaging studies   20–23, 27, 43
   pharmacological studies   24–25, 26, 27
   structure   40, 41, 42, 43
amygdala functions: acquisition   14
   associative representation   4
   cognitive-motivational network   216
   deficits following damage   43, 44, 45; *see also* lesion studies
   detection of negative stimuli   43, 105

---

[*] Page numbers in *italics* refer to figures and tables
Page numbers in **bold** refer to chapters

emotion   43–46, 150, 151
emotional memory formation
    4, 9, 13–14, 15, 20–23,
    27–30, 35
emotional response   44, 150
emotional/social judgment   23,
    43, 44
emotionally-significant events
    44, 45; *see also* reinforcers
evaluation   67
evaluative mapping   105–106
expression   14
facial expression, recognition
    43
fear conditioning   3, 13, 27,
    59,106
learning   14, 57
liking/wanting   53, 54, 60, 67
long-term emotional declarative
    memory   4, 9, 13–14, 15, 21
memory consolidation   18, 21,
    23, 24, 28
memory encoding   21, 23, 28
memory reconsolidation   28
memory retrieval   21, 23, 28
Pavlovian conditioning   44, 45,
    46, 47
physiological perception   30
reinforcement   44, 45, 46, 47,
    48, 49, 57, 58
anger   138
    free-floating   *173*
    and goal blockage   171, 179
    and joint errors   174
animal research studies   13, 14, 21,
    23, 24, 28–30, 44, 45; *see also*
    lesion studies
anterior attention system   249, 250,
    251, 252
anterior cingulate cortex (ACC)   27,
    149, 150
    and cognitive-motivational
      network   215, 216
    dopamine activation   249, 251,
      252, 254, 257, 263, 273, 274

locus of conscious awareness
    150
role in cognitive perspective
    249, 250
role in conflict monitoring   302
role in emotional control   120
role in executive attention   249,
    250, 251, 252
role in hypothesis generation
    250
role in metacognitive monitoring
    120
role in semantic tasks,
    neuroimaging studies   253
antidepressants   172
anxiety: and attentional bias   75, 81,
    100, 101, 102, 103–104
    drugs for combating   172
    evaluative learning in   75–76
    free floating   172
    information processing in   86,
      105
    interpretational bias   104–105
    and logical inconsistency   178,
      179, 180
    negative priming   100, 101, *102*
apomorphine   248
appetitive learning, in rats   40, 58
appraisals, emotional   138; *see also*
    evaluations; evaluative;
    judgment; somatic appraisals
approach-avoidance models of
    movement behaviour   202
approach-withdrawal related
    emotional function   291,
    293, 295, 296, 297, *298*, 299,
    303–310
    and emotional states   297, *298*
    network subsystem segregation
      303–304 , 306, 307–310
    reciprocal inhibition   303–304
arousal   10–13, 18
    and affect   246, 267–268,
      270–274

and attention   6, 10, 28, 80, 100–103, 221, 270
cognitive effects   272–273
and creative problem-solving   6, 245, 246, 247, 251, 258, 273
definition   267, 268
dominant response   268, 273
frontal cortex function   270–272
inducing   267, 268 245, 247, 267, 268
neurobiological basis of   268–270, 274
neurotransmitters   268–273
and problem solving   268, 273
states   138
and working memory   6, 270, 271, 272, 273
associative learning models   38; see also reinforcers
attachment love   *173*
attention
   to affective stimuli   81
   bottom-up processes   81
   and consciousness   146, 147, 152, 153
   distracters   *102, 103*
   and emotional arousal   6, 10, 28, 80, 100–103, 221, 270
   executive   249, 250, 251, 252
   models   101, 146–147
   neural circuitry of   147
   role of NE   269, 270, 271
   role of PFC   290
   selective   82, 83, 100–103, 221, 146, 147
   sustained   290
   top-down processes   81, 83
   and vigilance   146, 147
attention-focusing   295, 308
attention switching   250, 251
attentional avoidance   102
attentional bias   75, 80, 100, 105
   and anxiety   75, 81, 100, 101, 102, 103–104

and mood   6, 221, 222, 223, 224, 227, 240, 293
attentional processing   81
attractor neural network   121, 123
auditory fear conditioning   13
auditory verbal learning   16
automatic attention capture   83
autonomic conditioning, subliminal   77
autonomic responses   142, 143
averageness (prototypical stimuli)   125, 126, 129
awareness
   binary classification of   95
   contingency   76, 77, 78, 79, 82, 86, 87, 93, 95, 96, 99
   locus of conscious   150
   masking   44
   mere-exposure effect   126–127
   non-verbal   77
   phenomenal   149, 150
   reflexive   150
   see also consciousness

B
backward masking   4
backward/forward pairing   88–89, 90, 92, 94, 96, 99
basal forebrain: cholinergic cells   272
   and cognitive-motivational network   215, 216
   connections to amygdala   42
basic emotions   139, 172, *173*
basolateral nuclei of amygdala   40, 41, 42; see also amygdala; lesion studies
behaviour: cognitive control of see cognitive control
   observable   2
   role of emotion   1
   stream of   201
beliefs, role in emotion   5
beta-blockers   24, 29
bottom-up processes   81, 290, 304, 307

brain asymmetry *see* lateralization
brain function: and emotion   2, 3, 6
   and mind   2, 3
brain imaging *see* neuroimaging
   studies
brainstem   149, 150
   connections to amygdala   42, 43
   reticular formation   150
   role in arousal   268
Broca's area   309
Brodmann's Areas (dorsal PFC)   305
Burridan's Ass   240

C
catecholamines   27, 29; *see also*
   adrenaline; adrenergic;
   norepinephrine
categorization   80
caudate   13, 28, 42
   and cognitive-motivational
   network   215, 216
   and rule switching   250, 253
cerebellum, role in arousal   269
cerebral cortex: connections to
   amygdala   41, 42
   role in arousal   269
   role of NE   272
choice extinction tests   48
choice prediction   191–192
choice strategies   199
choice theory   192, 193
   cognitive   193
   emotion based *see*
   decision-making
cingulate cortex, anterior *see* anterior
   cingulate cortex (ACC)
cirazoline   271
classical conditioning   89
clonidine   271
cocaine   248
cognitive control, of behaviour   289
   adaptive function   294
   bottom-up influence of emotion
   290, 304, 307

   context dependent   290, 294,
   296
   emotion induction   292, 307
   emotion/working memory
   interaction   306–307
   emotional integration   289, 290,
   291–294, 309, 310
   emotional selectivity   291–294,
   295, 298, 307–309
   hemispheric specialization   290,
   291, 293, 294, 304, 307, 308,
   309
   information manipulation   289
   n-back task   293, 307, 308
   neural network model of brain
   function   290
   role of PFC   305
   spatial tasks   293
   subsystems of   289
   verbal tasks   293
   working memory   289, *292*, 295,
   303–304, 305, 308
   see also dynamic goal
   management
cognitive dissonance   120
cognitive-emotional integration
   289, 290, 291–294, 306–307, 309
cognitive flexibility, and affect   247,
   251, 252
cognitive load, and fluency   126
cognitive monitoring   119–121
cognitive-motivational conflicts
   experiment   199, 200, 212–214
cognitive-motivational network   *203*,
   215, 216
cognitive perspectives (set): and affect
   247, 265, 266, 273
   function, of ACC   249, 250
coherence   122, 123, 124, 125
communicative function, of emotion
   143–144
communicative theory of emotions
   171–173, 174
   basic emotions   172, *173*
   two-part hypothesis   172

compensatory function   95, *96*, 99
composite hypothesis   86, 80, 86, 87,
    88, 90, 99, 104, 105, 106
    augmented   98
computational mechanisms,
    perceptual fluency   121–125
computational models   1, 3, 6, 7
    algorithmic level   3
    computational level   3
    in evaluative learning   75
    implementational level   3
    neural network   121–125, 129;
        see also neural networks
computational theory of emotion
    137, 170
computerized   tomography (CT)
    neuroimaging studies   15
conceptual fluency   126; *see also*
    perceptual fluency
conditional response (CR)   36, 37, 38
conditional stimulus (CS)   36, 37, 57
conditioning: autonomic subliminal
    77
    classical   89
    fear   3, 13, 27, 39, 59, 106
    instrumental   38–40, 48, 49, 51,
        54, 61, 62, 63, 64, *66*, 67
    Pavlovian *see* Pavlovian
        conditioning
    second order   57, 58, 62, 89
    study   15
    see also learning
conflict: and emotion   179
    monitoring role of ACC   302
connectionism *see* neural networks
connectionist (neural network) model
    of brain function   80, 246,
    251–267, *253, 255, 257, 259,*
    273, 285–287, 290
conscious control   93; *see also*
    cognitive control
conscious processes   93
consistency *see* reasoning to
    consistency

consolidation, memory   13, 14, 18,
    21, 23, 24, 28
consumer choices   201–202
consumer research, variety seeking
    214–215
contempt   *173*
contingency awareness   76, 77, 78,
    79, 82, 86, 87, 93, 95, 96, 99
contingency memory   77, 105
contingent weighting theory   198
core relational themes   138, 140, 141,
    142, 143, 144
corrugator supercilii (brow) muscle
    117, 118
cortico-cortical projections   253, 254
cortisol, role in memory   24, 25, *26*,
    29; *see also* stress hormones
counterfactual reference points   183,
    184, 185, 188, 192
    downward   183
    negative outcomes, feelings
        183, 192
    positive outcomes, feelings   183,
        192
    upward   183
counterfactual thinking   79
creative problem solving   6
    and arousal   6, 245, 246, 247,
        251, 258, 273
    connectionist model   246,
        251–267, *253, 255, 257, 259,*
        273, 285–287
    dopamine modulated activation
        function   254–257, *255,*
        256, *257,* 257–267, 274
    Duncker candle task   6, 246,
        247, 252, 254, 260, 264–265,
        265, 266, 267, 268, 274, 275
    Remote Associates Test   6, 246,
        248, 251, 252, 260, 262–264,
        263, 264, 266, 267, 268, 274,
        275
    two-choice guessing task   254,
        258–260, *259,* 264, 274
    and verbal fluency   247

Subject index

word association   6, 246, 247,
    251, 252, 260–262, *261, 262,*
    266, 274, 293
creativity: Mednick's theory of   248
and mood   6

D

decision affect theory   5, 6, 184–186,
    188, 189, 190–194, 245
  decision utilities   185, 186–193
  and expectation/surprise   185,
    188, 192
  experienced utilities   185, 186
  judged expectations   186, 187,
    188, *189,* 190, *191,* 192, 193
  postdecision emotions   186,
    188–189, 192, 193
  predicting choices   191–192
  STEPIT subroutine   188
  subjective expected emotions
    (SEE)   186, 190, 191–193
  subjective expected utilities
    (SEU)   186, 190, 193
  subjective probabilities   186,
    190
  see also decision field theory
decision analysis   193
decision field theory   6, 202–217
  action theory   209
  applications, affect and
    decision-making   211–215
  attribute states   208–209
  certainty equivalents   202
  cognitive-motivational conflicts
    experiment   199, 200, 212–214
  cognitive-motivational network
    203, 215, 216
  competitive networks   205
  consumer research, variety
    seeking   214–215
  decision rules   203
  and deprivation-satiation   202,
    214, 217
  dynamic model   208, 209
  and environmental stimulation
    202, 211, 217
  motivational values   207–208,
    209, 211
  multi-alternative decision
    making   202
  multi-attribute decision making
    202
  needs   209, 210, 211, 217
  neurophysiological basis
    215–216
  preference states   204, 205, 209,
    210, 216
  rage and reason experiment
    199, 211, *212, 213*
  selling prices   202
  stopping rules   *204,* 205
  and uncertainty   202
  valence   205–207, 216
  see also decision affect theory;
    decision-making
decision-making   6
  adaptive models   198
  affective feedback   111
  Allais paradox   184
  behaviour   192
  counterfactual reference points
    183, 184, 185, 188, 192
  disappointment theory   184,
    192, 194
  dynamic cognitive model *see*
    decision field theory
  inferred emotions   184
  multi-alternative   202
  multi-attribute   202
  preference reversals   184
  reflection affect   184
  regret theory   184, 192
  role of economics   5
  role of emotion   5, 6, 7, 183, 193
  status quo as reference   183
  STEPIT subroutine   188
  see also decision affect theory;
    utility theory

decision theory *see* decision affect theory; decision field theory
decision utilities   185, 186–193; *see also* utility theory
declarative memory *see* memory, long-term declarative
delta learning rule   85
dentate gyrus   29
depression
  cognitive therapy for   178
  drugs to combat   172
  role of neurotransmitters   249
deprivation-satiation   199, 217
diencephalic amnesia   17
diencephalon   149
differentiation   122, 123, 124, 125
disgust   *173*
disappointment theory   184, 192, 194
distractibility, role of NE   271
distributed cognition   174
divinity, metaphor of   170
dominant response   268, 273
dopamine   245, 246
  and executive attention   252
  glutamine modulation   255, 256, 257
  PFC function   249, 250, 254, 257, 273
  receptors   255
  as reward signal   245, 248, 249
  role in emotion   6
  two-choice guessing   258–260
  see also neurotransmitters
dopamine agonists
  amphetamines   246, 248
  effect on probability learning tasks   258–260, 274
  effect on two-choice guessing task   254, 258–260, *259*, 266, 274
dopamine antagonists (neuroleptics)   248, 249, 251, 252, 253
  and cognitive set shifting   250, 251
  hypothesis   248–251
dopamine modulated activation function   249, 251, 252, 254–257, *255*, 256, *257*, 263, 273, 274
  tests of   257–267
dopaminergic theory of positive affect   245, 246, 248–251, 267, 273
dorsal PFC (Brodmann's Areas)   305
dorsolateral (DLPFC)   293, 307
  crossover stimulus x emotion interaction   293, 306
  activity, and mood   223
  see also prefrontal cortex
drug addiction   53, 59
drugs, effects on emotional memory   24
Duncker candle task   6, 246, 247, 252, 254, 260, 264–265, *265*, *266*, 267, 268, 274, 275
dynamic cognitive model *see* decision field theory
dynamic goal management   289, 290, 294–307
  active goals   296, *298*, 303, 304
  approach-withdrawal related emotional function   291, 293, 295, 296, 297, *298*, 299, 303–304, 306–310
  attention-focusing role   295, 308
  conflict monitoring   302
  consciousness of   295, 298
  context   294, 296
  emotional regulation   297–300
  explicit/pure approach goals   296
  evaluation   298, 299, 303
  goal definition   295
  goal hierarchies   296
  goal representations   295, 296, *298*, 299, 300–309
  implicit/approach-consistent goals   296
  lateralization   305–309

multiple goals 296–297, 298, 299
neural substrates 297, 304–307; *see also* PFC
potential reward/threat balance 301, 302
prioritization 295, 299, 304
dynamics of action 201
dynamics, processing 111; *see also* perceptual fluency

E
Easterbrook hypothesis 10, 11, 12
EEG (electroencephalogram) studies 223
elation 138
electroencephalogram (EEG) studies 223
embarrassment 172, 177, 179
emotion inducing photographs 152, 153
emotion induction 152, 153, 221, 223, 228, 235–236, 238, 292, 307
emotion signals 171, 172, 174, 180
    blaming 175, 179
    emotions as 169, 170–171, 172, 173
    goal plans 170, 171, 172, *173*
    joint errors 174, 175, 176, 177
    joint plans 170, 173–175, 176, 180
    mental models of others 175–176
    multiple goals 170, 172
    planning as reasoning 171
    negative trait ascription 175
    and trust 174, 175, 176, 180
emotional arousal *see* arousal; *see also* emotional memory
emotional cognition 1, 121
emotional consciousness 137, 144, 148–153
    attended intermediate level representation (AIR) theory 5, 146, 148, 150, 151–153

emotional control, role of anterior cingulate 120
emotional integration 289, 290, 291–294, 309, 310
emotional learning
    instrumental 36, 38–40
    neural bases of 35
    Pavlovian conditioning 36, 37–38
    reinforcer, role of 35
emotional memory 9, 11, 12, 13
    accuracy of 10, 11
    adaptive function of 9, 27
    beta-adrenergic activity 24
    consolidation 18, 21, 23, 24, 28
    encoding 21, 23, 28
    formation 4, 9, 13–14, 15, 20–23, 27–30
    lesion studies 14–19
    neurobiology of 9, 13–14
    neuroimaging studies 20–23
    pharmacology studies 24–25, *26*
    recall 9, 10
    reconsolidation 28
    retrieval 21, 23, 28
    role of amygdala 4, 9, 13–14, 15, 20–23, 27–30, 35
    /working memory interaction 306–307
emotional priming 176
emotional processing systems 1, 148
    automatic attention capture 83
    computational 1, 7, 137
    detection of bodily changes 148
    hierarchical levels 148, 149, 150, 151, 152, 153
    information processing 80, 83
    neural correlates 140, 149, 150
    recognition of somatic responses 148
emotional responses 113
    role of amygdala 44, 150
    and neuroanatomical regions 149, 150

Subject index 337

taxonomic hierarchy 149, 150, 151, 152
emotional selectivity 291–294, 295, 298, 307–309
emotional states 5
    and cognitive task demands 293
    and goal regulation 297
    taxonomic hierarchy 149, 150, 151, 152
    triune brain model 149
emotional Stroop task 100, 295
emotional valence 10, 11, 76, 86, 205–207, 216
emotional words study 18
emotionally-significant events 44, 45, 151; *see also* reinforcers
encoding 21
epilepsy, treatment of 14, 19, 43
epinephrine, role in memory 24, 25, 29, 30; *see also* norepinephrine; stress hormones
evaluations: automatic 111
    negative 127
    positive 4, 111–135
    see also perceptual fluency
evaluative inhibition 90
evaluative learning, human 4, 75–109
    and affective priming 90, 92, 93, 94
    assimilation effect 92
    compensation functions 95, *96*, 99
    composite hypothesis 80, 86, 87, 88, 90, 98, 99, 104, 105, 106
    conscious control 76, 77, 92–96, *94*
    and contingency awareness 76, 77, 78, 79, 82, 86, 87, 93, 95, 96, 99
    contrast effects 92, *94*, 95, 96
    counterfactual procedure 79
    exclusion-inclusion task 92

familiarity/recognition dissociation 92
forced-choice recognition tests 93
hedonic shifts 79
intrinsic hypothesis 79, 80, 82, 86, 87, 88, 90, 98, 106
learned association weighting 83, 84, 85, 86
nature of 78–80
network model 80–86
referential hypothesis 78, 79, 80, 82, 86, 87, 88, 90, 97, 98, 99, 106
revaluation studies 79, 98, 99
startle-probe response 104
subliminal 77, 78, 90–92, *91*, 92, 93, 94, 96, 99
valence 76, 86
evaluative maps 81, 82, 83, 100, 101, 105–106
evaluative mechanisms 80, 81, 111
evaluative memory, stable 76
evaluative priming 100, 101, *102*
evaluative response (ER) 86–87, 90, 124
    augmented 96
    backward/forward pairing 88–89, 90, 92, 94, 96, 99
    ES-NS associations 76, 78, 79, 82, 84, 86, 87, *88*, *89*, 92, 104
    feature-based sources 112–113
    fluency-based sources 112–113
    nature of 117–118
    and processing dynamics 111
    rate of acquisition 86, 87
    stability 97–99
    and stimulus attributes 111
evaluative stimuli (Es) 76, 78, 79, 82, 84
    long-term retention of 97–99
    subliminal 77
    supraliminal 96, *97*
evaluative weights 83, 84, 85, 86, 90, 97, 100, 101

event outcome studies   46, 47, 57
executive attention   249, 250, 251, 252
exclusion-inclusion task   92
experienced utilities   185, 186
The Expression of Emotions in Man and Animals   1
eyewitness testimony   10, 11

F
facial electromyography (fMEG)   117, 118
facial expression   112, 117, 139, 140, 142
   role of amygdala   43
fear   138, 142
   conditioning   3, 13, 27, 39, 59, 106
   free-floating   *173*
   and goal conflicts   171, 172
   neuroanatomical circuits involved in   3
familiarity attribution model   115
familiarity feelings   119, 127
feedback control theory   201
feeling of familiarity   119, 127
feeling-of-knowing phenomenon   119
feelings, and emotions   5, 30, 137, 138, 139, 143, 152
   bodily states   139
   cognitive   127
   fluctuations and cognitive processing   245
figure-ground contrast   114, 124–126
flashbulb memories   10, 11, 12
   accuracy of   10
fluency   125, 126, 127, 128
   conceptual fluency   126; *see also* perceptual fluency
   and negative evaluation   127
   and positive evaluation   111, 112

fluency-attribution model   115; *see also* perceptual fluency
fMRI *see* functional magnetic resonance imaging
focus-of-judgment effects   115
forced-choice recognition tests   93
forgetting rates   97; *see also* memory
forward/backward pairing   88–89, 90, 92, 94, 96, 99
free-floating emotions   172, *173*
freezing behaviour   45, 149, 152, *173*
frontal cortex   150
   and cognitive-motivational network   216
frustration   174, 178, 179
   and joint errors   174
functional fixedness   247
functional magnetic resonance imaging (fMRI)   15, 20, 21, 43, 44
   studies of emotion   291, 293
functional neuroimaging   9

G
GABA   272; *see also* neurotransmitters
gender differences   23
generalization   80
global precedence affect   225–227
   factors other than mood affecting   225–227
   time   226–227
   visual angle   225
   volitional control   226
glucocorticoids   29
   role in memory enhancement   24, 25
   see also stress hormones
glutamate   272; *see also* neurotransmitters
glutamine modulation   255, 256, 257
goal management *see* dynamic goal management
goal plans   170, 171, 172, *173*
   joint errors   174, 175, 176, 177

Subject index 339

joint plans 170, 173–175, 176, 180
mental models of others 175–176, 179, 180
multiple goals 170, 172
planning as reasoning 171
goal states 5, 6, 7

H
happiness 171, *173*
hedonic shift 79
hemisphere, left (left extrastriate cortex)
   high visual spatial frequency processing 222, 223
   left hemispheric word association task 223–224, 293
   verbal dominance 19
hemisphere, right (right extrastriate cortex)
   low visual spatial frequency processing 222, 223
hemispheric specialization 290, 291, 293, 294, 304, 307, 308, 309; *see also* lateralization
Herpes simplex encephalitis 14
heuristics 158, 170–180
   basic emotions 139, 172, *173*
   blaming 175, 179
   communicative theory of emotions 171–173, 174
   emotion signals 169–174, 180
   goal plans 170, 171, 172, *173*
   joint errors 174, 175, 176, 177
   joint plans 170, 173–175, 176, 180
   mental models of others 175–176
   multiple goals 170, 172
   negative trait ascription 175
   planning as reasoning 171
   trust 174, 175, 176, 180
   two-part hypothesis 172
high anxiety *see* anxiety
hippocampal amnesia 17

hippocampus 27, 28, 29, 120
   activation, and mood 223
   connections to amygdala 42
   damage 15, 17
   role in arousal 269
   role in memory consolidation 13, 14, 24
   role in memory formation 15, 20
   role of NE 272
histamine 268, 272; *see also* neurotransmitters
Hopfield network 121
hunger deprivation 200
hypothalamus 27, 28, 29, 140, 215
   connections to amygdala 42, 150
   and homeostatic mechanisms 216

I
implicit learning 78
impression formation 112
incentive magnitudes 201
incentive values 62
inconsistency, detection of 161, 162, 173, 178, 179, 180
   conditionals 162, 163
   disjunctions 162, 163
   generating emotion 179
   illusions 163
   see also reasoning to consistency
information processing
   and affect 111, 128
   expectations 127
   fluency 111, 112, 127
   neural network approach 121
instrumental conditioning 38–40, 48, 49, 51, 54, 61, 62, 63, 64, 66, 67
instrumental learning 36, 38–40, 49
   motivational processes 38
   reinforcement 38, 47, 59; *see also* reinforcers
insular cortex 27, 28, 67, 150

interference 100
intrinsic hypothesis 79, 80, 82, 86, 87, 88, 90, 98, 106

J
joint errors 174, 175, 176, 177
joint plans 170, 173–175, 176, 180
judged expectations 186, 187, 188, *189*, 190, *191*, 192, 93
judgments 111
    aesthetic 127
    and emotion 138, 139, 140, 142, 143
    morality 127
    non-evaluative 115
    preferences judgments 125–127, 129
    role of amygdala 23, 43, 44
    unconscious 78
    see also evaluations; evaluative
justice deprivation 199, 212

K
Kluver-Bucy syndrome 44–45
knowledge, limits of 170, 171

L
language memory processing 19
lateralization 290, 291, 293, 294, 304, 305–309
    amygdala activity 19, 23, 28, 44
    and emotional modulation of cognition 290
    of experienced emotion 305–306
    and gender 23
    high frequency processing 222
    low frequency processing 222
    of working memory 306
    see also hemispheres, brain
learned association weighting 83, 84, 85, 86
learning
    appetitive, in rats 40, 58

auditory verbal 16
evaluative 75–76
models, associative 38; *see also* reinforcers
motivated 14
response systems 53
role of amygdala 14, 57
types of 35
lesion method 9
lesion studies, of emotional memory 14–19, 20, 21, 23, 24, 27, 28, 29, 30, 43, 44, 45, *46*
    basolateral amygdala damage 43, 44, 45, *46*, 47, *48*, 49, *50*, 51, *52*, 53, 54, 55, *56*, 57, 58, 59, 60
    bi-lateral amygdala damage 16, *17*, 18
    conditioning study 15
    epilepsy treatment 14, 19, 43
    and evaluative function 67
    Herpes simplex encephalitis 14
    and preference acquisition 105
    Reisberg task 11, 12, 16
    unilateral amygdala damage 17, 18
    temporal lobectomy 14, 18, 19
    Urbach-Wiethe disease 14, 15, 43
    verbal vs. visual stimuli 19
liking/disliking
    and conceptual fluency 126
    and perceptual fluency 113–114, 116
    and recognition 114
liking/wanting 53, 54, 60, 67
limbic system 120, 149
lipoid proteinosis (Urbach-Wiethe disease) 14, 15, 43
local precedence effect 226, 233
locus coeruleus, role in arousal 268–269
logic, monotonic 160; *see also* reasoning, nonmonotonic

long-term declarative memory *see* memory, long-term declarative
long-term potentiation (LTP)   29

M

masking, backward   4
medial geniculate   41
medial nuclei, amygdala   43
medial temporal lobe memory system   14, 28, 29; *see also* ippocampus
Mednick's theory of creativity   248
memory: associative   99
  consolidation   18, 21, 23, 24, 28
  encoding   13, 20, 21, 23, 28
  illusions   120
  recognition   271
  reconsolidation   28
  reference   271
  retrieval   21, 23, 28
  role of hippocampus   13, 14, 15, 20, 24
memory, long-term declarative   4, 9, 13–14, 15, 21
  impairment   15
  modulation by emotion   4, 9–33; *see also* emotional memory
  role of amygdala   4, 9, 13–14, 15, 20, 21, *22*, 23
memory, working
  anatomical substrates of   6, 7
  and arousal   6, 270, 271, 272, 273
  cognitive control of   289, *292*, 295, 303–304, 305, 308
  and consciousness   147
  /emotion interaction   306–307
  impairment   250
  and positive affect   6, **245–287**
  role of prefrontal cortex   249, 250, 270, 271, 272, 273, 290, 305, 306
mental models, of others   175–176
  blaming   175, 179
  negative trait ascription   175
  and trust   174, 175, 176, 180
mere-exposure effect   113, 118–119, 123–127, 129
metacognition, and affect   119, 120, 121
  neuroimaging data   120
metacognitive feedback   119
metoprolol   24, 25
midbrain
  connections to amygdala   42, 43
  role in arousal   269
  role of NE   272
mind, levels of analytic description   145
mirror neurons   309
mismatch principle   163, 164, 165, 166, 168, 169, 178
Monte Carlo simulation   122, 123
mood: and attentional bias   6, 221, 222, 223, 224
  and behaviour   6
  and brain function   6
  and classification of stimuli responses   221, 227–228
  and cognitive bias   223–224
  global precedence affect   225–227
  hemisphere laterality effects   222, 223
  inducing   152, 153, 221, 223, 228, 235–236, 238, 292, 307
  informational value of   225, 240
  left hemispheric word association task   223–224, 293
  local precedence effect   226, 233
  as modulating factor   241
  and multidimensional models of classification choice   240, 241
  Navon stimuli   *222*, 222–225, 227, 228, 233, 234, 235
  object identification   224, 225
  possible reasons for   224
  prefrontal cortex activity   223

probabilistic classification task (PCT)   228–241, *234*
  and skill acquisition   221
  and visual spatial frequency attentional bias   222, 223, 224
  weighting function   241
  see also affect; emotions; feelings
mood, negative   6, 221
  and dorsolateral prefrontal cortex (DLPFC) activity   223
  global dimensional bias   227, 240, 241
  hippocampal activation   223
  low visual spatial frequency attentional bias   222, 224, 227, 240, 293
  right mid-prefrontal cortical activation   223
  systemic processing   309
  visual processing bias   6, 223, 293
mood, positive   221
  and creativity   6
  and dopamine   6
  heuristic processing   309
  high visual spatial frequency attentional bias   223, 224, 227
  left mid-prefrontal cortical activation   223
  and visual discrimination task performance   223, 293
mood-altering drugs   172
morality judgments   127
motivated learning   14
motivation, and cognition   200
motivational properties, reinforcers   37, 53, 55
motivational utility theories   199, 200, 201–202
  animal behavioural   201
  approach-avoidance models of movement behaviour   202
  consumer choices   201–202
  and decision theory   202
  drive states   201
  dynamics of action   201
  feedback control theory   201
  incentive magnitudes   201
  social/psychological   201
motor cortex   254
multi-alternative decision making   202
multi-attribute decision making   202
musculoskeletal system, emotional response   139

N
n-back task   293, 307, 308
need deprivation   199, 200, 217
need stimulation   199, 200, 217
negative priming *see* evaluative priming
negative trait ascription   175
neocortex   28
  role in arousal   269
neostriatum, and cognitive-motivational network   215, 216
network model   80–86
  modular network   82, *83*, 84
neural network approach   121
neural network model of brain function (connectionist model)   80, 246, 251–267, *253, 255, 257, 259,* 273, *285–287,* 290
neural networks   4, 6, 128–129
  affective response   123, 124
  architectures   121
  attractor   121
  clarity   124, 125
  coherence/differentiation   122, 123, 124, 125
  dynamic attractors   123
  dynamical parameters   121–125
  evaluative response   124
  figure-ground contrast   124, 125, 126
  neuroimaging studies   123

presentation duration 118, 124, 125, 126
priming 124, 125, 126
recognition response 123, 124, 128
simple attractors 121, 122
simulations 122, 123–126, 128
single cell recording studies 123
subsystems 303
volatility 122, 124, 125
neuroimaging studies 2, 20–23
    computerized tomography (CT) 15
    functional magnetic resonance imaging (fMRI) 15, 20, 21, 43, 44, 291, 293
    positron emission tomography (PET) 20, 23, 43, 44
    role of PFC in willed action task 253, 254
neurotransmitters
    acetylcholine (ACh) 268, 272, 273
    and arousal 268–273
    GABA 272
    glutamate 272
    histamine 268, 272
    and mood 249
    serotonin (5-HT) 249, 268, 272
    see also dopamine; norepinephrine; pharmacology studies
noradrenergic *see* adrenergic; norepinephrine
norepinephrine (NE) 246, 249, 268–272
    alpha/beta receptors 270, 271
    attentional function 269, 270, 271
    and distractibility 271
    neoromodulatory effect 272
    PFC function 270–272, 273
    signal-to-noise ratio enhancement 272, 273
    vigilance mediation 269

see also neurotransmitters
novelty monitoring 119, 120
nucleus accumbens *see* ventral striatum

O

orbitofrontal cortex 27
    and cognitive-motivational network 215, 216
orienting response 123
outcome devaluation studies 38

P

paralimbic areas 149
parietal cortex
    and cognitive-motivational network 216
    role in attentional processing 269
Parkinson's disease 250
Pavlovian conditioning 36, 37–38, 44, 45, 46, 47, 48, 51, 54, *56*, 57, 59, 61–64, *66*, 67
    reinforcers 37–38, 46, 47
    role of amygdala 44, 45, *46*, 47
perception
    conscious 144
    subliminal 146
perceptual fluency
    and affect connection 119
    boundary conditions 126–128
    cognitive monitoring 119–121
    computational mechanisms 121–125
    familiarity-attribution model 115
    figure-ground contrast 114
    fluency-attribution model 115
    and liking/disliking 113–114, 116
    measuring affective response 117, 118
    mere-exposure effect 113, 118–119, 123–127, 129

nature of evaluative responses
117–118
and negative evaluations   127
non-specific activation model
   115
and positive evaluations   4,
   111–135
and preferences   125, 126
presentation duration   114
selectivity   115–117
visual priming   113, 114, 116,
   118
see also neural networks
perceptual representation,
   amplification/inhibition   81
PET (positron emission tomography)
   neuroimaging studies   20,
   23, 43, 44, 253
PFC *see* prefrontal cortex
pharmacological interventions,
   emotional   172
pharmacological probes   9
pharmacology studies   24–25, *26*
   beta-blockers   24, 29
   catecholamines   27, 29; *see also*
      adrenaline; adrenergic;
      norepinephrine
   cortisol   24, 25, *26*, 29; *see also*
      stress hormones
   epinephrine   24, 25, 29, 30; *see
      also* norepinephrine
   metoprolol   24, 25
   yohimbine   24
   see also neurotransmitters
phenomenal awareness   149, 150
phenylephrine   271
planning as reasoning   171
plasticity-stability dilemma   121
pleasant-approach motivation   297;
   see also approach-withdrawal
   related emotional function
pons, connections to amygdala   42
positron emission tomography (PET)
   neuroimaging studies   20,
   23, 43, 44, 253

preference assessment   193
preference   123
   average stimuli (prototypical)
      125, 126, 129
   fluency effects   125, 126, 127
   symmetry   125, 126, 129
prefrontal cortex (PFC) 149
   acetylcholine   272, 273
   activity, and mood   223
   approach-withdrawal related
      emotional function   291,
      293, 305
   attention switching   251
   bottom-up influence of emotion
      290
   cognitive control functions   305
   dopamine   249, 250, 254, 257,
      273
   dorsal PFC (Brodmann's Areas)
      305
   dorsal-ventral specialization
      291
   dorsolateral (DLPFC)   223, 293,
      306, 307
   effects of lateralized damage
      305
   emotional states and cognitive
      task demands   293
   emotional states and goal
      regulation   297
   emotion/working memory
      interaction   306–307
   hemispheric specialization   290,
      291, 293, 294, 304, 305–306
   lateralization of experienced
      emotion   305–306
   lateralization of working memory
      306
   norepinephrine   270–272, 273
   role in emotional-cognitive
      information processing
      289
   role in willed action task,
      neuroimaging studies   253,
      254

sustained attention function 290
ventral PFC 305
working memory function 249, 250, 270, 271, 272, 273, 290, 305, 306
presentation duration 118, 124, 125, 126
primary emotions 139, 149
priming 124–126
   activation-based 124
   affective 90, 92, 93, 94
   visual 113, 114, 116, 118
   weight-based 124
prioritization, goal 295, 299, 304
problem solving, and arousal 268, 273
processing dynamics 111; *see also* perceptual fluency
prospect theory 198
protopathic properties, reinforcers 37, 53, 55
prototypical stimuli 125, 126, 129
psychological reactance 95
psychological/social utility theories 201
pulvinar nucleus, role in attentional processing 269
punishment
   avoiding 6
   /compassion needs 212
putamen 13, 28, 42
   and cognitive-motivational network 216

R
rationality, impossibility of 170, 171, 173; *see also* reasoning
reason, influence of emotion 1
reasoning, deductive, mental models 159–169
   fully explicit 160, 164
   model theory of causal relations 165, 166, 167, 168, 169

reasoning, nonmonotonic 161, 165, 178
reasoning to consistency 157–182
   abduction of explanation 161, 165, 166–169, 177, 179
   beliefs, editing 161, 163, 164, 165, 172
   communicative theory of emotions 171–173, 174
   computer program 161, 162, 166, 167
   detection of inconsistency 161, 162, 173, 178, 179, 180
   emotion signals 169, 170–174, 180
   goal directed action 171
   goal plans 170–180
   heuristics 158, 170–180
   illusory inferences 163
   joint errors 174, 175, 176, 177
   joint plans 170, 173–175, 176, 180
   limits of knowledge 170, 171
   mental models of others 175–176
   mismatch principle 163, 164, 165, 166, 168, 169, 178
   multiple beliefs 172
   multiple goals 170, 172
   planning as reasoning 171
recognition 21, 23, 122
recognition memory 271
recognition response 123, 124, 128
reference memory 271
referential hypothesis 78, 79, 80, 82, 86, 87, 88, 90, 97, 98, 99, 106
   augmented 98
reflexive awareness 150
regret theory 184, 192
reinforcers 35–73
   action discrimination 49, *50*, 57
   choice extinction tests *48*
   consummatory properties 37, 53, 56
   dissociable properties 53, 67

event outcome studies 46, 47, 57
idiopathic/sensory properties 53, 54, 55
incentive values 62
instrumental conditioning 38–40, 48, 49, 51, 54, 61, 62, 63, 64, 66, 67
liking/wanting 53, 54, 60, 67
models 60–67
Pavlovian conditioning 36, 37–38, 44, 45, 48, 51, 54, 56, 57, 59, 61, 62, 63, 64, 66, 67
preparatory properties 37, 53, 56
protopathic properties 37, 53, 55
reward discrimination 49–53, 52, 54, 56, 57, 58
role of amygdala 44, 45, 46, 47, 48, 49, 57, 58
second order conditioning 57, 58, 62, 89
S-R interpretation 51, 52, 54, 58, 59, 60, 61
S-S interpretation 58
Reisberg task 11, 12, 16
Remote Associates Test 6, 246, 248, 251, 252, 260, 262–264, 263, 264, 266, 267, 268, 274, 275
repetition, stimulus 113, 114
representations, mental, definition of 141
detection 141
emotional (somatic appraisals) 140–143, 148, 151
function 141
repression, memory 9, 10
retrieval, memory 21, 23, 28
retroduction 158
revaluation 79, 98, 99
reward
approaching 6; *see also* approach-withdrawal related emotional function

discrimination 49–53, 52, 54, 56, 57, 58
and dopamine levels 245, 248
neurobiology of 245
signals 245, 248, 249
rule switching 250, 253

S
sadness *173*
schizophrenia, behavioural deficits model 255
second order conditioning 57, 58, 62, 89
secondary emotions 139, 149
selective attention 82, 83, 100–103, 221, 146, 147
selectivity 115–117
self-organization 80
selling prices 202
senserimotor cortex 216
serotonin (5-HT) 249, 268, 272 *see also* neurotransmitters
sexual love *173*
Shannon entropy 230
signal learning 89
signal-to-noise ratio 122
acetylcholine enhancement 272, 273
simple attractor neural networks 121, 122
simulations, neural network 122, 123–126, 128
affective response 123, 124
clarity 124, 125
evaluative response 124
figure-ground contrast 114, 124, 125, 126
Monte Carlo 122, 123
presentation duration 124, 125, 126
priming 124, 125, 126
recognition response 123, 124, 128
single cell recording studies 123
skill acquisition 221

Skinner boxes   36
skin-conductance responses   18
sleep-wake cycle   272
snapshot approach   200
social/psychological utility theories   201
somatic appraisal theory   140–143, 148, 151
    somatic maps   150
somatosensory cortex   150
S-R associations   38
S-R habit   51, 52, 54, 58, 59, 60, 61
S-S learning   58
startle behaviour   45
startle-probe response   104
STEPIT subroutine   188
stimulus
    distinctive   21
    exposure duration   113
    repetition   113, 114
    speed of recognition   113; *see also* fluency; perceptual fluency
Stoics   1
stopping rules   *204*, 205
striatum
    connections to amygdala   42
    neurone firing rates   254
    role in memory consolidation   24
stress hormones   13
    role in memory   24, 25, *26*, 29, 30
Stroop task   100, 295
subjective expected emotions (SEE)   186, 190, 191–193
    maximizing   192, 193
    predicting choices from   191–192
    study   187–190
subjective expected utilities (SEU)   186, 190, 193
subliminal evaluative learning   78, 90–92, *91, 92, 93, 94, 96*, 99
subliminal presentation   77, 78
subliminal priming   114

superior colliculus, role in attentional processing   269
sustained attention function, PFC   290
symmetry   125, 126, 129

T
temporal cortex   215
temporal lobectomy   14, 18, 19
temporal processing   84
temporal weights   83, 84, 85, 86, 90, 97, 100, 101
thalamus
    and emotional responses   140
    neural connectivity   41, 42
    role in arousal   269
    role of NE   272
top-down processes   81, 83
triggering events (situation)   297
triune brain model   149
trust   174, 175, 176, 180
truth, principle of   159, 160
two-choice guessing task   254, 258–260, *259*, 264, 274
two-factor theory of emotion   115, 116, 138
two-step models   115

U
unconditional stimulus (US)   36, 37, 57, 58
    idiopathic properties   37, 38
    primary affective properties   37
    sensory properties   37
unconscious emotion   137, 139, 143–145, 153
unconscious processes   93
unpleasant-withdrawal motivation   297; *see also* dynamic goal management
Urbach-Wiethe disease   14, 15, 43
utility theory, in decision making   197–219
    attributes   197, *198*
    concept of   197

constructive   198, 199, 200
   and decision field theory
      202–217
   and deprivation-satiation   199, 217
   dynamic   199, 200, 201
   and emotions/moods   200
   and environmental variables   199
   motivational theories   199, 200, 201–202
   need deprivation   199, 200, 217
   need stimulation   199, 200, 217
   snapshot approach   200
   see also decision-making

V
vagus nerve, stimulation of   30
ventral PFC   305; *see also* prefrontal cortex
ventral striatum   67
   and cognitive-motivational network   215, 216
ventral tegmental area (VTA)   249, 250, 254
ventromedial prefrontal cortex   150
verbal fluency   247
verbal memory   19
vigilance   100, 146, 147
   mediation by NE   269
visceral emotional response   139

visual consciousness   145–146, 148
visual discrimination task performance   223, 293
visual priming   113, 114, 116, 118
visual processing bias, and mood   6, 223, 293
visual spatial frequencies   223
visuospatial memory processing   19
volatility   122, 124, 125
von Restorf effect   21

W
weight-based priming   124
willed action task, neuroimaging studies   253, 254
Wisconsin card sorting test   250
word association task   6, 246, 247, 251, 252, 260–262, *261*, *262*, 266, 274, 293
words stem completion task   16
working memory *see* memory

Y
Yerkes-Dodson effect   271
yohimbine   24

Z
zygomaticus major (cheek) muscle   117, 118

In the series ADVANCES IN CONSCIOUSNESS RESEARCH (AiCR) the following titles have been published thus far or are scheduled for publication:

1. GLOBUS, Gordon G.: *The Postmodern Brain.* 1995.
2. ELLIS, Ralph D.: *Questioning Consciousness. The interplay of imagery, cognition, and emotion in the human brain.* 1995.
3. JIBU, Mari and Kunio YASUE: *Quantum Brain Dynamics and Consciousness. An introduction.* 1995.
4. HARDCASTLE, Valerie Gray: *Locating Consciousness.* 1995.
5. STUBENBERG, Leopold: *Consciousness and Qualia.* 1998.
6. GENNARO, Rocco J.: *Consciousness and Self-Consciousness. A defense of the higher-order thought theory of consciousness.* 1996.
7. MAC CORMAC, Earl and Maxim I. STAMENOV (eds): *Fractals of Brain, Fractals of Mind. In search of a symmetry bond.* 1996.
8. GROSSENBACHER, Peter G. (ed.): *Finding Consciousness in the Brain. A neurocognitive approach.* 2001.
9. Ó NUALLÁIN, Seán, Paul MC KEVITT and Eoghan MAC AOGÁIN (eds): *Two Sciences of Mind. Readings in cognitive science and consciousness.* 1997.
10. NEWTON, Natika: *Foundations of Understanding.* 1996.
11. PYLKKÖ, Pauli: *The Aconceptual Mind. Heideggerian themes in holistic naturalism.* 1998.
12. STAMENOV, Maxim I. (ed.): *Language Structure, Discourse and the Access to Consciousness.* 1997.
13. VELMANS, Max (ed.): *Investigating Phenomenal Consciousness. Methodologies and Maps.* 2000.
14. SHEETS-JOHNSTONE, Maxine: *The Primacy of Movement.* 1999.
15. CHALLIS, Bradford H. and Boris M. VELICHKOVSKY (eds.): *Stratification in Cognition and Consciousness.* 1999.
16. ELLIS, Ralph D. and Natika NEWTON (eds.): *The Caldron of Consciousness. Motivation, affect and self-organization – An anthology.* 2000.
17. HUTTO, Daniel D.: *The Presence of Mind.* 1999.
18. PALMER, Gary B. and Debra J. OCCHI (eds.): *Languages of Sentiment. Cultural constructions of emotional substrates.* 1999.
19. DAUTENHAHN, Kerstin (ed.): *Human Cognition and Social Agent Technology.* 2000.
20. KUNZENDORF, Robert G. and Benjamin WALLACE (eds.): *Individual Differences in Conscious Experience.* 2000.
21. HUTTO, Daniel D.: *Beyond Physicalism.* 2000.
22. ROSSETTI, Yves and Antti REVONSUO (eds.): *Beyond Dissociation. Interaction between dissociated implicit and explicit processing.* 2000.
23. ZAHAVI, Dan (ed.): *Exploring the Self. Philosophical and psychopathological perspectives on self-experience.* 2000.
24. ROVEE-COLLIER, Carolyn, Harlene HAYNE and Michael COLOMBO: *The Development of Implicit and Explicit Memory.* 2000.
25. BACHMANN, Talis: *Microgenetic Approach to the Conscious Mind.* 2000.
26. Ó NUALLÁIN, Seán (ed.): *Spatial Cognition. Selected papers from Mind III, Annual Conference of the Cognitive Science Society of Ireland, 1998.* 2000.
27. McMILLAN, John and Grant R. GILLETT: *Consciousness and Intentionality.* 2001.

28. ZACHAR, Peter: *Psychological Concepts and Biological Psychiatry. A philosophical analysis.* 2000.
29. VAN LOOCKE, Philip (ed.): *The Physical Nature of Consciousness.* 2001.
30. BROOK, Andrew and Richard C. DeVIDI (eds.): *Self-reference and Self-awareness.* 2001.
31. RAKOVER, Sam S. and Baruch CAHLON: *Face Recognition. Cognitive and computational processes.* 2001.
32. VITIELLO, Giuseppe: *My Double Unveiled. The dissipative quantum model of the brain.* 2001.
33. YASUE, Kunio, Mari JIBU and Tarcisio DELLA SENTA (eds.): *No Matter, Never Mind. Proceedings of Toward a Science of Consciousness: Fundamental Approaches, Tokyo, 1999.* 2002.
34. FETZER, James H.(ed.): *Consciousness Evolving.* 2002.
35. Mc KEVITT, Paul, Seán Ó NUALLÁIN and Conn MULVIHILL (eds.): *Language, Vision, and Music. Selected papers from the 8th International Workshop on the Cognitive Science of Natural Language Processing, Galway, 1999.* n.y.p.
36. PERRY, Elaine, Heather ASHTON and Allan YOUNG (eds.): *Neurochemistry of Consciousness. Neurotransmitters in mind.* 2002.
37. PYLKKÄNEN, Paavo and Tere VADÉN (eds.): *Dimensions of Conscious Experience.* 2001.
38. SALZARULO, Piero and Gianluca FICCA (eds.): *Awakening and Sleep-Wake Cycle Across Development.* 2002.
39. BARTSCH, Renate: *Consciousness Emerging. The dynamics of perception, imagination, action, memory, thought, and language.* 2002.
40. MANDLER, George: *Consciousness Recovered. Psychological functions and origins of conscious thought.* 2002.
41. ALBERTAZZI, Liliana (ed.): *Unfolding Perceptual Continua.* 2002.
42. STAMENOV, Maxim I. and Vittorio GALLESE (eds.): *Mirror Neurons and the Evolution of Brain and Language.* n.y.p.
43. DEPRAZ, Natalie, Francisco VARELA and Pierre VERMERSCH.: *On Becoming Aware.* n.y.p.
44. MOORE, Simon and Mike OAKSFORD (eds.): *Emotional Cognition. From brain to behaviour.* 2002.
45. DOKIC, Jerome and Joelle PROUST: *Simulation and Knowledge of Action.* n.y.p.
46. MATHEAS, Michael and Phoebe SENGERS (ed.): *Narrative Intelligence.* n.y.p.
47. COOK, Norman D.: *Tone of Voice and Mind. The connections between intonation, emotion, cognition and consciousness.* n.y.p.